Title Page

**The Minister's Diary
Volume 1: 1936-1949**

**Mine Eyes Have Seen ~~The Glory~~…Verd*mont!
An Autobiography And Journal
By
The Reverend Albert Solomon Anderson
(Luke 2:30)**

✝ ✝ ✝

Transcribed, Co-Written, and Edited by Tira Pandolf
(Matthew 10:34)

March 2021

A Munificent Scribbler Press Production
Giving Is All There Is To Get

munificentscribbler.com
munificentscribbler@gmail.com

COPYRIGHT

The Minister's Diary, Volume 1: 1936-1949

Copyright © 2021 by Reverend Albert Solomon Anderson and Tira Pandolf
All Rights Reserved.

No part of this book may be reproduced by any method (including but not limited to being: copied, re-written, scanned, uploaded to the internet, photographed, recorded) or in any form without written permission by the copyright holder.

Library of Congress Control Number: 2021904935

ISBN-13: 978-1-947270-11-4 (Print version [Paperback]; First Edition

ISBN-13: 978-1-947270-09-1 (Ebook version [Epub]; First Edition

This print book is published by:

Munificent Scribbler Press
Northampton, MA

munificentscribbler.com
munificentscribbler@gmail.com

Published in the United States

The Minister's Diary, Volume 1: 1936-1949
Munificent Scribbler Press, First Edition: March 2021

This is book has been transcribed from the original diary of Reverend Albert Solomon Anderson, in the exact words as he wrote them. All details, including descriptions of events, news, books, movies, and people are based on the memory of Reverend Solomon Anderson at the time of writing his diary/journal.

Credits:

Book Cover by Tira Pandolf. The book's cover was created using Affinity Photo™ (version 1.5.2) and Affinity Designer™ (version 1.8.6) by Serif® (Europe) Ltd.

Composed with the aid of Scrivener (version 3.2.2) by ©Literature and Latte Ltd.

E-book created using Velum® (Version 2.7.3) by 180g

Editing by Tira Pandolf

Table of Contents

Title Page	1
Copyright	2
Synopsis	4
Dedication	5
Forward	6
First Sermon—Draft	8
Pictures of the Diary	10
Poems	28
1936	33
1937	59
1938	90
1939/1940	100
1939 (September - October)	131
1940 (January-September)	148
1941	172
1942	201
1943	246
1944	265
1945	290
1946	308
1947	331
1948	360
1949	374
Epilogue—Extra Memories	389
All of the Suggested Daily Spiritual Readings Listed the Book	401
All of the Suggested Further Readings Related to Diary Entries	414
A List of All the Suggested Popular Books by Year	465
A List of All the Suggested Popular Movies by Year	474

SYNOPSIS

Take a trip back in time and follow the life of a Methodist minister starting with his birth in Groton, Vermont in 1902. Read the stories of his newspaper printing escapades (including during the great influenza of 1917-1918), his time at Dartmouth and Harvard, his work with the New England Telephone & Telegraph Company, his ministry experiences, life during World War II, the many fishing trips, vacations on the farm, and trips to New York City (including a visit to the 1938 World Fair and the time he saw smoke billowing out of the Empire State Building after a B-25 bomber crashed into it in July of 1945). Meet a cast of exciting characters including Mr. Harry C. Whitehall—the owner of The Waterbury Record and WDEV radio, Henry S. Dennison (paper manufacturing magnate), and writer Edmund Ware Smith. Return to a simpler time when a love for God, Nation, Community, and Family dominated life in an America filled with decency, honesty, hard work, and appreciation.

DEDICATION

<u>To Mae, Janet, and ~~Junior~~ Albert Earl</u>

"...because no white in that time and place considered an Indian's motives or rights! And so this book is dedicated to all who have unjustly died. From the dawn of civilization, until time shall be no more, the heart of God must bleed for those who have known the inhumanity of men."

✝ ✝ ✝

Reverend Albert Solomon Anderson (November 11, 1936)

FORWARD

My grandfather, the Reverend Albert Solomon Anderson (1902-1992), kept a series of diaries/journals from November 1936 until he died. In this volume (1), I have only transcribed his entries from November 1936 through December 1949.

My grandfather, who I affectionately refer to as "The Reverend", was a Methodist minister from 1928 (26 years of age) until approximately 1978 (50 years of age); retiring when he was 76 years old.

The Reverend had a great sense of humor, as well as a love of history, astronomy, world affairs, science, nature, and above all else God. He was an intent listener, the best listener I have ever met. He would ask you a question, then sit back, joyfully puffing on his pipe, and listen without interrupting.

He loved people. Everywhere we went he would talk to everyone and anyone—whether it was the bikers hanging out on main street or the Church ladies he would pass on his walk to the library. Race, creed, color, financial position, criminal background, health status—none of it mattered to my grandfather; he ministered to everyone.

My mother remembers him greeting people who were down on their luck at the kitchen door, the back door of the parsonage, so as not to cause them any embarrassment. He always made sure they left with a full belly and a little coin in their pockets. The Reverend and his family (wife, son, and daughter) lived a very frugal life, sometimes not having money for Christmas or birthdays.

In his journaling, the Reverend focuses on what he thinks readers will want to know about if they happen to read his journals 5, 10, or 100 years from when he writes. For this reason, much of the focus of this first volume (1936-1949) is on the Reverend's upbringing, school years, work experiences, endearing stories from his ministry, World War II, his vacation time, nature, and his hobbies (hiking, astronomy, mineral collecting), as well as his children.

In my editing, I corrected punctuation and spelling when necessary. I attempted to identify all of the sources of the many quotes my grandfather inserted into his journal entries--sometimes correcting a quote or noting the correct quote.

When I included my own commentary/notes I added them in parentheses and in a different font (*italicized Times New Roman*). In addition, I moved a sentence if it was out of order (ex. November 13, 1936 - he wrote a sentence saying where he was born, right in the middle of explaining a field trip he took when he was young.)

From 1937 through 1940, the Reverend shuffled pages around in order to keep content intact.

It was my idea, as transcriber and editor, to add the following sections at the end of each diary entry: "Suggested Daily Spiritual Reading", "Further Reading Related to Diary Entry", "Popular Books of 19xx", and "Popular Movies of 19xx". I chose this action due to my grandfather's love of books and movies, and also because I found the content of his journaling of such great interest that it made me want to read more on the subjects he discussed. To create the "Suggested Daily Spiritual Reading" sections, I consulted the King James Version (KJV) of the bible. I am not sure what version of the bible the Reverend used; however, according to the website of the United Methodist Church:

"The United Methodist Church does not have an "official" version or translation of the Bible…When it comes to United Methodist teaching resources published by The United Methodist Publishing House in English, the Common English Bible (CEB) and the New Revised Standard Version (NRSV) are the preferred texts for curriculum, largely because these are the preferred versions of many of our pastors and teachers in the US." http://www.umc.org/what-we-believe/ask-the-umc-does-the-Church-have-an-official-bible [Accessed February 4, 2021].

During these difficult times, I hope the Reverend's diary will provide readers with inspiration, hope, and reassurance that even though every generation has its struggles, it is through faith, wisdom, truth, perseverance, love, and compassion that we survive and grow as souls; all connected to the same glorious energy known as God-Jesus-Holy Spirit. Amen.

Tira Pandolf - March 2021

FIRST SERMON—DRAFT

Below is the text from a handwritten draft of a sermon by Reverend Albert S. Anderson. It was written during his internship—at St. John's United Methodist Church in Watertown, MA—while under the tutelage/mentorship of Dr. Francis Taylor. This Sermon was given in the Reverend's final year at Harvard Theological School (circa 1927)

There are four influences which have definitely played a part in diverting my life toward the service of the Christian ministry. I owe first of all, to my mother, an unmeasured obligation for ~~bringing me up in a knowledge of the~~ guiding my first steps in the way of the Christian faith. A great philosopher has said that all true altruism has its roots in the maternal instinct. And I think it is generally true when I say that children can generally grasp the idea of loving God because they have known a loving mother.

The second great influence over my life, was the Church. One cannot ~~attend~~ be part of the Christian Church for years, particularly in the years of growth, without being moulded and oriented in spirit to its finest ideals and aims, its traditions and beliefs. And a man stands as ~~a~~ self-discredited ~~hypocrite~~ who partakes of the advantages and opportunities of the Christian fellowship while denying that he has any obligation thereto. The great spiritual grace of God descends freely upon all, but he who honors not the Father, honors not himself.

In the third place, I owe a profound debt to the world of nature. The psalmists say, "I will lift up mine eyes unto the hills from whence cometh my help." (Psalm 121:1) Who is there so blind that he cannot perceive the Creator in the limitless created? The endless panorama of the seasons; the birth, growth, and death of plants, animals, and man—the constant change of all living things—is enough to furnish food for speculation and thought to the most careless mind. What is the meaning of things—how did the stars originate, what is the purpose of the universe? These, and similar questions, led to a study of astronomy, philosophy, and science. Fortunate enough to enter upon a college training, I devoted much time to a study of the physical world—chemistry, physics, biology, astronomy, and other sciences—exact and inexact. Evolution strengthened my belief in God, as it has for so many others. And yet in all this study, I preserved almost a poetic passion for the beauty of nature—and I think I owe to the hills of New Hampshire my faith in the goodness of God and the immortality of the human soul.

The fourth ~~influence~~ factor was the influence of an eminently Christian preacher—your own Dr. Taylor. It was on Sunday morning, December 7th 1924 that Dr. Taylor spoke in the adjoining room (because the church was being re-modeled at the time) on the subject of "Glad Tidings". As I listened, I thought how good it must be to minister unto the spiritual needs of a people—truly it has its own reward. And from that day I resolved to be an ambassador of Christ. The following September, I entered upon a three-year course at the Harvard Theological School, and, at its close, I hope to begin my work in the ordained ministry and brotherhood of Jesus Christ.

Additional draft section written on back of sermon:

And ~~am~~ I do not feel I am presumptuous in thinking that there are other young people, here tonight, in whom similar influences and experiences are gradually taking form; who will in years to come take place in the ranks of Christian leadership—the great work of grinding souls to peace and salvation in our Lord, Jesus Christ.

Pictures of the Diary

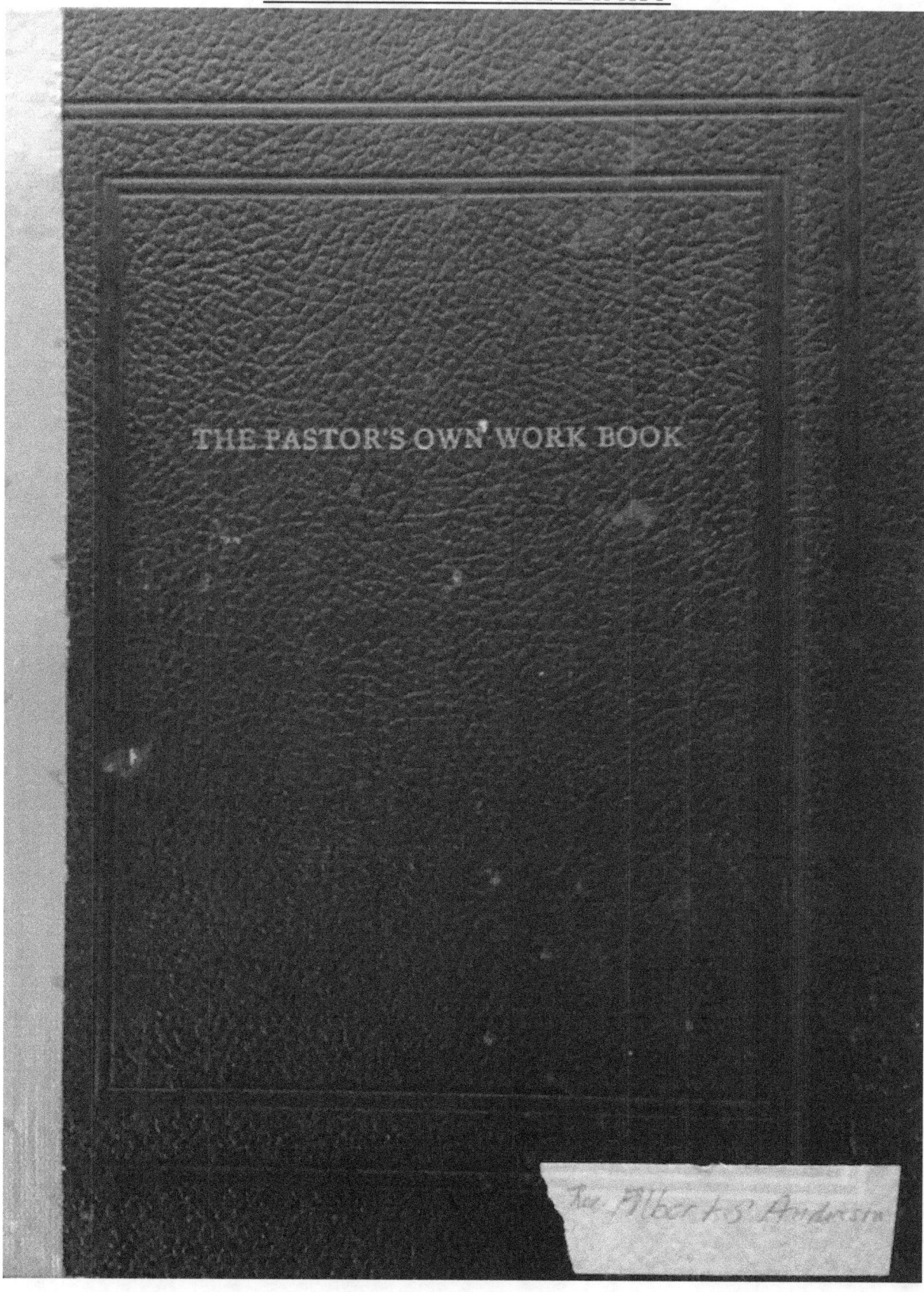

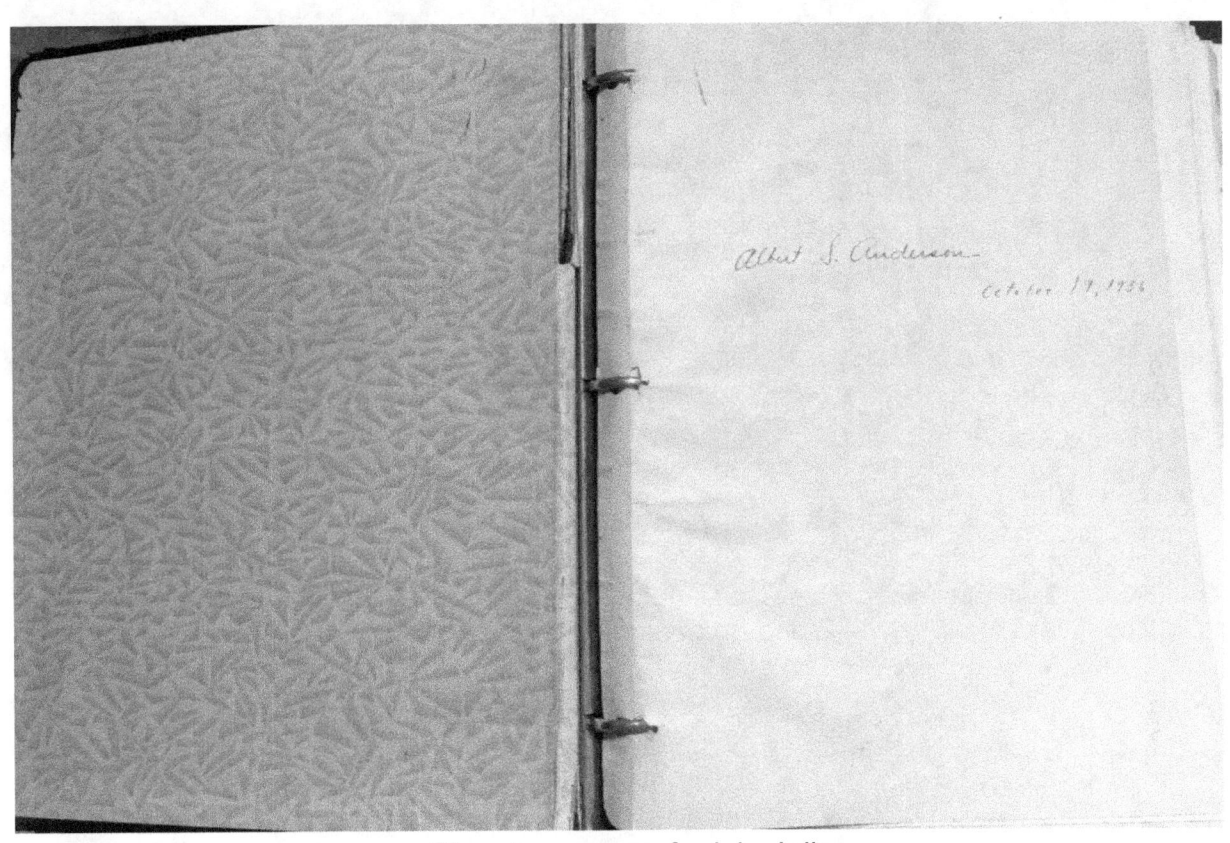
Signature page of original diary

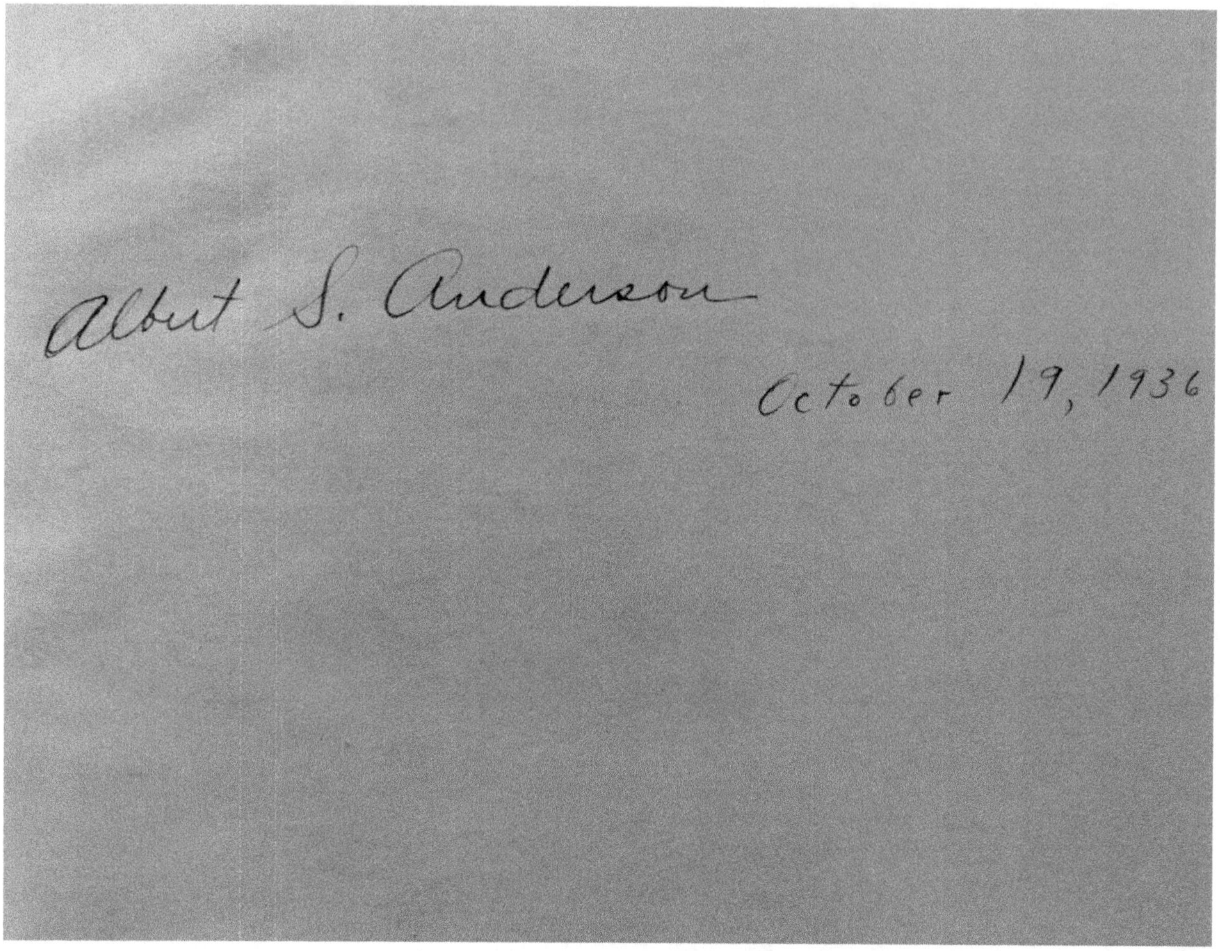

Close-up of signature page of diary

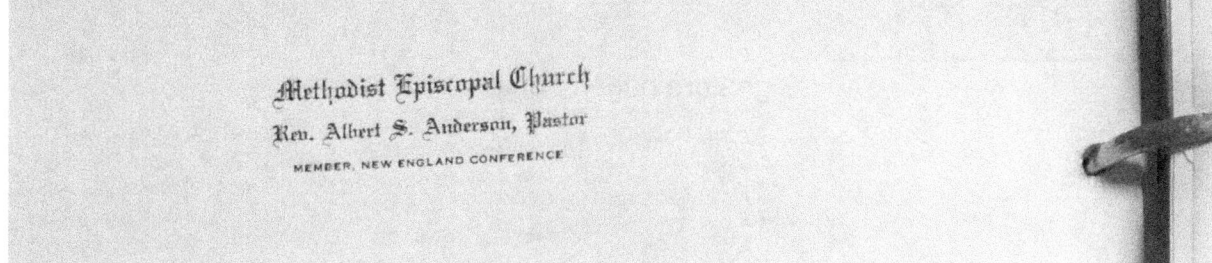

Diary letterhead

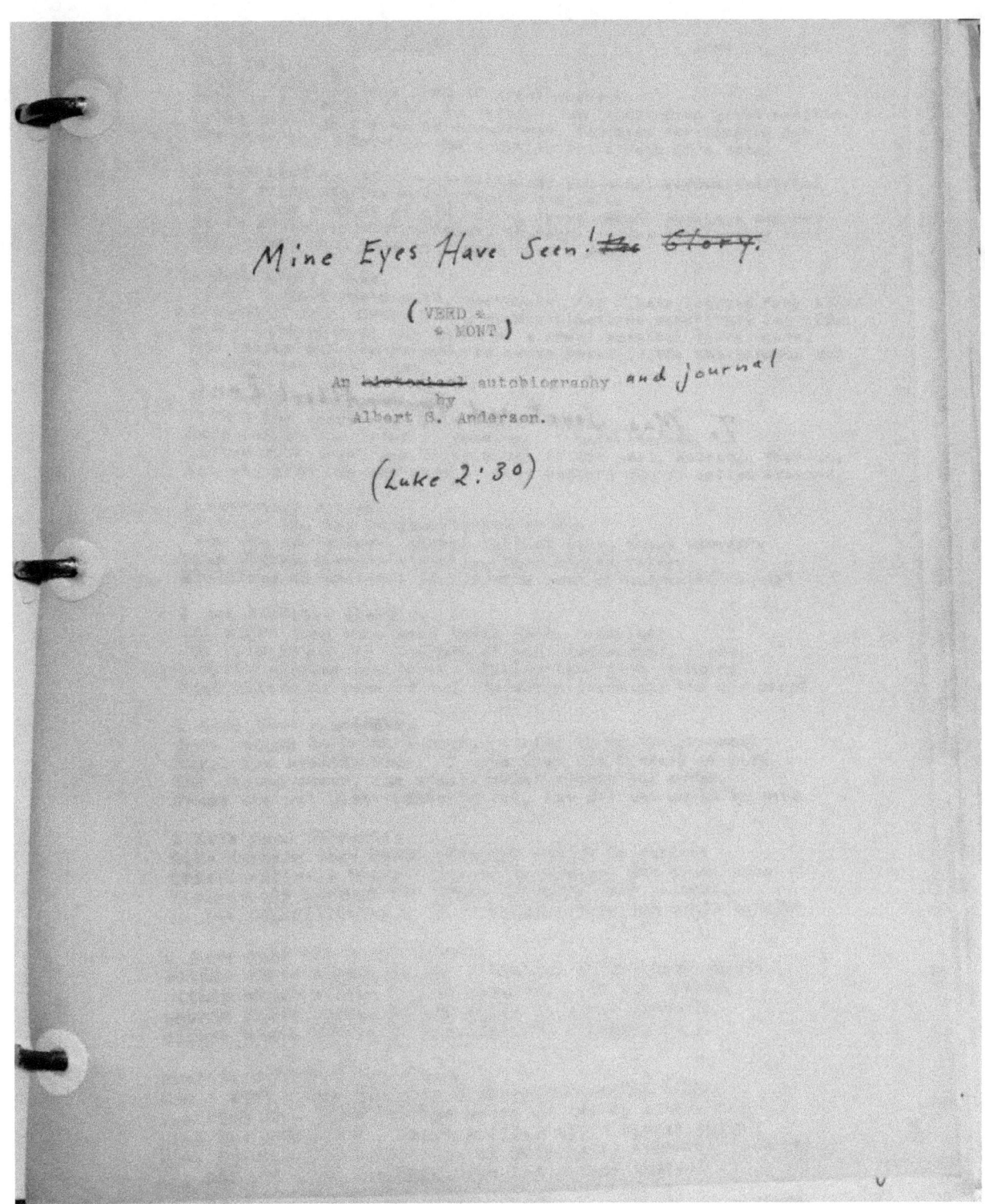

Introductory page of diary

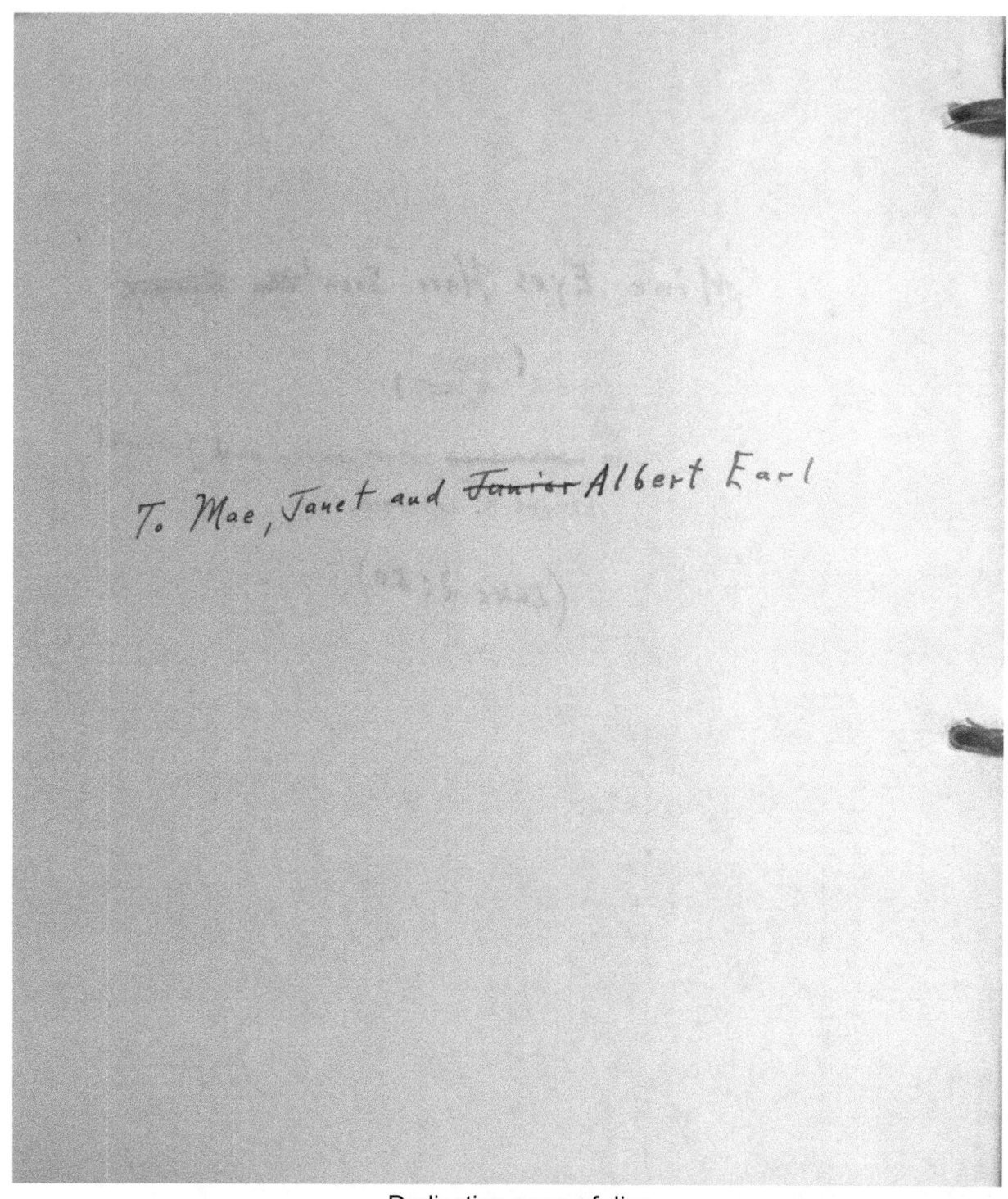

Dedication page of diary

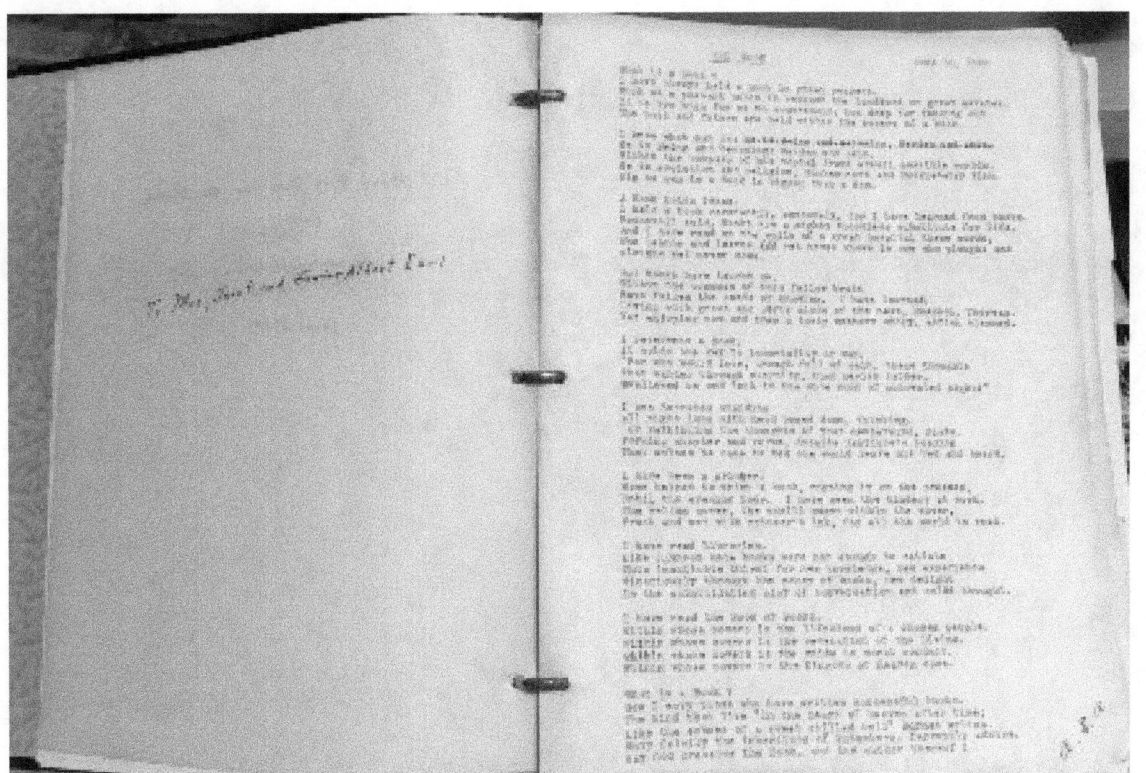

Poem *The Book*

Diary Letterhead

November 11, 1936

re is in the world!
uction of "Ramona"
tanding event in
assed in pictures
down by a rancher
so happily married
gravely ill of
, because his
ranch house
te in that time
ghts! And so this
From the dawn

Close-up of first entry in diary to show the date

1.

November 11, 1936

How much misunderstanding of motive there is in the world! I have just witnessed a Technicolor sound production of "Ramona" by Helen Hunt Jackson. The climactic and outstanding event in that drama of color and beauty hitherto unsurpassed in pictures is reached when Alessandro is ruthlessly shot down by a rancher whose horse he stole. Alessandro the Indian, so happily married to Ramona, shot down because his daughter was gravely ill of fever, because he must reach her with medicine, because his horse had gone lame, because no one was at the ranch house when he frantically sought aid, because no white in that time and place considered an Indian's motives or rights! And so this book is dedicated to all who have unjustly died. From the dawn of civilization until time shall be no more the heart of God must bleed for those who have known the inhumanity of men.

"Socrates drinking the hemlock,
And Jesus on the rood."

Eighteen years have passed since the guns ceased firing on the Western front. Eighteen years since the world was made safe for democracy! Eighteen years since six million men unjustly died. We are now a family of nations, but a family which has not learned to adjust its quarrels nor evaluate its personalities. Ironic must be the thoughts of the dead, bitter the souls whose memories haunt us still. Idealistic they may have been on the way to the front, but realistic they soon became in the muck and mud of the Masurian Lakes and Flanders Fields. For the most part they were caught in the woof and web of economic and social forces too complex for them to grasp. On Christmas eve in 1916 the story runs, the English and German soldiers met in No Mans Land and fraternized, under the spell of a little Child whose birth gave "Silent night, holy night" to a war-weary world. For Christ is born anew each Christmas eve. Years later a German radio announcer, Walther Wellman by name, was to play that piece on a harmonica beside a candle-lit pine in the Black Forest. He and his companions had gone there on skis through the soft snow. Still later on another Christmas eve (1935) he was to relate the incident over DJC and play that beautiful melody on his harmonica again. And I heard it, three thousand miles away. If the world could only live under the spell of Christmas eve through the year, war, the greatest social sin, would be incompatible with the human spirit!

I summon the presence of Him who said, "Love your enemies" and invoke Him to bestow his spirit of good will unto our family of nations. Then our loyalty will not be narrow and self centered, but we shall realize that truly the Father hath made of one blood all nations of men. And for those who have gone ahead with the white banners, for those who have unjustly died, may there be peace and fulfillment in Him who is our recompense!

"They shall not grow old, as we that are left grow old-
Age shall not weary them, nor the years condemn-
At the going down of the sun, and in the morning,
We shall remember them."

Full picture of first diary entry

Nov. 13, 1936

out a field trip.
oks which have
s, and through
lms beyond the
 that my circle
nant therefore
now, was my
 did I know
ther's heart.
inds in the

Close-up of second diary entry to show the date

Nov. 15, 1936

My earliest recollection centers about a field trip. I have ever loved to travel, by proxy through books which have taken me to the ends of the earth and the heavens, and through philosophic speculations which have gone into realms beyond the reach of any car, steamship or airplane. I hope that my circle of interest will widen to infinity. Quite consonant therefore with my later curiosity to know, and know, and know, was my earliest trip. To be sure, I did not go far, nor did I know that my absence had stirred up anxiety in my mother's heart. I was born in a little white house with green blinds in the outskirts of Groton, Vermont. The air was warm, the sun shining, the clouds fleecy, the birds singing, the treetops waving gently in a soft southern breeze, for it was early summer. Quite in order to wander afield, and so I did. Over a little rise and down into a field quite high with grass and flowers. I was about three years old. The sun was warm and inviting to sleep, and feeling drowsy, I lay down and took a nap. Thus I rested and refreshed myself on the bosom of the greatest mother of all. I was aroused by the footsteps of a man striding over the hill. Strong arms picked me up and transported me home, to a relieved mother and a mild scolding. The man? Well, he was the farmer next door, and I must describe him and his farm more fully later.

But now, I desire to record another little adventure in running away--this time when I was six years old. There being no school, I had gone to the village for a haircut. The quarter in payment thereof was clutched tightly in my hand, and was still so clutched when I emerged from the shop. A chum met me and suggested when I wished to return and pay the barber that the barber knew my father well, and that his credit was good. So the quarter was soon translated into candy--wafers in a yellow box, shaped a great deal like our matchboxes of today. Then we retired to the roof of a shed in another section of the town, and proceeded to eat the candy. This accomplished my erstwhile friend suggested we go swimming in the river. This I had no business to do, but being gullible then as now, I fell in with the suggestion. So we proceeded to the river bank and removed our clothes. Wells River is not deep except in places, and most of the river bed was sand and rocks, but I fear that I should have fared badly if I had ventured far into the swiftmoving current. The one o'clock whistle in the stonesheds blew about this time, and I knew I ought to be getti[ng] home, but still I tarried. And it was there my aunt found me, and somehow I was soon dressed and carried home to mother. My own children have been "lost" for a short period, and so I can well understand my mother's feeling. But there was a big dish of potato and a glass of milk awaiting me, after which I was [hustl]ed off to bed. Thus ended another misadventure. A

Full picture of second diary entry

Full page picture of a diary entry chosen at random

breeze blowing and the waves were running high. There was a stiff northwest ladder was much appreciated and exploited by Thoreau but as for me I [enjoy] the relative virginity of Lake Cochituate, unmarred as it is by any bathing or boating embellishments. I have read Wordsworth here. The lake, sky, wind and sun give a sense of "something far more deeply interfused, whose dwelling is the light of setting suns + the round ocean, and the blue sky, the living air, and in the mind of man." The spray opening on the shore had turned to ice, and the water was a deep blue contrasting with the lighter blue of the sky. Truly god is in this place — it is none other than the house of god and the gate of heaven. The spruces + pines, the oaks and swamp maples, an occasional beech + birch, and like a rara avis, the ducks lifting from the water silently. The sand of the beach is white and fine. The sun was warm + southerly. Nature is clean + beautiful. It bespeaks the true, the beautiful, the good and there is no evil there. There is no evil in nature. In human nature which stand between man and god, we find motivations of evil which reside in excess of good impulses instincts and habit patterns but none in god or his creation." And (in the words of Eunice Tietjens) I shall go down from this quiet place, this still white peace, and time shall close about me, and my soul stir to the rhythm of the daily round; yet having known, life shall not press so close, and I shall always feel time ravel thin about me for once I stood in the white windy presence of Eternity."   Cochituate   December 28, 1938

Handwritten entry in diary

Thursday, August 24, 1944

w York state and settling down to work
d, helping to make ice cream and keeping
ive gallon cans, we had assumed that
ight Fern and Helen Taylor came up and
 four days with them at Sprucehead, Maine.
rning and coming back on a Saturday. We
e on Sprucehead island right on the coast,
nd. The wooded islands of the bays, the
 the boats moored nearby made a pretty
wo mornings at five o'clock (awakened by
f the sea gulls, and went out lobster
 was a rare experience, giving us the
 markets are supplied with lobsters, a
ear the shore but in deep water is a
poles, where the herring are caught, and
 The Weirs were made by the Rackliffe clan,
o has been at it for 38 years, summer and
             All have built houses

Close-up of randomly chosen entry in diary

Resume of First Vacation Week.
August 2nd Sunday to August 9th

High Lights---Eagle perched on limb on bank of Connecticut.
Visit to Bill Yetten with three hour talk on minerals.
Boat ride on Lake Morey with the children.
Swimming at the river beach.

19.75 Sunday 2.00 Mon. 10.00 plus 2.50 Wed. 4.50 Thurs. .75 equals
Borrowed Fri. 1.50 dogfood plus Lake Morey Sat. hayfork 2.00

Sunday--nice ride up, no difficulty. Only about one-quarter traffic.
Stopped at Massabesic and Franklin diner. When we arrived Mother had lovely supper for us, chicken, coffee, veg. and ice cream.

Mon. Quiet restful day as I recall. Ride to Bradford with children. Went to beach. Three dogs and three children my responsibility.

Tues. Went up to see George and Bess in afternoon. Stonewall visited.

Wed. Got gas. Also haircut. Went up to Yetten's 2-6 p.m.

Thurs. Rode up the back road route 10. Examined electric fence switches.

Fril Took children to Lake Morey this evening. Boating. With Dad a.m.

Sat. Haying for first time in earnest. Broke hayfork. Saw Bald Eagle on river. Pure white on head and tail. Big as turkey. Do not know exact designation but it was first time I had seen and eagle up in this county. Very unusual and very patriotic. Also went up to see George and Bess again.

Sun. Raining. Went to creamery. Made plans this week to climb Mt. Moosilauke this next week. Chief difference is in lack of traffic on roads. We have no extensive plans as last year. Perhaps a short trip with Bill Yetten in search of minerals. Perhaps a game of golf with Stevenson. A little more haying on the lower meadow. But I for one appreciate the cool nights. And the low pressure vacation system, where you just take each day as it comes. Yesterday morning pitched hay back into the mow. Friday afternoon took Junior and Janet to the beach via the pool. Probably saw Eagle then. Sonny was ill on Thursday so he couldn't go swimming on Friday. We have had raspberries twice, blackberries twice, also blackberry pie.

Worldwide news--Germans have advanced to Maikop oil fields, and towards Stalingrad. Nothing in North Africa. In India Ghandi and all-India Congress open Civil Disobedience Campaign. This morning it is announced that Ghandi and some of his followers jailed. U.S. has attacked Solomon Islands. Japs claim 22 ships sunk. Six saboteurs executed yesterday, two given prison sentences. OWI reports our war effort below schedule in recent months. Systematic transfer of Dutch, three million, and others begugn to Ukraine fields for cultivation. Eventful week for diagnosis. Watch the Caucusus and India particularly.

Full page picture of a diary entry chosen at random

Full page picture of a diary entry chosen at random

During World War II, the Reverend always typed on the back of scrap paper—such as old letterhead or outdated bylaws from Church organizations or theater groups:

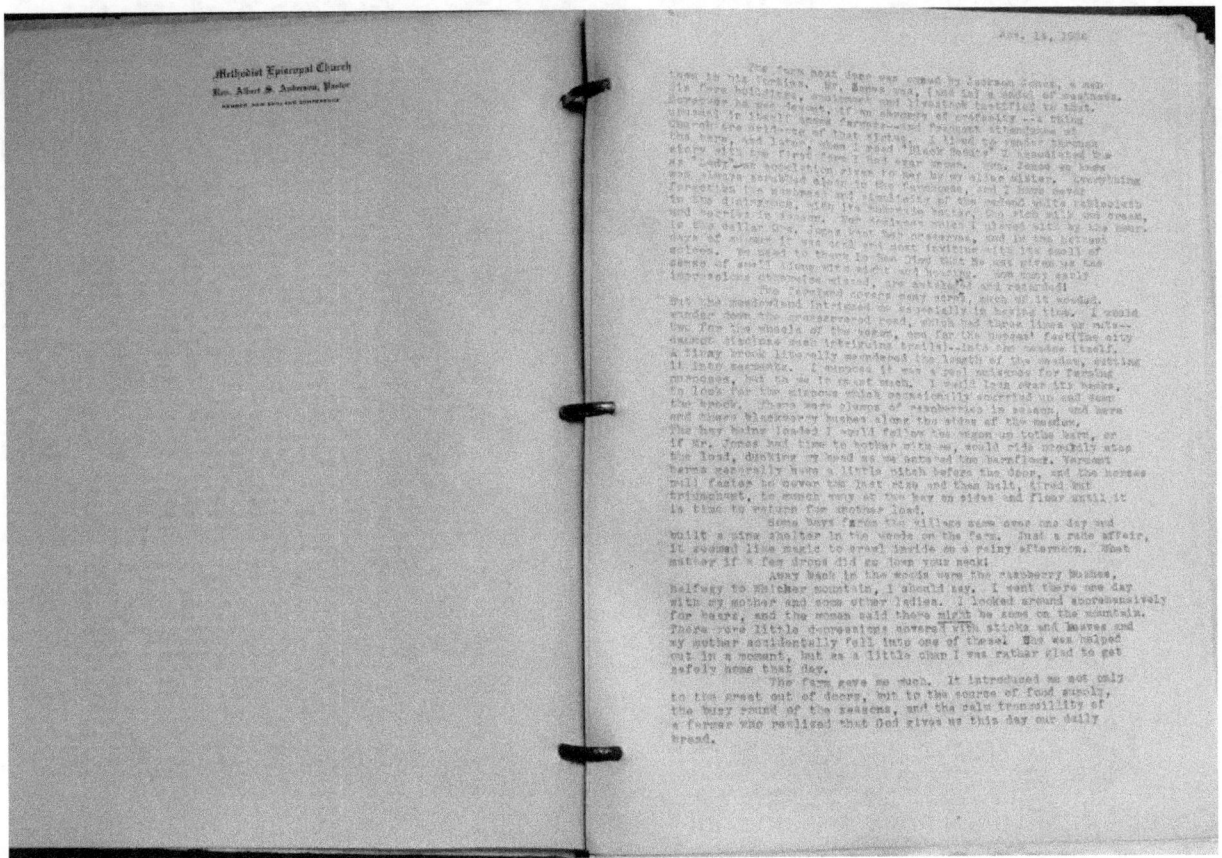

Picture of front side of scrap paper, showing typed diary entry

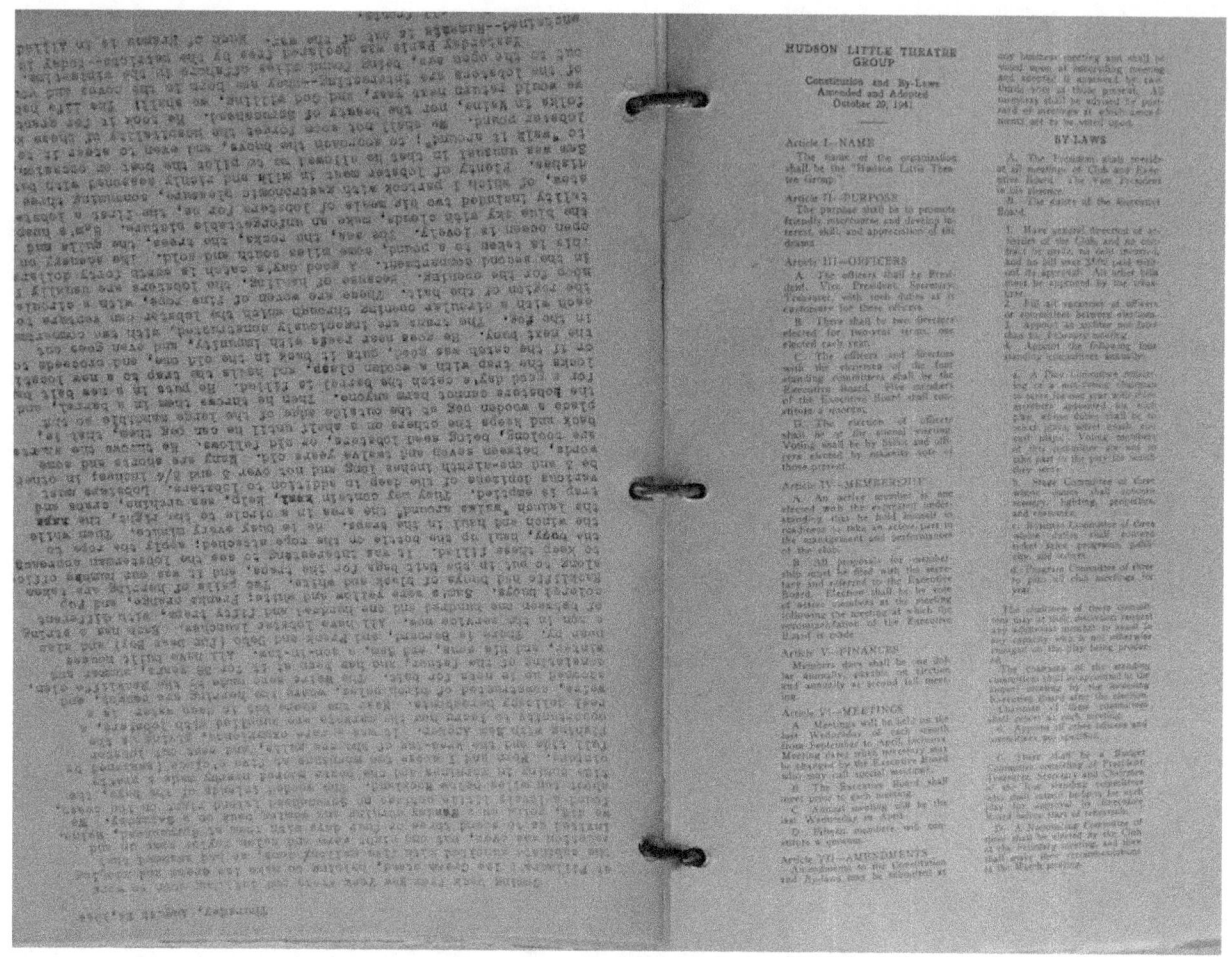

On left—typed diary entry, and on right—back side of a diary entry typed on scrap paper

HUDSON LITTLE THEATRE GROUP

Constitution and By-Laws
Amended and Adopted
October 29, 1941

Article I—NAME

The name of the organization shall be the "Hudson Little Theatre Group."

Article II—PURPOSE

The purpose shall be to promote friendly intercourse and develop interest, skill, and appreciation of the drama.

Article III—OFFICERS

A. The officers shall be President, Vice President, Secretary, Treasurer, with such duties as is customary for these officers.

B. There shall be two directors elected for two-year terms, one elected each year.

C. The officers and directors with the chairmen of the four standing committees shall be the Executive Board. Five members of the Executive Board shall constitute a quorum.

D. The election of officers shall be at the annual meeting. Voting shall be by ballot and officers elected by majority vote of those present.

Article IV—MEMBERSHIP

A. An active member is one elected with the expressed understanding that he hold himself in readiness to take an active part in the management and performances of the club.

B. All proposals for membership must be filed with the secretary and referred to the Executive Board. Election shall be by vote of active members at the meeting following the meeting at which the recommendation of the Executive Board is made.

Article V—FINANCES

Members dues shall be one dollar annually, payable on election and annually at second fall meeting.

Article VI—MEETINGS

[...] any business meeting and shall be voted upon at succeeding meeting and adopted if approved by two-thirds vote of those present. All members shall be advised by post-card of meetings at which amendments are to be voted upon.

BY-LAWS

A. The President shall preside at all meetings of Club and Executive Board. The Vice President in his absence.

B. The duties of the Executive Board.

1. Have general direction of activities of the Club, and no contract be made, no debt incurred, and no bill over $5.00 paid without its approval. All other bills must be approved by the treasurer.

2. Fill all vacancies of officers or committees between elections.

3. Appoint an auditor not later than the February meeting.

4. Appoint the following four standing committees annually:

   a. A Play Committee consisting of a non-voting chairman to serve for one year with three members appointed for each play, whose duties shall be to select plays, select coach, and cast plays. Voting members of this committee are not to take part in the play for which they serve.

   b. Stage Committee of three whose duties shall concern scenery, lighting, properties, and costumes.

   c. Business Committee of three whose duties shall concern ticket sales, programs, publicity, and ushers.

   d. Program Committee of three to plan all club meetings for year.

The chairmen of these committees may at their discretion request any additional member to assist in any capacity who is not otherwise engaged on the play being produced.

The chairmen of the standing committees shall be appointed at the annual meeting by the incoming Executive Board after the election. Chairmen of these committees shall report at each meeting [...] all other officers and

Close-up of scrap paper used in diary

POEMS

"The Book"

(Written on June 18, 1942 by the Reverend Albert S. Anderson, age 40)

What is a Book?
I have always held a Book in great respect.
Much as a peasant holds in respect the landlord on great estates.
It is too high for me to comprehend; too deep for finding out.
The past and future are held within the covers of a book.

I know what a man is.
He is Being and becoming; Werden und sein.
With the compass of his mortal frame are all possible worlds.
He is evolution and religion, Shakespeare and Huckleberry Finn.
Big as Man is, a Book is bigger than a Man.

A Book holds ideas.
I hold a book reverently, awesomely, for I have learned from books.
Roosevelt said, "Books are a mighty bloodless substitute for life."[1]
And I have read on the walls of a great hospital these words, "Who learns and
learns yet never knows, is one who ploughs and ploughs yet never sows."[2]

But books have taught me.
Within the compass of this fallow brain,
Have fallen the seeds of knowing. I have learned.
Living with great and lofty minds of the past--Emerson, Thoreau.
Yet enjoying, now and then, a lusty western story; action crammed.

I reverence a book.
It holds the key to immortality of man.
"For who would lose, though full of pain, these thoughts
That wander through eternity, than perish rather,
Swallowed up and lost in the wide womb of uncreated night?"[3]

I see Socrates standing
All night long with his head bowed down, thinking.
Or rethinking the thoughts of the mastermind, Plato.
Forming Chapter and verse, despite Xanthippe's coaxing
That unless he came to bed, she would leave his bed and board.

I have been a printer. Have helped to print a book; running it on the presses.
Until the evening hour. I have seen the bindery at work.
The vellum cover, the unlit pages within the cover,
Fresh and wet with printer's ink, for all the world to read.

I have read Libraries.

Like Johnson, mere books were not enough to satiate
This insatiable thirst for new knowledge, new experience
Vicariously through the proxy of books, new delight
In the scintillating play of conversation and solid thought.

I have read the Book of Books.
Within whose covers is the lifeblood of a chosen people.
Within whose covers is the revelation of the Divine.
Within whose covers is the guide to moral conduct.
Within whose covers is the Kingdom of Heaven come.

What is a Book?
How I envy those who have written successful books.
The kind that live "in the heart of heaven after time;
Like the echoes of the sweet stilled bell," Burnet writes.[4]
Envy faintly the inheritors of Gutenberg; reverently admire.
May God preserve the Book, and the author thereof!

---

[1] *The actual quote, from Robert Louis Stevenson, An Apology for Idlers, 1874, is: "…Books are good enough in their own way, but they are a mighty bloodless substitute for life…" (https://archive.org/stream/apologyforidlers00stev#page/12/mode/2up/search/books+are+good+enough+in+their+own+way) [Accessed January 21, 2021]*

[2] *This quote is from a poem called The Library by James Phinney Baxter. The actual quote is: "…Who learns and learns but does not what He knows, Is One who plows and plows but never sows." (https://baxterlibrary.org/contact/) [Accessed January 21, 2021]*

[3] *John Milton. Complete Poems. The Harvard Classics. 1909–14. Paradise Lost: The Second Book: "…Sad cure! for who would lose, Though full of pain, this intellectual being, Those thoughts that wander through eternity, To perish rather, swallowed up and lost In the wide womb of uncreated Night, Devoid of sense and motion?…" (http://www.bartleby.com/4/402.html) [Accessed January 21, 2021]*

[4] *This quote is from a poem called Dedication by Dana Burnet. The actual quote is: "…Mayhap if I sing bravely true and well, My song shall strike God's universal rhyme, And like the echoes of the sweet stilled bell, Live in the heart of heaven after time." Harper's Monthly Magazine, volume 131, 1915 (https://books.google.com/books?id=hW4yAQAAMAAJ&pg=PA196&lpg=PA196&dq=in+the+heart+of+heaven+after+time;+Like+the+echoes+of+the+sweet+stilled+bell&source=bl&ots=P--tNgwMG-&sig=7Q1sVkdaRBT4YQnody4tN40_c4M&hl=en&sa=X&ved=0ahUKEwj8tdqhip_aAhUm2oMKHaHDB2cQ6AEIJzAA#v=onepage&q=in%20the%20heart%20of%20heaven%20after%20time%3B%20Like%20the%20echoes%20of%20the%20sweet%20stilled%20bell&f=false) [Accessed January 21, 2021]*

THE BOOK   June 18, 1942

What is a Book ?
I have always held a Book in great respect.
Much as a peasant holds in respect the landlord on great estates.
It is too high for me to comprehend; too deep for finding out.
The past and future are held within the covers of a book.

I know what man is; ~~he is Being and Becoming, Werden und sein.~~
He is Being and becoming; Werden und zein.
Within the compass of his mortal frame are all possible worlds.
He is evolution and religion, Shakespeare and Huckleberry Finn.
Big as man is a Book is bigger than a Man.

A Book holds Ideas.
I hold a book reverently, awesomely, for I have learned from books.
Roosevelt said, Books are a mighty bloodless substitute for life.
And I have read on the walls of a great hospital these words,
Who learns and learns and yet never knows Is one who ploughs and
ploughs yet never sows.

But books have taught me.
Within the compass of this fallow brain
Have fallen the seeds of knowing. I have learned.
Living with great and lofty minds of the past, Emerson, Thoreau.
Yet enjoying now and then a lusty western story, action crammed.

I reverence a Book.
It holds the key to immortality of man.
"For who would lose, though full of pain, these thoughts
That wander through eternity, than perish rather,
Swallowed up and lost in the wide womb of uncreated night?"

I see Socrates standing
All night long with head bowed down, thinking.
 Or rethinking the thoughts of that mastermind, Plato.
Forming chapter and verse, despite Xantippe's coaxing
That unless he came to bed she would leave his bed and board.

I have been a printer.
Have helped to print a book, running it on the presses,
Until the evening hour. I have seen the bindery at work.
The vellum cover, the unslit pages within the cover,
Fresh and wet with printer's ink, for all the world to read.

I have read Libraries.
Like Johnson mere books were not enough to satiate
This insatiable thirst for new knowledge, new experience
Vicariously through the proxy of books, new delight
In the scintillating play of conversation and solid thought.

I have read the Book of Books.
Within whose covers is the lifeblood of a chosen people.
Within whose covers is the revelation of the Divine.
Within whose covers is the guide to moral conduct.
Within whose covers is the Kingdom of Heaven come.

What is a Book ?
How I envy those who have written successful books.
The kind that live "in the heart of heaven after time;
Like the echoes of a sweet stilled bell" Burnet writes.
Envy faintly the inheritors of Gutenberg; fervently admire.
May God preserve the Book, and the author thereof !

a. s. a.

"Where Vermont Comes In"

"Up where the north ends blow just a little keener,
Up where the grasses grow just a little greener,
Up where the mountain peaks rise a little higher,
Up where the human kind draws a little nigher,
That's where Vermont comes in.

Up where the snows of winter last a little longer,
Up where the heart beats just a little stronger,
Up where the hand clasp is just a little warmer,
That's where Vermont comes in.

Up where the lonesome pine its nightly requiem sighs,
Up where the unpolluted waters take their rise,
Up where the sons of toil have fought for freedom's sod,
Up where all nature's mood is a little nearer God,
That's where Vermont comes in.

Wherever manhood fights for honor,
And where woman shrinks at sin,
Where health is man's best riches,
That's where Vermont comes in.

Hon. Charles H. Darling

(Charles Hial Darling, 1859-1944, "Where Vermont comes in," Digital Vermont: A Project of the Vermont Historical Society, http://www.digitalvermont.org/items/show/43)[Accessed January 21, 2021]

"Up where the winds blow just a little keener,
Up where the grasses grow, just a little greener,
Up where the mountain peaks rise a little higher,
Up where all nature's mood is just a little nigher,
    That's where Vermont comes in!

Up where the lonesome pine its nightly requiem sighs,
Up where the unpolluted waters take their rise,
Up where the sons of toil have fought for freedom's sod
Up where all nature's mood is a little nearer God,
    That's where Vermont comes in!

Wherever manhood fights for honor,
And where woman shrinks at sin,
Where health is man's best riches---
    That's where Vermont comes in!"
                ---Quoted from memory.

1936

November 11, 1936

The Reverend is age 34, married to Mae, and has two small children—Albert Jr, age 7, and Janet, age 5.

How much misunderstanding of motive there is in the world! I have just witnessed a Technicolor sound production of "Ramona" by Helen Hunt Jackson. The climactic and outstanding event in that drama of color and beauty, hitherto unsurpassed in pictures, is reached when Alessandro is ruthlessly shot down by a rancher whose horse he stole. Alessandro the Indian, so happily married to Ramona, shot down because his daughter was gravely ill of fever, because he must reach her with medicine, because his horse had gone lame, because no one was at the ranch house when he frantically sought aid, because no white in that time and place considered an Indian's motives or rights! And so this book is dedicated to all who have unjustly died. From the dawn of civilization, until time shall be no more, the heart of God must bleed for those who have known the inhumanity of men.

```
"Socrates drinking the hemlock and Jesus on the rood."
```

(*Quoted from the poem "From Each In His Own Tongue" by William Herbert Carruth:* https://thebardonthehill.wordpress.com/tag/socrates-drinking-hemlock/ *[(accessed January 22, 2021]*).

Eighteen years have passed since the guns ceased firing on the western front (*reference to World War I*). Eighteen years since the world was made safe for democracy! Eighteen years since six million men unjustly died. We are now a family of nations, but a family that has not learned to adjust its quarrels, nor evaluate its personalities. Ironic must be the thoughts of the dead, bitter the souls whose memories haunt us still. Idealistic they may have been on the way to the front, but realistic they soon became in the muck and mud of Masurian Lakes and Flanders Fields (*reference to World War I. The Reverend was only 12 when the war started and 16 when it ended. Unbeknownst to him, his future wife's brother would be killed during that war.*). For the most part, they were caught in the woof and web of economic and social forces too complex for them to grasp.

On Christmas Eve in 1916, the story runs, the English and German soldiers met in No Mans Land and fraternized, under the spell of a little Child whose birth gave "Silent night, holy night" to a war-weary world. For Christ is born anew each Christmas Eve. Years later a German radio announcer, Walther Wellman, by name, was to play that piece on a harmonica beside a candle-lit pine in the Black Forest. He and his companions had gone there on skis through the soft snow. Still later, on another Christmas Eve, 1935 (*it is currently November 11, 1936 as he is writing*), he was to relate the incident over DJC and play that beautiful melody on his harmonica again, and I heard it three thousand miles away (*DJC was "The Radio Voice of Germany", available through short-wave radio [http://www.rfcafe.com/references/short-wave-craft/djc-radio-voice-germany-short-wave-craft-february-1935.htm [Accessed January 22, 2021]*). If the world could only live under the spell of Christmas Eve through the year, war, the greatest social sin, would be incompatible with the human spirit!

I summon the presence of Him who said, "Love your enemies," and invoke Him to bestow his spirit of goodwill unto our family of nations. Then our loyalty will not be narrow and self-centered, but we shall realize that truly the Father hath made of one blood all nations of men. And for those who have gone ahead with the white banners, for those who have unjustly died, may there be peace and fulfillment in Him who is our recompense!

```
"They shall not grow old, as we that are left grow old,
    Age shall not weary them, nor the years condemn
    At the going down of the sun, in the morning,
         We shall remember them."
```

(*Quoted from the poem "For the Fallen" by Robert Laurence Binyon, which was published in The Times newspaper on September 21, 1914.*)

Suggested Daily Spiritual Reading:
Luke 2:8-15
Matthew 5:44

Further Reading Related to Diary Entry:
- *For the Fallen* by Robert Laurence Binyon. Available at *The Great War (1914-1918)*: http://www.greatwar.co.uk/poems/laurence-binyon-for-the-fallen.htm [Accessed January 22, 2021].

- *The Guns of August* by Barbara W. Tuchman

- *White Banners* by Lloyd C. Douglas. Available at Project Gutenberg of Australia: http://gutenberg.net.au/ebooks06/0608861h.html [Accessed January 22, 2021].

Popular Books Published in 1936:
    Most Popular Books Published In 1936. Available at Goodreads.com: https://www.goodreads.com/book/popular_by_date/1936 [Accessed January 22, 2021].
    Ramona by Helen Hunt Jackson

Popular Movies Released in 1936:
    After the Thin Man (Myrna Loy, William Powell)
    Showboat (Irene Dunne, Allan Jones)
    Anything Goes (Bing Crosby, Ethel Merman, Ida Lupino)
    Ramona (Loretta Young, Don Ameche, Kent Taylor)

November 13, 1936

I was born in a little white house with green blinds on the outskirts of Groton, Vermont (*the year was 1902*).

My earliest recollection centers about a field trip. I have ever loved to travel, by proxy through books, which have taken me to the ends of the earth and the heavens, and through philosophic speculations, which have gone into realms beyond the reach of any car, steamship, or airplane. I hope that my circle of interest will widen to infinity. Quite consonant, therefore, with my later curiosity to know, and know, and know, was my earliest trip. To be sure, I did not go far, nor did I know that my absence had stirred up anxiety in my mother's heart.

The air was warm, the sun shining, the clouds fleecy, the birds signing, the treetops waving gently in a soft southern breeze, for it was early summer. Quite in order to wander afield, and so I did. Over a little rise and down into a field quite high with grass and flowers. I was about three years old. The sun was warm and inviting to sleep, and feeling drowsy, I lay down and took a nap. Thus, I rested and refreshed myself on the bosom of the greatest mother of all. I was aroused by the footsteps of a man striding over the hill. Strong arms picked me up and transported me home, to a relieved mother and a mild scolding. The man? Well, he was the farmer next door, and I must describe him and his farm more fully later.

But now, I desire to record another little adventure in running away--this time when I was six years old. There being no school, I had gone to the village for a haircut. The quarter in payment thereof was clutched tightly in my hand, and was still so clutched when I emerged from the shop. A chum met me and suggested, when I wished to return and pay the barber, that the barber knew my father well and that his credit was good. So the quarter was soon translated into candy--wafers in a yellow box, shaped a great deal like our matchboxes of today. Then we retired to the roof of a shed, in another section of the town, and proceeded to eat the candy. This accomplished, my erstwhile friend suggested we go swimming in the river. This I had no business to do, but being gullible then, as now, I fell in with the suggestion. So we proceeded to the riverbank and removed our clothes.

Wells River is not deep, except in places, and most of the riverbed was sand and rocks, but I fear that I should have fared badly if I had ventured far into the swift moving current. The one o'clock whistle in the stone sheds blew about this time, and I knew I ought to be getting home, but still I tarried. And it was there my aunt found me, and somehow I was soon dressed and carried home to Mother.

My own children have been "lost" for a short period, and so I can well understand my mother's feelings. But there was a big dish of potato and a glass of milk awaiting me, after which I was trundled off to bed. Thus ended another misadventure. A guiding spirit must have been hovering over my destiny, for on this, as on later occasions, no harm befell me.

Directly in front of our house was a pasture, of sorts. A trail led down the hill, across the brook, and up the railroad embankment, which divided the pasture from the stone shed where my father worked (*His father was a stonemason by trade.*). I often wandered down this little depression, which, to my mind, was a great valley, and as the train would speed around the curve of the hillside I used to wonder about the great big world on the "outside". And the little brook so often reminds me of Tennyson's poem of another brook: "…that makes a sudden sally… by coot and fern…to wander down the valley…" (*from the poem "The Brook" by Alfred Lord Tennyson. The first stanza of the poem is actually:*

> "I come from haunts of coot and hern,
> I make a sudden sally,
> And sparkle out among the fern,
> To bicker down a valley…"

Available at bartleby.com: https://www.bartleby.com/337/1288.html [accessed September 23, 2019]).

Wells River was one terminus of the railroad, and I well remember how my father returned from a business trip there, on one occasion, bringing with him a grapefruit, the first we children (I have two sisters, an older, Christina, and a younger, Lilla) had ever seen. He also brought some orchid-colored candy filled with peanut butter. How delicious it tasted! In connection with the valley, I later read Texas stories dealing with the days of the early settlers. I have forgotten the author and the titles, but one character stands out in bas-relief, one "Poke Stover", by name––and the incidents related therein seemed fitting for a place like my valley. And so I thrilled to think Indians might be lurking in the undergrowth.

Christina, Etta (mother), and Lilla, circa 1928

One winter's day, about noontime, I hurried down the trail and across a plank, on to meet my father, coming home for dinner. What boy is there who doesn't like to run and meet his father! I made the trip across the plank all right, thus proving that my guardian angel was with me, or else that I was more careful, but coming back I ran ahead, and because the plank was rounded with packed snow, I slipped and plunged off head first into the brook. My father was right behind me, and he waded in after me, pulling me from the icy water. I will not repeat what he said, for I do not remember, but I do remember, distinctly, his disgruntled look where upon reaching home he had to change his clothes "clear through" before eating dinner and returning to work.

Another picture I have of the pasture and the valley is that of my little fox terrier barking and running about when a chum called to see me. He was such a little watch dog, always barking fiercely if anyone so much as spoke to me. Alas, he went the way of all flesh, prematurely, when he absorbed too many porcupine quills and was shot and laid away. I have had a number of dogs since, but he was the first.

The only cow we ever possessed was led away one morning. She was purchased for me when I was baby, because I needed fresh cow's milk, and she supplied it. My father was a good artisan, but not a good farmer, and so the burden of milking fell to my mother. But the time came when the old brindled cow was no longer needed, and so she was sold and led away, out through the yard, which is still vivid and fresh in my mind after thirty years. There were birch trees there, and three birch stakes holding an iron pot; very fashionable in those days. The good earth and the animals thereof deserve a salute from us who live by them. There was a garden, too, always plentiful with fresh vegetables in season, and a big barn, which, after the cow went, housed only some hens. An old pig sty, too, where I was wont to play; pigs long since having left vacant. There are so many romantic spots for a boy of six or seven, around any place. My favorite playground was not on our property, however, but on that of our neighbor, the farmer, whose domain extended through field and forest to Whicher Mountain.

Suggested Daily Spiritual Reading:
Matthew 6:26
Timothy 4:9-15

Further Reading Related to Diary Entry:
- *Above, when mentioning the character "Poker-Stover, the Reverend is referring to a series of three books that were part of the Mexican War Series written by Edward Stratemeyer* [sometimes under the psuedonym, "Captain Ralph Bonehill"]: 1) *For The Liberty Of Texas*, 2) *With Taylor On The Rio Grande*, and 3) *Under Scott In Mexico*. Although the books in the *Mexican War Series* can still be purchased and found online for free, you can read the third book in the series, *Under Scott In Mexico,* from the Library of Congress: http://lcweb2.loc.gov/service/gdc/scd0001/2007/20070516002un/20070516002un.pdf [Accessed January 22, 2021].

- *You can read more about Stratemeyer* (creator of the "Rover Boys", "Nancy Drew" and the "Hardy Boys" series) and his syndicate of writers at http://stratemeyer.org/edward-stratemeyer/ [Accessed January 22, 2021].

- *The Pennsylvania Railroad: 1940s-1950s* by Ball Jr., Don

Popular Books Published in 1936:
The Diary of a Country Priest: A Novel by Georges Bernanos
Gone with the Wind by Margaret Mitchell
Journey Without Maps by Graham Greene

Popular Movies Released in 1936:
My Man Godfrey (Carole Lombard, William Powell)
Mr. Deeds Goes to Town (Jean Arthur, Gary Cooper)
Earthworm Tractors (Joe E. Brown, June Travis, Guy Kibbee)

November 14, 1936

The farm next door was owned by Jackson Jones, a man, then, in his forties. Mr. Jones was, and is, a model of neatness. His farm buildings, equipment, and livestock testified to that. Moreover, he was devout, if an absence of profanity--a thing unusual in itself among farmers--and frequent attendance at Church are evident of that virtue. I liked to wander through his barn, and later, when I read "Black Beauty", I associated the story with the first farm I had ever known. Mrs Jones we knew as "Lady"--an appellation given to her by my older sister. Everything was always scrubbed clean in the farmhouse, and I have never forgotten the neatness and simplicity of the red and white table cloth in the dining room, with its homemade butter, the rich milk and cream, and berries in season; nor the dominoes, which I played with by the hour. In the cellar, Mrs Jones kept her preserves, and in the hottest days of summer it was cool and most inviting with its smell of spices. We need to thank Le Bon Dieu that He has given us the sense of smell, along with sight and hearing. How many early impressions, otherwise missed, are catalogued and recorded!

The farmland covers many acres, much of it wooded. But the meadowland intrigued me, especially in haying time. I would wander down the grass-covered road, which had three lines or ruts--two for the wheels of the wagon and one for the horses' feet (the city cannot disclose such intriguing trails)--into the meadow itself. A tiny brook literally meandered the length of the meadow, cutting it into segments. I suppose it was a real nuisance for farming purposes, but to me it meant much. I would lean over its banks to look for the minnows, which occasionally scurried up and down the brook. There were clumps of raspberries in season and, here and there, blackberry bushes along the sides of the meadow. The hay being loaded, I would follow the wagon to the barn or, if Mr. Jones had time to bother with me, would ride proudly atop the load, ducking my head as we entered the barn. Vermont barns generally have a little pitch before the door, and the horses pull faster to cover the last rise and then halt, tired but triumphant, to munch away at the hay on sides and floor until it is time to return for another load.

Some boys from the village came over one day and built a pine shelter in the woods on the farm. Just a rude affair, it seemed like magic to crawl inside on a rainy afternoon. What matter if a few drops did go down your neck!

Away back in the woods were the raspberry bushes, halfway to Whicher Mountain, I should say. I went there one day with my mother and some other ladies. I looked around apprehensively for bears, and the women said there might be some on the mountain. There were little depressions covered with sticks and leaves and my mother accidentally fell into one of these. She was helped out in a moment, but as a little chap I was rather glad to get safely home that day.

The farm gave me much. It introduced me not only to the great out of doors, but to the source of food supply, the busy round of the seasons, and the calm tranquility of a farmer who realized that God gives us this day our daily bread.

Suggested Daily Spiritual Reading:
Jeremiah 17:5-8
Genesis 1:26-31

Further Reading Related to Diary Entry:
- *Vermont History*. Available from The Vermont Historical Society: https://vermonthistory.org [Accessed January 22, 2021].

- *Moses Robinson and the Founding* of Vermont by Robert A. Mello

- *Black Beauty* by Anna Sewell

Popular Books Published in 1936:
Drums Along the Mohawk by Walter D. Edmonds
Keep the Aspidistra Flying by George Orwell

Popular Movies Released in 1936:
Dodsworth (Ruth Chatterton, Water Huston)
Little Lord Fauntleroy (Freddie Bartholomew, Dolores Costello Barrymore)
Follow the Fleet (Fred Astaire, Ginger Rogers, Lucille Ball)

November 15, 1936

My grandsire's name was Albert S. Clark. His home was at the upper end of the township. It consisted of a house, barn, where he kept his horse, cow and pig, two or three acres of cultivated land--devoted to strawberries during his later years--and a hillside pasture. I recall with pleasure that near the woods, at the upper end of the pasture, was a beech tree, and the nuts in their furry coating, fallen with the first frosts, were delectable.

My grandfather's work was that of a charcoal kiln keeper. About a mile from his home were three coal kilns, cement covers fastened on, the wood set afire. It smoldered day after day until the slabs inside were converted to charcoal. Around the sides of the kilns, which were shaped like beehives, was a triple row of loose bricks. These would be removed to give the correct amount of draft. I have seen him take out a brick here and put in a brick there many a time. On a few occasions, the accumulated smoke and gas blew the covers high in the air. The job was not dangerous but exacting. There was a bunkhouse nearby where he would sometimes sleep when the kilns were going. It was a remembered adventure, as a boy, to be allowed to sleep there one night. Behind the kilns were tall raspberry bushes and, in season, added much to the tastiness of a meal.

My grandfather was descended from English stock. His father, Moody Clark, cobbled shoes in South Ryegate (*VT*) as did his father Thomas Clark before him. There must be something of Confucianism in my makeup, for I am compelled by an earnest desire to worship my immediate ancestors and to remember my friends through the medium of the printed word.

Next to the barn was the shed where the buggy was kept. It was great fun to sit in the buggy, covered up with the big fur robe, and take the whip in hand, pretending that I was on a long trip. And it was still more fun in the winter to ride to the village in a sleigh behind Old Bill the horse, listening to the crunch of the runners on the well-packed snow. The boy or girl who hasn't ridden in a buggy or sleigh has missed a great deal. We didn't have to watch for traffic in those days for, as I recall it, there wasn't a car in town until I was seven or eight years old. I moved away at that time.

One glorious afternoon, I had a ride behind a high-stepping horse all the way to the capitol of the state, Montpelier. The distance was twenty-eight miles. The road wound through the woods and over the hills until, from the top of Orange Heights, we could see Camel's Hump and the granite quarries of Barre in the distance. The next day, my grandfather came by train and in the afternoon took my cousin and I to see our first circus--Barnum and Bailey's (*so, this would have been about 1908 and the Reverend was about 6 years old).* That was a thrill long to be remembered.

We had no electricity in our home and so when electric lights were first installed at my grandfather's it was a treat to go around turning on the switches.

My grandfather was a good man, and my memory and affection for him is not dimmed. He loved to tease us, and I remember how one night, when my cousin and I were finding it difficult to sleep on the dining room floor, he playfully picked up the poker and brandished it over our heads.
He sleeps in the village cemetery. Requiescat in pace!

Suggested Daily Spiritual Reading:
Zechariah 8:5
Ecclesiastes 2:21-24

Further Reading Related to Diary Entry:
- *200 Years of Soot and Sweat* by Victor R. Rolando (1992). Available from the Vermont Archeological Society: https://www.vtarchaeology.org/publications/200-years-soot-sweat/ [Accessed January 22, 2021].
  - {**Note**: The Reverend's grandfather Albert S. Clark is mentioned in Chapter 6 of this book on page 172.} Also, a lecture film was created based on the book (11-28-2006): *Beyond 200 Years of Soot and Sweat: 19th Century VT iron, charcoal and limestone industries* by RETN, as part of the Harold Meeks Memorial Lecture Series, RETNVT, RETN, Victor Rolando, Brownell Library Events, Archaeology, Brownell Library: https://www.retn.org/show/beyond-200-years-soot-and-sweat-19th-century-vt-iron-charcoal-and-limestone-industries

- *Making Charcoal and Biochar: A Comprehensive Guide* by Rebecca Oaks

Popular Books Published in 1936:
In Dubious Battle by John Steinbeck
Eyeless in Gaza by Aldous Huxley

Popular Movies Released in 1936:
Theodora Goes Wild (Melvyn Douglas, Irene Dunne)
The Charge of the Light Brigade (Errol Flynn, Olivia de Havilland)
Hopalong Cassidy Returns (William Boyd, Gabby Hayes, Gail Sheridan)

November 16, 1936

Moosilauke, circa 1939.

One cannot mention Groton without mentioning that out in Westville, about a mile beyond the turn where my Aunt Lilla use to "keep alcohol", there is a marker to the memory of William Scott, the sentinel who fell asleep on duty during the Civil War. Oddly enough, I never heard that story in my boyhood, and although I heard of the sleeping sentinel pardoned by Lincoln, later on in school days, it wasn't until my college days, or after that, Groton (*Vermont*) was named to me as the place of his birth. The marker is relatively new. I saw it in 1934. No farmhouse there now, only fields and the woods, and far to the South, Mt. Moosilauke limned against the sky. The mind of a Vermonter can easily picture, however, the farm of those days, and a young farm boy, with uncut hair and smooth face, enlisting as a Volunteer in Company K. Going perhaps to Barre or Montpelier for his enlistment. Days of training. Then one night after a long tour of duty, informed that his buddy supposed to relieve him was ill, Scott continued to tour the camp, and fell asleep on duty. An offense in wartime punishable by death. Lincoln heard of the mitigating circumstances and pardoned him. I can imagine Scott's gratitude, and almost envy him the experience, since it resulted—correct me if I err—in his gazing upon the living face of the mightiest American. Twenty-three years and one week from the day of his birth on the little Vermont farm, he died of wounds received in action, at the battle of Lee's Mills (*Virginia*).

"That life is long which answers life's great end." (Edward Young)

The inscription of the marker carries its own pathos and glory:

"IN MEMORY OF WILLIAM SCOTT, THE SLEEPING SENTINEL PARDONED BY ABRAHAM LINCOLN, SEPT 9TH, 1861. BORN ON THIS FARM APRIL 9TH, 1839. ENLISTED IN COMPANY K, 3RD VERMONT VOLUNTEERS, JULY 10TH, 1861. DIED OF WOUNDS A

Lee's Mills April 16th, 1862."

It is a well known fact that Vermont supplied more soldiers in the Civil War, according to her population, than any other state. The words which Lincoln is said to have uttered concerning the Methodist Episcopal Church might well be paraphrased and attributed to this state—small in size, but big in deeds. "She has sent more nurses to the hospitals, more soldiers to the battlefield, and more prayers to heaven than any other."

While I am in a boasting mood concerning my native state, let me mention that in "Who's Who" there are more native-born Vermonters listed than inhabitants of other states; or so I have been informed. But Vermonters have a way of keeping their feet on the ground, and so do not readily contract swellheaditis. I "get a rise" out of my mother when I tell her that a lot of big men come from Vermont, and the sooner they come the bigger they are. However, as Walter Hard, a Vermont writer, has expressed it, they seem to bring something with them in the way of materials.

Half my life was spent there, and I like to go back through the village each summer on my vacation, not only to see Jack and "Lady" Jones, but more especially to visit Groton Pond, for this body of water has changed least of all the old things I knew. My birthplace, the farm, my grandsire's place, even the stores in the town have been altered. But Groton Pond, a lovely three mile body of water to the north of the town, has kept its virginal aspect, and still invites those who truly love nature.

Suggested Daily Spiritual Reading:
Titus 3:4-6
James 1:3-4

Further Reading Related to Diary Entry:
- *Bishop Chase's Reminiscences: an Autobiography*. Comprising a history of the principal events in the author's life to A.D. 1847. Seventy-first Psalm:17,18. Volume 1, second edition by Philander Chase. James B. Dow, Boston.
  Available at the Internet Archive:
      Volume 1: https://archive.org/details/bishopchasesremi01chas/page/n10 [Accessed January 22, 2021].
      Volume 2: https://archive.org/details/bishopchasesremi02chas/page/n8 [Accessed January 22, 2021].

- *The Story of Groton's Historical Sleeping Sentinel. His Memory Lives On* by Marilyn Hatch-Ruiter. Available at http://www.grotonvt.com/AboutGroton/

Groton%20Sleeping%20Sentinel.htm [Accessed January 22, 2021].

Popular Books Published in 1936:
    Fighting Angel by Pearl S. Buck
    Madame Curie: A Biography by Evé Curie

Popular Movies Released in 1936:
    Rose Marie (Nelson Eddy, Jeanette MacDonald)
    The Story of Louis Pasteur (Paul Muni, Josephine Hutchinson, Anita Louise, Donald Woods)
    The Amazing Adventure (Cary Grant, Mary Brian)

November 16, 1936
(Continued)

To reach the Pond, in years gone by, it was necessary to take the train to Lakeside, or go by team (*horse and buggy*) to Ricker's Mills--the oldest continuously operating lumber mill in the United States, Mr. Ricker informs me--and then walk up the track for about two miles until you come to the "big" pond; for Ricker's Mills is at the lower end of the "little" pond, which is about a mile in length and not nearly as wide or beautiful as Groton Pond. Once arrived at the Pond, however, over a new dirt road constructed by the CCC boys (*Civilian Conservation Corps boys*), now stationed at Rickers' Mills, the view is majestic. You can see across the lake three hills of peculiar contour, the one to the left being called Owl's Head. It is shaped like the forehead of an owl and faces toward the Southwest. The hill on the right is shaped likewise and faces southeast. Thus is formed a balanced symmetry very pleasing to the eye.

The Pond has many memories for me. I have stayed in several cottages in the upper end, where there is a beach of whitest sand. My father and mother have taken me there in years gone by, and my grandfather, uncles and aunts have been there with us.

My father was born in Boras, Sweden, loved to fish, and would spend a few days at the Pond each year. The sun still shines as brightly as ever, there are few new cottages as yet, and the cold brook water still courses down to the lake from back in the hills. I remember going out fishing early one morning with my father, grandfather, and uncle. The sun had risen but was red in color, a fiery red. I recall my grandfather telling me, and trying to make me believe, that it was the moon which had just risen. I didn't quite believe him, though I was considerably puzzled. Anyhow, the fish seemed to be biting pretty good. There were lots of blueberries in season, too, not far from the lake.

Two summers ago my wife and I spent a day and a night at the upper end of the Pond. The day was lovely, but the night was different from our anticipations. We decided to sleep out beside a fire on the sands of the beach. After the sun went down it grew cold rapidly. The fire was very comforting, but its radiated heat didn't serve to warm all of the surrounding atmosphere. We huddled together, fully dressed, beneath blankets, but still we were cold. To make it worse, fog covered the lake and the stars were blotted out. About two in the morning we could stand it no longer. We arose and cooked a breakfast, which we ate while shivering, and then packed our materials into the boat, having decided to return to my wife's folks home in Piedmont, N. H., where we were staying. We couldn't see two feet ahead of us, and could only dimly discern the outlined blackness of the shore. I was rowing by dead reckoning. For some distance the red glow of the campfire helped us, but then that too died away. Just the blackness of the night; the mist and the cold accentuated the dip of the oars. My wife huddled in the back seat with a blanket huddled over her shoulders, undoubtedly wishing she was anywhere but there at the moment. It was impossible to tell how near we were to the shore, and we didn't wish to get too near on account of large boulders, which project out into the lake. We heard the crackling of underbrush, once, on the shore of the lake. Moose or bear? More likely a doe down for a drink. Even the longest night wears to dawn, and about two-thirds of the way down the lake the false dawn appeared and the stars faded. Then came the rosy tint of the true dawn, and a welcome sight it was. Toward the end of our journey, we caught the ghostly outline of the framework of an old mill, and soon we had docked. The car started easily, though there was ice on the seat of the boat, and soon we were on our way to warmth and shelter.

Suggested Daily Spiritual Reading:
   Ephesians 6:1-4
   Ezekiel 47:9-10

Further Reading Related to Diary Entry:
- *Ricker Pond State Park*. Available from the VT Dept. of Forests, Parks and Recreation: https://vtstateparks.com/ricker.html [Accessed January 22, 2021].

- *Ricker Pond*. Available from the Vermont Campground Association: https://campvermont.com/campground.html?site=423 [Accessed January 22, 2021].

- *The Forest Service and The Civilian Conservation Corps: 1933-42*. Chapter 10: Region 7—The Eastern Region; Region 9—The North-Central Region (Last Updated, January 7, 2008). Available from the U.S. National Park Service (NPS): https://www.nps.gov/parkhistory/online_books/ccc/ccc/chap10.htm [Accessed January 22, 2021].

Popular Books Published in 1936:
   How to Win Friends and Influence People by Dale Carnegie
   You Can't Take it With You by Moss Hart

Popular Movies Released in 1936:
   Intermezzo (Ingrid Bergman, Gösta Ekman)
   Lloyd's of London (Tyrone Power, Madeleine Carroll)
   Meet Nero Wolfe (Edward Arnold, Lionel Stander, Dennie Moore)

November 17, 1936

I have just come across a copy of Thompson's Gazetteer of Vermont, published in Burlington in 1853 by Zadock Thompson. It is a storehouse of information, and while common to libraries and editorial offices, it has never been my privilege to peruse it heretofore. In connection with Groton, let me record Thompson's early history of the town. The name Hosmer, and Osmore alike, are named in the early history. I quote:

"Groton, a township in the South part of Caledonia County is in lat 44 degrees 14 min., and long 4 degrees 45 mins., and is bounded north by Peacham, east by Ryegate, south by Topsham, and west by Harris' gore. It lies 16 miles east from Montpelier, and 15 northwest from Newbury. It was granted November 7, 1780, and chattered to Thomas Butterfield and his associates, October 20, 1789, containing 28,300 acres. The settlement of the township was commenced in 1787 by Messrs. James, Abbott, Morse, and Osmore. John James was the first male child born in the town. The town was organized March 28, 1797, and Nathaniel Knight was the first town clerk. The wife of Mr. Page, in this town, was in 1819, delivered of four male children at a birth. The religious denominations are Baptists and Methodists. The ministers are Elder Lyman Culver, Baptist and Elder James Smith, Methodist. The surface of this township is generally uneven, rough, and stoney. There is, however, some very good land, both in the Northeast and Southwest parts. The timber is mostly spruce and hemlock, interspersed with maple, beech, and birch. This township is watered by Wells River, and some of its branches, which afford several good mill privileges. There are also several natural ponds. Wells River Pond, through which Wells River passes, is in the north part, and is three miles long and three quarters of a mile wide. Little Pond, in the southeastern part, covered about 100 acres, and lies in the course of the Wells River. Kettle Pond, so called on account of Mr. Hosmer, a hunter, having lost a small kettle in its vicinity, lies in the Northwest corner and covers about 40 acres. The South branch rises in Harris' gore, and running nearly east through the south part of the town, joins Wells River just below Little Pond. In the South part of the township, is an extensive bank of white clay or marl, which is a very good substitute for chalk, and which has been used instead of lime in plastering, and is said to answer a very good purpose. There are here one grist, seven saw and one fulling mill, two stores, and two tanneries. Statistics of 1840: Horses, 169; cattle, 1,138; sheep, 2,061; swine, 605; wheat, bus. 2,185; barley, 306; oats, 13,618; Indian corn, 2,967; potatoes, 31,095; hay, tons, 2,009; sugar, lbs., 20,530; wool, 4,001. Population 928."

Quadruplets, the loss of a kettle--of such simple things is history made. Statistics can tell much, but how many fascinating stories might be written of any town if we could divine the lives and the thoughts of the inhabitants thereof! A traveler from Australia said, to a famous bishop in London, "Your cathedrals are fine, but you should see the church at Austin's Mills!" The bishop went to Australia, visited the little township, and saw what was dearer to the traveller's heart than any cathedral--a little wooden church standing in a bare field! All of us hold dear these centers of our affections.

Suggested Daily Spiritual Reading:
Ephesians 2:18-22
Colossians 3:13-17

Further Reading Related to Diary Entry:
- *Zadock Thompson and The Story of Vermont* by Kevin Graffagnino. Available from the Vermont Historical Society: https://vermonthistory.org/journal/misc/ZadockThompsonVermont.pdf [Accessed January 22, 2021].

- *History of Vermont, Natural, Civil, and Statistical, in three parts, with an Appendix* (1853) by Zadock Thompson. Available at the Internet Archive: https://archive.org/details/historyofvermo00thom/page/n10 [Accessed January 22, 2021].

Popular Books Published in 1936:
Language, Truth and Logic by Alfred J. Ayer
The Snows of Kilimanjaro by Ernest Hemingway

Popular Movies Released in 1936:
- *Secret Agent* (John Gielgud, Madeleine Carroll)
- *Flash Gordon* (Buster Crabbe, Jean Rogers)
- *San Francisco* (Clark Gable, Jeanette MacDonald, Spencer Tracy, Jack Holt, Jessie Ralph, Ted Healy)

November 18, 1936

Vermont mountains, circa 1930s.

"Oh! The high trails, the hill trails,
The winding trails of brown,
Seeing first the sun arise,
And last its going down—
Ever calling to the heart,
With your windings far;
Luring feet to follow on,
Where peak is friend to star!"

In these understanding words, Arthur Wallace Peach intimates the lure of the mountains. There are higher mountains than those in Vermont, but none lovelier. From boyhood I have been lured by the mountains, and have taken advantage of it as opportunity has permitted. I have climbed Monadnock (3,000 ft.) no less than eight times, Camel's Hump (4,000 ft.) twice, and Moosilauke (5,000 ft.) and Washington (6,000 ft.) once each. It isn't simply the peaks that lure, though the view I had of the entire ranges of the Green and White Mountains from Monadnock, one day last fall, was breathtaking. No, the lure lies in the trail itself. The stream that comes coursing down its boulder deep bed on the mountainside, the sun shining through the pines, the birds and occasional squirrel, even the rotting deadwood beside the trail--all these have lure.

And the Psalmist of old did not lift his eyes unto the mountains, but unto the hills whence came his help. Who can ever forget--one having seen--the cold and forbidding, yet majestic, aspect of Vermont hills in winter! With pine, spruce, and hemlock standing out, warm in color against the grayness of the maples, beech, and ash! Then is the time for the fire-lover to snuggle closer to the hearth and pile the fire high to keep out the "great white cold that stalks abroad". Then also is the time for the true nature lover to put on a heavy mackinaw, toque, boots and leggins, mittens, and other accessories, and brave the cold with a brisk walk into the hills, or if the snow be deep enough, to don skis or snowshoes. One moonlit night at Dartmouth two of us did that very thing and skied eight miles to Moose Mountain cabin. The ghostly light on the hills, and the fact that we were lost a couple of times on the way, made the journey memorable.

And I can still see, in retrospect, the great double six-foot high snowroller, manned by two drivers, and pulled by four horses, coming through the drifts and blowing snow up the lane, which stretches out in front of my Groton birthplace, on the cold wintery days when their presence was needed to pack down the snow. Not many of those rollers are still in use, I fancy, certainly not on our well plowed main roads, which are kept open for traffic all winter. But at that time and place, there was no traffic, save in sleighs, and no cars to create the necessity of open roads. Still, we had to walk to school, and to get supplies; hence, the roller service.

And then consider the hills in spring, when the advancing sun loosens the icy grip of winter; when the rivulets and creeks are full to overflowing, and the mayflowers are found deep in the woods. And in the summer when the hillsides are lush and green, and tourists are plentiful. And in the fall, when the alchemy of nature brings out the yellow of the beech, the bronze of the oak, and the scarlet of the swamp maple. None has expressed the mood of the hills better in verse than Bliss Carman, the Vagabond Poet:

```
"There is something in the autumn that is native to my blood—
            Touch of manner, hint of mood;
          And my heart is like a rhyme,
With the yellow and the purple and the crimson keeping time.

    The scarlet of the maples can shake me like the cry
              Of bugles passing by—
           And my lonely spirit thrills
   To see the frosty asters like a smoke upon the hills.
```

> There is something in October sets the gypsy blood astir—
> We must rise and follow her—
> When from every hill of flame
> She calls and calls each vagabond by name."

(*From "A Vagabond Song" by Bliss Carmen [Louis Untermeyer, ed. {1885–1977}. Modern American Poetry. 1919]. Available at bartleby.com:* https://www.bartleby.com/104/24.html *[Accessed January 22, 2021].*)

The hills have all seasons for their own.

Have you ever heard how Vermont got its name? Again, I am indebted to Zadock Thompson who gives an account of it on page 4 of his Vermont History:

> "The name is said to have been adopted upon the recommendation of Dr. Thomas Young (understood generally, though without proof, to have drafted the original constitution the state, submitted to and adopted by the Council of Safety). The following account of the christening of the Green Mountains is given by the Rev. Samuel Peters in his life of the Rev. Hugh Peters, published at New York in 1807. Verd-mont was a name given to the Green Mountains in October 1763 by the Rev. Dr. Peters, the first clergyman who paid a visit to the 30,000 settlers in that country, in the presence of Col. Peters, Judge Peters, and many others who were proprietors of a large number of townships in that colony. The ceremony was performed on the top of a rock standing on a high mountain, then named Mount Pisgah, because it provided, to the company, a clear sight of Lake Champlain, at the West, and at the Connecticut River, at the East, and overlooked all the trees and hills in the vast wilderness at the North and South. The baptisms performed in the following manner: Priest Peters stood on the pinnacle of the rock, when he received a bottle of spirits from Col. Taplin; then haranguing the company with a short history of the infant settlement, and the prospect of its becoming an impregnable barrier between the British colonies on the South and the late colonies of the French on the North, which might be returned to their late owners for the sake of governing America by the different powers of Europe, he continued 'We have here met upon the rock Etam, standing on Mount Pisgah, which makes a part of <u>the everlasting hill</u>, the spine of Asia, Africa, and America, holding together the terrestrial ball, and dividing the Atlantic from the Pacific ocean—to

> dedicate and consecrate this extensive wilderness to God manifested in the flesh, and to give it a new name worthy of the Athenians and ancient Spartans—which new name is <u>Verd</u> <u>Mont</u>, in token that her mountains and hills shall be ever green and shall never die.' He then poured out the spirits and cast the bottle upon the rock Etam."

No spot in the state could more fittingly have been chosen than the rocky height of Mt. Pisgah on Lake Willoughby. This lake has been called the Lucerne of America.

Suggested Daily Spiritual Reading:
Psalm 121
Psalm 104:5-6

Further Reading Related to Diary Entry:
- *History of Vermont, Natural, Civil, and Statistical, in three parts, with an Appendix* (1853) by Zadock Thompson. Available at the Internet Archive: https://archive.org/details/historyofvermo00thom/page/n10 [Accessed January 22, 2021].

- *Vermont Prose: A Miscellany* by Arthur Wallace Peach (Editor), Harold Goddard Rugg (Editor)

- *Roads Taken: Contemporary Vermont Poetry* by Sydney Lea (Editor), Chard deNiord (Editor)

Popular Books Published in 1936:
The Autobiography of G.K. Chesterton by G.K. Chesterton
The Trouble I've Seen by Martha Gellhorn
A Further Range by Robert Frost

Popular Movies Released in 1936:
The General Died at Dawn (Gary Cooper, Madeleine Carroll)
Rembrandt (Charles Laughton, Gertrude Lawrence)
Thank You, Jeeves! (Arthur Treacher, Virginia Field, David Niven)

November 23, 1936

Quoted from Thompson's Gazeteer of Vermont:

"Waterbury, a post town in the western part of Washington County, is in lat. 44d 23m and long. 4d 17m, and is bounded North by Stowe, East by Middlesex, South by Winooski River, which separates it from Duxbury and a part of Moretown, and West by Bolton. It lies 12 miles Northwesterly from Montpelier and 24 miles Southeast from Burlington; and was chartered June 7, 1763, containing 21,220 acres. In June 1784, Mr. James Marsh moved his family, consisting of a wife and eight children, into this township from Bath, N. H., and took possession of a surveyor's cabin, which was standing near Winooski River. Mr. Marsh was induced to move his family hereat the time he did by the promise of the proprietors, that several other families should be procured to move into the town in the following Fall. This promise was not fulfilled, and for nearly a year this solitary family scarcely saw a human being but themselves, and for more than two years their nearest neighbors were in Bolton, 7 miles distant. In the spring of 1785, Hon. Ezra Butler visited this town, and spent some time in preparing a place of residence. In September 1786, he moved his family from Weathersfield Vermont to this town. In 1788, Mr. Caleb Munson moved into the town with his family, and soon after was followed by several others. The town was organized March 31, 1790. Hon. Ezra Butler was ordained elder of the Baptist church, with which he was connected till his death. In 1803, the Rev. Jonathan Hovey was ordained and settled as pastor of the Congregational church of this town. He was dismissed about four years after his settlement. The Rev. Daniel Warren was settled over this church from 1826 to 1839. The present minister, the Rev. J.F. Stone, was settled in 1839. There are two small but pleasant villages. The largest, called <u>Waterbury Street</u>, is in the South part, near Winooski River, and contains a Congregational meeting house, built in 1824; a Methodist meeting house, built in 1841; a village school house; a tavern; three stores; a post office bearing the name of the town; and the usual variety of mechanics. The other village is near the centre of the township, and is called Waterbury Centre…The intervale on Winooski River, and on several smaller streams, is not surpassed in fertility by any in the state, and the lands in every part of the town produce in a manner that amply repays the labor of the skillful farmer. The rocks are principally chlorite and mica and slate and quartz; the former containing sulpheret of iron and sulpheret of copper. The timber is generally hard wood, with a considerable mixture of spruce and hemlock…There are in town 4 meeting houses, 17 school districts, 2 post offices, 4 stores, 1 tavern, 2 grist and 10 saw mills, 3 tanneries, 1 clothing works and woolen factory…Population 1,192."

Suggested Daily Spiritual Reading:
Isaiah 43:2
Ezekiel 47:9

Further Reading Related to Diary Entry:
- *Zadock Thompson and The Story of Vermont* by Kevin Graffagnino. Available from the Vermont Historical Society: https://vermonthistory.org/journal/misc/ZadockThompsonVermont.pdf [Accessed January 22, 2021].

- *History of Vermont, Natural, Civil, and Statistical, in three parts, with an Appendix* (1853) by Zadock Thompson. Available at the Internet Archive: https://archive.org/details/historyofvermo00thom/page/n10 [Accessed January 22, 2021].

Popular Books Published in 1936:
Fighting Angel by Pearl S. Buck
Man Makes Himself by V. Gordon Childe
Hamilton Fish: The Inner History of the Grant Administration by Allan Nevins

Popular Movies Released in 1936:
The Trail of the Lonesome Pine (Sylvia Sidney, Fred MacMurray, Henry Fonda)
The Plainsman (Jean Arthur, Gary Cooper)
Yellowstone (Judith Barrett, Alan Hale)

1937

January 4, 1937

One of the profoundest forces in shaping our lives is the influence of environment and persons in early life. I understand that young Russians cannot enter places of worship until they are twenty-one. We change little emotionally after twenty-one, or even fifteen. I distinctly recall uniting with the Methodist Episcopal Church when fourteen years of age, and thinking to myself, at that time, "Now I may grow older, and acquire more knowledge, but I can never be more aware that I am alive and that things are what they are than right now." I was sure of it then. I am still sure of it twenty years later.

Dominating the village of Groton, for it faces the village street, is a Methodist Church. I was born a Methodist, even as I was born a Republican. I know not who established it there, nor how deviating the way of John Wesley and his evangelistic fervor to the New England expression in wood and stone in this little town, but I do know it altered my life. A neighbor, her whom I called "Lady" Jones, said to my mother when I was about three years of age, "He's cut out for a Methodist preacher". The idea was repressed sternly until long after college days, until I was impressed, not only by its inevitability, but also by its desirability. But there is a beginning, make of it what you will. I went to Sunday school and Church as regularly as to day school. Undoubtedly, its influence was deep, although seemingly superficial. I used to squirm and fidget with the other children, and chiefly enjoyed the long walk home in the sunshine, knowing that a good dinner awaited me. And now the pastor of the Methodist Church in a neighboring town, Stead Thornton, by name, was pastor of the Groton Church during the war years. Such a small world, after all!

I left Groton when eight years of age. My father found work in Waterbury, and thither we moved. I remember seeing with awe the capital of the state, and learning the difference between capital and capitol. Standing on the platform of Montpelier Junction, I gazed upon the Montreal Express, a great monster on the rails, puffing and panting, about to take me to a new home. I had heard that old poem:

>   "The Montreal Express, was speeding at its best,
>   Near Hartford bridge it struck a broken rail—
>   Then with a fearful crash, to the river it was dashed,
>   And no one lived to tell the horrid tale."

(*From the poem "The Wrong Rail in the Wrong Place at the Wrong Time: The 1887*

West Hartford Bridge Disaster" by J.A. Ferguson. Available from The Vermont Historical Society: <u>https://vermonthistory.org/journal/81/VHS8101TheWrongRail.pdf</u> *[Accessed January 22, 2021].)*

And now I was seeing the Montreal Express "in person". Small wonder it impressed me! It bore us swiftly up the Winooski valley--the valley of the Onion River--to our new home. We arrived long after dark, and all we could do that first night was to light up two or three kerosene lamps, and Mother fixed up the beds, and we went to sleep.

Appended as taken from Thompson's Vermont is a birds eye view of Waterbury Vermont of the early days. It has changed considerably since those days, but that is the beginning, and I am still interested greatly in early beginnings. They often lead to strange endings.

Outside of the technical treatises that are written for the preservation and development of the knowledge of the past, I fancy that a large share of the poetry and prose that has been written has been done with this thought in mind, consciously or otherwise--to project or extend in time the thought and personality of the writer. As Hugh Browlley expressed it so ably:

```
"There is something within us that can be without us, and
will be after us, though indeed it hath no knowledge of
what it was before us, or how it came to enter into us."
```

(Actually, the above quote is similar to Sir Thomas Browne's, from his book "Religio Medici: The Religion of a Doctor": "Thus we are men, and we know not how, there is something in us, that can be without us, and will be after us, though it is strange that it hath no history, what it was before us, nor cannot tell how it entered in us.")

As I write, I think of the lives that are to be lived in long, long years to come, and my thought goes out to those lives hoping they will find in their turn those supreme satisfactions of the individual self that make life so worth while. To you of ten, a hundred, a thousand years hence, greetings! To you who have not unjustly died but justly live, my best wishes for the more abundant life. I have found such a life and, like St. Paul of old, the life I now live in the flesh I live in faith by the Son of God, who loved us and gave himself for us. These descriptions, this autobiography, are aimed toward that goal, of showing one man's development of thought through childhood, boyhood, manhood, and the influences at work therein.

> "There is a Divinity that shapes our ends, roughhew them how we will." (*Shakespeare—a quote from "Hamlet"*)

My inclinations and aptitudes culminated in the ministry as a satisfactory expression of the ego in service. Why are we more happy in helping others than in living selfishly? Why did Christ come not to be ministered unto, but to minister? Why is that life incomplete which does not in some measure include the outreach of self into other lives? A current writer, a clergyman of Wellesley, Mass., points out the tremendous dynamic obtainable from the sayings of Jesus, who knew how to live supremely. In "Magnificent Obsession" Lloyd Douglas preaches a great sermon. The dynamic found there and displayed in the lives of his heroes and heroines is that in the sixth chapter of Luke:

> "Let not thy right hand know what the left hand doeth."

And Charles M. Sheldon, great pastor of the First Church in Topeka, wrote a book at the close of the last century (*1896*) which captured the attention of the world. It was called "In His Steps" and was based on I Peter 11:

> "For hereunto we ye called, because Christ also suffered for us, leaving us an example, that ye should follow His steps."

The answer to the question, "What would Jesus do?" profoundly changed many lives.

Now, it is very interesting to recall that the first parish which Charles M. Sheldon served was the Congregational Church in Waterbury, Vermont. I did not know that until the other day. I have attended services in that Church during the World War (*WWI*). I distinctly remember the affable and outstanding pastor of the Church, Rev. William Boicourt, who served as chaplain in the War. The site of the Church is just about where the first settler of the town built a little hut for the storage of his corn that first unfortunate winter. Marsh was his name. He returned in the dead of winter to find his corn crib ransacked by predatory animals, and had to leave his children to get along as best they could until his return. He found them on his return at the home of the nearest neighbor, in Richmond, some ten miles away. I can see in fancy Waterbury as a wilderness, with occasional bands of Indians walking through the forest, along the banks of the Onion River. There is no record, so far as I know, of Indians settled on the site of the town. But they used the valley as a trail to and from Canada. A fine concrete road now meanders up the valley, and there are so many places of interest to tell about in connection with my eleven years residence there that I scarcely know where to begin.

(Above, the Reverend references the fact that at the age of 8 years old, his family moved from Groton, Vermont, to Waterbury. So, it seems that he lived in Waterbury until he was 19.)

Suggested Daily Spiritual Reading:
1 Peter: 11
John 14:6

Further Reading Related to Diary Entry:
- *Religio Medici: The Religion of a Doctor*. Available at Sir Thomas Browne website, University of Chicago: https://penelope.uchicago.edu/relmed/relmed.html [Accessed January 22, 2021].

- *Magnificent Obsession* by Lloyd Douglas. Available at the Internet Archive: https://archive.org/details/magnificentobses00byll [Accessed January 22, 2021].

- *In His Steps* by Charles M. Sheldon. Available at Project Gutenberg: https://www.gutenberg.org/ebooks/4540 [Accessed January 22, 2021].

Popular Books Published in 1937:
Most Popular Books Published In 1937. Available at Goodreads.com: https://www.goodreads.com/book/popular_by_date/1937 [Accessed January 22, 2021].

Popular Movies Released in 1937:
A Day at the Races (The Marx Brothers)
Captains Courageous (Spencer Tracy, Freddie Bartholomew, Lionel Barrymore)
The Emperor's Candlesticks (William Powell, Luise Rainer, Robert Young, Maureen O'Sullivan, Frank Morgan)

January 6, 1937

The village of Waterbury lies in the valley of the Onion River. I would never have guessed, during my eleven years of residence there, that "Old Man Ribber" would or could go on such a rampage as it did in November of 1927 (*he would have been 25*), just a little more than ten years ago. Thatcher's Brook, a tributary, coming down from "Mill Village", often overflowed in the spring, so that it covered the "twin bridges" in the northern end of the town, and I have seen where the Winooski, too, backed up and overflowed its banks coming a short distance up Winooski street, but to even imagine that the inundation of the river would one day carry nearly to the top of "Bank Hill", in the center of the town, was unthinkable. And yet it happened.

I visited the village about six weeks before the flood and three weeks after, and such a contrast! The newly painted houses were muddy up to the second story, all along the main street, and two of the bridges to the South were quite washed away. The loss of life was heavy, too; the toll being 27, if I remember aright. Toward Middlesex we crossed the river on a swaying footbridge, without railings, and near the Palisades the mud was piled high in the roadway to the depth of three or four feet, the Macadam Road, washed out entirely, and two white houses set back from the road several yards were completely absent. I picked up a doorknob on the spot—all that was left of former homes. Houses nearer the village were askew, and to the north of the town they were upended. We ferried across the river to the Main Street, and after passing a mile of desolation, in the form of despoiled homes, arrived, finally, at the white Congregational Church on the hill, where Dr. Sheldon had once preached, and where now a corps of relief workers were serving meals to the needy. That was Waterbury in 1927.

Now for the Waterbury of 1910 and thereafter. I suppose a boy remembers summer best. I use to run away with the others and go swimming in Thatcher's Brook. I remember the triumph I felt when at last I could coordinate feet and arms and really swim, even if it was only a "dog paddle". I have taught many children to swim since then, my own son included, but that was a banner day. Among my playmates were four boys who have since gone their separate ways. Those separate ways are of interest in themselves. One became a doctor, one a lawyer, one an electrical engineer, one a school teacher, and I became a clergyman! Yet, back there in the old swimmin'-hole, we were just boys, out for a good time, and let the world go hang! Indian weed on the bank, white downy thistles, willow trees, and the warm sun overhead; these the concomitants of youth. I have always had an appreciation of nature, and there was ample outlet for it in Waterbury. We threw crabapples at each other to the west of town, made bows and arrows of hemlock and ash, built a log cabin on Sunset Hill, and climbed Camel's Hump (4,006 feet).

The centers of my life were the home, the school, the Church, and the out-of-doors. Perhaps I should add to these the printing office, for there I was shaped for college and given a start in life by a versatile near genius in applied business and philanthropy, the late and truly lamented Harry C. Whitehill.

Let us consider these centers one by one. First, my home life. Whistler's portrait of his mother suggests repose of infinite calm. I cannot recall my mother so (*his mother Etta [nee Clark] Anderson*). She has always been active, loving her family with inordinate pride and sacrificing for it unceasingly. She has lived in and for her children, and I hope we have not disappointed her overmuch.

Christina, my older sister, after high school, decided to take up nursing, and during this period went to Rochester, New York, and attended the Homeopathic Hospital of that city, called the "City of Flowers", and renowned for its Kodaks and Eastman music hall. Upon her graduation, after a short period of private nursing, she became connected with the Henry Street Settlement nursing service in New York, which service the Metropolitan Life Insurance Company likewise uses for its nurses. Here she labored for twelve years.

Christina's (back row, 4th from left) graduation from nursing school, circa 1920.

Lilla, my younger sister was born in Groton in 1909, and was but a year old when we migrated to Waterbury.

Suggested Daily Spiritual Reading:
Psalms 118:24
Romans 12:9-15

Further Reading Related to Diary Entry:
- *History of the 1927 Flood*. Available from the University of Vermont, Land Change Program: https://www.uvm.edu/landscape/1927_flood/about_1927_flood.htm [Accessed January 22, 2021].

- *History of Waterbury, Vermont, 1763-1915*; edited by Theodore Graham Lewis; Published by Harry C. Whitehill (1915); The Record Print, Waterbury, Vermont. Available at the Internet Archive: https://archive.org/details/HOW_vtrbms [Accessed January 22, 2021].

Popular Books Published in 1937:
The Cost of Discipleship by Dietrich Bonhoeffer
Beat to Quarters by C. S. Forester

Popular Movies Released in 1937:
Shall We Dance Fed Astaire, Ginger Rogers)
Topper (Cary Grant, Constance Bennett, Roland Young)
Green Light (Errol Flynn, Anita Louise)

Page 15 - No Date - 1937

My father worked as a granite carver for the Perry Granite Company in Waterbury

(A *1938 picture of Waterbury showing the Perry Granite Company building is available from Martin McGuirk's Central Vermont Railway website at http://centralvermontrailway.blogspot.com/2016/12/then-and-now-perry-granite-later-cooley.html [Accessed January 22, 2021]. The building is still standing today*.).

Our home life was a happy one and especially happy were the days later on when my father considered me old enough to go fishing with him on Lake Champlain. Those days--two or three each year for a period of years--are very precious in my memory. I shall speak of them in their due place.

As regards the school, Waterbury takes just pride in its educational system. I was held back a year since we moved late in the Spring, and it was rather difficult for me to "get onto" the long division then being employed. I can still see the rows of figures on the blackboard, and I believe the teacher's name was Miss Joslyn. After that there was no major difficulty and the years up to high school passed without incident. I took as my subject in graduating from grammar school (there was no junior high school in those days and at that place) "The Industries of Vermont". Waterbury had, at that time, the second largest talc mine in the state--the talc being used mostly for roofing, automobiles, etc., and only about one percent going into talcum powder. I once visited the mill and mine, situated to the south of the village, shortly after there had been a cave-in at the mine. I penetrated the mine to the scene of the cave-in--about a quarter mile--and recall, vividly, the dampness of the passage. Talc comes in large chunks, which are conveyed to the mill in little cars, similar to those used in coal mines--and then the talc is crushed to necessary fineness. That graduation essay helped me to understand more about the resources of the state--lumber, granite, marble, maple syrup, and Morgan horses!

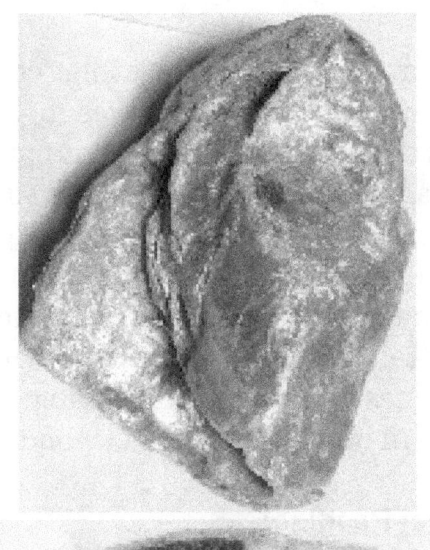

Talc (top and bottom) from the Reverend's mineral collection.

The high school years passed pleasantly and swiftly. We use to sing in assembly "Through the four long years of high school", but even at the time, I dimly realized that they were short years indeed. Later on at Dartmouth, I once saw an old grad looking out over the campus, and I wondered if I would ever be as old and out of things as he. Well, I am, and can understand his silence in surveying the past.

```
"The moving finger writes, and having writ
    Moves on; nor all your piety nor wit
   Can lure it back to cancel half a line
  Nor all your tears wash out a word of it."
```
(*From "The Moving Finger", from the Rubaiyat of Omar Khayyam; a sermon by Reverend E.F Dinsmore*)

In high school, I didn't have much time for athletics, for I was working in my spare hours. In my last year, incongruously, I was made president of the athletic association, but the extent of my duties, under that high sounding title, were to take tickets at the basketball games. Buck O'Brien was the athletic genius of the school. He is a lawyer now, I believe, at least he attended Fordham with that intention. His father, at one time, ran the motion picture theater in town. What a thrill it was when, on one or two occasions, we as special friends of "Buck", christened Leo, were admitted free to an afternoon matinee. There was a popcorn machine in the orchestra pit, and the piano was out of tune, and perhaps John Bunny flickered some in outline, but it was wonderful just the same!

Suggested Daily Spiritual Reading:
1 Timothy 3:2-8
Proverbs 17:17

Further Reading Related to Diary Entry:
- *The Moving Finger* of Omar Khayyam; a sermon by Reverend E.F. Dinsmore, Unity Church, Santa Barbara, CA. Available at the Internet Archive: https://archive.org/details/movingfingerofom00dinsrich/page/n4 [Accessed January 22, 2021].

- The Book of Omar and Rubáiyát (Being a book of miscellanies—biographical, historical, bibliographical, and pictorial notes on Omar Khayyam of Naishapur, and his inspired quatrains.) The Bankside Press. M.F. Mansfield, publisher; New York and London, 1900. Available at the Internet Archive: https://archive.org/details/bookofomarrubai00newyuoft/page/n11 [Accessed January 22, 2021].

- *John Bunny* biography. Available at imdb.com: https://www.imdb.com/name/nm0120544/bio [Accessed January 22, 2021].

Popular Books Published in 1937:
Men of Mathematics by Eric Temple Bell
The Importance Of Living by Lin Yutang

Popular Movies Released in 1937:
Black Legion (Humphrey Bogart, Ann Sheridan)
You Only Live Once (Sylvia Sidney, Henry Fonda)
Jim Hanvey, Detective (Guy Kibbee, Tom Brown, Catherine Doucet)

Page 16 - No Date - 1937

To the east of the village of Waterbury lies Mill Village, so called from an old tannery that used to be there. Just opposite the grist mill, where I often went for chicken corn, was a steep hill admirably adapted for skiing and tobogganing, and on barrel staves improvised and on sleds we made the most of the hill in winter. (I can well imagine it is in use today, for boys are eternal.) Above Mill Village, the road gradually winds upward until you come to Blush Hill, and from here began the mile-long rides on a traverse, which were the real thrill of the winter. Packed six or eight on the long bobsleds, with the leader in firm control of the ropes, we would ride with deepest pleasure a hundred yards below the gristmill. The long trek back wasn't such a thrill! In Mill Village, too, was the Mill Pond, which made an ideal skating place, when the backwash from the river wasn't quite solid enough. Snow-trains and buses now take the skier to the slopes of Mount Mansfield, just outside the village of Stowe, connected in those days by trolley car with Waterbury.

In the days before the war (*WWI—the Reverend was 12 years old when the war began and 16 when it ended.*), we had as teacher of agriculture and athletics in school a man by the name of Perry Aldrich. During the summertime he hired a field across the brook, and planted beans. There was, and still is, to the best of my knowledge, a large canning factory in the town. When the beans came up they had to be cultivated. I led the horse while Perry guided the cultivator. I was proud of that experience afterward for in the fall Mr. Aldrich enlisted in the air corps of the Army and went to France, where he was shot down while acting as observer over the enemy lines. He was our first contact with the casualties of war. Infantile paralysis invaded the community about this time, and while isolated at home, I learned to knit, with my mother's help, a khaki sweater. Hence, a feeling of kinship with all knitters.

The day came, when, all examinations passed, I stood to deliver the salutatory address on the platform of the theater. I chose for my subject this time "Overcoming the Impossible", and this recital of the deeds of Admiral Peary, Columbus, and others has often been in my mind, when I have heard it said, "It can't be done". Not long thereafter, armed with my mother's blessing and the promise of a job in the college print shop, I took the train south, headed for Dartmouth College, and my high school days were at an end. Gone but not forgotten--these many memories of associations with splendid young people. An unusually large percentage of the class of nineteen twenty-eight went on to higher education and larger opportunities. All-in-all, I shall not look upon their like again.

Suggested Daily Spiritual Reading:
Philippians 4:13
Romans 15:13

Further Reading Related to Diary Entry:
- *World War I: Camp Vail, 1916*. Available from the Vermont Historical Society: https://vermonthistory.org/world-war-i-camp-vail-1916 [Accessed January 22, 2021].

- *Waterbury Village Historic District*. Available from the U.S. National Park Service, Department of the Interior: https://www.nps.gov/nr/travel/centralvermont/cv8.htm [Accessed January 22, 2021].

Popular Books Published in 1937:
The Bachelor of Arts by R.K. Narayan
Northwest Passage by Kenneth Roberts

Popular Movies Released in 1937:
The Prince and the Pauper (Errol Flynn, Claude Rains, Henry Stephenson)
The Prisoner of Zenda (Ronald Colman, Madeleine Carroll, C. Aubrey Smith)
The Life of Émile Zola (Paul Muni, Joseph Schildkraut, Gale Sondergaard)

Page 17 - No Date - 1937

The third center of influence, and a not inconsiderable one, was the Church, the Methodist Episcopal Church. It has had a long and honorable history in Waterbury. A venerable gentleman, Rev. Mr. Douglas was pastor when we first went to Waterbury, and while I do not remember his sermons, I do remember one fine Sunday afternoon when he invited me to ride down the other side (the western side) of the Winooski River to a little church in South Duxbury where he conducted a service. It was simple, but very impressive, and there was a saintliness about the preacher, which lent dignity and beauty to the service. The ride down and back with horse and buggy was enjoyable also. He had a charming daughter, Florence, a companion of my sister, who died a year or so later. It was a grievous loss for him.

I attended Church and Sunday school regularly. My first teacher was a Miss Crossett, then nearly ninety, whose low, pleasing voice and gaily-colored, little, religious cards she distributed are still remembered. Verne L. Smith became pastor after Mr. Douglas, and he organized the first Boy Scout troop in the town. He was a boy with the boys, and inasmuch as he had been a carpenter before entering the ministry, he employed that craft to our advantage, and we helped him build a cabin on Sunset Hill, to the north of town. Stones from the fireplace we carried from a little brook to the cabin in our kerchiefs. It was a good substantial cabin and we had a number of outings there. I often use to visit it when berrying or wandering over the hillside while living on "Farrar's Addition", as the suburb of the north of town was called. Our Scout troop was organized about 1915 (he was 13), just five years after the movement came to this country from England. I derived a great deal of benefit from Scouting, although attaining only to the rank of second class Scout. Unfortunately, Mr. Smith was called to Beverly, Massachusetts, where he assisted in building a new Church-- unfortunately for us I mean, for our Scout work languished.

The Reverend's Boy Scout Troop (he is third from left), circa 1915.

At this time, while living on the Addition, whither we had moved from Main Street, I had one of the most enjoyable periods of my life. We were happy in our home life, I was attending high school, I loved to wander over the hills nearby, and I had as a chum a boy named Dustin Cooley, who was more blessed in this world's goods than I, and also was gifted with considerable scientific ability. He later studied electrical engineering at U.V.M, as the University of Vermont is locally called, and worked for General Electric at Schenectady. His father sold diesel engines in and around Boston. Before the war, we were interested in wireless, and he rigged up wireless telephone and telegraph sets between our homes. What a thrill it was to hear Arlington, Virginia, give the time signals in code at ten pm! The news of Admiral Dewey's death came via wireless shortly before amateur stations were dismantled by government order at the outbreak of war (*WWI*). Dustin had the first De Forest audio tube in town--a two-element tube, which displaced the galena crystals we were using as detectors. I still have the spark coil which I used to send messages to him in that far-off era. Today, the far corners of the world come to my door in code and voice through the magic and genius of shortwave, but I shall always feel privileged to have been associated with the early days of ham radio. Even the word "radio" was unknown to us then.

Mr. Smith was succeeded in the church by a Mr. Locke, whom I remember chiefly for his pronunciation of "to-wards", always making it two words. The Church, through services and socials, filled a real need in my life at that time. I united with the Church when fourteen years of age.

<u>Suggested Daily Spiritual Reading:</u>
Exodus 20:8-11
John 14:6

Further Reading Related to Diary Entry:
- *Roots (1736–1816), John and Charles Wesley and the Evangelical Revival in England*. Available from the United Methodist Church: http://www.umc.org/who-we-are/roots [Accessed January 22, 2021].

- *The Boy Scout and Other Stories for Boys* by Richard Harding Davis; copyright, 1891, 1903, 1912, 1914, 1917, by Charles Scribner's Sons. Available at Project Gutenberg: https://www.gutenberg.org/ebooks/30953 [Accessed January 22, 2021].

- *The History of the Radio Industry in the United States to 1940*. Available from the Economic History Association: https://eh.net/encyclopedia/the-history-of-the-radio-industry-in-the-united-states-to-1940/ [Accessed January 22, 2021].

Popular Books Published in 1937:
The Complete Works of O. Henry by O. Henry
The Devil and Daniel Webster by Stephen Vincent Benét

Popular Movies Released in 1937:
The Good Earth (Paul Muni, Luise Rainer)
Make Way for Tomorrow (Victor Moore, Beulah Bondi)
The Shadow (Rita Hayworth, Charles Quigley)

Page 18 - No Date - 1937

The out-of-doors has always appealed to me. My favorite Psalm is the 121st—"I will lift up mine eyes unto the hills whence cometh my help." The highest point in Middlesex County (*Massachusetts*), where this is written, is a little hill called Nobscot, some 300 feet (Nobscot Hill is located in Framingham, MA). I have climbed the tower countless times and looked longingly toward Mount Monadnock in southern New Hampshire, some ninety miles away, knowing that from the top of that I could see the Vermont and New Hampshire ranges in all their glory—as I did on a clear day a year ago last fall.

Monadnock is a little more than 3,000 feet high, and I have climbed it eight or ten times, by all the trails, save the Long Dublin Trail. Spread out in a vast panorama to all points of the compass are over sixty lakes. It is a beautiful spot on a clear day. I have also climbed Moosilauke near Warren, New Hampshire, 5,000 feet in height, and Mt. Washington, 6,000 feet. But these mountains, delightful as they are, do not have the personality and picturesqueness of Camel's Hump (4,000 ft), which is monarch off all it surveys, some eight miles to the northwest of Waterbury. True, it looks like the hump of a camel, but the Indian name fits it better—Tah-wah-bede-ee-wadso, meaning Saddle Mountain. The early French explorers called it Le Lion Couchant—the crouching lion. It is a splendid sight from the waters of Lake Champlain. I have climbed it twice, staying overnight once, but on both occasions the mountain was enshrouded in fog, and I have never had the privilege of knowing what the view from the peak really is.

Mt. Washington train

Mt. Washington Train (Ammonoosuc)-Albert & Janet, circa, 1941.

The Reverend and his mother—possibly at Mt. Washington observatory, circa 1941.

Back in 1910 (*he was 8 years of age*), our neighbors across the street, McNally by name, invited us to go to Camel's Hump with them, and one Sunday morning we set out, riding in a two-seated carriage with a frilled canopy to keep off sun or rain. A span of horses carried us in good time to the base house, a mile or so from the top of the mountain, and there the women and children (including myself) stayed until the men returned. It was thought too hard a climb for and eight-year old boy, although my son and daughter, seven and five, respectively, climbed Monadnock with us Labor Day last, and were less fatigued than we. While waiting their return, we amused ourselves around the barn and orchards. I remember the plums we picked. They were small blue ones and a trifle sour, but they tasted delicious to us. The wooded slopes of the mountain towered above us like a great sentinel. Emerson once gave an address in the Divinity School at Harvard, which I later attended, in which he used the text "The sun shines today, also". The same warming rays of sun, which illumine the earth in the year of our Lord 1937, came from the same source which gave such luster and magic to that far-off day. The ride to the mountain and home again was memorable. Mountains lend themselves readily to contemplation. They are challenges to climbing to be sure, but above that they exhibit a calm aloofness and patience, which are much needed in the restless mind of man.

> "Our little systems have their day—
> They have their day and cease to be—
> They are but broken lights of Thee,
> And thou, O Lord, art more than they."

(*From "In Memoriam" by Alfred Lord Tennyson. Available at The Poetry Foundation:* https://www.poetryfoundation.org/poems/45328/in-memoriam-a-h-h-obiit-mdcccxxxiii-prelude *[Accessed January 22, 2021].*)

It would take many pages to express my indebtedness to the Vermont hills. Suffice it to say that there is a deep-seated nostalgia for them that not even the varied charm and appeal of Singing Beach at Manchester by the sea, nor the sands and sails of Nantucket have been able to dispel.

Suggested Daily Spiritual Reading:
Psalm 121
1 Peter 5:8

Further Reading Related to Diary Entry:
- *Nobscot Scout Reservation*. Available from the Sudbury Valley Trustees at https://www.svtweb.org/properties/page/nobscot-scout-reservation-conservation-restriction-sudbury [Accessed January 22, 2021].

- *Hiking Overview. Available from the* Vermont Department of Forests, Parks, and Recreation at https://vtstateparks.com/hiking.html *[Accessed January 22, 2021].*

- *A 1940s Monadnock Childhood* by Tom Shultz

Popular Books Published in 1937:
- *The Flivver King: A Story of Ford-America* by Upton Sinclair
- *Pecos Bill: The Greatest Cowboy of All Time* by James Cloyd Bowman

Popular Movies Released in 1937:
- *Maytime* (Jeanette MacDonald, Nelson Eddy, John Barrymore)
- *Lost Horizon* (Ronald Colman, Jane Wyatt, Edward Everett Horton)
- *Super-Sleuth* (Jack Oakie, Ann Sothern, Paul Guilfoyle)

Page 19 - No Date - 1937

Next to Camel's Hump in its appeal in those days (and now) were the blue waters of Lake Champlain. My father loved to fish, and in my high school years we spent two or three days at the Lake trolling for pickerel. We visited, successively, Shelburne Bay near Burlington, then Mallet's Bay where in the early 1900s he caught Pickerel or Pike weighing 21 pounds, a record catch at that time--then Kellet's Bay in North Hero on Grand Isle--a long island in the middle of Lake Champlain.

The year we went to Mallet's Bay, he (*his father*) was successful in catching a nice string of pickerel, one weighing ten pounds, another six, and several three or four. I have the snapshot at hand to prove this assertion, if proof were needful.

The Reverend (on the left) with his Father Solomon Anderson after a fishing trip in which many pickerel were caught.

The ten-pounder was quite a large pickerel, of course, and a gaff was inadequate for the landing. So my father reached over the side of the boat, caught the pickerel by the gills, and hauled him into the boat. You can be sure my father's eyes were sparkling, then, and he was chuckling. We anchored the fish with the boat chain and thrust him under the seat. Surprisingly, he didn't struggle much. Probably, he had done all of his fighting previously. On another occasion, we rowed a long distance around the shore of the Lake and up the Lamoille River, where we camped overnight. Those who have been to Kellet's Bay will recall the railroad bed, which had for its construction across the Lake, hundreds of marble blocks cast off from the Proctor quarries. In the morning sun, with the sky intensely blue, the white marble gleamed a most enhancing white. The fellow at whose camp we stayed at in North Hero was arrested for rum smuggling not long after our departure. Of course, we knew nothing of his activities, although we often passed the ice house where he kept the liquor hidden--indeed we even borrowed some ice to keep our fish fresh, if I remember aright.

We arose early one morning, on Mallet's Bay, and went out for fish. There was a fresh breeze, the sky was cloudless, the sun ascending, and far to the Southeast Camel's Hump outlined the sky. We anchored among some lily pads, or rather near them, and while my father fished, I gave myself over to contemplation of the beauty of the morning. I see, in retrospect, the white house on the shore nearby, the tilled fields, the birds wheeling overhead, and to me it seems like the beginning of the world. Indeed it could not have been more beautiful in that far-off dawn when the Spirit of light moved upon the face of the waters. If this account moves another to meditation and retrospect of Lake Champlain as pleasing as mine, it will not be labor lost but satisfaction gained. I have no doubt that Europe has its lovely lakes and Alps, but even though Lake Willoughby in Vermont has been called the Lucerne of America, and though I have seen it also in the morning, I grant the palm of loveliness to Lake Champlain. When I feel the rocking of a rowboat and the clug-clug of the anchor chain, I am transported back to the incomparable coloring of sky and sea in that day and place.

On our way to Lamoille River, we passed a Boy Scout cabin set back in the pines on the shore of the Lake and facing west toward the New York skyline. Although I have had scout troops under my charge and we have visited interesting places, I have always regretted the fact that I could not attend a summer camp. The Abenaki Indians used to roam these shores, and undoubtedly fished in their canoes (I wonder if they caught pickerel or knew anything about trolls). They camped on the shores of the great lake and built their fires. The Boy Scouts lived the life of the Indians vicariously with modern conveniences the Indians never knew. I suppose their ghosts are still there, and in their Happy Hunting Grounds the warriors still find ghostly fish for their ephemeral diet. But there will be others, in years to come, who will likewise claim these fishing rights--those who have been captivated, as I was, by the peacefulness and grandeur of the Lake. Perhaps the Indians will solemnly welcome, if they have not already done so, the spiritual forms of Sieur de la Champlain and his fellows explorers who travelled down the Richilieu River and discovered the lake which bears his name. About its shores cluster the legends of many years--some forgotten now--but its beauty is there for all to discover anew.

Suggested Daily Spiritual Reading:
Ephesians 6:10-11
Philippians 4:4

Further Reading Related to Diary Entry:
- *Lakes and Ponds*. Available from the State of Vermont, Department of Environmental Conservation at https://dec.vermont.gov/watershed/lakes-ponds [Accessed January 22, 2021].

- *Lake Champlain History*. Available from the Lake Champlain Maritime Museum at https://www.lcmm.org/explore/lake-champlain-history/ [Accessed January 21, 2021].

- *Benedict Arnold's Navy: The Ragtag Fleet That Lost the Battle of Lake Champlain but Won the American Revolution* by James L. Nelson

- *Lake Champlain Islands* by Tara Liloia

- *The Battle of Lake Champlain: A "Brilliant and Extraordinary Victory"* by John H. Schroeder

Popular Books Published in 1937:
A Hermit in the Himalayas: The Journal of a Lonely Exile by Paul Brunton
Amateur Telescope Making - Advanced by Albert G. Ingalls; Scientific American Inc.
Everybody's Enquire Within (Volume 1) edited by Charles Ray

Popular Movies Released in 1937:
A Damsel in Distress (Fred Astaire, George Burns, Gracie Allen)
Shall We Dance (Fred Astaire, Ginger Rogers)
You're Only Young Once (Mickey Rooney, Lewis Stone, Cecilia Parker)

Page 20 - September 28, 1937

The fifth and last, but by no means least, of early influences in Waterbury was my connection with the printing office and stationary store, preceded over by the genial proprietor, Harry C. Whitehill. Mr. Whitehill not only gave me work in his office during high school days, but furthered my education by securing a scholarship for me at Dartmouth and a job in the printing office there, as well, which job enabled me to "earn my way" through college.

Mr. Whitehill was also born in Groton (which accounts in part, I presume, for his interest in my welfare), the son of Moses and Ella Whitehill. I have heard Moses Whitehill driving his team of oxen in the woods of an early morning on the neighboring lumber lot, a "wohish there" accompanying the flick of the whip. Ella Whitehill was a lovely soul, who took great pride in the success of her sons (George, the other son, lives in St. Johnsbury and has been connected for many years with the Fairbanks Scale Company). Harry Whitehill was educated at Montpelier Seminary, coming soon afterwards to Waterbury where he courted and married Mary Moody, whose father, a fine, bearded gentleman, published the Waterbury Record and Stowe Journal, did job printing, and sold newspapers and stationery. Upon his death, Harry Whitehill took over the management of the store. Since the period when I worked for him (1917 - 1921 [*ages 15 - 19*]), he has built and operated a radio station, WDEV, with its concomitant modernization of his office by the addition of teletypewriters etc., bringing latest news from the news-gathering agencies. This station was the crowning achievement of a long and busy life. Mrs. Franklin Roosevelt visited the town and station in 1933 or 1934 (*so, 3 or 4 year ago, as he is writing this*) and was escorted to the station by Mr. Whitehill. At Dartmouth, in 1924, he helped to arrange a meeting of Republicans of Vermont and New Hampshire with Vice President Calvin Coolidge as speaker, but I imagine his pleasure and pride on that occasion did not match his privilege of escorting the First Lady of the land to the station he had erected.

I first went to work for Mr. Whitehill in the capacity of newsboy. I think I was in my sophomore year of high school, then. After a few weeks of this, I was asked to serve as office boy in the store. First job of the day was sweeping out the office and the store with broom and Dustbane, a green compound which I remember well. One morning, shortly after I had begun work, Mr. Whitehill came in and began talking with me. He told me then he desired that I should go to college, preferably Dartmouth. It opened a new world to me, and the vision was duly realized in 1920.

In the office, I learned the printer's trade. All type was set by hand. A weekly paper was published and there was considerable printing on the side. I also looked after the furnace, which required huge quantities of soft coal during the winter. Let me relate a little incident which shows how important it is to keep your mind on your work. One morning I had opened the valve to fill the boiler, when I heard footsteps in the store upstairs. Being alone, I went up to wait on the customer, and then promptly forgot about the boiler. Half an hour later I was informed that water was leaking from the steam radiators on the floor above, in the typesetting room. I had to carry out forty or fifty pails of water to bring the gauge down to the proper level, and you may be sure I never forgot to tend to it faithfully after that, customers or no customers!

Printing was to me an interesting art, though it often entailed long hours. Type, of course, is set in reverse and obverse of normal letters. A "p" looks like a "b" when you're putting it into a stick, a "q" looks like a "d" and vice-versa. It is like learning a new language. To be fully educated in printing, one should work in a small country office, where all phases of the work are encountered. Setting news columns and ads, running the job presses and the old-fashioned cylinder press, cutting up paper, running the folder--these are educational indeed!

Suggested Daily Spiritual Reading:
Ephesians 6:23
Colossians 3:15-17

Further Reading Related to Diary Entry:

- *History of Waterbury, Vermont, 1763-1915*; edited by Theodore Graham Lewis; Published by Harry C. Whitehill (1915); The Record Print, Waterbury, Vermont. Available at the Internet Archive: https://archive.org/details/HOW_vtrbms [Accessed January 22, 2021].

- *The Printing Trades* by Frank L. Shaw. Copyright 1916 by The Survey Committee of the Cleveland Foundation (Charles E. Adams, Chairman). Published by WM. F. Fell Co. Printers, Philadelphia. Available at the Internet Archives: https://archive.org/details/printingtrades00shawrich/page/n7/mode/2up [Accessed January 22, 2021].

- *American Dictionary of Printing and Bookmaking*. A History Of These Arts In Europe And America, With Definitions And Technical TermsAnd Biographical Sketches. By Wesley Washington Pasko. Howard Lockwood and Company Publishers, New York, 1894.

- *Gallegher and Other Stories* by Richard Harding Davis (Copyright, 1891, By Charles Scribner's Sons). Available at Project Gutenberg: https://

www.gutenberg.org/ebooks/5956 [Accessed January 22, 2021].

- ♦ *The Club of Queer Trades* by G. K. Chesterton

Popular Books Published in 1937:
Last Flight by Amelia Earhart
The Mystery of the Grail: Initiation and Magic in the Quest for the Spirit by Julius Evola

Popular Movies Released in 1937:
Easy Living (Jean Arthur, Edward Arnold, Ray Milland)
Think Fast Mr. Moto (Peter Lorre, Virginia Field, Thomas Beck)
West Bound Limited (Lyle Talbot, Polly Rowles)

Page 21 - No Date - 1937

In high school, I learned many a long poem--Longfellow's "Legend Beautiful", and parts of Lowell's "Vision of Sir Launfal", for example--while feeding the presses. I would set the book nearby, look at a line or two, and then learn the versus while feeding the sheets through the press.

Often tramp printers would come into the office looking for work. One had a red beard. He worked long enough to draw his pay on a Saturday night, then left us, never to return. Another was an actor who became stranded in the local theater. He became foreman for a while. He was an excellent checker player. I was able to win only one game from him. He taught me how to pronounce words after the manner of the theater. "Duty" was never to be pronounced "dooty". In his cultured voice in became "deeuty". Similarly with "beauty" and other words. I think, in retrospect, that his histrionic talent was greater than his printing ability. One day he too drifted.

Printing opened up a whole field of possibilities--newspapers, publishing, books, art, and life. We recalled, with secret pride, that Warren Gamaliel Harding had been a printer. Books were read with new interest. Mr. Whitehill once said to me, "printing is good clean work." I often recalled that remark as I tried in vain to scrub off all the printer's ink, which had invested the crevices of my hands. Indeed, I have never gotten the feel of printer's ink out of my system. It is an early love which abides. I have visited the great presses in the cities, and the rows of Mergenthaler linotypes, have met distinguished reporters and editors, and have even taken a college course in journalism, and yet none of these are as typically American, in my judgement, as the country printing office. That is the backbone of the nation, and a profound force, educationally and politically.

One week, back in 1919 (*he was 17*), I think it was, during the great influenza epidemic, I went to bat on all fronts in the struggle to get out the Wednesday weekly. That we succeeded in getting it out the following Monday, instead of Friday as usual, was no cause for opprobrium, considering the circumstances. Many of the help were at home ill, and the office was without a foreman. Mr. Whitehill was in Boston on Liberty Loan work. So, it devolved on me to write up such news as I could gather, then help to set it into type. After which (with Mr. Whitehill's help in closing the "forms"; he coming from Boston for that purpose) I ran off the sheets on the old cylinder press, four pages to a side--took them to the folder, then stamped them with the mailer, and carried them in a big basket to the post office. That was a week's work, combined with other duties!

There are many interesting reminisces of my life in the office, but to recount them all would require a volume as large as the "History of Waterbury, Vermont" by Theodore Graham Lewis, which was published in the office. But to show his diversity and ability, I should like to recount the activities of Mr. Whitehill, which were known by me. He was proprietor of the stationery store, and publisher of the weekly. He was a director in the local bank. He dealt in hay. He owned a farm on Blush Hill, where the radio station is located, which was operated on shares by a Mr. Will Ather. I used to gather a number of things on that farm, from Christmas trees to blackberries, and I hope retribution will not catch up with me by confession at this late date. He sold maple syrup and sugar to the bankers of the West; the advertising letters printed in his office. He was in charge of a part of the Liberty Loan drive in New England during the war (*WWI*). He was appointed as collector of customs for Vermont at the port of St. Albans, and served in that capacity for a number of years. He introduced notables and made speeches on important local occasions. He interested men in and chartered the Vermont Special, which toured the nation displaying the products and handiwork of Vermont. He was a charter member of the Green Mountain Club. He was intensely and genuinely interested in his town, state, and nation. He was a trustee of the Methodist Church, and for a time superintendent of the Church School. He was president of the Board of Trade. But supremely he was interested in principles and people. And as long as his radio station endures, he will be remembered as the founder.

Suggested Daily Spiritual Reading:
Proverbs 3:3
Matthew 7:1

Further Reading Related to Diary Entry:

- *The Theologian's Tale; The Legend Beautiful* by Henry Wadsworth Longfellow. Henry Wadsworth Longfellow. Available through the Maine Historical Society at https://www.hwlongfellow.org/poems_poem.php?pid=2064 [Accessed January 22, 2021].

- *The Vision of Sir Launfal* by James Russell Lowell (1848). Available fromThe Camelot Project; A Robbins Library Digital Project, University of Rochester, at: https://d.lib.rochester.edu/camelot/text/lowell-vision-of-sir-launfal [Accessed January 22, 2021].

- *An Evening with Longfellow* by Henry Wadsworth Longfellow; publisher: Sherwin Cody School of English, 1907. Available at the Internet Archive: https://archive.org/details/aneveningwithlo00longgoog/page/n6 [Accessed January 22, 2021].

- *For the Record. A look at the Waterbury newspaper's past and future* by Monica Mead (January 25, 2007; updated July 10, 2013). Availale from Stowe Today at https://www.stowetoday.com/waterbury/archives/for-the-record/article_557e6e08-4a99-5df7-8c2d-efa695f3bf2a.html [Accessed January 22, 2021].

- *1918 Influenza: the Mother of All Pandemics* by Jeffery K. Taubenberge and David M. Morens. Emerging Infectious Diseases; vol.12 (1), January 2006. Available from the Centers for Disease Control and Prevention (CDC) at https://wwwnc.cdc.gov/eid/article/12/1/05-0979_article [Accessed January 22, 2021].

- *History of Waterbury, Vermont, 1763-1915*; edited by Theodore Graham Lewis; Published by Harry C. Whitehill (1915); The Record Print, Waterbury, Vermont. Available at the Internet Archive: https://archive.org/details/HOW_vtrbms [Accessed January 22, 2021].

Popular Books Published in 1937:
Towers in the Mist by Elizabeth Goudge
Think and Grow Rich by Napoleon Hill

Popular Movies Released in 1937:
True Confessions (Carole Lombard, Fred MacMurray, John Barrymore)
Fire Over England (Laurence Olivier, Flora Robson, Vivien Leigh)
Join the Marines (Paul Kelly, June Travis, Reginald Denny)

Page 22 - No Date - 1937

He (*Mr. Whitehill*) had a genius for making money. Everything he turned his hand to seemed profitable for him. That he staked it all in his last venture, is understandable to one who worked under him. That too would make money, for his was an incurable optimism that hard work combined with initiative must necessarily be profitable; but the money to be accrued was incidental to the making of wider contacts. These he gloried in, and the memorial edition of his weekly attests to a wide circle of acquaintances and friends in every walk of life, from governors to neighbors.

This is not an obituary, but an evaluation. I have met quite a few business men, but none has impressed me with such acumen and versatility as the late Mr. (*Harry*) Whitehill. As to people, he liked to help them to help themselves. He gave me no money for my college venture, and I can truthfully say, I think that I earned any money he ever gave me for working for him. But his influence gave me something better--a real chance to further my education. A scholarship, a job at college, even a job after college, he secured for me by speaking a good word in time. These were invaluable in providing me an opportunity to advance myself, and I hope I have, in some small measure, repaid him for his continued interest in me. As with me, so with others whom he helped. He might have adopted for his motto that used by Morgan Memorial--"Not charity but a chance". I recall two remarks characteristic of him in letters to me. The first concerns dignity of personality. He wrote, "A man may not have expensive clothes, but it always makes a good impression if they are neat and he keeps his shoes shined." The second concerns the dignity of labor. "A minister," he wrote, "should be the busiest person in the community."

I have not written of his home life. He was earnestly devoted to his wife, a cripple for many years. He did everything he could for her medically. They were close spiritually. Soon after his passing, she followed him. Life seemed intolerable to her without his protection and comfort. They were childless in the flesh, but in the mind he fathered many children--ideas and practices which are a permanent memorial to him. Requiescat in pace!

This brief account, logically, closes the period of my residence in Waterbury. Thanks to Mr. Whitehill, the morning came when I bade goodbye to my mother, standing on the platform of the station as my train pulled out bearing me to new scenes and new experiences. I anticipated, wonderingly, what Dartmouth would be like, whether I could make my way, and what the future had in store for me. It is a red letter day when one starts off for college! (*1920*)

Suggested Daily Spiritual Reading:
Jude 1:17-21
3 John 1:11

Further Reading Related to Diary Entry:
- *The History of Printing in America, with a Biography of Printers, and an Account of Newspapers* by Thomas, Isaiah and Thomas, Benjamin Franklin (publication date: 1874); publisher: Albany, N. Y., J. Munsell, printer. Available at the Internet Archive: https://archive.org/details/aey4217.0005.001.umich.edu/page/IV [Accessed January 22, 2021].

- *The Vermont Historical Gazetteer: A Magazine, Embracing a History of Each: Civil, Ecclesiastical, Biographical, and Military*; edited by Abby Maria Hemenway. Available at the Internet Archive: https://archive.org/details/vermonthistorica01heme/page/n12 [Accessed January 22, 2021].

Popular Books Published in 1937:
The Hobbit, Part One by J.R.R. Tolkien
The Citadel by A.J. Cronin

Popular Movies Released in 1937:
Souls at Sea (Gary Cooper, George Raft, Frances Dee)
A Family Affair (Lionel Barrymore, Cecilia Parker, Eric Linden)
God's Country and the Woman (George Brent, Beverly Roberts, Barton MacLane)

1938

Page 23 - No Date - 1938
(Sometime After September 1937, But Before 1939)

It was a beautiful day in the fall of the year (*1920*) when I stepped off the train at Norwich (*Vermont*) on the west bank of the Connecticut River and walked across the old wooden and covered bridge which spans the river. It was mid-afternoon and the green of the pines along the banks together with the blue sky and fleecy clouds above made an arresting picture. Just beyond the bridge the road forks, the one to the right going up into the village of Hanover (*New Hampshire*) to the college; the one to the left going up to the college by way of Tuck Drive--named after Amos Tuck, famous benefactor of Dartmouth College. The macadam roads lead up through a grove of pines, past a small meadow on the river bank wherein is found a monument to the memory of John Ledyard, Dartmouth freshman of many a long year past, who carved out a canoe, from a log on this spot, and drifted down to the sea to adventures which carried him halfway around the world. Near this spot, too, a group of Indians, who had been invited down to the college from Canada, suddenly bolted--terrified, perhaps, of the nearness of so much learning--and swam across the river to return to their native haunts.

My first view of college property was an entrancing prospect, and I have never lost my love for it. A bit farther up Tuck Drive, and to the right, is the old cemetery where lie, in their eternal sleep, Eleazar Wheelock and other early builders of the college, which was founded in 1769. Rev. Eleazar Wheelock had left an Indian charity school in Connecticut to found this new Indian school in the wilderness. An old college song runs as follows:

```
         "O' Eleazar Wheelock was a very pious man,
        He went into the wilderness to teach the In-di-an.
         With a Gradus ad Parnassum, a Bible, and a drum—
            And five hundred gallons of New England rum.
       Fill the bowl up, fill the bowl up, drink to Eleazar,
                    And his primitive Alcazar,
    For he taught the In-di-an in the goodness of his soul!"
```

I imagine there are many Dartmouth students who have never visited this hallowed spot, but as you stand in the woods on this eminence, which overlooks Tuck Drive and the Connecticut Valley, you instinctively thrill to the historical significance of this life so well lived in the sight of God, and the flat stone partly covered with moss makes real the deeper meaning of this and all colleges--that here they stand to serve their day and generation by grace of men of faith who risked everything to make their visions and ideals become true and living. Here lies all that is mortal of that worthy divine, but this immortal soul has transcended body and books and dwells in the Dartmouth spirit.

I did not see all that on this first day, but the quiet hush of the woods was a fitting prelude to my contact with the college buildings and personnel. I soon came out on the campus, which is a beautiful one, flanked as it is on the east side by the historic Georgian halls--Dartmouth, Reed, Thornton. Twice burned (or is it thrice?), but ever rising anew, and more glorious, like a Phoenix from the ashes. I made my way to College Hall, on the West side of the campus, past the Administration building, and Tuck Business School, and Robinson Hall--to College Hall, with its tall Corinthian columns, where I was to spend my first year eating in its Commons and sleeping in its dormitory.

Suggested Daily Spiritual Reading:
Titus 3:3-6
James 2:14

Further Reading Related to Diary Entry:
- *John Ledyard Departs Down the Connecticut River* by Jim Collins. Available from Dartmouth College: https://250.dartmouth.edu/highlights/john-ledyard-departs-down-connecticut-river [Accessed January 22, 2021].

- *Dartmouth Undying: A Celebration of Place and Possibility*, edited by David Shribman and Jim Collins

- *American Traveler: The Life and Adventures of John Ledyard, the Man Who Dreamed of Walking The World* by James Zug

- *Memoirs of the Rev. Eleazar Wheelock, D.D., Founder and President of Dartmouth College and Moor's Charity School* by David McClure, D.D and Elijah Parish, D.D. Published by Edward Little and Company, 1811. Available at the Internet Archive: https://archive.org/details/memoirsreveleaz00parigoog/page/n8 [Accessed January 22, 2021].

- *History and Traditions*, Dartmouth College. Available from Dartmouth College at https://home.dartmouth.edu/life-community/explore-green/history-traditions [Accessed January 22, 2021].

Popular Books Published in 1938:
Most Popular Books Published In 1938. Available at Goodreads.com: https://www.goodreads.com/book/popular_by_date/1938 [Accessed January

22, 2021].

Popular Movies Released in 1938:
    The Adventures of Robin Hood (Errol Flynn, Olivia de Havilland, Basil Rathbone, Claud Rains)
    Boys Town (Spencer Tracy, Mickey Rooney)
    Love Finds Andy Hardy (Mickey Rooney, Judy Garland, Lewis Stone)
    White Banners (Claude Rains, Fay Bainter, Jackie Cooper)

Page 24 - No Date - 1938

Its large foyer contains a huge fireplace and easy leather chairs, and I consider it an ideal dormitory, in spite of being somewhat noisier than the others. It initiated me into the swirl of college life. My room was on the second floor of College Hall, and I soon found my roommate. A New Yorker, Sidney Fish, by name, his metropolitan upbringing made a contrasting foil to my semi-rural upbringing. He used to awaken early in the mornings, unable to sleep because of the quietness and the birds calling! I have since visited New York a number of times and can readily understand the contrast. He gave me a new outlook on many things and made a good roommate. I, early, made the acquaintance of another chap, Ralph H. Richardson from Ayer, Mass, who remained throughout college days a boon companion.

The first night, after eating in the Commons, I remember I visited the town which is immediately adjacent to the college property, and went to the movies. The first show then, and I suppose now, was given over to peanut throwing--at the screen, the piano player, and at all and sundry. Altogether different from the sedate movies I attended before and since.

The following day we registered, after standing long in line, and received, along with our credentials, a handshake from the President, Ernest Martin Hopkins, a gentleman and great educator. He was outstanding in a subsequent commencement address in which he championed the aristocracy of brains. Essentially democratic, he made us feel at home in the college. He often presided at chapel, and his scholarly voice and bearing and bushy eyebrows are well remembered.

College began in earnest a day or two later, and we were busy with books and classes. Among other things, I elected Latin, English, Political Science, Sociology (then taught by Jerome Davis), French, and a course demanded of all called Evolution, which was really a melange of all the sciences.

I had no time for extracurricular activities, for I was soon at work in the printing office, working nights on the pony cylinder press, putting out 1,100 copies of the Daily Dartmouth. This I continued for two years. I might add that I did have to take up athletics, this being likewise compulsory, along with chapel, the first two years I was there. I chose cross country running, and we all had gym training, en masse, under the active guidance of Doc Bowler and Pat Kean.

It would take volumes to express all my impressions of the Dartmouth campus, faculty, students, and activities. The memories come back with a flood of impressions--the first football games, the first Dartmouth carnival, the skiing in the vale of Tempe, the hikes to Happy Hill and Mooses Cabins--so many, in fact, I scarcely know how or where to begin.

Shortly after our arrival, we engaged in a tilt with the sophomore class. A huge ball, higher than a man, was put in action on the campus one night, and the object of the struggle (and struggle it was, for many clothes were torn) was to see which side could first get the ball across the road. The pressure almost unbearable near the edges, as over a thousand husky, young men began to push the ball--it was overwhelming the/in center. I think the sophomores won, for they possessed a coordination we lacked at the time.

Suggested Daily Spiritual Reading:
Luke 13:29-30
Proverbs 17:28

Further Reading Related to Diary Entry:
- *The Storied History of Dartmouth* by Aziz G. Sayigh, Boris V. Babson, A.S. Erickson, Charles S. Dameron, Adam I.W. Schwartzman, and Nicholas P. Desatnick. Available from The Dartmouth Review at http://dartreview.com/history-of-dartmouth/ [Accessed January 22, 2021].

- *Papers of Jerome Davis*, 1912-1965. Available from the Franklin D. Roosevelt Presidential Library and Museum, National Archives, Marist College at http://www.fdrlibrary.marist.edu/archives/pdfs/findingaids/findingaid_davis_jerome.pdf [Accessed January 22, 2021].

Popular Books Published in 1938:
The Coming Victory of Democracy by Thomas Mann
The Anatomy of Revolution by Crane Brinton

Popular Movies Released in 1938:
A Christmas Carol (Reginald Owen, Gene Lockhart)
Algiers (Charles Boyer, Hedy Lamarr)
Suez (Tyrone Power, Loretta Young)

Page 25 - No Date - 1938

The period of hazing came along shortly, too--three days of it called Delta Alpha. We of College Hall wore our clothes inside-out, wore wooden neck ties, and built paddles for the use of the overweening sophomores. We dragged our books to classes in a desk drawer propelled by a string. Other dormitory freshman wore bathrobes with clocks pinned to them, or tripped up and down the walks like fairies. Freshman, at noon, had to stand on the watering trough on the South side of campus, and give a talk on "There's a Reason" with a mouth filled with Grape-nuts (*cereal*), or some other absurd and low comedy, with the alternative a good dunking in the trough. At night, we underwent further hazing, being called up to engage in rowing contests on a dormitory floor, the water supplied liberally from pails splashed over our heads; orchestral efforts with paddles supplying the motivation; grease fights, and a whole repertory of other interesting games devised by the ingenuity and diablerie of the crowing sophomores. Speaking of crowing, we had to line up on the porch of College Hall each morning at seven o'clock and say "cuckoo" every time the clock struck. Before entering the building we had to kneel and repeat a little poem written, if I remember correctly, by a senior named Franklin McDuffee, and which went, somewhat, as follows:

```
        "Here before your lefty portals,
           O ye gods of College Hall;
            I the lowliest of mortals,
           Doff my baby bonnet small;
        My brains are few, my costume shabby;
          My wit is nil my muscles flabby—
             Great Hall as now I enter in,
         Maintain me pure and free from sin,
         From verdant greenness pardon me,
              Forgive my raucous roar—
         Three cheers for nineteen twenty-three,
                To h— with twenty-four!"
```

Along with these pleasantries, there were sundry admonitions, such as "keep off the grass" and "no smoking for freshman", at least while out of doors, and our duties were defined to the edification and comfort of the upper classes. Life was truly hectic during this hazing period, but our turn came the following year when, sore heads forgotten, we lambasted and befuddled the incoming freshman to our hearts content.

After the heat and burden of the week, it was always a well-remembered pleasure to attend chapel hour on Sunday nights. The tones of the organ and the religious service lent a charm and power to soothe an otherwise disordered jumble of activities and impressions, and the walk across the campus afterward to the grill room or Commons for the evening meal was a benediction lent by heaven. Perhaps I was more sensitive than most, but so it seemed to me. Then was I ready for another week of study, work, social intercourse, and recreation.

> "Men of Dartmouth give a rouse
> For the college on the hill;
> For the lone pine above her,
> And the loyal men who love her;
> Give a rouse, give a rouse, with a will!"

Suggested Daily Spiritual Reading:
Ruth 1:16
Psalm 25:1-2

Further Reading Related to Diary Entry:
- *A Dartmouth History Lesson for Freshman* by Francis Lane Childs. The Dartmouth Alumni Magazine, December 1957. Available from the Dartmouth College Library at https://www.dartmouth.edu/~library/rauner/dartmouth/dartmouth_history.html [Accessed January 22, 2021].

- *A History of Hazing* by Michael J. Perkins (October 24, 2016). Available from The Dartmouth Review at http://dartreview.com/a-history-of-hazing/ [Accessed January 22, 2021].

Popular Books Published in 1938:
The Evolution of Physics by Albert Einstein and Leopold Infeld
Cause for Alarm Paperback by Eric Ambler

Popular Movies Released in 1938:
A Yank at oxford (Robert Taylor, Vivien Leigh, Lionel Barrymore)
The Dawn Patrol (Errol Flynn, Basil Rathbone, David Niven)
Young Doctor Kildare (Lionel Barrymore, Lew Ayres, Lynne Carver)

Page 26 - No Date - 1938

My second and third years at Dartmouth leave but hazy impressions. I was rooming off-campus at the time, and was very busy. I worked at night in the printing office, going to work at ten o'clock, and finishing at 4 a.m. Ed Boyle, the white-haired compositor, who became very angry with me for no reason I could discover and made life difficult, and Charlie Burgess, placid compositor, who was fond of saying, "Another day, another dollar," as he quit work, left the building early and I was alone in the press room to get out another addition of the "Daily Dartmouth" on the press. These long nights, I improvised by quoting poems to myself and thinking the long, long thoughts of youth, when I wasn't interrupted by mechanical difficulties. In winter the friction in the moving paper was great, and a gas flame was used on the press to correct this difficulty. It was a pony press and as the cylinder revolved I would get sleepy. I fell asleep one night standing up at work, coming to rapidly enough, when the tip of my finger was caught in the gripper. No damage done, but I was alert from then on!

One of the verses I remember from the darkest hours:

"Be thou a hero, let thy might
Tramp on eternal snows its way,
And through the dark (ebon) walls of night
Hew down a passage unto day."

(From the poem "Press On" by Park Benjamin)

In the later part of my junior year, work ran out for me at the office, and I did all sorts of jobs, working for a time washing dishes for a professor's wife, who taught me how to wash dishes correctly--a fact that I have tried to conceal from my wife who might capitalize on it--tending children at night, carrying out ashes, beating rugs, and working for a while at the "Greasy Spoon" as a waiter. There I met a man who invited me to go with him as a traveling salesman for the summer, selling office supplies in the New England states. I did this, and it was fine culturally, but profitless financially.

The first summer vacation was spent in the record office in Waterbury, Vermont, writing articles; and the second as a bell-hop at one of the hotels at Bethlehem, N.H. In the White Mountains.

Not a fraternity man, I did not enter into the social life of the college much, and, thereby, missed a great deal, undoubtedly. But I did make a number of interesting acquaintances--Earl Borglum, nephew of the sculptor and one

Spargo, son of the well-known socialist, John Spargo, among them. I likewise had for Sociology professor, Jerome Davis, who has been ousted from several fine colleges since (or is it one?) for his radical opinions. I did not hear him utter any heresies politically, and I question whether in his further career he did other than teach doctrines which were rightly in his province to teach. After all, if one is to understand Russia, one must read and discuss "Das Kapital" and Hitler would be incomprehensible without "Mein Kampf".

During these years I skied and walked and enjoyed the lovely campus, visiting among other places the grave of Eleazar Wheelock and speculating upon the vital issues of life. Others had exciting experiences to record, visits to the dens of Lebanon and the Junk, and to Montreal, but my life seemed grooved in a prosaic round. I have read Ovid, Martial Augustine, Cellini, and Dreiser with pleasure, but their titillating amatory contacts have not been mine. College held something of a monastic discipline and regularity, and perhaps it was all together well it was so. When the mind is in the formative state, love and studies are mutually exclusive. Perhaps I am as misogynistic as Schopenhauer in saying this, but educators will applaud the sentiment, I am sure.

> "If I had a daughter, sir, I'd dress her up in green
> And put her on the campus to coach the freshman team.
> And if I had a son, sir, I'll tell you what he'd do,
> He would yell the hxxx with Harvard, like his daddy use to do!
>
> (The collegiate tradition, Sic!)

Suggested Daily Spiritual Reading:
Genesis 1:1-26
Philippians 4:4-7

Further Reading Related to Diary Entry:
- *The "Pony" Press and the Patent Model Collection* by the National Museum of American History (NMAH), Smithsonian Institution, January 4, 2013. Available from the NMAH at https://americanhistory.si.edu/blog/2013/01/the-pony-press-and-the-patent-model-collection.html [Accessed January 22, 2021].

- *The History of Dartmouth College* by Baxter Perry Smith; Houghton, Osgood, and Company, Boston; The Riverside Press, Cambridge (1878). Available from Project Gutenberg at https://www.gutenberg.org/ebooks/28641 [Accessed January 22, 2021].

- *The Dartmouth.* America's Oldest College Newspaper; founded in 1799.

Available from Dartmouth College at https://www.thedartmouth.com [Accessed January 22, 2021].

♦ *A Sociological Interpretation of the Russian Revolution* by Jerome Davis (Political Science Quarterly; Published Jan 1, 1922). Available from the Internet Archive: https://archive.org/details/jstor-2142509/page/n1 [Accessed January 22, 2021].

♦ *Lost Songs of Old Dartmouth*. Available from The Dartmouth Review at http://dartreview.com/lost-songs-of-older-dartmouth/ [Accessed January 22, 2021].

Popular Books Published in 1938:
Epitaph for a Spy by Eric Ambler
Scoop by Evelyn Waugh

Popular Movies Released in 1938:
The Saint in New York (Louis Hayward, Kay Sutton, Sig Ruman)
Of Human Hearts (Walter Huston, James Stewart, Beulah Bondi)
Room Service (The Marx Brothers)
Cipher Bureau (Leon Ames, Charlotte Wynters, Joan Woodbury)

1939/1940

(Pages from 1939 and 1940 have been moved around [by the Reverend] in order to maintain content continuity)

Page 27 - No Date - 1939

As I look back in retrospect, over sixteen years to my last year at Dartmouth, I realize how altogether inadequate are words to describe the experiences of one's last year in college. There is a looking forward and a wondering, and a looking backward too, with a realization, poignant like pain, that these swiftly passing days can be lived but once in their fullness. One absorbs tradition over four years of time; and Daniel Webster knew of whereof he spoke when he declaimed before the Supreme Court, relative to Dartmouth, "It's a small college, sir, but these are those who love it!" All alumni and most undergraduates are sensitive to that declaration.

One absorbs tradition over four years of time; and Daniel Webster knew of wherein he spoke when he declaimed before the Supreme Court, relative to Dartmouth, "It's a small college, sir, but there are those who love it!" All alumni and most undergraduates are sensitive to that declaration. One absorbs the tradition, the learning, and the fellowship, just as his lungs absorb the clean New Hampshire air. The cities are discovering the joys of skiing in the sports regions of New Hampshire in increasing numbers, but the members of the Dartmouth Outing Club, from 1911 on, thanks to Fred Harris and the environs of the Vale of Tempe, discovered them long ago. It was a thrill to watch Johnny Carlton and Dick Bowler turn somersaults on skis, over the big ski jump, the height of which on foot is enough to take one's breath away. Forward somersaults at that! That was at the winter carnival in 1924, and it would take a small brochure to describe the beauty of a winter carnival--the torches on the ice lighting the fancy skaters, the schusses and slaloms, moonlight on the golf links, and the gayety and sparkle of the ball in the gym.

I roomed in Wheeler Hall, near the chapel, in my senior year, and enjoyed it greatly. In my junior year, in company with my grandfather (his mother Etta's father), I had visited old friends of his about twenty miles north of Hanover. There I met for the first time she who has been my faithful wife and loyal companion for twelve years. Her father lived on a farm, at that time, in Orford (NH), and I found occasion to the road north, out of Hanover, to visit Mae (Brock) quite often.

Mae on the farm with father, Ernie, circa 1922

    The Brocks lived about three miles up the valley from Orford, which has been described by a traveler of world renown as the loveliest village in America. Mae would drive me back to the station in a sleigh on winter nights behind Old Bill, and a lovely ride it was in the moonlight. The year went swiftly and every day was precious. I was working at the Dartmouth Press again, setting up ads and the like and becoming an embryonic Ben Franklin, whose autobiography I read with pleasure and profit about this time. Later in Boston, I saw his printing press at the old state house. I didn't become a Franklin, but as compensation, Mae and I have two fine children, a boy, Albert Earl, and a girl, Janet Elisabeth, age ten and eight, respectively (the ages of the children indicate that the year is 1939 when he is writing). As Stevenson wrote with such inanity, and perhaps asininity, "Life is so full of a number of things, I am sure we should all be as happy as kings." But occasionally those words express a mood of gratitude toward life which cannot be ignored and this is one of them.

The Reverend, Albert Jr., Mae, and Janet, circa 1935 or 1936.

My acquaintances widened and deepened during this last year and I hope my learning did too. I majored, the last two years, in Political Science, studying such things as Constitutional and International law, under big Jim Richardson, and learning, generally, how the government should be run (shades of the new deal!). I also gained a lot from Logic and Philosophy, which later I have perused with profit in the later years.

Come graduation, with the gathering at the Bema, and the breaking of the peace pipe, the caps and gowns, the carving of the senior canes surmounted with an Indian's head, the last visit alone to the old tower in the college park, the reception of diplomas and hurried leave-takings from friends and relatives and classmates.

Graduation from Dartmouth, 1924. From left to right: Etta Anderson (mother), Solomon Anderson (father), Lilla Anderson (younger sister, 15 years of age), Albert Solomon Anderson (22 years of age—soon to become a minister).

Then, in company with my father, who had recently secured work in Brighton, Mass, I entrained for Boston, which I had visited but once and which held the lure and magic of all places strange and new. I was to secure employment as clerk in the engineering department of the New England Telephone and Telegraph Co., but I did not know that as Hanover and four long years (sic!) of college receded into the background of my life.

Suggested Daily Spiritual Reading:
Galatians 3:26
Job 42:10

Further Reading Related to Diary Entry:
- *The Writing and Speeches of Daniel Webster* edited by Fletcher Webster. Volume Two. National Edition. Available from the Internet Archive: https://archive.org/details/cu31924092900590/page/n16 [Accessed January 22, 2021].

- The Dartmouth Alumni Magazine, issues from 1924, available at http://archive.dartmouthalumnimagazine.com/issues/1924 [Accessed January 22,

2021].

- *Autobiography of Benjamin Franklin* by Benjamin Franklin; Frank Woodworth Pine (editor); E. Boyd Smith (illustrator). Henry Holt and Company, New York (1916). Available from Project Gutenberg - [EBook #20203 {release date, December 28, 2006}]: http://www.gutenberg.org/files/20203/20203-h/20203-h.htm [Accessed January 22, 2021].

- *The American Political Science Review*; Vol. 18, No. 4, Nov., 1924. Published by the American Political Science Association: https://www.jstor.org/stable/i306617 [Accessed January 22, 2021].

Popular Books Published in 1939:
Johnny Got His Gun by Dalton Trumbo
Gadsby by Ernest Vincent Wright

Popular Movies Released in 1939:
Mr. Smith Goes to Washington (James Stewart, Jean Arthur, Claude Rains)
The Wizard of Oz (Judy Garland, Frank Morgan, Ray Bolger)
Gone with the Wind (Clark Gable, Vivien Leigh, Leslie Howard, Olivia de Havilland, Hatie McDaniel, Butterfly McQueen)

Page 28 - No Date - 1939

I remember vividly our first night in Boston. I had read about Boston, years before, in a book--the old houses in Louisburg Square, Paul Revere, and all the rest--and it is always interesting to square reality with imagination. The summer previously, I had visited Boston overnight, coming in by the Elevated (*Boston Elevated Railway, similar to street cars*) from Malden, and that which impressed me most was the immensity of the apartment houses with thousands of lights, and the gas lamps on the corners of the dimly lighted streets (the Third Avenue Elevated [*street car*] in New York, later, impressed me in the same manner, but to a lesser degree). For in Vermont and New Hampshire, there are no cities comparable to Boston and New York. Well, on this first night of our arrival, my father took me into the Park Street subway, where we boarded a car for Allston, where he had secured a room. After boarding the car, and before the door was closed, we heard a cry, and turning, learned that a child's arm had been caught in the door while it was being closed by the motorman. At that time, I concluded it must be a common occurrence, but in all the years since, I have never witnessed a repetition of the incident.

I secured employment for the summer (the time was to extend to a year and a half) with the New England Telephone and Telegraph Co., on Oliver Street. My longtime employer and friend in Waterbury (*Whitehill*) had spoken to the president, Matt Jones, and a place was made for me in the engineering department, division of the budget. The experience was invaluable. Our clerical force of four, with the help of stenographers, spent the year on just one sheet to be incorporated in the budget to be presented to the stockholders, at the annual meeting; the sheet representing new construction in the New England area over a five-year period.

The company was spending, at that time (1925), approximately thirty-million dollars a year. Estimates, with blueprints, were submitted in detail for two years' work, and contingently and sketchily for the following three years. It was very interesting work, the hours were congenial, as were the personnel, and the company paid us well. Most of the men in the department were graduates of the Massachusetts Institute of Technology (MIT), as was natural, and they initiated me into the mysteries of radio construction, among other things. One, Stevenson, was the son of a doctor, or more properly, doctors, as both of his parent were physicians. He related two things concerning them--one was that his mother saved a would-be suicide by going into a saloon and tying off the ends of a severed jugular vein. The capillaries take care of circulation of blood through the head. The man recovered. His father made the following remark, which his son repeated to me, "I believe in letting every man go to hell in his own way."

There was another chap in the office, nee John, who went down to Providence (*RI*) one night and, by his own admission, "got plastered" and drove home in his bid Stevens-Duryea coupe. He fell asleep and his car turned turtle on a bend. John came to work the next day, none the worse for the experience. The nosepiece on his glasses was tied together with a piece of string. That was the sole casualty.

Then there was another chap, brilliant mentally but erratic to say the least. A bohemian sort of chap. He brought an alarm clock to work in his overcoat pocket. During lunch hour, we secured the clock and set the alarm. While we were all quietly working at two o'clock the alarm went off with a loud whirr and clang. We guffawed at the joke and his face assumed the color of a beet. We never saw the clock again.

While working for the company, I had occasion to visit other departments. The research department was located in the basement, and that was interesting. So also was the records department, where the directories were kept on file. I was shown one going back to the '80s (*1880s*) where the customers were listed in longhand. It was a Boston University professor, Alexander Graham Bell, who invented the telephone in 1875. He taught the deaf pupils in the University, and while seeking some way to alleviate their affliction, he chanced on his great discovery. I believe there were seventy-three subscribers in the first directory. I have never seen the first telephone, although this past summer (1939) I saw the ether cone which William Thomas Green Morton employed for the first anesthetic operation at the Massachusetts General Hospital. Morton was a practicing dentist at the time.

Suggested Daily Spiritual Reading:
Obadiah 1:3-4
Luke 4:8

Further Reading Related to Diary Entry:
- *Boston in the 1920s* . Available from the Marion Ringwood Scrapbook Digital Library, Simmons College : https://slis.simmons.edu/mringwood/exhibits/show/life-and-times/boston-in-the-1920s [Accessed January 22, 2021].

- *Elsie Venner* by Oliver Wendell Holmes. 1859. Available from Project Gutenberg at https://www.gutenberg.org/files/2696/2696-h/2696-h.htm [Accessed January 22, 2021].

- *The City-State of Boston: The Rise and Fall of an Atlantic Power, 1630-1865* by Mark Peterson.

- *A City So Grand: The Rise of an American Metropolis, Boston 1850-1900* by Stephen Puleo.

- *Censorship of the Theatre in Boston* by Daniel M. Doherty. Available from Boston University at https://open.bu.edu/handle/2144/4569 [Accessed January 22, 2021].

- *The Telephone Gambit: Chasing Alexander Graham Bell's Secret* by Seth Shulman.

Popular Books Published in 1939:
The Big Sleep by Raymond Chandler
Alcoholics Anonymous, The Big Book by Bill Wilson, Dr. Bob Smith

Popular Movies Released in 1939:
Only Angels Have Wings (Jean Arthur, Cary Grant)
Young Mr. Lincoln (Henry Fonda, Alice Brady)
t's a Wonderful World (Jimmy Stewart, Claudette Colbert)

Page 29 - No Date - 1939

Another interesting department (*at the New England Telephone and Telegraph Co., on Oliver Street, Boston*) is the collection room where 25,000 nickels, dimes, and quarters are sorted in a special machine in an hour's time. These are taken from the telephone booths, and the man in charge told about attempts to evade the charge. He showed us a box half full of all sorts of foreign currency, which had been put in the machines. Best of all was his story of a man who came in one day quite incensed. A new collector had taken away his supply of BL tags (of tin), which he kept at hand in place of nickels. It was his custom to redeem them at the end of the month. In the early days the barkeepers used to keep a club at hand, under the counter, when they wished to call the operator, but that practice has been circumvented.

Over on Milk Street is a large exchange, and it fascinated me to watch the operators completing the calls over the trunk lines, as well as the local switchboard. Here also were machines like typewriters to care for calls coming from manual offices and going to the machine-switching offices, and vice-versa. On a visit to the Liberty Exchange we saw the machine-switching or dial system in operation, with four frames or boards to select the correct trunk lines for the calls. Miles upon miles of cords, and hundreds upon hundreds of calls. Here truly is the nerve center of a great city. The conduits underground that carry the tiny wires have as many as 1,212 in one cable (the extra twelve are for spares), and perhaps today the number has increased. Of course, each conduit, a nonconducting tile of rectangular form, has many cables. Mirabile dictu! The wires carry the messages and the vacuum tubes, like those of radio, which the telephone companies first utilized to the full, amplify the signals. A message to Europe must be amplified many billions of times.

The company gave me insight into a great public utility and I have always treasured the experience. But during my days there, my mind was on a profession, and the law seeming impracticable, my mind turned toward the ministry (*He had once considered becoming a lawyer*). I noted later, going over the writings for the period, that I was more interested, in the total, in life than in any of its parts, interesting as those parts undoubtedly were and are. During the noon hours I would browse around Corn Hill, much after the manner of Benjamin Franklin, and buy an old book here and there. Phillips Brooks' sermons, Autocrat of the Breakfast Table, Emerson's essays, and other New England authors, were among these. And so in the summer of 1925 I turned my steps toward Harvard Divinity School, and the ancient spiritual home of Emerson. I interviewed Dean Willard Learoyd Sperry, one of the finest educators I have known, and made plans to enter the school in the fall of that year.

Before leaving the telephone company, I had an interview with the president, Matt Jones, which was instructive. He talked for a time about the telephone in general, mentioning the service prevailing in Europe, especially Stockholm. I stayed for about half an hour with him. He was a Vermonter, as was also one of the vice presidents, the chief engineer, and a host of lesser officials. The country injects new blood into the cities and manages its institutions, a fact well known in sociology. The country, especially Vermont, is a good place in which to be born.

Suggested Daily Spiritual Reading:
   Psalm 57:1
   1 John 1:1-7

Further Reading Related to Diary Entry:
- *The Telephone: A Description of the Bell System with Some Facts Concerning the So-Called Independent Movement* by New England Telephone and Telegraph Company (1906)

- *The Innovators: How a Group of Hackers, Geniuses, and Geeks Created the Digital Revolution* by Walter Isaacson

- *The Autocrat of the Breakfast-Table* by Oliver Wendell Holmes. James R. Osgood and Company, Boston, 1873. Available from Project Gutenberg at https://www.gutenberg.org/ebooks/751 [Accessed January 22, 2021].

- *The Consolations of God: Great Sermons of Phillips Brooks* by Phillips Brooks

- *Twenty Sermons* by Phillips Brooks, Rector of Trinity Church, Boston. Fourth Series. E.P. Dutton and Company, New York, 1887.

Popular Books Published in 1939:
   The Secret Life of Walter Mitty by James Thurber
   The Confidential Agent by Graham Greene
   Western Union by Zane Grey

Popular Movies Released in 1939:
   The Hunchback of Notre Dame (Charles Laughton, Maureen O'Hara, Cedric Hardwicke)
   Gunga Din (Cary Grant, Joan Fontaine, Victor McLaglen)
   Goodbye, Mr. Chips (Robert Donat, Greer Garson, Terry Kilburn)

Page 30 - July 23, 1940

There is sometimes a hiatus in the lives and minds of men, and the period from 1925 to present is no exception. The process of becoming a minister, and the duties of the office, are not conducive to absorbed reading, except in the realm of things immaterial, and few, besides other ministers, would be especially interested. Hence, I will make this section short except insofar as it can be relieved by anecdotes.

At Harvard Divinity School I met such interesting personalities as Dean William Wallace Fenn, James Hardy Ropes, Henry Joel Cadbury, George Foote Moore, and Kirsopp Lake, who all helped, with Dean Sperry, to shape my theological outlook or weltanschauung. I am deeply indebted to them each and several, and if I didn't meet up with their expectations from an educational standpoint that was not the fault of their excellent teaching.

During my first year, I had charge of young people's work at the Harvard Congregational Church in Brookline, where Dr. Leavitt was, and is, pastor. Thanks to scholarships, the other years of preparation could be spent partly at home in Watertown, where I regularly attended the Methodist Church, coming under the pastorate of Dr. Francis Taylor, who, when the time came, helped to get me into the New England Conference, on trial in 1928, in full in 1930. I was ordained deacon in 1928 by Bishop William Anderson at Worcester, and ordained elder in 1930 by Bishop William Frazier MacDowell in Cambridge.

My first pastorate, of two years, was in West Quincy (all places Massachusetts unless otherwise specified). This was in 1928. Mae Thelma Brock and I were married that fall (*she dropped out of the University of Vermont just before her senior year to marry*), and went overnight to Sugar Hill in New Hampshire, staying in a cottage which overlooks the Presidential Range. An auspicious beginning to a very happy marriage, and rather realistic too when we discovered a flat tire on the car in the morning! But I have always said it is better to have a flat tire on the car than in the car. And with Mae along I've never had that!

We made many friends in West Quincy, particularly the Francis family who have remembered us at Christmas through the years, and Dr. Thomas J. Dion, who presided at the delivery of our first born. Our salary was small, being only twelve dollars a week on occasion, and so when Albert Earl came into the world I found work at a printing office in Boston to help out with expenses. But we managed pretty well, and at the end of the year there was an extra sum to help out. (*His daughter, Janet, would later note that there were many Christmases when they didn't have enough money for gifts and that the Reverend often had second jobs.)*

The Reverend with a newborn Albert Junior, circa 1929.

Albert Jr., circa 1930

"Hardscrabble Hill" is a good place for a young man to begin--things seem easier thereafter. And West Quincy was a good training ground. Our first District Superintendent, Dr. Edward A. Elliot, dropped in for a cup of tea at quarterly conference time, and as he always upheld and stood by his ministers, it helped greatly to overcome minor administrative difficulties.

I remember my first funeral, the first Sunday I preached there, a little girl baby, in a home exceedingly modest, and the majesty of the minister's task was borne in upon me as I stood in the presence of the eternal, as God's man, to try to bring comfort to those bereaved hearts. There was also a sweet little girl across the way who met in a tragic end. Stricken with diphtheria on Tuesday, she died on Friday next, and was buried the following day, in a sealed casket. "Suffer the children to come unto me...," said the Master, and millions have heeded the call to come to newer playgrounds.

My list of serio-comic weddings began there. In one, the groom dropped the wedding ring on the floor and it rolled across the room, stopping near a register (heater). In another, the groom was Portuguese and didn't understand when I told him he could kiss the bride. So the attendant sister punched him in the ribs and said, "Beso, beso," which is their word for "kiss".

Suggested Daily Spiritual Reading:
John 3:16
1 John 2:15
Matthew 19:13-15

Further Reading Related to Diary Entry:
- *History and Mission*, Harvard Divinity School, available at: https://hds.harvard.edu/about/history-and-mission [Accessed January 23, 2021].

- *Methodist Church* (last updated 7–12-2011). Available from the BBC at https://www.bbc.co.uk/religion/religions/christianity/subdivisions/methodist_1.shtml [Accessed January 23, 2021].

- *Wesley and the People Called Methodists*, 2nd Edition by Richard P. Heitzenrater

Popular Books Published in 1940:
The Trees by Conrad Richter
The Ox-Bow Incident by Walter Van Tilburg Clark

Popular Movies Released in 1940:
The Grapes of Wrath (Henry Fonda, Jane Darwell, John Carradine)
The Long Voyage Home (John Wayne, Thomas Mitchell, Ian Hunter)
Night Train to Munich (Margaret Lockwood, Rex Harrison, Paul Henreid)

Page 31 - July 23, 1940
(Continued)

A clergyman has his store of memories of odd weddings at which people cry, at funerals in which they indulge in a certain amount of subdued hilarity. I have read a certain bishop was asked to conduct a funeral, who arrived in time to see a lady in mourning with two or three children at the bier of the deceased gentleman, and who naturally assumed they were matrimonially kin. He began his service immediately, speaking of the virtues of the deceased as a fine husband, and stressing comfort to the widow and children. The men present could not suppress their smiles, so left the church and went outside where they rolled in the grass in glee, with great guffaws. The bishop, sensing the situation, finally shouted, "Well, who is dead around here anyway?" He was told by the minister, to his eternal discomfiture, that the dead brother was a bachelor, and a misogynist to boot!

After two years at West Quincy we were transferred to South Hamilton, pleasantly situated on the North Shore. Nearby are some lovely beaches--in Gloucester, Beverly, and Manchester. In Hamilton, and environs, are some large estates constituting, as it were, an English colony, and including such figures as Frederick Prince, famous locally for allegedly assaulting a fellow polo player with a mallet, and internationally as the father of Norman Prince of the Lafayette escadrille; the then editor of the Boston Transcript, whose name has eluded me for the nonce, George von L. Meyer, one time ambassador to Germany, I believe; and another gentleman who entertained H.R.H. the Prince of Wales, later King Edward. It was here we first saw polo games and fox hunts with the ladies and gentry in red coats on sleek horses, following the hounds, like the old English prints of country landscapes. Here too I met Norman Vaughan of Ipswich who, with Eddie Goodale, had charge of sled dogs for Byrd on his expedition to the South Pole. And at this reception to Vaughan and Goodale, who autographed a book for me, I also met Leverett Saltanstall, later Governor of Massachusetts. I was scheduled to give the invocation at the meeting in the town hall, but Jonathan Lamson, chairman and local selectman, was so flustered with details he did not call upon me until the meeting was nearly over! Here too, as in other towns, I greatly enjoyed the meetings of the local clergymen, when we could meet socially and talk over our common problems.

There is not a great deal to say about South Hamilton, with a few exceptions. Our daughter Janet was born while we resided here, and she and Junior were very dear to the heart of one of the neighbors--"Auntie Durkee". We also made other friends here, who have abided through the years.

The Reverend bathing Janet, circa 1931.

The Reverend and Janet, circa 1936

Over in East Hamilton, I had a little church of which I am especially proud. There were only a few families resident there, but they were deeply interested in their children. The women bought an old schoolhouse for five dollars and converted it into a worshipful little church. In the two years previous to my coming, they had added a kitchen, at a cost of seven hundred dollars, enabling them to serve suppers more easily. In the two years of my residence, they renovated the schoolhouse at a cost of fifteen hundred dollars, adding a cupola, for which I secured a bell from the nearby town of Beverly. The mayor came over one night to dedicate it. There was a fine group of boys in the church, and we organized a scout troop. We stayed overnight at Little Neck, in Ipswich, and had a splendid time, going swimming at midnight in water that sparkled with phosphorescence. Most of the boys joined the church, and I was proud of them all. We shall remember East Hamilton, and the saintly people there, with enduring gratitude. Our superintendent here was Dr. C.C.P. Hiller, one of the finest men in any conference.

Suggested Daily Spiritual Reading:
Romans 8:31
Micah 7:8

Further Reading Related to Diary Entry:
- *The Star Book for Ministers, Third Revised Edition, 1814-1901* by Edward T. Hiscox. Available from the Internet Archive at https://archive.org/stream/starbookforminis00hisc/starbookforminis00hisc_djvu.txt [Accessed January 23, 2021]

- *Nelson's Minister's Manual, NKJV Edition* by Thomas Nelson

Popular Books Published in 1940:
For Whom the Bells Toll by Ernest Hemingway
How to Read a Book by Mortimer J. Adler

Popular Movies Released in 1940:
The House of Seven Gables (George Sanders, Margaret Lindsay, Vincent Price)
Pride and Prejudice (Greer Garson, Laurence Olivier, Mary Boland)
Broadway Melody of 1940 (Fred Astaire, Eleanor Powell, George Murphy, Frank Morgan)

First Page Following Last Dated Page (7/23/40)

Methodist Church in Cochituate, circa 1933

Parsonage in Cochituate, circa 1935

Here (*in Cochituate, MA*), Janet, who was a babe in arms (*1 year old-1932*) when we came, has grown to her present estate (*Lynn, MA; age 9*), and here too, Junior developed from a baby of two (*in Cochituate, MA*) to a young man of eleven, with all a healthy boy's interests. They will always remember our neighbors, Uncle and Auntie Fiske, into whose home they went frequently. They use to run over each night, before going to bed, to bid them goodnight. Their daughter Marion, practically clothed Janet. The children will certainly remember Cochituate.

Albert Jr. (about 6 years old) and Janet (about 4 years old), in Cochituate, circa 1935.

Cochituate—Albert Jr. And Janet and friends, circa 1935.

My father, who had moved to Cochituate shortly after we did, died in July of 1932, and lies buried in the beautiful lakeside cemetery in Cochituate. Here may he rest in blessed memory! As stated before, born in Sweden he had travelled far in time and custom--spanning the years from the older era of the relatively simple life where his father was foreman of a farm in Sweden, to the modern age of airplanes and nylon stockings! In his last years he suffered greatly from the ravages of silicosis (*His father was a stonemason by trade.*), but his application for compensation for industrial disease, and its granting by the Supreme Court of Massachusetts, after three years of litigation, was instrumental in defining the rights of other workmen, whose employers were want to discharge when old, leaving them without redress. The fairness of the justices, whom he never saw, and the majesty, if slow working, of the law, are matters of great satisfaction to me. There are no rump courts, nor peremptory decisions by one-man judicial bodies in America! No man shall be deprived of life, liberty, or property without due process of law, is ingrained in our system of jurisprudence, stemming as it does from the Magna Carta—obtained by the barons from King John at Runnymeade.

One of the most interesting exhibits at the World's Fair (*He went to the New York World's Fair in 1939.*), for me, was Lincoln's copy of the Magna Carta, kept in Lincolnshire Cathedral for 725 years. Having studied the rise of English law and the development of its traditions, it is remarkable that one can view, with one's own eyes, this ancient Latin document. It is an indispensable heritage for the ages, and we trust that all the might of totalitarian states will not be sufficient to submerge its protection for the civilized man.

My mother continued to live in Cochituate (*MA*) until about 1935, when she moved to Natick (*town next door*), where she still resides with my younger sister (*Lilla*), a technician in the laboratory at Palmer Memorial, a part of our great Deaconess Hospital (*Boston*). My older sister (*Christina*) is still at the Henry Street Settlement in New York, a part of the visiting nurse service.

We made many new friends in Cochituate, and these constitute a great compensation for a family of the manse. We went down (*he means "up"*) to Maine in the summer of 1938 with the Scotlands, as hereinafter related. The Taylor family--Fern Taylor is a tree surgeon, brought up in the company of Davey Tree Surgeons and now on his own--went on many an excursion with us. Fern and I, in particular, went to the New Brunswick border with Henry S. Dennison (*President of Dennison Manufacturing Company, Framingham, MA*); and also to Portland, Maine, where we went on a fishing trip in a commercial vessel. (*When my grandfather passed away, Fern showed up at his funeral and told stories of the Reverend and Dennison and their fishing trips.*)

Then there were the Lewis's; Mrs. Albert Felch, widow of a former pastor who gave me many of his books; Charles Fullick, who educated me in the collection of stamps; Prof. James R. Martin, teacher of geology at Boston University, who helped me in that field (*My grandfather had a huge rock collection! I have some of these rocks, still, today.*); his son Erven, deceased in an auto accident, with whom I played chess; the Schleichers, and many others. I had charge of the Boy Scout Troop for three years, and this was instrumental in helping me to become better acquainted with the young men in my own Church. Nor should I neglect to mention the fellowship of the Natick clergymen--for at our regular meetings, I learned they were regular fellows. Then, too, the Worcester ministers' meetings of Methodist preachers added much theologically, under the leadership of the superintendents, Dr. Robert Pierce and Dr. John Cairns. One of the finest associations was with a group of Methodist men called the Worcester Clerics; of which group I was secretary and later vice president. These were happy years.

The Reverend with Janet and Albert Jr., circa 1935

Suggested Daily Spiritual Reading:
    Genesis 3:19
    2 Timothy 2:4

Further Reading Related to Diary Entry:
- *Boston Holds a Water Celebration in 1848* (chronicles the use of Lake Cochituate to supply water for Boston). Available from the New England Historical Society at http://www.newenglandhistoricalsociety.com/flashback-photo-boston-holds-a-water-celebration-in-1848/ [Accessed January 23, 2021].

- *Magna Carta*. Available from the U.S. National Archives and Records Administration at https://www.archives.gov/exhibits/featured-documents/magna-carta [Accessed January 23, 2021].

Popular Books Published in 1940:
    The Transposed Heads by Thomas Mann
    Oliver Wiswell by Kenneth Roberts

Popular Movies Released in 1940:
    The Santa Fe Trail (Errol Flynn, Olivia de Havilland, Raymond Massey)
    Our Town (William Holden, Martha Scott, Fay Bainter)
    The Westerner (Gary Cooper, Walter Brennan, Doris Davenport)

Second Page Following Last Dated Page (7/23/40)

The summer of 1938 was enlivened by a week's vacation in the Moosehead Lake region of Maine. It is a wonderful country, with wide vistas, quite unlike New Hampshire or Vermont, where the mountains are close to one another. And lakes abound. We stayed on the shores of one, with friends, in a modern camp, and drove to nearby lakes for fishing. A country storekeeper, who was willing to close the store to go fishing at any time, a guide of 45 years experience in the northeastern woods and a mutual friend, went with us. We were regaled with stories. We visited and fished Moose Pond, a u-shaped body of water several miles long. We left our cars at Pickerel Cove, beautiful in the morning light, with hundreds of white pond lilies. We cast and trolled, with one eye on the lines and the other in spying out new spots of beauty. It being summertime, no salmon were caught, but enough white perch were snared for the noon meal. We landed on the rocks and the guide soon had a fire going and cooked a delicious meal. Fried fish, sandwiches, and tea strong enough to stay by you, filled us to repletion. The green woods of pine, spruce, and hemlock along the shore, the rocky shoreline with a large island mid-pond, the freshening breeze, the blue sky with racing clouds, remained fixed, unforgettably, in memory.

The Reverend with Mae, Janet, and Albert Jr., circa, 1934.

How great a thing is memory so we can relive our experiences over, and especially memories of scenes that are universalized, so to speak, for lakes have been fished by countless Izaak Waltons, and scenes recorded as well as contents noted! I am very grateful to my friends for making that day possible. It recalled many happy hours spent fishing with my father on Lake Champlain. After dinner a thunderstorm came out, but we rode out the rain, and the white perch took hold in good shape. I lost a new plug in the morning, and at this time lost a nice trolling spoon to "a big one that got away". But I managed to bring in a few and, if I remember rightly, we beat the guide and storekeeper who were in the other boat. "We" consisted of my friend Carlisle Scotland and Val Lippold. Returning to Pickerel Cove, in the afternoon, we saw two loons who were creating a weird cacophony. They were racing a motorboat, at first, and actually out-distanced it, and then disappeared under water, coming up a half mile away. I believe Moose Pond is in the town of Harmony--certainly it was a harmonious fishing trip and one long to be remembered.

Next day, we--this time meaning my wife and daughter Janet, Mrs. Scotland and son Richard, Mr. Scotland, and myself; yes, and "Duggie", as Douglas Scotland is known to his friends--motored to Moosehead Lake. We saw the mountain range along the way, and visited Greenville, at the foot of the lake, where we purchased several articles as souvenirs at the Indian Store. A certain lady of that region, called Effie, was once asked how she would get to Boston, and she replied she would go to Greenville and take the boat! And she added that while she was in Boston she "allowed as how she might as well visit the United States." A few miles up the right side of the lake, from Greenville, we climbed an eminence whence we could see ten miles of the 44-mile lake in panorama. Squaw Mountain, Mount Kineo, and Lily Bay, opened to the view, and the deep blue of the lake, contrasted with the green of the boundless forests and lighter blue of the sky, was entrancing.

The day following our fishing was resumed with a trip to Smith pond, twenty miles from nowhere. We went by Kinsbury Pond and followed a lumber road to a lumber camp set well back in the woods, where at this season, doubtless, there is excellent hunting. It was a dreary day, misty and rainy and cold, but one outstanding nevertheless. Smith Pond is perhaps a mile long, and is uninhabited except for the lumber camp, which maintains a skeleton crew in summer. While Carl and Henry the guide were having sundry adventures at a beaver dam nearby, looking for rainbow trout--you could hardly expect a rainbow to appear in that drizzle--we went out fishing in canoes.

In the morning I had a canoe without a keel and it was almost impossible to turn it around. But in the afternoon I had the use of the guide's canoe, which he had made, and although Chet, the storekeeper, who sat in the middle of the canoe, and Val, who certainly is no lightweight, sat in the other end, or prow, it navigated easily, and I had the satisfaction of not only piloting the canoe, but also of bringing aboard a good sized pickerel and the largest white perch caught during the day. At noon, we cleaned several white perch and again partook of a bounteous meal. We found shelter in a lean-to, and although Chet dropped some of the fish on the ground, sending forth some strong expletives because of it, the meal was thoroughly enjoyed. It rained harder in the afternoon, and we were quite chilled when we docked, finally. One of the lumber men hospitably gave us shelter, and a roaring fire in the camp stove helped to thaw us out. Henry, the guide, came in dripping wet, in his rubber poncho, and showed me a trout no longer than his finger with the remark it had "got crushed" on the way in from the beaver dam. It must have been a big one when he started, but then fish have a way of becoming diminutive when you show them to your friends. The ride home was uneventful.

"Duggie" had been staying with his uncle and aunt at a farm in Dexter, and one of the days we were there we went berrying on the farm. The raspberries were fairly plentiful, and we soon had enough for our evening meal. What a pleasure it is to "go forth under the open sky" in God's great out of doors, and pick the natural fruits of the field. Where there is open slash, whether in Vermont, New Hampshire, or Maine, raspberries or blackberries just naturally grow, and some of my most contented moments have been spent picking them. I remember picking several quarts of luscious blackberries from just one clump of bushes in a certain spot in New Hampshire, a few days later--I'm not telling just where!--and they certainly tasted good both then and later, in retrospect. Long may they flourish!

Another fishing trip of moment, this summer, was undertaken with yet another friend, who is a tree surgeon, Fern Taylor by name. We left Portland Harbor in a little fishing smack, which boasted a captain and crew of three, for the fishing ground ten miles beyond Portland light ship. This boat is a seiner. We left the pier at three in the morning and returned at eleven with 2,000 pounds of mixed fish aboard. The impressions of the trip are many. Advancing through the swell by starlight and a pale half moon, with a light haze, we heard the fog horn and saw the lights, colored red, of the Portland light ship, long before we saw her actual shape. Beyond the light ship, we ran into real fog, and the captain steered by compass. We found the buoy--a white flag on a barrel--promptly, and the crew set to work. Four miles of seine were laid the day before, and as it came up over the winch there were revealed many kinds of fish I had never seen before. Cod weighing up to 75 pounds, pollock, red fish, blue fish, hake, flounders, and the ever-present dogfish, which look like small sharks. The crew slit the mouths of these and threw them back to the deeps whence they came. Little eels and a huge starfish were other yields. It was rather eerie to be driving along in a fog, which obliterated all sight beyond a few yards. I lay on the forward deck and listened for the fog horn of the light ship. When the net had been fully hauled in, we went back over the same course, and laid out another one. These nets look like tennis nets, are weighted with lead on the bottom, and supported with small buoys on the top. The net is linked piece by piece, and sinks slowly to the bottom, about seventy fathoms at that point. Barrels with flags are posted at other end. The fish are cleaned on the way to port. I am proud of the fact that I was not seasick on this voyage. The captain was proud of his ability to read the compass. Truly, "they that go down to the sea in ships, that do business in great waters, these see the works of the Lord, and His mighty wonders in the deep." (*Psalm 107:23-24*)

Shortly before we emerged from the fog into the clear sunshine of Portland Harbor, I encountered a picture which will long remain in my memory. Fog, fog, and nothing but fog was ahead of me, and yet the caption said that nearby was an island whose name I have forgotten. All at once it loomed up ahead, dimly like a dream at first, and then sharply and swiftly, and I saw the breakers pounding on a white beach, with rocks in the background. I recommend a deep sea fishing trip to any who suffers ennui—boredom with life. It stabs the spirit broad awake.

Suggested Daily Spiritual Reading:
John 20:19-22
Luke 8:5-8

Further Reading Related to Diary Entry:
- *Fishing in Maine: Best Places to Catch Fish* . Available from *Wilderness Today* at https://www.wildernesstoday.com/fishing-maine/ [Accessed January 23, 2021].

- *Introduction to Portland's Waterfront*. Available from the City of Portland in the State of Maine at https://www.portlandmaine.gov/1281/Introduction-to-Portlands-Waterfront [Accessed January 23, 2021].

- *Places to Fish*. Available from the Maine Department of Inland Fisheries and Wildlife at https://www.maine.gov/ifw/fishing-boating/fishing/fishing-resources/maine-fishing-guide/regions/index.html [Accessed January 23, 2021].

- *Moosehead Lake*. Available from the Maine Office of Tourism at https://visitmaine.com/things-to-do/parks-natural-attractions/moosehead-lake [Accessed January 23, 2021].

Popular Books Published in 1940:
The Long Week-End by Alan Hodge and Robert Graves
History of the Iranian Constitutional Revolution by Ahmad Kasravi

Popular Movies Released in 1940:
Road to Singapore (Bing Crosby, Bob Hope, Dorothy Lamour)
Waterloo Bridge (Vivien Leigh, Robert Taylor, Lucile Watson)
The Bank Dick (W.C. Fields, Cora Witherspoon, Una Merkel)

Third Page Following Last Dated Page (7/23/40)

Two events this fall (*1938*) are worthy of record. One was a hurricane, which took a freak course and roared over New England, going up the Connecticut Valley and cutting a swathe 200 miles wide, doing great damage to trees and buildings. It came on September 21st, about 4 p.m., and reached its peak of velocity of 100 miles an hour. Church steeples were toppled, houses unroofed, enormous trees did great damage to buildings in falling, light and telephone service were completely disrupted, and highways littered with falling trees. Pines were the greatest victims, with countless thousands down. Whole groves were decimated, and the maple trees of Vermont and New Hampshire suffered casualties up to 70% of the sugar crop. Together with a flood that ravaged Central Massachusetts and a tidal wave which inundated the coastal regions causing many deaths, untold havoc was wrought. Monetary losses ran into the millions. In one small cemetery, nearby, nearly 80 pines were felled, and I have stood in a woodlot in New Hampshire and counted 200 or more trees down. The trees fell slowly, soundlessly, carrying with them great patches of sod. The tree roots had been softened by recent rains. Windows were smashed, Churches and other buildings had sides torn out, highways were blocked, wires carried away. It was days before lights were restored to use, and weeks before telephone service was normal. Generally speaking, the nut-bearing trees, which had taproots, escaped damage, while the surface feeders--maples, pines, and birches--were hard hit. It will be a lifetime before these can be replaced and the woods cleaned up. The latter constitutes a fire hazard of grave proportions. All together, New England would prefer that tropical hurricanes be read about rather than seen. Still it was a nine days wonder.

About this same time, international events moved swiftly. Hitler had risen to power in Germany and, under a "blood and soil" policy, was clamoring for the dismemberment of Czechoslovakia and the return of Sudetenland. For days the world lived under a cloud of war, for it was evident that Nazidom intended to back up her demands with the sword, or rather a powerful new bomb made of liquid air, recently invented by two young Americans and bought by the German government. In this threatening atmosphere, tense with the possibility of such devastation as the world has never seen before, moved Prime Minister Neville Chamberlain of England. He took a courageous initiative and volunteered to go to Germany and talk things over with Hitler. Mussolini, the Duce of Italy, paved the way, and the result was a conference at Munich which virtually granted all of Hitler's demands, with reference to Czechoslovakia, and yet averted a general war. That little country was the last to be informed. By shortwave I had heard the terms of the agreement from London, and tuned in Praha to discover, with a sense of shock, that the capital of Czechoslovakia was still ignorant of the outcome. So rapidly do events move today, and so effectively is power concentrated in the hands of the big four namely London, Paris, Rome, and Berlin. And so a virile democratic nation created at the close of the World War (*I*) was thrown to the dogs of threatened war as sacrifice to avert a greater calamity. Time alone will tell whether the sacrifice was made in vain.

Suggested Daily Spiritual Reading:
1 John 3:8
2 John 1:7

Further Reading Related to Diary Entry:
- *The Great New England Hurricane of 1938*. Available from the U.S. Department of Commerce, National Oceanic and Atmospheric Administration, National Weather Service at https://www.weather.gov/okx/1938HurricaneHome [Accessed January 23, 2021].

- *Timeline of Events (1933-1938)*, the holocaust. Available from the United States Holocaust Memorial Museum at https://www.ushmm.org/learn/timeline-of-events/1933-1938 [Accessed January 23, 2021].

- *Foreign relations of the United States diplomatic papers, 1938, Volume I*; U.S. Government Printing Office, 1938; United States Department of State, Washington, D.C. Available from the University of Wisconsin, Digital Collections at http://digital.library.wisc.edu/1711.dl/FRUS.FRUS1938v01 [Accessed January 23, 2021].

- *Appeasement: Chamberlain, Hitler, Churchill, and the Road to War* by Tim Bouverie

- *Fair Labor Standards Act of 1938: Maximum Struggle for a Minimum Wage* by Jonathan Grossman. Available from the U.S. Department of Labor at https://www.dol.gov/general/aboutdol/history/flsa1938 [Accessed January 23, 2021].

- *Fourth Annual Report of the Archivist of the United States, 1937-1938*. Available fromThe National Archives at https://www.archives.gov/files/about/history/sources/reports/1938-annual-report.pdf [Accessed January 23, 2021].

Popular Books Published in 1940:
Farewell My Lovely by Raymond Chandler
To the Finland Station by Edmund Wilson

Popular Movies Released in 1940:
   The Sea Hawk (Errol Flynn, Brenda Marshall, Claude Rains)
   The Mark of Zorro (Tyrone Power, Linda Darnell, Basil Rathbone)
   The Ghost Breakers (Bob Hope, Paulette Goddard)

Fourth Page Following Last Dated Page (7/23/40)
(First Handwritten Page - Dated December 28, 1938; Cochituate, MA)

I took a walk around Lake Cochitutate today. There was a stiff northwest breeze blowing and the waves were running high, with white caps showing. Lake Walden was much appreciated and exploited by Thoreau, but, as for me, I prefer the relative virginity of Lake Cochituate, unmarred as it is by any bathing or boating embellishments. I can read Wordsworth clear. The lake, sky, wind, and sun give a sense of "...something far more deeply interfused, whose dwelling is the light of setting suns, and the round ocean, and the living air, and the blue sky, and in the mind of man..." (*From the poem "Lines Composed a Few Miles above Tintern Abbey, On Revisiting the Banks of the Wye during a Tour. July 13, 1798" by William Wordsworth*)

The spray spitting on the shore had turned to ice, and the water was a deep blue, contrasting with the light blue of the sky. Truly God is in this place--it is none other than the house of God and the gate of heaven. The spruces and pines, the oaks and swamp maples, an occasional beech and birch, and, like a rara avis, the ducks lifting from the water silently. The sand of the beach is white and fine. The sun was warm and southerly. Nature is clean and beautiful. It bespeaks the true, the beautiful, the good, and there is no evil there. There is no evil in nature. In human nature, which stands between man and God, we find motivations of evil which reside in excess of good impulses, instincts, and habit patterns, but none in God or His creation. And (in the words of Eunice Tietjens) "...I shall go down from this quiet place, this still white peace, and time shall close about me, and my soul shall stir to the rhythm of the daily round; yet having known, life shall not press so close, and I shall always feel time ravel, thin about me, for once I stood in the white, windy presence of eternity..."

<u>Let it be noted that the actual excerpt from Eunice Tietjens' "The Most Sacred Mountain" is as follows</u>:
...But I shall go down from this airy space, this swift white
peace, this stinging exultation.
And time will close about me, and my soul stir to the rhythm
of the daily round.
Yet, having known, life will not press so close, and always I
shall feel time ravel, thin about me;
For once I stood
In the white windy presence of eternity."

Suggested Daily Spiritual Reading:
Romans 12:21
2 Peter 1:4

Further Reading Related to Diary Entry:
- *Lines composed a few miles above Tintern Abbey* by William Wordsworth (1770–1850). Nicholson & Lee, eds. The Oxford Book of English Mystical Verse 1917. Available fom bartleby.com at https://www.bartleby.com/236/67.html [Accessed January 23, 2021].

- *The Most-Sacred Mountain* by Eunice Tietjens. Jessie B. Rittenhouse, ed. (1869–1948). The Second Book of Modern Verse. 1922. Available from bartleby.com at https://www.bartleby.com/271/83.html [Accessed January 23, 2021].

Popular Books Published in 1938:
The Unvanquished by William Faulkner
Facing Mount Kenya by Jomo Kenyatta

Popular Movies Released in 1938:
Angels with Dirty Faces (James Cagney, Pat O'Brien, Humphrey Bogart)
Alexander's Ragtime Band (Alice Faye, Tyrone Power)
The Lady Vanishes (Margaret Lockwood, Michael Redgrave, Paul Lukas)

1939 (SEPTEMBER - OCTOBER)

September 6, 1939

"We strive toward heaven and lay hold on hell,
With starboard eyes we stumble in dark ways,
And to the moments when we see life well,
Succeeds the blindness of bewildered days."

(*From "A Battle Song of Failure" by Amelia Josephine Burr*)

The world is at war again; Munich was not enough, and like the old Russian legend, more had to be thrown to the wolves or they must be faced. England and France have faced Germany again, after Hitler's troops had wantonly invaded Poland. Hitler stands condemned before the judgment bar of the conscience of mankind. Napoleon was ambitious. Hilter is demonic. My greatest indictment of National Socialist dictatorship is that it has prostituted the free mind and the free conscience. He has committed the unforgivable sin in denying the Holy Ghost within himself. He has attacked learning, religion, and lives. I have been keeping a record of the newspaper headlines for the past momentous week. Someday they will be history; indeed, are already so. The four horsemen of the apocalypse are riding again--imperialism on the white horse, Mars on the red horse, famine on the black horse, and death is on the pale horse (Revelations 6). The carnage is renewed and the blackouts are begun. I made a prophecy from the pulpit last Sunday--as long as England and France are winning, the United States will remain neutral; if they are losing heavily and seem in imminent danger of surrender, this country will join on their side, for we cannot contemplate the extinction of English civilization as we know it. I make a further prophecy--that the countries with the most economic resources, meaning the Allies, will win the war.

"One by one the lights are going out all over Europe and they will never be lighted again in our time," said Lord Grey in 1914. There are many interesting parallels today. Once more Germany complains of an iron ring encircling her; once more the Germans torpedoed, from a submarine, and unarmed ship, the Athenia, with 1,400 aboard, provoking world indignation. Her claim, as reported from a German newspaper today, is that Winston Churchill, first lord of the admiralty, sunk the ship with a British submarine to bring us into war; once more Britain has established a blockade in the North Sea; once more the French and German troops face each other on the Rhine, this time on the famed Maginot and Siegfried lines. Propaganda is rampant, the English planes having dropped some six million pamphlets over the German border; and once more censorship is strictly imposed; very little news coming through.

The German drive is converging on Warsaw in the East, successfully it seems, and, at the present writing, it seems that Poland is doomed as a political entity for a time. But it seems inconceivable that the poles, who rose from a thousand years of serfdom to freedom, will long remain subjects of the German Empire. German culture is at its lowest ebb in history; the Barbarians were forthright and did not practice Machiavellianism, at least.

I like the German people individually, as I have known them, and it has been a pleasure to listen to the German music via shortwave radio and to copy their code messages, which has constituted one of my hobbies, but their imprisonment of Pastor Martin Niemoeller in a concentration camp at Dachau; their subjugation of universities, newspapers, and churches, by nefarious methods; and their sickening technique of atrocity stories to whip up enthusiasm for conquest, have cooled my admiration for the undoubted good that Hitler has accomplished in restoring the morale of the German nation. "Truth crushed to earth, shall rise again--the eternal years of God are hers." (*From "The Battlefield" by William Cullen Bryant*)

Suggested Daily Spiritual Reading:
1 John 4:3
Proverbs 3:25

Further Reading Related to Diary Entry:
- *A Battle Song of Failure* by Amelia Josephine Burr. The Literary Digest, Volume 45, October 19, 1912, page 691.

- *The Battle-Field* by William Cullen Bryant (1794–1878); Thomas R. Lounsbury, ed.; Yale Book of American Verse. 1912. Available from bartleby.com at https://www.bartleby.com/102/23.html [Accessed January 23, 2021].

- *The Works of John Bunyan, Volume 1: Experimental, Doctrinal, and Practical* by John Bunyan, edited by George Offor, Esq. (1855)

- *The Complete Works of Thomas Brooks, Volume 4—The Crown and Glory of Christianity* by Thomas Brooks (1662)

- *1939: Germany invades Poland*. On This Day. Available from the BBC at http://news.bbc.co.uk/onthisday/hi/dates/stories/september/1/newsid_3506000/3506335.stm [Accessed January 23, 2021].

- *The Coming of the Third Reich* (Book 1 in a series) by Richard J. Evans

- *World War II: The Definitive Visual History from Blitzkrieg to the Atom Bomb* by DK (part of Penguin Random House)

Popular Books Published in 1939:
Most Popular Books Published In 1939. Available from Goodreads.com at https://www.goodreads.com/book/popular_by_date/1939 [Accessed January 23, 2021].

Popular Movies Released in 1939:
Another Thin Man (Myrna Loy, William Powell)
The Four Feathers (John Clements, Ralph Richardson, C. Aubrey Smith)
Dark Victory (Bette Davis, Humphrey Bogart, George Brent)

First Page Following September 6, 1939

Last winter I took up the hobby of mineral collecting. I have gathered quite a number of specimens. This summer I visited a limestone quarry in Bolton, Mass; an old graphite quarry on Mount Monadnock; a feldspar mine in Grafton, N.H.; the emery quarries at Warren, N.H.; and an abandoned copper mine at West Fairlee, Vermont.

Some of the minerals the Reverend collected over the years.

I have been studying the atomic theory--the protons, neutrons, electrons, positrons, and deuterons--constituting interesting material. What interests me, particularly, in this connection is that when the atomic circle is complete, the gas becomes inert. Helium with two electrons, neon with ten, argon with 18, then krypton, xenon, and radon successively do not unite with the other elements, for their circles are complete. Sodium (Na) with three electrons around the nuclear proton, has one to spare, while chlorine (Cl) has seven and lacks one to complete its circle, so they rush together and adhere by electrical attraction, forming salt.

Then, too, crystals in minerals have definite patterns, and practically all minerals and rocks, barring the extrusive igneous rocks (eg. lava) which cool too rapidly, conform to one of the seven general patterns--these are isometric, tetragonal, orthorhombic, monoclinic, triclinic, hexagonal, and rhombohedral. I plan to attend my second meeting of the mineral club of the Boston Museum of Natural History on the evening of September 12th.

I have also kept up my hobby of stamp collecting, and have the collection complete and mint for the regular United States' issues for the past 16 years, with one present exception. The current issue of general stamps in use is rather expensive to collect complete as it contains the one, two, and five dollar stamps.

This summer, a part of our vacation was spent on the farm in New Hampshire belonging to my wife's folks, where I hayed, and went swimming with Junior and Janet, now nine and seven, respectively. We ascended Cannon Mountain in the newly built aerial tramway owned and operated by the state of New Hampshire. At the top we lunched, then journeyed over the summit path where we saw the Richard Taft ski trail; and saw, also, where the snow was 20 feet deep last winter, as marked on the pines. I saw, too, a fat partridge with two chickens, who were quite tame.

We went to Cape Cod for a week, staying with friends at a cottage in Eastham, but my stay was cut short when I was called home to officiate at four funerals and a wedding. But we enjoyed Cape Cod, visiting Provincetown, and seeing the many Cape Cod style of cottages with central chimney and low white fence in front of the house. We visited two lighthouses, and was impressed, particularly, with Highland Light, where a huge radio beam tower has been installed. The rollers coming in from the broad ocean led me to recall Keats and Tennyson. We swam and fished and enjoyed frankfurters cooked over a brazier on the beach. There were many cultural values to be discovered on the Cape, and it would take long to evaluate that beautiful section of our state. In the town of Eastham we saw an old windmill built in 1791. The moon was full the nights we were there, and as I stood in the water fishing and looking out across the bay, "over the moonlit waters," I recalled Matthew Arnold's great poem--"Self Dependence":

> "...Unaffrightened by the silence round them,
> Undistracted by the sights they see,
> These demand not that the things without them
> Yield them love, amusement, sympathy.
>
> And with joy the stars perform their shining,
> And the sea its long moon-silver'd roll--
> For self-poised they live, nor pine with noting
> Serene they live, nor note with pining
> All the fever of some differing soul..."

(*From "Self Dependence"* by Matthew Arnold. Available at the Poetry Foundation: https://www.poetryfoundation.org/poems/43602/self-dependence [Accessed January 23, 2021].

Suggested Daily Spiritual Reading:
Revelations 21:19-20

1 Corinthians 15:41

Further Reading Related to Diary Entry:
- *National Audubon Society Field Guide to Rocks and Minerals: North America* (National Audubon Society Field Guides) by National Audubon Society

- *Every Stamp Tells a Story: The National Philatelic Collection* (Smithsonian Contribution to Knowledge) by Cheryl Ganz (Editor), Richard R. John (Foreword), M. T. Sheahan (Contributor).

- *The World Encyclopedia of Stamps & Stamp Collecting: The Ultimate Illustrated Reference To Over 3000 Of The World's Best Stamps, And A Professional Guide to Starting and Perfecting Perfecting A Spectacular Collection* by James Mackay.

- *Physics for Poets* by Robert H. March

- *Men Who Made A New Physics* by Barbara Lovett Cline

- *Thirty Years that Shook Physics: The Story of Quantum Theory, Revised Edition* by George Gamow

Popular Books Published in 1939:
Ask the Dust by John Fante
Wind, Sand and Stars by Antoine de Saint-Exupéry

Popular Movies Released in 1939:
The Adventures of Sherlock Holmes (Basil Rathbone, Nigel Bruce, Ida Lupino)
Union Pacific (Barbara Stanwyck, Joel McCrea, Akim Tamiroff)
Babes in Arms (Mickey Rooney, Judy Garland)

Second Page Following September 6, 1939

The Morse International Code, with its dots and dashes, has long enabled men to send their thoughts around the globe. This, as Thoreau suggested, may be an improved means to an unimproved end. But once the syncopated hieroglyphics are mastered, neither time nor space, nor specious weather stay these couriers from their appointed rounds. And the interesting thing is that any language with Roman characters, Japanese or German, for example, may be sent and copied; although, the operator may not have the slightest knowledge of the language. I have copied Scandinavian, Portuguese, Spanish, German, and Japanese without difficulty.

Having mastered to some extent the reception of code, a new world is opened to the listener, for CW (*continuous waveform or carrier wave*), as it is called, travels a hundred times farther than phone or voice. This enables the Dutch, English, and others to keep in contact with their empires when phone sending and receiving would be out of the question because of atmospherics.

Of course, in commercial work and military messages it is essential that further secrecy be employed, and resort is made to a code within a code. I have often copied these without translating them. They run in a series of five letters, usually (eg. UQXVH, MJFET, LSPVX, etc.). Those who are familiar with Edgar Allen Poe's story The Gold Bug, will recall how codes are made up. Letters are transposed, advanced, or otherwise arranged in such manner as to baffle detection. I have read it stated that no code is unbreakable if enough is given. The analysis of the Rosetta stone by Champollion is a case in point. During the last World War (*I*), according to books I have read, the code experts of the various governments could unravel or "break" almost any code, given time enough, and so it was essential to change code keys frequently. I imagine that one of the most difficult to interpret would be common agreement on a certain book, then reference to page and word number for the word to be used. Figures like 11-24, 35-67, 22-34 would not give much to work on unless one stumbled on the book by chance, which is extremely unlikely. Suffice it to say that cracking codes must call for great patience as well as perseverance, but it all sounds most interesting.

Before the World War (I) a friend and I had wireless sets, with their galena crystals, tuning coils, and loose couplers for receiving, and spark coils for sending. It was a thrill to hear the Arlington, VA time signals, which were sent out in code at ten p.m. But the government suspended the activities of amateurs in 1917, and I lost interest in radio. Not until 1924 did I regain it again, when I went to work for the New England Telephone Company in Boston. There I came in contact with several Massachusetts Institute of Technology (MIT) graduates who were making kit sets, and I made two or three small sets at that time. But radio has made such rapid advances that while, through a study of physics in college and a perusal of many QST magazines, I have quite a bit of theoretical knowledge of the subject, the practical difficulties along the way have precluded the possibility of my making a transmitter on short waves and applying for an amateur's license. But it has not prevented my listening to and appreciating the efforts of others. And the world is still open to anyone willing to give the effort necessary to read and copy the International Morse Code as it is sent today. One can literally take the wings of the morning and dwell in the uttermost parts of the sea. Einsteinian concept of the relativity of time and space becomes a bit clearer if you listen to Australia at six on a winter's morning and realize that there it is 9:30 of a summer's evening! It bears out my contention that time is but the relative position bodies in space and that space is a negative abstraction.

Suggested Daily Spiritual Reading:
Matthew 17:7
Luke 6:28

Further Reading Related to Diary Entry:

- *International Morse Code (Instructions)* by U.S. Department of Defense; Departments of the Army and the Air Force, September 1957. Available from the Internet Archive at https://archive.org/details/Tm11-4591957 [Accessed January 23, 2021].

- *Compendium of Automatic Morse Code* by Ed Goss

- *Ham and Shortwave Radio for the Electronics Hobbyist* by Stan Gibilisco

- *On the Short Waves, 1923-1945: Broadcast Listening in the Pioneer Days of Radio* by Jerome S. Berg.

- *The Short Wave Magazine* (April 1939, Volume III, Number 2); published by the Short Wave Magazine Ltd., London. Available from WorldRadioHistory.com at https://worldradiohistory.com/UK/Short-Wave-UK/30s/SWM-1939-04.pdf [Accessed January 23, 2021].

- *Hammarlund Short Wave Manual, 1938, 4th edition*. Published by the Hammarlund Manufacturing Co. Inc., New York. Available from WorldRadioHistory.com at https://worldradiohistory.com/Archive-Early-Radio-Assorted/Hammarlund/Hammarlund_SW_Manual-1938.CV01.pdf [Accessed January 23, 2021].

Popular Books Published in 1939:
    Finnegans Wake by James Joyce
    After Many a Summer by Aldous Huxley

Popular Movies Released in 1939:
    Stanley and Livingstone (Spencer Tracy, Nancy Kelly, Richard Greene)
    Confessions of a Nazi Spy (Edward G. Robinson, George Sanders, Francis Lederer)
    You Can't Cheat an Honest Man (W.C. Fields, Edgar Bergen, Charlie McCarthy)

October 31, 1939

    Down in Maine, about 30 miles from the New Brunswick border, there is one of a chain of lakes called "Sysladobsis", meaning "maiden" in the language of the Passamaquoddy Indian tribe. To the Northwest lies a smaller lake called "Sysladobsis-sis" or "little maiden". Beginning at "little maiden" lake you can traverse a chain of lakes--Sysladobsis, Pocumcus, Big Lake, Grand Lake, Louis Lake, and one or two others--until you come to the headquarters of the St. Croix River and moose country. I should like to make the entire trip in a canoe--some thirty or forty miles by water--as it is a most interesting country. Wilderness for miles upon miles, and although the great northern paper companies have passed this way and still pass--for I understand that paper for the Boston Globe, for example, is furnished by the St. Croix Paper Company--yet it has left hardly a dent in the unbroken wilderness. The panoramas are magnificent, with Katahdin rearing its lofty head some forty miles northward, and with sunrise and sunset and the night sky to cast a spell over the distances. I have purposefully waited a month to write down my impressions of Sysladobsis, thinking the glow would fade, but it is still there. Truly up there the heavens declare the glory of God and the firmament sheweth His handiwork! We spent but a day and a half in that hallowed wilderness but its impress will remain for life.

Here's how I came to visit this section of Maine. I have a friend who is a tree surgeon, Fern Taylor, by name. He sometimes takes care of the trees on the lovely Nobscot estate of Henry Dennison, president of the Dennison Manufacturing Company, located in Framingham (*MA*), but known throughout the world as a necessary adjunct to any successful party, supplying as it does crepe paper and all sorts of novelties in the paper line. We have been out to Nobscot together and chopped down gray birches with Mr. Dennison, and so it came about that he invited both of us to go with him to his camp at Sysladobsis.

Mr. Dennison is a remarkable man. He has not only built up a successful business, but he has taken the time to develop himself physically and socially. He spent hours each day out of doors in active exercise, complementing this with piano playing, for he is an especial admirer of Bach. He holds a responsible position with the Resources Board in Washington, which deals with water conservation. He has been connected with the League of Nations. He is a Harvard man, and remembers his college chemistry in detail. I hope that someday his son-in-law, Edmund Ware Smith, successful in his own right as contributor to several sporting magazines and writer of short stories, will give the world a biography of this unconventionally interesting person called Henry Dennison. A wealthy man, he is most democratic; a conservator of the best things in life, he is liberal in politics and outlook. He has collaborated in the writing of books. Well along in years, he can hold his own in the woods with canoe or pack. I greatly enjoyed the stimulus of his personality on this trip (*The Reverend is 37 years old as he writes this and Henry Dennison was 62*).

We set out from Cochituate (*MA*) very early one morning, the last of September, and were well on our way by sunrise. We ate our breakfast at the railroad station in Portland (*MA*). At Wicasset Mr. Dennison showed us, on a side street, the Cape Cod-style house where his grandfather lived; the barn out back where he began his paper box industry; the magnificent elm in front of the house. We had a lobster sandwich for lunch. About three in the afternoon we arrived at the head of Sysladobsis, where were met by Ed Smith (*son-in-law*) and Pop Thorton (*caretaker of the Dennison camp*). We covered the nine or ten miles to camp in a launch, admiring the wilderness, and watching the many loons on the lake. The camp used to be a clubhouse for a group of wealthy men, and its history goes back to the time Mr. Dennison's grandfather.

<u>Suggested Daily Spiritual Reading:</u>
Ecclesiastes 1:7
Genesis 1:6-10

Further Reading Related to Diary Entry:
- *Sysladobsis Lake, Lower*--a map; Maine Department of Inland Fisheries and Wildlife. Availble from The State of Maine at https://www.maine.gov/ifw/docs/lake-survey-maps/washington/sysladobsis_lake_lower.pdf [Accessed January 23, 2021].

- *Chickens, Gin, and a Maine Friendship: The Correspondence of E.B. White and Edmund Ware Smith* by E.B. White (Author), Edmund Ware Smith (Author), Martha White (Introduction)

- *American Paper Mills, 1690–1832: A Directory of the Paper Trade with Notes on Products, Watermarks, Distribution Methods, and Manufacturing Techniques* by John Bidwell

- *Henry S. Dennison papers*. Available from the Baker Library Special Collections, Harvard Business School, Harvard University at https://hollisarchives.lib.harvard.edu/repositories/11/resources/621 [Accessed January 23, 2021].

- *Dennison, Henry Sturgis* (March 4, 1877– February 29, 1952) by Daniel Nelson. Available from the American National Biography at https://doi.org/10.1093/anb/9780198606697.article.1000406 [Accessed January 23, 2021].

Popular Books Published in 1939:
Selected Poems by W.B. Yeats, John Kelly (Editor)
Nutrition and Physical Degeneration: A Comparison of Primitive and Modern Diets and Their Effects by Weston A. Price

Popular Movies Released in 1939:
Jesse James (Tyrone Power, Henry Fonda, Nancy Kelly, Randolph Scott)
Andy Hardy Gets Spring Fever (Lewis Stone, Mickey Rooney, Cecilia Parker, Fay Holden)
The Hound of the Baskervilles (Basil Rathbone, Nigel Bruce)

First Page Following October 31, 1939

There were at least six canoes at the camp, which is located on the small stream that unites Sysladobsis with Pocumcus at the foot of the former lake. Two of the canoes had "kickers", as Mr. Dennison described the motors. There are three main buildings--Honeymoon camp, the clubhouse with five or six bunks, and the farmhouse. There is a barn and outhouses with two small camps for guides appended to the farmhouse.

The camp has its own electric generator, and in the house there was a radio and there were lights in the camp. I spent the evening looking about, playing horseshoes with Ed, and reading his book "A Tomato Can Chronicle"--dealing with hunting and fishing incidents at Sysladobsis--and also the old journals of the camp.

Edward Filene of Boston had visited here, and along the wall is a rack of clay pipes, which were used by former guests. There is also some fine tackle and rods in the clubhouse, some belonging to Mr. Dennison, some to Ed. After watching the wheeling of the planets in the blue vault above, we retired early for we had a busy day ahead. May I say, by way of parenthesis, the food at the camp, as prepared by the capable hands of Mrs. Thorton, and served by Ed Smith, was most enjoyable.

About five in the morning we were awakened by Ed and invited to come out and see two buck deer grazing at the forest edge a quarter mile away. Seen through the binoculars, they made an unforgettable picture as their bodies faced east, their antlered heads east, and their tails lifted like white flags. On the way home, the next day, we were to see a doe with fawn, but those deer were the high point of interest to me. They walked sedately into the woods and disappeared. After a hearty breakfast we visited the eel trap at the dam, and saw quite a number of eels, which had been caught in transit. We also spent some time with the cameras taking pictures of the group and lovely environs.

Ed, Fern, Mr. Dennison, and myself then entered a canoe--with kicker--and went to see the sites on Lake Pocumcus, to the east of us. The lake is narrow and at its northern end the water was a deep blue; the sun brilliant, the sky filled with fleecy clouds. There was a wind blowing and kicking up the spume and altogether the scene was entrancing. Ed was in the bow and Mr. Dennison did the navigating. It was a morning to remember. We discoursed on many matters, including Santayana's "Sense of Beauty", and Ed and I agree that beauty lay in the mind and soul of the beholder. We crossed a channel, skirting a sandbar, and stopped for a little while on the bank nearby before turning back.

On returning, in company with Pop Thorton, we went up the lake

(Sysladobsis), a mile or two, and dug up about five or six small pines, which were transported back to camp by canoe and transplanted to replace a large pine blown down by the hurricane. We then had lunch on a nearby beach, and such a lunch--great hunks of steak, with coffee, potatoes, corn on the cob, and cookies. It was a grand feed and Ed prepared it for us. Before dinner, Fern and I went swimming, in the altogether--and who cared for there were no camps for miles. Fern took a picture of me as I was getting dressed minus my pants. The swim was invigorating and we did full justice to the splendid meal. I spent most of the afternoon looking for arrowheads on Pocumcus Point, where there was a great Indian battle one hundred years ago, but I found nary a one. The Passamaquoddy Indians have a reservation down near Princeton (*Maine*), and there are Indian relics in abundance in these parts, but I wasn't fortunate enough to find them in a short hunt. I did find some flakings, in the evening, on the point thanks to Pop Thornton's helper, who assisted me and showed me how to dig for them in the sand.

After our evening meal, the four of us--Ed, Fern, Mr. Dennison, and myself--crossed Sysladobsis in another canoe, with a "kicker",and witnessed a sunset, without parallel in my experience. The sun, in setting, flooded the sky with magenta-colored clouds, and the shadings and overtones simply emphasized the glory of them. To the south, the cloud linings were of opalescent pearl. The dark water and green of the great pines provided colorful support to this display of nature's spectacle. On the way home, we saw a red fox on the shore, which Ed took for a bobcat, at first. The sky that night was clear and we had free seats at the greatest show on earth--Venus, Mars, Jupiter for planets; the Pleiades, Ursa Major, and Cassiopeia for constellations; and early the next morning I saw Orion for good measure.

Suggested Daily Spiritual Reading:
Jonah 1:17
Proverbs 3:5

Further Reading Related to Diary Entry:
- *Upper Sysladobsis Lake*; Lakeville, Penobscot, Maine. Available from the LakesOfMaine.org (a product of Lake Stewards of Maine, in collaboration with state and federal agencies and nonprofits) at https://www.lakesofmaine.org/lake-overview.html?m=4688 [Accessed January 23, 2021].

- *A Tomato Can Chronicle: And Other Stories of Fishing and Shooting* by Edmund Ware Smith (Author), Ralph L. Boyer (Illustrator).

- *The Sense of Beauty: Being the Outline of Aesthetic Theory* by George

Santayana.

- *Early Labor Economics: Its Debt to the Management Practice of Henry S. Dennison*. History of Political Economy, 2007 by Kyle Bruce. Available from Academia.edu at https://www.academia.edu/31731484/Early_Labor_Economics_Its_Debt_to_the_Management_Practice_of_Henry_S._Dennison [Accessed January 23, 2021].

- *Native American Tribes of Maine*. Available from the Native Languages of the Americas website at http://www.native-languages.org/maine.htm [Accessed January 23, 2021].

- *Maine Native Studies Resources*. Available from the Maine Department of Education at https://www.maine.gov/doe/learning/content/socialstudies/resources/mainenativestudies/resources [Accessed January 23, 2021].

Popular Books Published in 1939:
Systematic Theology by Louis Berkhof
The Man Who Came to Dinner by Moss Hart, George S. Kaufman

Popular Movies Released in 1939:
The Three Musketeers (Don Ameche, Gloria Stuart, The Ritz Brothers, Binnie Barnes)
Buck Rogers (Buster Crabbe, Constance Moore, Jackie Moran)
Destry Rides Again (James Stewart, Marlene Dietrich)

Second Page Following October 31, 1939

    We had to leave in the morning, before sun-up, but then all good things come to an end, we are told. However, scenes may go, but beauty lingers. Going up the lake on the launch (it was rather chilly until the sun came out and the fog lifted), I looked back down the length of Sysladobsis and saw a vivid painting on a great canvas; one which only the greatest painter of all could produce. There was, first, the white spray on the water, with a trace of fog; then, the green of an island slanting water-ward; then, the blue of the farther water; the lighter blue of the distant mountain—Duck Mountain, perhaps—then, the pink of the sunlight's reflection on the white clouds; and, above all, the sky-blue of the open vault of heaven. It formed a composite and majestic whole, and the rest was anticlimax-- the doe and fawn, the distant view of Katahdin's peak, the ultimate richness of the Maine woods, and the smooth, flowing ride home.

    I am indebted greatly to Mr. Dennison, not only for his gracious hospitality, but also and primarily for the opportunity of seeing some of the grandest country in the world. When the lake is frozen over, and the great white cold stalks abroad, it is good to be back in civilization. However, when the summer is present, and the fish are alluring, and the distant waters call, and the teal, ducks, and loons make a grand picture overhead, and the buck deer stand like sentinels looking curiously toward man-made things, then the place to be is northern Maine, and the time to be alive is youth.

    A word about Pop Thorton--he seems like a fine guide to "ride the river with". He showed me an Indian grinding stone, hollowed out for or by the constant use of the pestle of the Indian women; he told me about the wildlife in the woods; and he showed me his cap-an-bunk fences, which ought to last in the neighborhood of a hundred years--long enough for any fence, I think. Pop is handy with tools, and he has made some ingenious things, but the fence impressed me most. Not a nail in it, but solidly held. Two posts are set parallel in the ground, and over them is put a slab with two holes bored to fit the posts. A big log is then inserted between the posts; another slab with holes put on for a binder, and so on until about four logs are in place, firmly held by the bored slabs. This is called a cap-an-bunk fence. Although I have travelled over New England a great deal, I have not seen them elsewhere; although, other farmers may have them. Pop is a fine caretaker; works up his own wood; has even built a saw rig to saw the wood with this winter, and the place is kept up "ship-shape and in Bristol fashion". Mr. Dennison is fortunate in having such a versatile fellow for superintendent.

    The summer has been a rich one in out-of-door experiences--Monadnock, Newfound Lake, Cape Cod, and to round it off nicely, a day and a half on the hospitable shores of Sysladobsis. May other summers bring like memories!

Suggested Daily Spiritual Reading:
John 7:7
John 3:17-18
Genesis 1:16

Further Reading Related to Diary Entry:
- *Explorer's Guide Maine, Including the Coast and Islands* by Nancy English and Christina Tree

- *Cape Cod* by Henry David Thoreau

- *The Outermost House: A Year of Life On The Great Beach of Cape Cod* by Henry Beston

Popular Books Published in 1939:
Lost on a Mountain in Maine by Donn Fendler, Joseph B. Egan
Selected Writings by Thomas Aquinas, Ralph McInerny

Popular Movies Released in 1939:
It's a Wonderful World (James Stewart, Claudette Colbert)
On Borrowed Time (Lionel Barrymore, Sir Cedric Hardwicke, Beulah Bondi)
Idiot's Delight (Clark Gable, Norma Shearer, Edward Arnold, Charles Coburn)

1940 (January-September)

January 22, 1940

I have been looking up at the clock and the weathervane on the Church tower, and thinking how one might well write an essay or poem on "Time and the Weather". How important both have been in the minds of men! What time is it? What's the weather going to be tomorrow? The weather is an ever present reality--it is stormy or clear or lowery or warm or cold; but as regards time, I am not so sure. It is a convenient reference point to be sure, but as an absolute, I am convinced there is none such. Time is but the concept for the relative positions of bodies in space, and space is but a negative abstraction, where matter is not!

This is my thirty-eighth birthday. My wife gave me "Dana's Mineralogy" (14th edition). My mother and sister gave me money to buy mineral specimens. It seems good to have one's loved ones around at such a time--to have people that really care for you. I met a Greek in a nearby hospital the other day--a Greek from Smyrna; a bachelor with white hair and high blood pressure, condemned to a lengthy period of hospitalization. No relatives, no loved ones, no family, and no friends. There were tears in his eyes after I prayed with him, and in gratitude that an absolute stranger should take the time to converse with him he offered me an orange, about the only thing he had. It gave me pause to think how great were my blessings, with a healthy son and daughter, and many of the good things of life, and best of all, a profound faith in God and His benevolent ultimate purpose for this spinning planet. I am sure of the benevolence of nature--the tooth was not made for aching, but for mastication. The tree was not made for firewood, but for fruit. The poet may well write of the great outdoors, "Where every prospect pleases, and only man is vile" (*from "The Missionary Hymn" by Reginald Heber*).

And yet man, essentially, wants only lebensraum, or "living room", as the Germans say, and ultimate harmony in the relationships of mice or men involves not competition but cooperation. The lion does not kill promiscuously and indiscriminately, but quickly and for food. Battles among men seem to contradict this, but this war is bearing it out amply. The Maginot and Siegfried lines have launched no major offensives--preservation and conservation of lives is the guiding principle, for the common man is tiring of war, except to achieve that principle.

No blitzkrieg has struck the English shores from Germany--retaliation would be too swift and complete. A stalemate is reached, for the moment, militarily. In the economic realm, the objective is to starve the enemy, but after starvation and revolt, and the setting up of new governments, food relief is quickly instituted, as witness to the end of the last war. I foresee a time when war will be outlawed as an instrument of national policy, because it is contrary to the fundamental law of nature, and in the present age decides nothing. Economic expansion, peaceful penetration--these will supersede military destruction. Let an international police force maintain order among the nations. I foresee in the next hundred years either a United States of Europe voluntarily arrived at, or an Imperium akin to that of ancient Rome. If the later, then man will have retrogressed by exactly 2,000 years, and must painfully and slowly learn the way to sovereignty and self-government. But the current is all in the other direction. The Russo-Finnish war simply bears out the contrast between men fighting for their homes and freedom, and hirelings of the state who have no real interest in the struggle, and who would gain nothing thereby.

```
"Till the war drums throbbed no longer, and the battle flags were furled
   In the Parliament of Man, the Federation of the World.
 There the common sense of most shall hold a fretful realm in awe
 And the kindly earth shall slumber, lapped in universal law."
```
(*Paraphrased from the poem "Locksley Hall" by Alfred, Lord Tennyson*)

Suggested Daily Spiritual Reading:
Philippians 1:29
Mark 4:37-41

Further Reading Related to Diary Entry:
- *Dana's Textbook of Minerology (With an Extended Treatise on Chrystallography and Physical Mineralogy)* by Edward Salisbury Dana and William E. Ford Publisher: John Wiley & Sons, Inc.; 4th edition (January 1, 1932)

- *Dana's Manual Of Mineralogy For The Student Of Elementary Mineralogy, The Mining Engineer, The Geologist, The Prospector, The Collector, Etc* by James Dwight Dana and William Ebenezer Ford

- *The Weather Machine: A Journey Inside the Forecast* by Andrew Blum

- *Reality Is Not What It Seems: The Journey to Quantum Gravity* by Carlo Rovelli

Popular Books Published in 1940:
Most Popular Books Published In 1940. Available from Goodreads.com at https://www.goodreads.com/book/popular_by_date/1940 [Accessed on January 23, 2021].

Popular Movies Released in 1940:
 Behind the News (Lloyd Nolan, Doris Davenport, Frank Albertson)
 Edison, the Man (Spencer Tracy, Rita Johnson, Charles Coburn)
 The Great McGinty (Brian Donlevy, Muriel Angelus, Akim Tamiroff)

March 4, 1940

Since February 8th, we have lived in the city of Lynn (*MA*). I was transferred to the South Street Methodist Church on the 4th of February, and since then we have been extremely busy, making the necessary contacts in the Church, and moving into the home. We like our new home very much--it's set upon a hill overlooking the city, and, also, overlooking the ocean, so that I can sit at my desk and see the waves breaking on the shores of Nahant. It is a cozy six-room, bungalow-type house, and has quickly become a real home. And the Church is responsive and interesting, with its increased number of services, and different type of problems. It has excellent leadership and a finely developed spirit of loyalty. I am sure I shall have a fine pastorate here.

About a week after we moved in, a blizzard, in the form of a prolonged snowstorm, settled over the country and it was two days before the street in front of the house was plowed out, with a powerful snowfighter, and it was three days before I was able to get my car back up on the hill and into the garage, which I rent down the street. The snow with its whiteness was a beautiful sight, and must have been especially lovely in New Hampshire. How much I enjoyed my four years at Dartmouth, and the white, unbroken snow, with the pines developing a pattern of green on the landscape. But while it is a little difficult adjusting ourselves to city life, and there is a definite nostalgia for friendships formed over a period of years. I am sure we will acclimate ourselves to our new environment. Like the chambered nautilus:

```
"...Stretched in the newfound home,and knew the old no
```
more..." (*From the poem "The Chambered Nautilus" by Oliver Wendell Holmes, Sr.*)

It is like the barrier of death, which says we may look back on the old scenes and old relationships, but as in the poem...

```
"Break, break, break, on thy cold grey stones, O sea,
And I would that my tongue could utter, the thoughts that
                       arise in me."
```

And again:

```
"Break, break, break, on thy cold grey stones, O sea,
But the tender grace of a day that is dead, can never arise in
                           me."
```
(*Paraphrased from the poem "Break, Break, Break" by Alfred, Lord Tennyson*)

The sea is symbol enough of my state of mind, and mood. My life began in the rolling hills of Vermont; will it end beside the never resting waves? The poet tells it...

"Then he knows or thinks he knows,
The hills where his life rose,
And the sea where it goes."
(*Paraphrased from "The Buried Life" by Matthew Arnold*)

Rolling Hills of Vermont, circa 1930s.

To break with something cherished, and not to be attained again, is to give one sympathy with all lost causes, and hard-pressed peoples. My heart aches in sympathy for the people of Finland. Communism in Russia was to usher in a golden era of brotherhood and economic equality. Russia has more resources than any single country in the world. But the great experiment, with its denial of God and the theistic way of life, reverts to the pattern of the savage, who is not content with enough. He must have it all. In Finland, today is one of the crucial points of civilization. Charles Martel at Tours in 1215 (?) turned back the tide of the Mohammedan hordes and saved the peoples of Europe for Christianity, but what if it be lost in our century by greed and stupidity. Christ has suffered most in the house of his friends. If Czarism had been nearer the people, perhaps a revolution might have been averted. And if England and France had been less vindictive in 1919, perhaps the second world war would not have arisen. It is a moot question, and much debated. Will the allies come to the aid of Finland? If Finland is conquered, and reduced to serfdom, would Germany, with her dependence on Swedish iron ore, allow Scandinavia to be overrun by the menace from Moscow? The modern ideological war has supplanted the former religious one. May the mercy of God and His peace abide with those who suffer amid the grotesque tragedy of war!

Suggested Daily Spiritual Reading:
John 6:16-20
Luke 20:46

Further Reading Related to Diary Entry:
- *Finland at War: The Continuation and Lapland Wars 1941–45* by Vesa Nenye, Peter Munter, Toni Wirtanen, Chris Birks

- *Frozen Hell: The Russo-Finnish Winter War of 1939-1940* by William Trotter

Popular Books Published in 1940:
A Technique for Producing Ideas by James Webb Young
Clock Without Hands by Carson McCullers

Popular Movies Released in 1940:
Foreign Correspondent (Joel McCrea, Laraine Day, Herbert Marshall)
Rebecca (Laurence Olivier, Joan Fontaine)
Escape (Robert Taylor, Norma Shearer, Conrad Veidt)

July 24, 1940

The advice of an old Scot divine to a young man about to enter the ministry is good advice for all ministers on all occasions. "Sonny," he said, "in every sermon, put in a good word for Jesus Christ." Especially in these days when the word "Jew" is anathema in some quarters abroad, and, by implication, Christianity, founded by a son of Nazareth, is called in Nietzschean terms, a slave morality. Personally, I am proud that Christ was a Jew by birth--that out of that persecuted and misunderstood people, who gave Monotheism to the world, has come a Savior of the world. And the world, beset by force, cruelty, and Machiavellian deceit, is badly in need of a Savior. He came not His own, and His own received him not, but uncounted millions have received Him with comfort and blessings to themselves. We have all sinned and come short of the glory of God, and every man needs to remember:

```
"There is a fountain filled with blood, drawn from Immanuel's
                              veins,
And sinners, plunged beneath that flood, lose all their guilty
                              stains.
 The dying thief rejoiced to see that fountain in his day,
  And there may I, though vile as he, wash all my sins away!"
         (From the hymn, "There is a Fountain Filled with Blood")
```

"This bread is my body broken for thee," (*Matthew 26:26*), and "This…blood…is shed for thee and for many for the remission of sins," (*Matthew 26:28*) are the most sacred words from human lips. Of Jesus it may be said in his own words, "Greater love hath no man than this, that a man lay down his life for his friends. And ye are my friends…" (*John 15:13-14*)

Earth has many fine things to give us. I am writing these words on a lovely beach beside the Connecticut River in New Hampshire. A great elm in the meadow is foreground for Black Mountain. The sun shines brightly, and my son and daughter, with nephew and niece, are playing in the sand at the water's edge. On the other bank, in Vermont, is a white flagpole, from which flew yesterday, in proud splendor, the Stars and Stripes, symbol of our liberty under law. And I am enjoying, in my bathing suit, all the peace and tranquility of the morning.

Back Row: Olive ("Mother Brock"—Mae's mother and the Reverend's mother-in-law), Aunt Bess (Ernie's sister-Mae's aunt), Carl (Mae's brother), Millie with cigar (Carl's wife), George (Bess' husband), Ernie with hat on stick ("Father Brock", Mae's father). Front row: Carl Jr., Janet, Joyce (Carl Jr.'s sister), Albert Jr., and the Reverend. Circa 1937.

Yet, as I said recently in a sermon, if one dwells in peace and prosperity, yet without Christ, he is nothing; but even in the midst of war and carnage, with the world falling about his ears, if he have Christ, he is wealthy beyond price; having both, one is blessed indeed. Now having spoken a "gude (*result of the word "good" when being said with a Yankee accent*) word" for Jesus Christ this morning, let me resume my narrative.

After spending two pleasant years in Hamilton, preaching the Word to the best of my ability, under conditions trying at times, I was transferred to Cochituate (*Janet 1 year old and Albert Jr 3 years old*), which is part of Wayland (*Massachusetts*), where we spent eight years before coming to Lynn (*Massachusetts*), where we are now situated (*Janet 9 years old and Albert 11 years old*). During those eight years our roots went quite deeply into community life, and it is with hesitation and nostalgia that I record, in cold type, the impressions of our itinerancy in a lovely community and Church.

On the material side, I had the satisfaction of helping to put the Church edifice in better condition, with interior and exterior renovated and painted. Above all, we put a cross in the Church and used lighted candles each Sunday, to emphasize the Light of the world. With the help of the town highway department, for a number of years we went into the woods and cut enough fuel for the winter. C.O. Baker, who owns a power saw, each year would come down, and without compensations financially, would cut all the wood needed. I have heard of a preacher who left a Calvinist denomination because he could not accept the doctrine of total depravity of men, having known six who could not possibly be in that category; and I know how he feels, having met such men and women myself. When I say the people in the Church were like the people in East Hamilton, I have paid them the highest reciprocal compliment. During my incumbency, we organized a men's club, which was highly successful in bringing the men of the community into closer social contact with the Church.

Suggested Daily Spiritual Reading:
John 15:13
Mark 14:22-24

Further Reading Related to Diary Entry:
- *Jesus Through Middle Eastern Eyes: Cultural Studies in the Gospels* by Kenneth E. Bailey

- *Simply Jesus: A New Vision of Who He Was, What He Did, and Why He Matters* by N. T. Wright
- *Three Simple Rules: A Wesleyan Way of Living* by Rueben P. Job

- *Five Means of Grace: Experience God's Love the Wesleyan Way* (Wesley Discipleship Path Series) by Elaine A. Heath

- *Spurgeon on Prayer & Spiritual Warfare* (anthology of six of Spurgeon's classic books on prayer: *The Power in Prayer, Praying Successfully, The Golden Key of Prayer, Finding Peace in Life's Storms, Spurgeon on Praise, Satan: A Defeated Foe*) by Charles H Spurgeon.

Popular Books Published in 1940:
A Mathematician's Apology by G. H. Hardy
Country Squire in the White House by John T. Flynn

Popular Movies Released in 1940:
Stranger on the Third Floor (Peter Lorre, John McGuire, Margaret Tallichet)
Boom Town (Clark Gable, Spencer Tracy, Claudette Colbert)
The Shop Around the Corner (Jimmy Stewart, Margaret Sullivan)

July 30, 1940

Lynn (*MA*) is an interesting place geologically. A great deal of it is rhyolite, a volcanic rock. Over in Nahant there are many points of interest--Swallow's cave, near the home of John Roosevelt (son of the President); the sedimentary rock in strata on the Lodge estate, where lived and worked, overlooking the sea, Henry Cabot Lodge, and prior to him, according to Lewis' "History of Lynn", Francis Parkman, who wrote "Conquest of Mexico", and other works. There is a stone building with corinthian pillars used by Lodge as a workshop, which overlooks the restless sea--I should like to own it. Then there is Castle Rock--of gabbro (feldspar plus pyroxene) and the Spouting Horn, and a ledge of hornblende (Ca, Al, Mg, Fe, Si_3O_6), and an ancient rock temple made of sedimentary rocks from the other side of the island. Then there is a fort, built many years ago, and Crystal Beach, where we did <u>not</u> find hornblende crystals, which Lewis spoke of in his history as being there. Just off (*the coast of*) Nahant is Egg Rock, where the gulls lay their eggs, and which is probably gabbros.

About a mile behind our home begins the Lynn Woods, covering two or three thousand acres, and containing, among other things, Mt. Gilead with tower; a tower on Burrill Hill made mostly of hornblende glacial granite; several lakes of remarkable beauty; the Wolf Pits, built in 1635 by the early colonists, used for trapping wolves. The pits are about four by two feet, two in number, and lined with granite. Originally quite deep, they have been filled in with debris until they are no more than four feet in depth, at present. Then, too, the Woods are filled with granite boulders, obviously exotics, and undoubtedly brought down by the glaciers of remote times. There is also some rhyolite in the park. The trees are of many varieties and escaped the ravages of the 1938 hurricane. Most interesting place in the Lynn Woods is Dungeon Rock (diorite), which has quite a history. Legend tells of a pirate escaped from the British who fled to a cave in Dungeon Rock and was buried there, by an earthquake, with his treasure chest, presumably. A few years before the Civil War, along came one William Marble of Charlton, Mass.; a spiritualist who began digging a tunnel to the buried treasure. He and his son, who is buried on the site, worked for fifteen years in response to inner urgings and spiritualistic directions, and dug a tunnel 193 feet in depth and seven feet in diameter; apparently carrying the rock out on their backs, and using only gunpowder for blasting; dynamite not having been invented.

Lewis tells in his book, written seventy-five years ago, of their progress--over 160 feet at that time. Marble came with $1,500; a goodly sum in those days, but not enough to last him fifteen years. Visitors who came, contributed to the work, and spiritualist meetings were held, in which the illiterate pirate's instructions played a prominent part, according to Lewis. But they never found the treasure, and water filled the tunnel; until now one may only descend sixty-five feet. Many take advantage of the opportunity, as it is a unique tunnel with a unique history. Working fifteen years at hard labor voluntarily with a visionary promise of reward is indeed unique. I have a feeling that the work to which he was accustomed were like a prisoner's chains, with which marble was loathe to part. So strong does habit grow. As a friend once said, "if you take the "h" from habit, you still have a "bit"; if you take away "a" and "b", you still have "it"!"

On the edge of the Woods, near Breed's Pond, I have found dendrites--patterns in rock-like trees and plants, made by manganese dioxide--and Lewis tells again, in his history, of a man finding these seventy-five years ago on the same spot. I suppose the earliest settlers ran across them also, and, possibly, the Indians. From a geological standpoint, Lynn has many points of interest to one interested! And I am, quite definitely! As another friend put it, I am a "bug on rocks"!

Suggested Daily Spiritual Reading:
Psalm 27:1
Matthew 18:33

Further Reading Related to Diary Entry:

- *History of Lynn* by Alonso Lewis. Available from the Internet Archive at https://archive.org/details/historyoflynn02lewi/page/n10 [Accessed on January 23, 2021].

- *The Legend of Dungeon Rock and the Pirate Treasure It Holds* (updated in 2020). Available from the New England Historical Society at https://www.newenglandhistoricalsociety.com/legend-dungeon-rock-pirate-treasure/ [Accessed on January 23, 2021].

- *Dungeon Rock, Lynn Woods*. Available from the Swampscott Public Library, Swampscott, Mass. at https://digitalheritage.noblenet.org/swampscott/items/show/277 [Accessed on January 23, 2021].

- *Lynn Woods Reservation*. Available from the City of Lynn at http://www.lynnma.gov/departments/lynnwoods.shtml [Accessed on January 23, 2021].

- *The Book of Roses* by Francis Parkman. Published in 1871 by J. E. Tilton And Company, Boston. Available from The Project Gutenberg at http://www.gutenberg.org/files/47232/47232-h/47232-h.htm [Accessed on January 23, 2021].

- *France and England in North America*, volumes 1-8 by Francis Parkman.
  - *A Half-Century of Conflict*. France and England in North America, part 6. Published by Little, Brown, and Company, Boston in 1910. Available from Internet Archive at https://archive.org/details/franceandenglan06parkgoog/page/n11 [Accessed on January 23, 2021].

Popular Books Published in 1940:
Zen and Japanese Culture by D.T. Suzuki
Miss Hargreaves by Frank Baker

Popular Movies Released in 1940:
The Philadelphia Story (Cary Grant, Katharine Hepburn, James Stewart)
The Mortal Storm (James Stewart, Margaret Sullavan, Robert Young, Frank Morgan)
The Howards of Virginia (Cary Grant, Martha Scott)

August 7, 1940

My father-in-law was telling me, last night, about the time he worked on a construction job in Enfield, New Hampshire, and the tricks they used to play on the foreman of the project--a big, red-headed, six-footer. He used to swear at the men, cursing them roundly and finding fault when there was none; in consequence, no one liked him. The job was the erection of a big mill dam to supply power for the shoe shops and woolen mill located there. Dad (*Ernie*) Brock had me laughing so much at the deserved misfortunes of Red Head that I developed the hiccups.

On one occasion, the foreman, Red Head, was down in the bastion-hole or caisson (I'm not quite sure of the terminology of places where cement is poured) when Dad Brock came along with a wheelbarrow full of cement and poured the whole thing over him; quite accidentally of course. Red Head's bellows could be heard quite a distance away, but he never discovered who did it. There was a sluiceway near the big shoe shop, and one day while Red Head was looking down into it, one of the girls in the factory poured down a bucket of water from the third floor, which struck him squarely on the head, and almost tipped him into the sluiceway. He was all right, but not his ten gallon hat, costing five dollars or more, which he never recovered. His outburst of profanity on that occasion was only equalled a few days later when, down in the hole again, the men played another trick on him. When dinnertime came, all the men except Red Head left the hole via the ladder, and one of the men--his identity is hidden forever--pulled up the ladder after him, and went off to dinner. Red Head's absence at the dinner table was duly noted and comments passed, and when the men returned, after taking their time, his bellowing could be heard for a hundred yards! There was a plank across a cut on the job, supported by two wooden horses, and on another memorable occasion someone pulled out one of the horses, unbeknownst to Red Head, and he took a header into the ditch, skinning his knee, and ruining what was left of his disposition! His objurgations, when he emerged, had best be omitted. Such was the jolly life led by the men on the job--the whole of whom he threatened to discharge collectively and summarily more than once.

Anyone who knows him can tell you that Ernest Brock has always been a hard worker. Now past sixty-two and with graying hair, he has slowed down slightly, but only slightly. He gets up at four o'clock and helps the hired man milk the cows, goes to the creamery about seven, comes home, and goes to haying until milking time. Then, perhaps, after milking he will get a load of wood or sawdust, as on last evening. The other night at nine o'clock my wife and I took him way out to West Newbury, some ten or twelve miles, where he practiced the old square dances with the West Newbury Grange team, which for several years past has been first in the state contests! Last winter he got out 175,000 feet of lumber—to bring in extra money he sells Christmas trees, maple syrup, and each summer for the past seven years he has spent a month or so selling strawberries. He has twice the vitality of most people, and although not tall is thickset and very strong. I have seen him lift things around like Jean Valjean, and it is always a pleasure to come up on the farm, as we do each summer, and work with him. He is very even tempered, and even after a hard day's work will fool with the children or the dog. The farm has been a real burden for many years past, because of the low price of milk ($1.65 a hundredweight in the current market—a pint equals one pound, roughly), and what with taxes, interest, insurance, feed, replacement of machinery, repairs, etc., it entails a lot of expense to run a farm. Mother (Olive) Brock is a very good cook, and a good helpmate. In spite of trouble with her feet, which bother her considerably, she manages to look on the best side of things, and she makes things very comfortable for us during the weeks we spend here.

This summer has been one of the most restful we have known.

Ernest (Ernie) Brock, circa 1940

<u>Suggested Daily Spiritual Reading:</u>
Psalm 18:49
Ecclesiasticus 29:21-23

Further Reading Related to Diary Entry:
- *The Last of the Hill Farms: Echoes of Vermont's Past* by Richard W. Brown

- *Historic Photos of Vermont* by Ginger Gellman

Popular Books Published in 1940:
Darkness at Noon by Arthur Koestler
New World Order by H.G. Wells

Popular Movies Released in 1940:
The Great Dictator (Charlie Chaplin)
Brother Orchid (Edward G. Robinson, Ann Sothern, Humphrey Bogart)
Northwest Passage (Spencer Tracy, Robert Young)

August 7, 1940
(Continued)

    The farm, located on the River Road in Piermont, New Hampshire, sits on the brow of a hill overlooking the beautiful Connecticut River Valley, and out the back window one can look fifteen miles upstream. There are four magnificent maples and an elm in the yard, and as I type a refreshing breeze sweeps through the yard. Junior and Gypsy, the collie, have just gone down the road after the mail. The house is white with green trimmings, and one has a feeling of spaciousness for it is not hemmed in by other houses as in the city. Black Mountain rears its majestic peak to the North, capped by its observation tower, and to the West lie the Vermont hills. The unpainted barn houses twenty-six cows, four calves, the bull, two horses—Harry and Prince—and some forty tons of hay, newly gathered. The farm land slopes westward to the river (*the Connecticut River*), and covers the oats, potatoes, and corn, besides the grassland which is several acres in extent. To the South, on a hill, are some eighty acres of pasture and timberland. Other occupants of the farm, who live upstairs, are the hired man, one Arthur Joyal, and his housekeeper, Minnie Scott, who celebrates her fifty-ninth birthday today. We are having dinner together, prepared by her, and there will be a nice homemade birthday cake and presents. It is an occasion to be remembered. The war, business, and politics seem very far away.

    For outside interests, we have visited an abandoned gold mine or quarry in Lyman, where specimens were secured of quartz crystals, iron pyrites, and possibly gold. We also visited a place near Pearl Lake in Lisbon where we found garnets and staurolite. And Ore Hill in Warren yielded specimens of pyrites, lead, copper, and tremolite. We have visited friends in Barre and Groton, Vermont, and taken many rides up and down the valley. It has been a delightful summer, and what with Lynn Beach and the hayfield, the children and I have become well tanned.

    Speaking of haying, let me tell you of the intelligence of Harry, the gray horse. Hitched to a rope which pulls the hayfork, he will, on command, go out to the rope's end, turn about and come back to the stable door, and turn around once more in position without further guidance. Quite a remarkable horse. The haying is done almost mechanically. A tractor with cutter is used to mow the hay; it is raked with a side-delivery rake and truck; loaded with truck and hay loader; and hauled up into the mows with a big fork. Only Harry is indispensable in the final operation, and that could be done with a truck if need be. Henry Ford said recently that in fifty years the farms of America will be completely mechanized, but the older farmers still prefer to keep a span of horses.

Possibly Harry the horse, circa 1940.

The weather has largely been unsettled, there being only two cloudless days, to my recollection; but with the exception of a few humid days in July, the weather has been cool and lovely. There has been a breeze for several days past, which has made swimming in the river rather unnecessary to cool off. We have had one or two wiener roasts on the beach, and many enjoyable days of swimming. We also picked two or three quarts of raspberries, the other day in Newbury, which Mother (*Brock*) translated into delicious raspberry pies. I enjoy blackberrying, but that will come later in August, and we will be treading the city streets by then. But for all-around pleasure during vacation one would look far for a place to equal the farm, and especially this farm--where my wife and I were joined in marriage, and to which our children have come each year with renewed pleasure. As a centerpiece, here on the lawn Mother (*Brock*) has a tub filled with peonies atop of an old stump, and surrounded with wire to keep the cows at their proper distance.

The men have just come to their dinner, with a load of green feed on the truck for the cattle, and festivities are about to begin.

In Bath, I met a chap named Woods who is a mining prospector, and also a seismologist, who gave me some good hints, and at Pearl Lake we met two members of the Boston mineral club--Professor Taylor of Boston University and Dr. Fernald a dentist, with whom we exchanged minerals and information. It makes for good fellowship!

Suggested Daily Spiritual Reading:
Ecclesiasticus 29:10
Mark 3:7

Further Reading Related to Diary Entry:
- *Smithsonian Handbooks: Rocks & Minerals* by Chris Pellant

- *National Geographic Pocket Guide to Rocks and Minerals of North America* (Pocket Guides) by Sarah Garlick

- *Geophysics for the Mineral Exploration Geoscientist*, 1st Edition by Michael Dentith and Stephen T. Mudge

- *Growing Up: Farm Life & Basketball in the 1940s & '50s* by Harold L. Schoen

Popular Books Published in 1940:
Memory Hold-The-Door. The Autobiography of John Buchanan by John Buchanan
Drums and Shadows by Mary Granger

Popular Movies Released in 1940:
Charlie Chan at the Wax Museum (Sidney Toler, Victor Sen Yung, C. Henry Gordon, Marc Lawrence)
Christmas in July (Dick Powell, Ellen Drew)
Strange Cargo (Clark Gable, Joan Crawford, Peter Lorre, Paul Lukas)

August 26, 1940

Home, again, from our summer vacation, with the family intact. We did have our festivities and I was surprised, most agreeably, to be informed that the 7th of August was the 12th anniversary of the wedding of myself and my "favorite" wife! Mrs Scott presented us with four jars of preserves, and we presented her with a paddle, among other things, and a birthday cake. The memories of twelve years ago, with the presence of my father, among others, came in for a few moments--whenever I hear "Traumerei" (*by Robert Schumann*) played it brings back the memories of that day, also--but we do not live long in the past, nor would the actors wish us to--the more unselfish of them. Christina Rosetti writes, "Better that you should forget and smile, than that you should remember and be sad." (*from her poem "Remember"*). And Shakespeare--"All the world's a stage, and all the people in it merely players..."

Ah, but the little while we are on the stage we live it to the full, and we leave it lingeringly. We like the encores, and yearn for them; and, so, sometimes the dead hand of the past intrudes itself into the lives of men. Some solicitous lady left a fund for red, underwear flannels for divinity students, forgetting autre temps, autre mores. While writing these words (about wedding anniversaries) I have had a telephone call requesting me to officiate at a wedding Monday--making three in all since my return!

Summer idylls are fast crystallizing, or else the imminent draft bill has its measure of compulsion. London was bombed for six hours last night, but thus far the Royal Air Force seems to be holding its own, inflicting severe damage on German airports, junctions, and supply depots, as well as converting Junkers into junk. No less a conservative paper like the Boston Herald in an editorial today states that "the average American exults at the German losses and suffering." I do not believe I measure up to the average, for while I can sympathize with a desire to help punish those who inflict cruelty, the victims are probably women and children who never desired war, who may not desire Hitlerism, who may love life as we love it, and wish only to be allowed to live in peace. War is a tragedy for all concerned in its dislocation of all values--and my deepest resentment lies in the fact that the leaders have, through supine stupidity, allowed the world state to come to such a sorry plight, that one man could upset the whole applecart of peace and plenty. This is democracy with a vengeance. Eternal vigilance is the price of liberty, and if the world regains its freedoms, the first ideology that must be established is that in the name of world justice and Christian brotherhood there must be no more Napoleons! But as a realist I fear the time is far distant when any nation or group of nations can make such a disposition of the situation. For I feel that even if Britain survives the

Battle of Britain, the result will be a stalemate, with economic maladjustments concomitant with Europe for Europeans, Asia for Asiatics, America for Americans, and Africa for the one who can get there fastest and with the most men. The world will be in a state of armed truce for a long time, with rival ideologies--totalitarianism of whatever color versus Christian democracy--vying for new conquests. It is a blessed thing to look out over the ocean, and observe no hostile aircraft nor men of war approaching our shores, and we should appreciate such blessings to the full. The free nations need a strong will and resolute purpose, like that of Ulysses who said, "And this is my purpose, to sail beyond the paths of all the western stars until I die--to strive, to seek, to find, and not to yield." We have too many freedoms and too much enjoyment in our Christian democratic heritage to yield anything to anybody!

My sister, Lilla, came up on the farm the last Sunday we were there, and the following day we journeyed to Waterbury, Vermont, where we had lived for eleven years (*as children*), then went four miles upriver to Bolton, where we (our family and Lilla) climbed Camel's Hump.

Suggested Daily Spiritual Reading:
Luke 6:20-23
Hebrews 11:1-3

Further Reading Related to Diary Entry:
- *Ordinary Church: A Long and Loving Look* by Joseph S Beach

- *At Home in Mitford* by Jan Karon

- *Home to Harmony* by Philip Gulley

- *World War II Map* by DK and Smithsonian Institution

Popular Books Published in 1940:
The Birth and Death of the Sun by George Gamow
An Agricultural Testament by Sir Albert Howard

Popular Movies Released in 1940:
A Dispatch from Reuters (Edward G. Robinson, Edna Best)
East Side Kids (Leon Ames, Dennis Moore, Joyce Bryant, East Side Kids)
My Favorite Wife (Cary Grant, Irene Dunn)

August 26, 1940
(Continued)

As stated previously, I had climbed Camel's Hump twice, but was poorly rewarded. This time, however, after a brief lunch (we left Mother Brock [*Olive*] in the car), we arrived at the top, over the Callahan Trail (named for the farmer who lived highest up the mountain) to find a clear view in all directions. There was some haze, but we could make out Lake Champlain, Mount Mansfield, and mountains to the East. The children arrived first, as usual, and stood the trip very well. The Callahan Trail is about 2 1/2 miles long and is rather rough, but shorter than the Forest Service Trail (3 1/2 miles) by which we descended. The lady caretaker at the top tells me that Callahan, for whom the trail is named, is still living, but that Professor Will Munroe, who bought his farm, and who is chiefly responsible for laying out the Skyline Trail, has died. We met a man atop the mountain who had just come over a good section of it, having spent nearly a week on the trail. An employee of the Sperry Gyroscope Company, he was taking his vacation in this interesting way. His hirsute adornment resembled the House of David ball team, and he requested me to take a picture of the same.

On the way up the mountain our thirst was amply quenched at the picturesque brook, whose trickle was sweet music to our ears. Descending we met but one party coming up--five girls who were spending the night on the top. Lilla lost her sunglasses, but, apart from this minor mishap, there were no casualties and we ate a lunch on our return to the car, which satisfied our gastronomic requirements. I am convinced that life is basically emotional, and the visceral satisfaction that comes from climbing a mountain, or sorting out my minerals, or keeping my stamp collection and diary up-to-date are adequate compensations for the time and labor spent. We came home the following Wednesday and are adjusting ourselves to the routine again.

The night before we came home, my father-in-law told us a story which made me laugh heartily. It was about a horse trade, like unto that in "David Harum", and I wish I might reproduce it as he gave it. (*"David Harum" was written by Edward Noyes Westcott and published in 1898—was a best seller in 1899—and later made into a movie in 1915 and 1934.*)

He had purchased a horse--an army calvary horse--and it was too skittish for the children to drive to school, so he wished to trade it. He met Otis Smith, of Wells River, Vermont, one day. Otis was driving a mare which was quite suitable, and Mr. (*Ernie*) Brock offered to trade, which he did, with six runts to boot. The catch was that when Otis got the horse home and tried to drive him on the street of Wells River, he knew he had been trimmed properly, for the horse balked in the middle of the street, and Otis had to drag him home with an Ox team, much to the amusement of his fellow citizens. Finally, in disgust he told his stable boy to take the horse just as far as he could go and trade him in for anything; a jackass if nothing else was offered. The boy took ten dollars and the horse, and was gone three days. When he showed up one morning, as Otis was coming from the stable, he was minus the ten dollars and was riding, of all things, a jackass! Otis never lived that down, and it was one time that he, a horse dealer, was really beaten in a horse trade! Otis is long since deceased, but in the Valhalla of memories he will certainly live by proxy. Stories are immortal even if we are not.

It has been a fine summer, and it is drawing to an end. But it has been spent well, and its memories are added to those of other summers, to be lived over again at will.

Junior has been entertaining his former playmate from Cochituate, James Tufts. They have encompassed the pleasures of Lynn Woods and the beach, and yesterday I took them fishing. The boys caught flounders, perch, and sculpin, and I caught a good pollock. Jimmy also caught a hake. We threw them away on our return home. It saves cleaning them. The boys have also been flying kites and shooting a BB gun. There is no time like youth, and none values it less. Wisdom comes with age.

Suggested Daily Spiritual Reading:
Matthew 15:35-38
1 John 3:16

Further Reading Related to Diary Entry:
- *AMC's Best Day Hikes in Vermont: Four-Season Guide To 60 Of The Best Trails In The Green Mountain State* by Jen Lamphere Roberts

- *White Mountain Guide: AMC's Comprehensive Guide to Hiking Trails in the White Mountain National Forest* by Steven D. Smith (Editor)

- *David Harum: A Story of American Life* by Edward Noyes Westcott. Published by D. Appleton & Company in 1898.

Popular Books Published in 1940:
The Artist's Handbook of Materials and Techniques by Ralph Mayer
Utrecht Atlas by Marcel Minnaert, Gerard Mulders, Jakob Houtgast

Popular Movies Released in 1940:
His Girl Friday (Cary Grant, Rosalind Russell)
The Marines Fly High (Richard Dix, Chester Morris, Lucille Ball)
Rhythm on the River (Bing Crosby and Mary Martin)

Friday September 13th, 1940

The moon waxing is shining upon the rolling waters at the beach tonight, and it evokes a response which manifests itself in prose. So calm and serene--

> "And with joy the stars perform their shining,
> And the sea its long moon-silvered roll—
> Serene they live, nor note with pining
> All the fever of some differing soul…"
>
> (*Paraphrased from the poem "Self-Dependence" by Matthew Arnold*)

I wonder if the chaps in the sky looking eastward from England, toward the continent, notice that same moon, or are they too busy fighting wave after wave of German bombers and fighters coming across the channel to view nature's grand spectacle? In the words of Winston Churchill, Prime Minister and, erstwhile, dictator of England, "war is a melancholy business". Winston is a good phrase-maker.

For a week London has been subjected to devastating air raids, her important buildings hit, whole blocks destroyed, vital utilities damaged, a multitude of fires raging. I assume that things are far worse than we hear about. Rotterdam was virtually erased in two-and one half hours; and while London has defenses, of course, tons and tons of bombs have been dropped on the city incessantly for days. To me it is a source of wonder that there is anything left of the city. Buckingham Palace was hit last night and three workmen injured--plumbers they were--privileged casualties, so to speak, compared with the countless unnamed and unknown who are innocent victims of "Teutonic fury"--an overworked metaphor for the impersonal annihilation of war. The chance drop of a bomb negatives all human values--reducing a living personality to the status of inorganic material. That is the melancholic part of war to me--that the machine transcends, indeed eclipses, the man.

Can England hold out against an expected (next week) invasion? Military experts are unanimous in saying that she can, provided Germany does not obtain superiority in the air. But the merciless bombings of the capital during the past week, without reference to the customary "dog fights" over the city mordantly, suggests that Germany has a decided edge in the air already. Granted that her airmen are inferior personally, to a devotee of chess, it is patent that she can swap two planes to one and still maintain the advantage. Her factories are underground--England's in the open. Her planes are protected with armored cockpits and gas tanks and her bombers and fighters have a shorter range (100 miles) by far than the English bombers. Yet, the English are bulldogs in breed, and they have not wrested a world empire without the élan-vital necessary for successful attack and defense, and, so, we shall pray for England--Dieu defend le droit!

In all fairness, Germany deserves a place in the sun, but as Americans we do not wish to see her occupy it at the expense of England, nor other neutral nations; hence, our immense defense program, with conscriptions, five billion for armaments, a new navy, and all the rest. (A year hence, there may be decided change in the status quo, or a week hence, for that matter, and so I like to record my views form time to time with relation to world conditions. They may be ancient history in a week, but ancient history has its lessons.)

Shortly after returning to Lynn, I was invited to speak over a neighboring radio station, and in this connection a record was made of my talk, which I hope to play next summer on the radio-phonograph at the farm. The interesting thing is that one's own voice sounds utterly alien--it is like listening to another person, to hear a recording of one's own voice. The announcer tells me it is the same with all whom he has recorded--they do not recognize themselves either. "Would some power the giftie gie us, to see oursils as ithers see us," said Bobby Burns, long ago. Perhaps it well we live in our own conceits. Otherwise we might perish from shame.

Suggested Daily Spiritual Reading:
Matthew 14:27
Hebrews 10:22

Further Reading Related to Diary Entry:
- *The Ghost Army of World War II: How One Top-Secret Unit Deceived the Enemy with Inflatable Tanks, Sound Effects, and Other Audacious Fakery* by Rick Beyer and Elizabeth Sayles

- *Double Crossed: The Missionaries Who Spied for the United States During the Second World War* by Matthew Avery Sutton

Popular Books Published in 1940:
Inside the Gestapo: Hitler's Shadow OverThe World by Hansjrgen Koehler
The Encyclopedia of World History compiled and edited by William L. Langer

Popular Movies Released in 1940:
Pastor Hall (Wilfrid Lawson, Nova Pilbeam, Seymour Hicks)
Remember the Night (Barbara Stanwyck, Fred MacMurray)
Turnabout (Adolphe Menjou, Carole Landis, John Hubbard)

1941

Saturday January 25, 1941

There is a time for everything under the sun--a time to write and a time to refrain from writing. Theoretically, a journal like this should be most interesting, because unhurried. It would be with Emerson, Thoreau, or Winston Churchill editing the same, undoubtedly, or Pepys recording in his own shorthand--but with your humble and obedient servant at the keys (in olden time I would say, "Taking pen in hand.") The outlook is not so good. Without any passion for it, I have anonymity, and while the world leaves me in peace, I am afraid that for all of me, the world will remain at war.

Paraphrasing Keats:
```
"On the shores of the wild world I stand and think
   Till fame and love to nothingness do sink."
```

Which reminds me to get on with my journal, which I have neglected of late. I started to say that I am in the right mood for reportorial reminiscence, and when the typewriter and mood coincide, then who knows, there may be literary immortality! Having received so much in the way of entertainment, instruction, and inspiration from the world of books whose authors have not faintly imagined my being--from the Song of Deborah (1300 BC) and before, to the present day--to the latest ebullition of Bernard Shaw, it is only natural to wish that you who read these lines should derive something of entertainment, instruction, or inspiration from my writing. We cannot all be great--there is but one best seller to fifty writers, at a conservative estimate--but we can all be interesting, if we try. Life has so many facets. Each individual sees the diamond from a fresh and different viewpoint. No combination of molecules like myself has ever existed before--not like yourself, either. Every little man is a unique, too. Then why not tell the world about it. There is still shelf room in the libraries. May our words, "...like the echoes of a sweet, stilled bell, live in the heart of heaven after time." (*From the poem "Dedication" by Dana Burnet*)

Two days ago, I celebrated my 39th birthday anniversary; one of the pleasantest I have ever had. My wife gave me a splendid supper--steak, coffee, ice cream, and things between--and a mineral specimen, amethyst, cut and polished, which surprised and please me greatly. My mother and sister, Lilla, gave me a volume of the world's best religious poetry, which I shall surely use a great deal, while Junior and Janet have sent for some Indian relics to add to my collection. Today I visited a friend who has a nice collection of minerals, including a trilobite fossil, a denizen of the deep hereabouts some fifty-million years ago; a meteorite, which came from outer space; agates and crystals and many others of rare beauty. Truly minerals are a thing of beauty and a joy forever. I would like about a thousand dollars to invest in them. I would compromise on a hundred.

Amethyst from the Reverend's mineral collection.

Since last observations, the Greeks have driven back the Italians in Albania; the Imperial Army of the Nile has captured Sidi Barrani, Bardia, and Tobruk in Libya; the Germans have invaded (peacefully) Romania and Hungary; London has been bombed and burned (with 10,000 thermite, two-pound, incendiary bombs on December 29th), and our country has passed a $28,000,000,000 defense bill. We have called into being, also, a draft army of a half a million men for training. England is still uninvaded, and the war in the air seems to have reached a stalemate, for the time being; events of tremendous and far-reaching importance, yet not conclusive to the outcome of the war. It looks highly improbable that England can be successfully invaded, since she is rapidly attaining parity in the air; and it seems equally improbable that for a year or two, at any rate, the continent can be invaded.

Three inches of snow have fallen today, and continues. It reminds me each winter of Whittier's Snowbound. Hemmed in from all the world without--and good books to read.

("Whittier's Snowbound" is reference to the poem "Snow-Bound: A Winter Idyl" by John Greenleaf Whittier)

Suggested Daily Spiritual Reading:
James 5:1-6

Matthew 6:28

Further Reading Related to Diary Entry:
- *The Artist's Way* by Julia Cameron

- *On Writing Well: The Classic Guide to Writing Nonfiction* by William Zinsser

- *Writing About Your Life: A Journey into the Past* by William Zinsser

- *The Liberator: One World War II Soldier's 500-Day Odyssey from the Beaches of Sicily to the Gates of Dachau* by Alex Kershaw

Popular Books Published in 1941:
Most Popular Books Published In 1941. Available from Goodreads.com at https://www.goodreads.com/book/popular_by_date/1941 [Accessed on January 23, 2021].
Escape from Freedom by Erich Fromm
The Mind of the Maker by Dorothy L. Sayers

Popular Movies Released in 1941:
The Maltese Falcon (Humphrey Bogart, Mary Astor, Sydney Greenstreet, Peter Lorre, Elisha Cook Jr., Ward Bond)
Adventure in Washington (Herbert Marshall, Virginia Bruce)
Arkansas Judge (Roy Rogers, Veda Ann Borg)

Saturday January 23, 1941
(Continued)

And now for a bit of philosophical dissertation. An English writer, who has sent his family abroad, where they are relatively safe, while he joins the forces at home, has written an article for the Atlantic monthly entitled, "I'll go to bed at noon". He is writing to his son, and he says he would like to live long enough to find out whether pacifists will, in the future, be regarded as saints to be revered or criminals to be shot. Most men want peace, except they be underdogs, and yet most men today face war. It must be especially hard for the patriotic Quaker in these stirring times, since this is not a war of trade balances but a war of revolution, of ideologies. Is war ever justifiable? Do the freedoms gained compensate for the lives lost? Historically, if we examine the Battle of Tours (1215 AD) and realize that Charles Martel saved Europe from being overrun by the Saracens, we may get an approximate parallel. If the Saracens had won, Christianity could not have survived in Europe, at least Christianity as we know it. And if the totalitarian powers win today, civilization as we know it--the sanctity of treaties, the observance of laws, the rights of small states, freedom to practice religion according to the dictates of conscience, equality of the individual, and democracy itself will be abrogated. Leaving nationalism aside, and we will grant that selfish nationalisms as contrasted with a universal City of God have caused most wars, we are faced with the spectacle of two opposing ways of life--one in subservience to the state, with slave classes, and abolition of morality--the other with some semblance of freedom for individual development.

Is our way of life worth preserving and, if so, how can it be preserved without fighting for it, with force of arms? Even the criminal has to be subdued by police power, which is only a delegation of force to one branch of society. Even the Quaker will restrain violence by exercise of muscles. Jesus said, "My kingdom is not of this world. If my kingdom were of this world, then would my servants fight." I firmly believe that the kingdom of Christ transcends all national boundaries--it encompasses all races--it dwells in the spirit of man, just as do the ideas of Truth, Beauty, and Goodness. But men are not organized as spiritual forces alone. If so, they would not need to fight. Men are organized into nations, with homes and loved ones. Even a world state must be founded on the rights of its constituent members, to work out their several destinies, while letting others do the same. This implies order, justice, and peace for all. But it must be policed to subdue the pernicious elements as in every well-regulated society. If the world order, der Weltraumpelitik, be one in which one dominant race seeks to impose its will on all others, there is a negation of the values Christianity has known. Under the Roman empire, religion was relatively free to develop. But when anti-Christ rules of necessity, there is reversion to martyrdom, as in the case or Nero, Caligula, and others. Perhaps this line of cleavage is again indicated. Certainly it is true in Germany where Martin Niemoeller languishes in Sachsenhausen while Hitler dominates the German empire. But whether Christianity wills it or not, and a supine Christianity would hardly be in a position to retaliate through martyrdom under Hitler or Stalin; the free nations of the world will decidedly not chance such a survival. It will fight for its rights, and most men will assume the armor, rather than be classed with inferior races, so called. With a great price have we obtained this freedom--and the subjugated nations and the suppressed Germans call silently for liberation. On assuming leadership at Nazareth, Christ said, "The spirit of the Lord is upon me, for He hath anointed me...to preach deliverance to the captives--to set at liberty them that are bruised..." (*Luke 4:18*) We cannot achieve that goal through ideas alone. We must implement them with all means at our disposal, bombs, planes, tanks. "To seek and to strive, and not to yield." (*Paraphrased quote from the poem "Ulysses" by Alfred, Lord Tennyson*).

Suggested Daily Spiritual Reading:
John 18:36
Acts 18:9-10

Further Reading Related to Diary Entry:
- *No Cross, No Crown. A discourse, shewing the nature and discipline of the Holy Cross of Christ* by William Penn. A New Edition Revised, 1842; Harvey and Darton publishers, London. Available from Project Gutenberg at http://www.gutenberg.org/ebooks/44895 [Accessed on January 23, 2021].

- *Living the Quaker Way: Discover the Hidden Happiness in the Simple Life* by Philip Gulley

- *A History of Fascism, 1914–1945* by Stanley G. Payne

- *Exile in the Fatherland: Martin Niemöller's Letters from Moabit Prison* by Martin Niemöller (Author), Hubert G. Locke (Editor)

Popular Books Published in 1941:
Under the Sea Wind: A Naturalist's Picture of Ocean Life by Rachel Carson.
All in a Lifetime by Frank Buck, with Ferrin Fraser

Popular Movies Released in 1941:
All Through the Night (Humphrey Bogart, Kaaren Verne, Conrad Veidt)
The Big Store (Marx Brothers, Tony Martin)
Citizen Kane (Orson Welles, Joseph Cotten, Everett Sloane, Paul Stewart)

February 17, 1941

Cosmology, biology, herpetology, etymology, ichthyology, psychology, teleology, palaeology, seismology, zoology, ontology, ollogy--logy...O'Gee!

All the past is prology (pardon me, I mean prologue)--we start from here. This encouraging theme was developed in a sermon last night in historic First Methodist Church in Lynn (*MA*)--now celebrating its 150th anniversary--by Rev. Dr. William L. Stidger, better known to his acquaintances as Bill Stidger. The first part of the sentiment is found on a bronze statue at the entrance of the Archives building in Washington, D.C. A maiden is leafing a book, and is nearing the end of it--symbolizing the fitness of our knowledge in an infinite world.

Man has learned a lot in the relative second of recorded time on the clock of history, but there is so much more to be learned, and verified. When the trilobites were swimming, or crawling, near these shores, in the Cambrian epoch of the Palaezoic era, some five hundred million years ago, such things as neoplastic were unconcealed in the womb of time. And when one is interested in all things from the trilobites to the neoplastics, time becomes an important consideration. Dinosaurs to dynamics--how interesting it would be to take a voyage back in time and space, to the beginning of things, then watch them develop over the immensity of the ages; just as you can watch a flower grow through the process of taking consecutive motion pictures, compressing centuries into minutes of time. "A thousand ages in Thy sight are but as yesterday when it is past, or as a watch in the night." (*Psalm 90:4, paraphrased*)

Atomic changes, hydrogen to helium--or radium to helium to lead in the sun masses--the magmas of chemical constituents cooling the earth's crust to form granite, beryl, fluorite, zircon, and diamonds; the first vegetation, the first cell creatures, the slow growth of fauna and flora covering the continents; the ice-caps and the glaciers; the volcanoes and earthquakes; the emergence and subsidence of the seas--what a melodrama that would be! If some producer could provide such a spectacle, it would be well worth seeing. Well, the great Producer has done so, and the Architect of the Universe has left abundant evidence of his handiwork for us to read, if our eyes are keen to see. The finest college to me would be one in which some geologist could take one around the world to see these vestigia, a la Darwin; a biologist to recreate life and perhaps dissect it; a chemist to construct the essential compounds, and a physicist to show the interplay of matter and energy; perhaps an archeologist to show how history is littered on its shores with the forms whence substance has fled, such as the Parthenon and the Pyramids; a philosopher surely to correlate the motivations of men, a botanist to make live the beautiful things in the world of plants, and a painter to reveal the artistry of nature; and, of course, a musician to reveal the dissonances and the harmonies of composition. Such a college would be beyond compare--we have libraries which help vastly in this direction, but there is nothing comparable to personal instruction. It is the Mark Hopkins education of the future, perhaps. All the past is but prologue--we start from here, to see life, steadily, fully, and to see it whole.

Suggested Daily Spiritual Reading:
Psalm 36:1-3
Proverbs 16:2

Further Reading Related to Diary Entry:

- *Evangelism's First Modern Media Star: Reverend Bill Stidger* by Jack Hyland

- *The Time Machine* by H.G. Wells

- *Earth (Second Edition): The Definitive Visual Guide* by Douglas Palmer, Robert Dinwiddie, John Farndon, Michael Allaby, David Burnie, Clint Twist, Martin Walters, and Tony Waltham

- *In Six Days: Why Fifty Scientists Choose to Believe in Creation* by John F. Ashton

- *Temperance and Education*: *The relation of the social drinking customs to the educational interests of the nation*, by Mark Hopkins, D.D. Published by the National Temperance Society, New York, 1876. Available from University of Michigan, Making of America Books at https://quod.lib.umich.edu/cgi/t/text/text-idx?c=moa;idno=AAW8208 [Accessed January 23, 2021].

- *Lectures on Moral Science* by Mark Hopkins, D.D. Available from the University of Michigan, Making of America Books at https://quod.lib.umich.edu/cgi/t/text/text-idx?c=moa;idno=AJF1419 [Accessed January 23, 2021].

- *Online Books by Mark Hopkins* (Hopkins, Mark, 1802-1887). Available from The Online Books Page, University of Pennsylvania at http://onlinebooks.library.upenn.edu/webbin/book/lookupname?key=Hopkins%2C%20Mark%2C%201802-1887 [Accessed January 23, 2021].

Popular Books Published in 1941:
Mildred Pierce by James M. Cain
The Keys of the Kingdom by A. J. Cronin

Popular Movies Released in 1941:
   Confessions of Boston Blackie (Chester Morris, Harriet Hilliard)
   Dangerously They Live (John Garfield, Nancy Coleman)
   Dive Bomber (Errol Flynn, Fred MacMurray)

April 22, 1941

Professor Alfred North Whitehead of Harvard University gave the Ingersoll Lecture on Immorality, in Appleton Chapel this afternoon at four-thirty at the conclusion of an interesting and worthwhile Day of Visitation at the Harvard Divinity School. He stressed the relevance of all things--God is the unity of the many; man is the multiplicity of the one--and decried the Greek conclusion that things can have independence (How tragically true is that statement in view of the modern Greek's heroic, but unequal, fight for independence!). He related the transitory world of fact to the immortal world of value, and told how each is sterile without relation to the other. An apple tart, he said, has no meaning with relation to a moment in time, but does have meaning with relation to our mood, i.e. value, contingent upon antecedent hunger and appeasement. He spoke of personal identity bridging the gap between the sensations of the moment and the abiding timeless values. To me, this was his strongest point. For he himself, venerable and full of years, was the focal point between long years of learning and the future life of values. For a moment the Word became flesh, and dwelt among us... He did not, but might well have concluded with the words of St. Paul in Galatians, "The life I now live in the flesh, I live by the faith of the Son of God, who loved me and gave himself for me." Perhaps, I have not reported him faithfully, but I did listen attentively; for it was a real intellectual and spiritual treat. There were about two hundred auditors--students and clergymen.

This biography is degenerating or, perhaps, ascending into a sort of journal, but perhaps this is all to the good. Pepy's diary and Emerson's journals are among the literary classics, and a journal captures the essence of living, transmutes it, and gives it a sort of permanence.

We bought a collie puppy six weeks ago. He is named Rover. We have had a difficult time raising him, for he has been subject to dysentery, but is now greatly improved. He is a well-mannered, little dog, and obeys as well as one may expect of a puppy. He sniffs his way along in life--especially when I take him for a walk. The olfactory organs are far more strongly developed in dogs than in men, seemingly--at least, they are used more in interpreting life. Memory and anticipating are relatively weak compared to man. These are integral parts of the world of value, according to Professor Whitehead, so that a dog lives more fully than we in the world of fact. Perhaps we do not live enough in that world-- we long for the good old days, and anticipate the future with foreboding all too often. Emerson said, in a famous divinity school address, "The sun shines today, also. The rose gives of itself without reference to past or future roses." We might live more fully if we lived truly in the present, above time, "heart within and God overhead," but we are not constituted. From the atom to the nebula we see development in terms of advancement or retrogression. What has a future life in store for us more glorious than the present life?

Junior had a little chameleon, which died the other day. It's life span was about 5 months. It was running around vigorously on the day it died, then it suddenly ceased to be. Is there a Valhalla for chameleons, I wonder? In the great scheme of life, there is a purpose for every living thing. If we cannot believe in a literal resurrection, surely we can believe in personal identity--and that is beyond time and space. I give salute to this tiny descendant of the dinosaurs and commend its soul to the Giver of Life. In the life and light of ten thousand years, we are as transitory as the chameleon, and perhaps no more important. But having faced the Eternal with equanimity, we can go down into the valleys of time with renewed confidence in One who said, "I am the Way, the Truth, and the Life!"

Suggested Daily Spiritual Reading:
Deuteronomy 11:1
Samuel 22:32-33

Further Reading Related to Diary Entry:
- *The Quantum of Explanation—Science, logic, and ethics, from a Whiteheadian Pragmatist perspective (go figure)* by Gary L. Herstein. Available from garyherstein.com at https://garyherstein.com/2017/11/01/reading-between-the-texts/ [Accessed January 23, 2021].

- *Alfred North Whitehead* by Andrew Irvine and Ronny Desmet (first published May 21, 1996; substantive revision Sep 4, 2018). Available from the Stanford Encyclopedia of Philosophy, Stanford University at https://plato.stanford.edu/entries/whitehead/ [Accessed January 23, 2021].

- *The Diary of Samuel Pepys* by Samuel Pepys. Available from The Gutenberg Project at http://www.gutenberg.org/files/4200/4200-h/4200-h.htm [Accessed January 23, 2021].

- *Emerson and the Art of the Diary* by Lawrence Rosenwald

- *Journals of Ralph Waldo Emerson with Annotations* by Ralph Waldo Emerson, edited by Edward Waldo Emerson and Waldo Emerson Forbes. Published by Houghton Mifflin Company, Boston, 1909. Available from Internet Archive at https://archive.org/details/journalsofralphw02emeruoft/page/n12 [Accessed January 23, 2021].

Popular Books Published in 1941:

The Physics of Blown Sand and Desert Dunes by Ralph Alger Bagnold
Grey Eminence by Aldous Huxley

Popular Movies Released in 1941:
Footsteps in the Dark (Errol Flynn, Brenda Marshall, Ralph Bellamy)
High Sierra (Ida Lupino, Humphrey Bogart, Joan Leslie, Arthur Kennedy, Cornel Wilde, Henry Travers)
The Lady Eve (Barbara Stanwyck, Henry Fonda)

August 30, 1941

A lot of time has elapsed since my last entry in this journal. We returned from our vacation yesterday, and a fine one it has been. We spent two weeks at home, with my mother (*Etta*) and my sister Lilla, here; and then went up on the farm (*Brock farm-Olive and Ernie*). Lilla and I have taken up golfing this summer, and so we enjoyed going around the courses (*The Reverend is 39 and Lilla is about 32*), especially at Happy Valley, where the outlook on various lakes would have pleased Thoreau. I often think of him as I go through the Lynn Woods and beside the various lakes here--Birch, Breed's, Flax, Glen-Lewis, and Walden. These and the stars shall endure when our cities are rubble. Can we not still see with our own eyes the cellar-foundation for Thoreau's cabin at Walden pond in Concord?

Lilla and Janet, circa 1942.

The Reverend and Janet, circa 1942.

On the farm, besides golfing, fishing, haying, wood-cutting, manure-carting, and the like, we found time for two major trips in the car, both of lasting interest, I think. One Sunday, the 17th, with Mother and Dad Brock, we took a 280-mile trip to Fort Ticonderoga, coming back via Crown Point and the new Lake Champlain bridge. We went first to White River Junction, then over Mendon Mountain to Rutland and Whitehall. This road, to my mind, equals anything in the East. You are snuggled up close to the mountains, whose green-wooded slopes in the morning sun meander with the silver ribbon of the brook. The scenery is truly beautiful, and I felt I had not really seen my native state (*Vermont*) until I had covered that historic road across the center of it. It probably began as an old Indian trail to Canada. (I have been reading Collins' History of Vermont with a great deal of interest since returning home.) Near Whitehall, we cross the lower end of Lake Champlain, and motor through the sedimentary ledges to restored Fort Ticonderoga. This interesting fortress was first called Fort Carillon, by the French who built it, after Vauban, in the form of a six-pointed star; with demi-lunes separated from the main fort, thus making, in effect, seven forts. The outer bastions were taken by an American general, Warren, but the inner fort was never taken by direct assault. When Allen captured it with 82 men, there were only 12 men on duty (or off). The French held it for a time--there are two cannons which were captured from Napoleon on view there--then the British occupied it to 1680, except for a short period when the Americans held it. It was from here, in the winter of 1775, that General Henry Knox carried over a hundred cannons to (*General*) Washington in Cambridge to help in the siege of

Boston. At the water's edge is a gunboat of the 1812 vintage, which was sunk in one of the many battles on the lake. The museum houses uniforms and souvenirs of the French, British, and Americans. On the third floor of the museum are Indian relics and early American house-hold and farm equipment. A letter in the handwriting of Ethan Allen addressed to General Washington—while in command of the fort—brings the past vividly before one. I had not realized how instructive, from a historical standpoint, the fort really was until I saw it. Outside the fort, in the park, are the old breastworks occupied by 1,300 French troops under Montcalm, who defeated, decisively, the British attacking force of 2,000 in a battle long since silent, except in memory. Junior and Janet ought to find early American history more interesting because of the visit. The colonial flag, the fleur-de-lis of France, the Union Jack, and the stars and stripes fly side-by-side over the fort. We returned to Peirmont, N.H. Via Vergennes and Burlington, which route afforded magnificent and changing views of the Adirondacks, the Green Mountains, and Lake Champlain—which widens from one mile to thirty in a short space. How pleasant, in retrospect, is such a trip when it can be lived over again and assimilated to the full in enjoyment! We missed seeing Lake George, but another day is coming!

Suggested Daily Spiritual Reading:
Luke 6:37-38
Romans 16:20

Further Reading Related to Diary Entry:

- *Henry David Thoreau : A Week on the Concord and Merrimack Rivers / Walden; Or, Life in the Woods / The Maine Woods / Cape Cod (Library of America)* by Henry David Thoreau

- *Walden; or, Life in the Woods* by Henry David Thoreau. Available from Lit2Go, University of South Florida at https://etc.usf.edu/lit2go/90/walden-or-life-in-the-woods/ [Accessed January 23, 2021].

- *A History of Vermont* by Edward Day Collins, Ph.D.; Ginn and Company Publishers, Boston, The Athenaeum Press, 1903. Available from the Internet Archive at https://archive.org/details/historyofvermont00co [Accessed January 23, 2021].

- *Fort Ticonderoga*. Infoirmation available from the Council of the Arts, New York State at https://www.fortticonderoga.org [Accessed January 23, 2021].

- *Battles - Fort Ticonderoga*. Available from the American Battlefield Trust at https://www.battlefields.org/learn/revolutionary-war/battles/fort-ticonderoga

[Accessed January 23, 2021].

Popular Books Published in 1941:
    The Snow Goose by Paul Gallico
    Strategy by B.H. Liddell Hart

Popular Movies Released in 1941:
    Mr. And Mrs. Smith (Carole Lombard, Robert Montgomery)
    No Hands on the Clock (Jean Parker, Chester Morris)
    One Foot in Heaven (Fredric March, Martha Scott, Beulah Bondi, Gene Lockhart)

August, 30, 1941
(Continued)

Our next trip came the following Thursday when we went into Maine via Gorham to Black Mountain. We took with us Mr. William Yetten of Benton (N.H.), who collects New Hampshire specimens (minerals/rocks). The mountains looked lovely in the morning sun as seen from near Jefferson. They towered into the sky and were utterly clear--Washington, Adams, Jefferson, and Madison. Patriarchs of the North Country, in the finest sense of the word. Near Jefferson, also, we saw the newly laid oil pipe line, which carries oil from Portland to Montreal. At Gorham we stopped to buy some Maine minerals from Leggatt and Verrill, and there met Peter Zodac, secretary-treasurer of the Rocks and Minerals Association. He asked me for a specimen of molybdenite, which I found at Warren, N.H. I gave it to him gladly.

Then we went on through Gorham, where beside the road and near the lake are some lovely birch trees; on into Maine for seventy-five miles to Black Mountain, near Rumford, which we climbed. We visited a mica mine there and obtained specimens of rubellite. The mine is run by a very obliging fellow by the name of Trajiano. The trail to the mine is very steep. The children climbed with us, while my wife remained in the car at the foot of the mountain. Janet feared the blasting operations, at first, but after the blast went off did not seem to mind at all. Far from finding gem tourmaline, we didn't even find good samples of watermelon stone (rubellite surrounded by green tourmaline). I didn't imagine we would, which is why I purchased specimens at Gotham before starting. A wise fisherman always buys a few fish just in case! Mr. Yetten is a true amateur, however, and so far has never bought a thing, to my knowledge. The trip was too long, and very tiresome except for the view of the mountains at Jefferson, and the birches near Gorham.

Reverend's Mica samples

Rover has grown to a fine dog. He and the collie on the farm, Gypsy, had the time of their lives playing together this summer.

Other trips included a visit to the old Palamo mine in North Groton, where we found heterosite, altered from triphyllite, and graftonite; Ore Hill in Warren, which Junior had not visited; the old "gold" mine in Warren--a vein of pegmatite, where feldspar crystals, beryl, and black tourmaline were found; and the old iron mine on Sugar Hill in Lisbon where hematite, and not much else, is plentiful. Altogether it has been a fine summer collecting, inasmuch as on a previous trip home we stopped at North Grafton (Ruggles Mine) and found splendid samples of autunite, torbernite, gummite, uranophane, and uraninite.

Some of the Reverend's mineral collection

I also bought a 1941 Crosley short and long wave radio for ten dollars from "Scotty", a former hired man at the farm. The present hired man is called "Clint" and cannot be five feet tall. But his muscles are big, and he is always good-humored, which is a great asset, I think.

With regard to the international scene, this summer marks the entry of Germany into Russia, England into Syria and Iraq and Iran. Nine weeks of blitzkrieg have given the Germans large slices of the Ukraine, but no major Russian cities have been taken as yet. The Russian campaign has given England a much needed breathing spell, and if Germany bogs down in Russia it may mean the turning point of the war in the long run. Sabotage has reared its head in the New Order, and Germany is well occupied in keeping any kind of order in the overrun countries. We have intensified our war efforts and a stern attitude has so far prevented Japan from invading Thailand, the critical area overlooking Singapore. There has been considerable newspaper talk of shortages--gas, oil for ranges, and coal--but, as yet, only advancing prices on many commodities mar the peaceful scene.

We return to work rested in mind and body, and ready for the fall labour in the vineyard of the Lord. May it be fruitful, for His sake, who created the hills and the valleys for our enjoyment! In the words of the 42nd Psalm, "Why art thou cast down O my soul, and why art thou disquieted within me. Hope thou in God, for I shall yet praise Him who is the health of my countenance and my God."

Dad Brock is on the dancing team from West Newbury, Vermont, which won the Governor's Cup in the annual contest at Plainfield this year. Last night the team danced at the Governor's Ball at Barre, with thirteen governors present-- occasion, 150th anniversary of admission to statehood for Vermont.

Suggested Daily Spiritual Reading:
Psalm 42:11
Wisdom of Solomon 9:15

Further Reading Related to Diary Entry:
- *Fodor's New England: with the Best Fall Foliage Drives & Scenic Road Trips* by Fodor's Travel Guides

- *Lonely Planet New England's Best Trips - 32 Amazing Road Trips* by Lonely Planet, Gregor Clark, Carolyn Bain, Mara Vorhees, Benedict Walker

- *To Lose a Battle: France 1940* by Alistair Horne

- *Russia's War: A History of the Soviet Effort: 1941-1945* by Richard Overy

- *The 40s: The Story of a Decade. The New Yorker.* By The New Yorker Magazine (Author), Henry Finder (Editor), David Remnick (Introduction), W. H. Auden (Contributor), Elizabeth Bishop (Contributor)

Popular Books Published in 1941:
Blithe Spirit by Noël Coward
Consider the Oyster by M.F.K. Fisher

Popular Movies Released in 1941:
Penny Serenade (Irene Dunne, Cary Grant, Beulah Bondi, Edgar Buchanan)
Red River Valley (Roy Rogers, Gabby Hayes)
The Sea Wolf (Edward G. Robinson, Ida Lupino, John Garfield)

September 4, 1941

  A sparrow taking a bath in an outdoor pool yesterday set me thinking. As a rule we devour too much of life; at least I do. We ingest without savoring, greedily like the wolf, and have consequent spiritual and mental indigestion. Do I go to the library? I bring home six or eight books, all of which must be "read" in an evening. Dryden said of Johnson that he devoured not books, but libraries. I am like that. Is it golf? Then I must play 51 holes in a day, until I am utterly weary of the game for a month. Is it calling? The same holds true to a lesser extent; although, no preacher can ever do too much of that. Radio, minerals, books, sermons, even friends—there is a tendency to overwork even them. There must be a term for this hyperactivity in the normal cyclothymic swing. But when zest of life's great, and there is so much to learn and do, perhaps it is a good thing to obtain satiety by this method. The government overdid comparative stamps last year—it tired us trotting to the postoffice. This year the rest has been a great relief.

  Thomas Wolfe, to my mind the greatest prose writer of the century, had this hunger and thirst in his soul from the time he left Catawba till he died; you can read it in his eyes; you can read it in the splendid cadences of words set to the rhythm in "Of Time and the River" and "You Can't Go Home Again". Did he ever finally learn two things, I wonder? First, the saying of Jesus, "...blessed are they that <u>hunger</u> and <u>thirst</u>,...after <u>righteousness</u>" (*Matthew 5:6, paraphrased*), or in the opening words of the 42nd Psalm, "...as the hart panteth after the water brooks, so panteth my soul after thee, O God. My soul thirtieth for God, for the living God..." The second thing: with Augustine to discover (*paraphrased*), "For Thyself thou hast made us, and our souls are restless until they rest in Thee." Wealth, in ideas, or money or land, is not for those who possess it; it is for those who enjoy it. Does the great God need burnt offerings or our poor sacrifices? All things are mine, He proclaims—the cattle upon a thousand hills—the cathedral spruces on Sugar Hill, the lovely birches beside the lake, the baby ducks that took to the river when danger threatened, sunrise over Moosehead Lake when the busy world is hushed and solemn—all things are mine, and what is mine is also <u>thine</u>. Hurry and take it, this evanescent beauty, which will endure long after the gold has been melted away and the mountains crumble into dust.

  How beautifully the Savior lived this doctrine in his Father's world! How poor we are with our misread treasure! What I have kept I have lost—what I gave I have. "...hope thou in God, for I shall yet praise Him who is the health of my countenance and my God." (*Psalm 42:11*)

  Only the spiritual can discern spiritual things; deep still calleth unto deep—the Lord still commands his loving kindness in the daytime, and in the night his song shall be with us, a prayer unto the God of our lives. Awake, thou sleeper, and open thine eyes to the beauty, the wonder, the treasure of the infinite resources of God. Watch a sparrow take a bath!

For eleven days, the Russians have been counter-attacking in the central sector of the Russian front, and claim to have retaken over twenty towns. The Germans have penetrated the Ukraine to the Dneiper, but apparently have not crossed; Leningrad, Moscow, Kiev, are still free and active. Perhaps the panzer divisions are running out of gas, but for the first time in this war, a blitzkrieg has failed to blitz, and that is good news for England and the Empire. England and Russia have established liaison through Iran. England's RAF heavily bombed Berlin, Mannheim, etc., night before last; and carry out daylight sweeps over northern France daily using new plans, Stirlings, Halifaxes, Manchesters, and the new American flying fortresses, which operate in the sub-stratosphere, from 30,000 to 40,000 feet. The Reich is manifestly short of gasoline for planes, as no heavy raids have been carried out over London for a month.

Rover, the dog, and I took a five-mile hike to the old wolf pits (built 1635) in the Lynn Woods, yesterday. Met no one. Few people in Lynn have ever hiked to the pits, apparently.

Suggested Daily Spiritual Reading:
Psalm 42:1-2
Matthew 5:6

Further Reading Related to Diary Entry:
- *Ben Hogan's Five Lessons: The Modern Fundamentals of Golf* by Ben Hogan (Author), Herbert Warren Wind (Author), Anthony Ravielli (Illustrator)

- *Look Homeward Angel* (1929) by Thomas Wolfe

- *Of Time and the River* (1935) by Thomas Wolfe

- *The Journey Down* (1938) by Thomas Wolfe

- *You Can't Go Home Again* (1940) by Thomas Wolfe. Available from The Project Gutenberg - Australia at http://gutenberg.net.au/ebooks07/0700231h.html [Accessed January 23, 2021].

- *Yanks in the RAF: The Story of Maverick Pilots and American Volunteers Who Joined Britain's Fight in WWII* by David Alan Johnson

Popular Books Published in 1941:
    A Testament of Devotion by Thomas R Kelly
    Thomas the Obscure by Maurice Blanchot

Popular Movies Released in 1941:
    Sergeant York (Gary Cooper, Walter Brennan, Joan Leslie)
    The Shepherd of the Hills (John Wayne, Betty Field)
    Sullivan's Travels (Joel McCrea, Veronica Lake)

September 25, 1941

On the sixth of this month it was my pleasure to hear Moscow on the radio via shortwave; directly from the capital of the USSR. They broadcast in English for an hour, eleven to twelve Eastern daylight savings time, which is 15.00 hours Greenwich Mean Time. The reception was excellent with volume of R9, as the amateurs say. The official communique was given with commentary following, and then music by Russian composers. It gave me a real thrill, as I have been trying for years to get Moscow. I listened to them for several mornings regularly, but other affairs have intervened and I have not heard them of late. The little 1941 shortwave set I purchased this summer has fulfilled its mission for me; Rome, London, Berlin are heard regularly, too. I used to imagine, when radio first came into being that the second world war would be vastly more interesting than the first, since it would cross the barriers of frontline, and perhaps give a close-up of the fighting at times. But outside of recorded bombings of London, it has consisted mainly of questionable communiques and interminable propaganda from all the capitals.

The following week, eight people interested in minerals met one night at the home of Lester Spear, 194 Essex Street, in Lynn, and organized the Lynn mineral club. It is patterned on the lines of the Boston club, save that we have no dues, as of yet. Mrs. Speed of Saugus was elected president; Albert King of Lynn, vice president; and Alden Jacobs of Swampscott, secretary-treasurer. Members have the privledge of selling minerals at the meetings, and we hope to have a speaker at each session of the club. It ought to prove very interesting.

For my collection, I have been interested, of late, in getting a few cut gems. I have a diamond now, and emerald crystal from Russia, an aquamarine, which my daughter, Janet, found; a synthetic ruby given to me by Lester Spear, and four genuine ruby crystals from Ceylon from the same source; have ordered a Montana sapphire--blue and facet-cut; and have received today in the mail three diamond-cut zircons, which I recently ordered. Also have turquoise, tourmaline, topaz, opal, apatite of gem quality, opals, garnets, and many others including lapis lazuli from Chile, all of which are used as gems. My minerals include gold, silver, copper, lead, tin, etc., etc. And for rocks I have a good supply of the igneous, sedimentary, and metamorphic types. So, my mineral collection is progressing nicely.

Junior and his friend, Richard Woodworth, have been constructing a pigeon loft for two homing pigeons they recently acquired. Junior also has been busy with his chemical set, so kindly given him by Mr. Spear, and Janet has been busy with her school, her friends, and her dolls. So, we have been a busy and, fairly, happy family the past several weeks.

We have with us a guest, a little girl by the name of Louise Taylor, five years old, of Cochituate. Her mother expects to go to the hospital soon for another arrival in the family. Louise is very quiet and very interested in everything that goes on in the family life.

Rover and I take a walk by the lake (Breed's Pond) nearly every day. I hike about a mile to an island, which I call Treasure Island. It gives me an opportunity to work up sermons, and plan my work; and it gives him the chance to investigate every thing of importance to a dog in the woods, and to chase, ineffectually, the birds. So we have a good time together, and it is much cheaper than playing golf.

My darling wife is on her way to a meeting of the Fisher Maids, a local organization within the Church, this afternoon, so the duty of looking after the children devolves on me. But the task is not very arduous, as they look after themselves pretty well. Fall is nearly here with all its pretty colors.

Suggested Daily Spiritual Reading:
Colossians 1:25
1 Timothy 3:16

Further Reading Related to Diary Entry:
- *Citizens of London: The Americans Who Stood with Britain in Its Darkest, Finest Hour* by Lynne Olson

- *The Secret History of World War II: Spies, Code Breakers, and Covert Operations* by Neil Kagan and Stephen G. Hyslop

- *Foxhole Radio: the ubiquitous razor blade radio of WWII* by Brian Carusella

- *Crystal Set Projects: 14 Radio Projects You Can Build* by Patricia M Anderson and Members of Xtal Set Society

- *The Voice of the Crystal* by H. Peter Friedrichs

Popular Books Published in 1941:
Space, Time and Architecture: The Growth of a New Tradition by Siegfried Giedion
The Hammer of God by Bo Giertz

Popular Movies Released in 1941:
   Suspicion (Cary Grant, Joan Fontaine, Nigel Bruce, Cedric Hardwicke, Dame
      May Whitty, Leo G. Carroll)
   Western Union (Randolph Scott, Robert Young)
   Sun Valley Serenade (Sonja Henie, John Payne, Glenn Miller)

October 14, 1941

About two weeks ago I purchased a motor and buffing head, which rotates an emery wheel and a polishing cloth for me. With this simple lapidary equipment, I have been enjoying myself cutting out and polishing cabochon and other objects from serpentine. Simple equipment it is from the standpoint of modern lapidaries who use special saws, and horizontal laps, but elaborate to the eyes of the native in India or Ceylon, whose emery wheel is propelled by hand or foot power, and whose equipment is most primitive. Yet, on this primitive equipment, cut stones and precious things, like jade, are fashioned. Patience and skill they have. They even facet the stones by hand using the hand-propelled emery wheel to eat away the stone--lapis, Latin for stone, hence, lapidary, worker in stone. An artist has well said that to carve a statue, all you need to do is cut away the non-essentials. So with gem stones. Having tried to emulate nature in fashioning a stone after barytes, which forms in the orthorhombic system, and only partially succeeding, I pay my deep respects to atomic affinity, which creates such symmetrical designs. But I am learning slowly--design and patience and skill--and, incidentally, enjoying myself greatly, for this is creative, and may endure for a time, for no one willingly throws away a beautiful object; not if he has the slightest sense of appreciation! I get my precious serpentine from a quarry called Devil's Den in the nearby town of Newbury, Mass. Serpentine, apparently, alters into asbestos if given time. Ground and smoothed and polished, the dark green serpentine varies with the light to give a pleasing effect. I have ordered a diamond saw--a saw of copper or steel with diamond boart pressed into the edges and hammered down--to cut my serpentine, quartz, whatnot, more readily. I have been handicapped in this respect, but hope soon to be able to fashion even more lovely pieces.

A word about the war situation at the present time. The Germans have penetrated the lines around Smolensk and Orel and are nearly the distance to the outer defenses of Moscow. Leningrad and Odessa still hold out, but Budyenny's army is in retreat, if not cut off, and the Germans there are headed toward the rich Donet's River basis, where about forty percent of Russia's industrial strength is concentrated; and beyond lie the Caucasus Mountains with their oil wells and manganese ore. The situation is grave for Russia. England has resumed twenty-four hour raids on Germany, but these do not relieve the eastern front. What is needed is the establishment of a western front, but the English do not feel capable of this at the present juncture, and I cannot say that I blame them, for they have lost everything at Dunkirk except their Navy, their courage, and the Royal Air Force. With these, they are gallantly recovering, but it will be long before the armies of the Reich feel the impact of invasion in Europe. Meanwhile, Hitler is master of all he surveys, and he can survey just about the whole of Europe.

My sapphire arrived and it is lovely--about half a carat and sparkling blue. A week ago I went into town and bought a carved piece of jadeite from China; that is, it was carved in China. Jadeite, a form of pyroxene, comes from Burma or Turkestan. Nephrite, which is the dark green jade, comes from New Zealand. Thus I have achieved one of my desires, mineralogically speaking. I still hope to get some boulder opal from Australia, someday. In the mineral club meeting in Boston, last Tuesday evening, we heard an interesting lecture on industrial uses of diamonds, and also saw a fine display of stones which the Schortmann brothers brought from Easthampton. I bought Janet a large almandine garnet from South Dakota.

Mother Brock is visiting with us at present. She and the children have been playing games together. Junior had a fistfight with Albert Chassis yesterday and won with a bloody nose!

Suggested Daily Spiritual Reading:
Acts 15:18
Romans 1:16

Further Reading Related to Diary Entry:
- *Gemstone Tumbling, Cutting, Drilling & Cabochon Making: A Simple Guide to Finishing Rough Stones* by James Magnuson

- *Handbook for the Amateur Lapidary* by James Harry Howard

- *Amateur Gemstone Faceting Volume 1: The Essentials* by Tom Herbst

- *The Mantle of Command: FDR at War, 1941–1942* by Nigel Hamilton

Popular Books Published in 1941:
The Impersonal Life by Joseph Benner
Between Two Worlds by Upton Sinclair

Popular Movies Released in 1941:
You're in the Army Now (Jimmy Durante, Jane Wyman, Phil Silvers)
Topper Returns (Joan Blondell, Roland Young, Carole Landis, Dennis O'Keefe)
Here Comes Mr. Jordan (Robert Montgomery, Evelyn Keyes, Claude Rains)

December 9, 1941

World history is being written at such a shocking pace that even the teletypewriters are unable to take it all down! Two days ago, on a Sunday dawn, The Japanese, without warning, attacked, with bombs and sudden death, Pearl Harbor and Honolulu in the Pacific, killing at least two hundred boys in the army camps and naval base alone, and damaging an unknown number of ships and planes. This was part of a concerted attack throughout the Pacific, undoubtedly for two purposes--to cripple our navy and to advance on the Dutch East Indies. Guam, Wake, and Midway Islands are reported captured. Manilla and the Philippines have been under attack several times; the Japanese soldiers landed in British North Borneo; Singapore and Hong Kong bombed; and Thailand surrendered after a token resistance. The Japanese also landed at Malayan beaches. "This is a day that will live in infamy," in the words of our President, Franklin D. Roosevelt.

Yesterday, noon, after a ringing speech by the President, in which he condemned the duplicity of the Japanese for carrying on peace negotiations while deliberately carrying out war strategy, the Congress declared war on Nippon. So did England, Holland, China, Mexico, Canada, and several Central and South American states. The number of World War II belligerents is expected to rise today to 40 in number, as compared to about 35 in the first world war.

Last night a squadron of enemy planes approached the Golden Gate, but finding the coast alert, and meeting interceptor planes, sheared off southward. Yesterday afternoon I heard a first-hand account from Manilla on the bombing there. The announcer was atop the Hickok Building--oil stores were afire at nearby Nichols Field, the half-moon was shining brightly, and the stars, and Japanese planes were actually bombing Manilla at that time. Three hundred soldiers were reported killed at nearby Clark Army Camp. Quite thrilling to hear a first-hand account. The reporter climbed eight fire escapes to reach the roof for the story.

Winston Churchill spoke from London at three EST, or 20 hours GMT, summing up the situation. "In the past," he said, "we had a candle which flickered! In the present, we have a candle which flames (with typical Churchillian pronunciation of flames), and in the future we shall have a candle which shall shine steady and resplendent," when this scourge shall have been driven from the land and from the sea. Inexact quotation, but it is always a pleasure to hear the doughty Churchill speak. He is England incarnate, yes even the "Empire". President Roosevelt outlines the gravity of the situation at eight o'clock tonight.

I am taking the air raid warden's course, and find it very interesting. The air warden is the eyes of the city. His chief duty is to report damage, casualties, and dangers. His work is also educational, teaching air raid precautions. He is not a policeman, fireman, nor doctor. I received an interesting letter the other day from a man in England who is also a warden--author and dealer in gems--Louis Kornitzer, who wrote "The Jewelled Trail". His home was bombed three times, his office once. He is also an auxiliary firefighter.

The West Coast was blacked out last night, and radio stations went off the air for a time. It seems futile to compress such tremendous events into the narrow confines of one page, but Wordsworth did pretty well with the sonnet in 14 lines and I always remember the description of the burning of Pompeii written by an eyewitness, whose name eludes me at this time.

Germany has given up the Russian campaign for the winter. Bitter cold is blamed, but the Russians jeer, "Napoleon reached Moscow--Hitler isn't able to get that far." Oil freezes in the crankcase, men freeze to the ground. The battle of Rostov decided the issue, I think.

Suggested Daily Spiritual Reading:
Revelations 22:21
Matthew 3:1-3

Further Reading Related to Diary Entry:
- *All the Gallant Men: An American Sailor's Firsthand Account of Pearl Harbor* by Donald Stratton

- *Brothers Down: Pearl Harbor and the Fate of the Many Brothers Aboard the USS Arizona* by Walter R. Borneman

- *Day Of Deceit: The Truth About FDR and Pearl Harbor* by Robert Stinnett

- *Churchill's Ministry of Ungentlemanly Warfare: The Mavericks Who Plotted Hitler's Defeat* by Giles Milton

- *A Handbook for Air Raid Wardens* prepared by Training Section, Office of Civilian Defense, revised edition. U.S. Government Printing Office, April 1942, Washington D.C. Available from the Illinois Digital Archives; Illinois State Library at http://www.idaillinois.org/cdm/ref/collection/isl3/id/10981 [Accessed January 23, 2021].

- *The Jewelled Trail* by Louis Kornitzer. Available from Online Books by Louis Kornitzer, The Online Books Page, University of Pennsylvania at http://onlinebooks.library.upenn.edu/webbin/book/lookupname?key=Kornitzer%2C%20Louis [Accessed January 23, 2021].

Popular Books Published in 1941:
   Clarence Darrow for the Defense by Irving Stone
   The Captain from Connecticut by C.S. Forester

Popular Movies Released in 1941:
   Harvard, Here I Come (Maxie Rosenbloom, Arline Judge)
   Dr. Jekyll and Mr. Hyde (Spencer Tracy, Ingrid Bergman, Lana Turner)
   The Devil and Miss Jones (Jean Arthur, Charles Coburn)

1942

Saturday Morning, January 24, 1942
130 Bellevue Road, Lynn, MA

My bench here in the basement where I ordinarily write is occupied by a chemistry set belonging to one Richard Armstrong, Albert's friend. The two boys have enjoyed skiing, chemistry, and diverse other recreations together. They made candles from special moulds--star, heart, diamond, and other shapes--this past week, and did very well in getting orders at five cents each, but now they have tired of that, temporarily, and have returned to chemistry. Next week it may be model planes or some other of a dozen hobbies, but that is as it should be.

Life itself has infinite variety, and I have prided myself in being interested in every aspect of it. A clergyman does well to interest himself professionally in the hobbies of his parishioners, but my interest is usually genuine. I do like to see well-made table-spreads, and good gardens, and fine photographs, and collections of little animals, and all the rest. People are most interesting of all--as I ride on the bus about the city I try to study the kaleidoscope of their lives--quite impossible of course, but nevertheless quite interesting to me.

Janet is helping her mother this morning, dusting the furniture.

Thursday I passed my 40th birthday--life begins at 40, they say--and I found it very enjoyable. My sister Lilla came down Monday and gave me a wrist flashlight; Janet made me some special candles—a set of patriotic ones, red, white, and blue; Junior gave me a huge chocolate bar and mints; and my darling wife gave me a sweater just suited to wear in the cold while calling (There have been a lot of sick folks the past two weeks). In the evening, some friends, Mr. And Mrs. William Fisher, invited us to attend the annual banquet of the Boy Scouts, held at the Oxford Club on Broad Street. The tickets were $1.25 and the meal was catered by Hicks (no charge for mentioning same!)—one of my parishioners works for him! Chicken, and plenty of it, ice cream, and plenty of it, coffee, and rolls; there were other things too, like relishes, but I like chicken and ice cream! The speaker was one James Harold Williams, scout executive from Providence, and he had the ability to make us laugh about people of whom we had never heard, which is genuine ability. He didn't tell jokes, but we were laughing regularly, which is a real tribute to his genius for finding the humorous. He used a great deal of expression, particularly facial. He told about coming through Boston in his Scout uniform and campaign hat, and people whispered, "Oh, are they still wearing campaign hats in the army? He's not in the Army? He's a Boy

Scout? Oh!" After the meeting, games were played, and then we joined in the grand march. Laus Deo, they actually played waltzes, and I danced for the first time in many years—with Mrs. Fisher first, and then my wife. Felt like Samuel Pepys--how I enjoyed reading his diary. And so to bed!

The war is shaping up in the world front. Like a big chess game, it is. The British have defeated the Germans and Italians in Libya; the Russians are still driving the Germans back in Russia, having recaptured Mozhaisk (pronounced by our best commentator "Mo-ji-eesk"); and in the far East, Japan threatens Singapore. MacArthur still holds Corregidor and the Bataan Peninsula in the Philippines. Parts of Sumatra, Borneo, and the Celebs have been taken by the Japs. Our navy, which was to have joined the Far Eastern Fleet at the outbreak of war, according to the Grand Strategy, has not been heard from as yet--either the Japs crippled too many ships at Pearl Harbor or it was decided not to risk the remainder without adequate air support. It will be hard to dislodge the Japanese from some 1300 islands down the far eastern Pacific archipelago. We have a real problem on our hands this time, as Hitler is far from beaten in Europe and Japan is reported to have two years supply of essential materials on hand at the present time. Eventually, economic power will win, however, and the moral forces of humanity.

Suggested Daily Spiritual Reading:
Wisdom of Solomon 12:22
Colossians 2:6

Further Reading Related to Diary Entry:
- *The Diary of Samuel Pepys* by Samuel Pepys. Available from The Project Gutenberg at http://www.gutenberg.org/files/4200/4200-h/4200-h.htm [January 23, 2021].

- *Boy Scouts Handbook: The First Edition, 1911* by Boy Scouts of America (Author). Available from The Project Gutenberg at http://www.gutenberg.org/files/29558/29558-h/29558-h.htm [January 23, 2021].

- *Girl Scouts Handbook: The Original 1913 Edition* by W. J. Hoxie

- *Scouting for Girls*. Official Handbook of the Girl Scouts, 1925 (Sixth Reprint) by Girl Scouts, Inc; editor: Josephine Daskam Bacon. Release Date: April 4, 2009. Available from The Project Gutenberg at https://www.gutenberg.org/files/28490/28490-h/28490-h.htm [January 23, 2021].

- *The Secret of Sherwood Forest* by Guy Woodward

- *Building for War: The Epic Saga of the Civilian Contractors and Marines of Wake Island in World War II* by Bonita Gilbert

- *The Aleutian Islands Campaign: The History of Japan's Invasion of Alaska during World War II* by Charles River Editors

- *Spearhead: An American Tank Gunner, His Enemy, and a Collision of Lives in World War II* by Adam Makos

Popular Books Published in 1942:
Most Popular Books Published In 1942. Available from Goodreads.com at https://www.goodreads.com/book/popular_by_date/1942 [January 23, 2021].

Popular Movies Released in 1942:
Casablanca (Humphrey Bogart, Ingrid Bergman, Claude Rains, Paul Henreid, Dooley Wilson, Peter Lorre)
Across the Pacific (Humphrey Bogart, Mary Astor, Sydney Greenstreet, Charles Halton)
Bells of Capistrano (Gene Autry, Virginia Grey)

January 31, 1942

There is always a sense of indescribable finality when I put my pen to these pages. Time hurries us along willy-nilly, and while we realize above all others the mediocrity of these observations a faint hope rises within us that they will not wholly die. This will be true only insofar as the particular is sublimated to the universal.

I have just returned from conducting a funeral service for one of my parishioners, a man who served the Church for fifty-five years as trustee and treasurer. Among the friends present was Dean Earl Marlatt of the Boston University School of Theology, and author of that inspiring hymn "Are ye able, said the Master, to be crucified with Me?" He came principally out of respect for the daughter, who is secretary for the school. One of the sons is, at present, librarian at the public library in the center of Boston. A large number were present to pay their last respects to the deceased. My remarks centered around the thought that we are immortal in three ways--through our children; through our good works ("Remember me, O Lord, for good," said Nehemiah), though we are not justified by work; and through our trust in the promises of Christ. There is probably a fourth--if spirit or idea be an entity apart from matter (throws off, just for evidence, this overcoat of clay--Sandburg) as idealism suggests; is transcendent as well as immanent, regardless of how it controls matter--then there may well be a Conservation of Spirit, as well as conservation of matter and energy.

My real self is not in my hands, nor in my brain, nor yet the sum total of all I have been and shall be. My real self, as Wordsworth suggests, comes from the great reservoir of Being which is coeternal with God. "...Our birth is but a sleep and a forgetting; the soul that rises with us, our life's star, hath had elsewhere its setting and cometh from afar...from God, who is our home..." (*From "Ode on Intimations of Immortality from Recollections of Early Childhood" [1804] by William Wordsworth*). These thoughts are not intended to be somber, but to affirm pragmatically, ideologically, and religiously the tremendous fact that we can never really die. We simply pass from the stage into the wings to await the disposition of the Director--"that Being only, who hath known each one from the beginning, can remember each unto the end" (*From "A Nameless Epitaph" by Matthew Arnold*) Can love change? "...the heart which has truly loved never forgets, but as truly loves on to the close..." (*From "Believe Me, If All Those Endearing Young Charms" [1808] by Thomas Moore*) Hereby we know that we have passed from death unto life, because we love the brethren! My Father's spirit is with me still, and will be all my days. And my spirit shall reside in those I love, forever and ever, Amen.

The transient scene discloses that the protagonists on the field of Mars are shifting positions. Japan now besieges Singapore, a hundred thousand strong. Rommel in Africa has recaptured Benghazi. Timoshenko in Russia is striking into the Ukraine. Hitler delivered a self-justificatory address yesterday in the Sportspalast, blaming the weather, as did Napoleon, for the reverses in Russia. U-boats claim the 21st victim off the East Coast. Amboina, a strong Dutch naval base in the East Indies, is attacked by invasion troops. These are headlines, and reveal the shifting fortunes of war. But who is going to write about the heartbreak of the individual caught in the toils of disaster; the loss of homes, loved ones, freedom, and all that life holds dear? We need another Tolstoi with a larger canvas to portray all this. The quivering nerves, the quickening heartbeat, the sense of impending disaster that must inevitably accompany the surprise attack, the demoralizing scream of bombs, the maimed and bleeding limbs--this requires a faith commensurate with the magnitude of the battle. "What time I am afraid, I will trust in Thee." (*Psalm 56:3*), writes the psalmist, and no better advice was ever given.

In minerals, salts of strontium give us red, barium--green, sodium--yellow, lithium--purple, copper--red or green, titanium--blue. A little chromium accounts for the greening in the emerald and the red in the ruby. Odd isn't it? We had a fine mineral club meeting Thursday night at the home of Albert King on Whiting Street.

Junior has been collecting magazines and books for the boys in the service. Janet has gone to the movies with her friend, Ann.

Suggested Daily Spiritual Reading:
Psalm 56
John 3:3

Further Reading Related to Diary Entry:
- *No Death, No Fear: Comforting Wisdom for Life* by Thich Nhat Hanh

- *William Wordsworth - The Major Works: including The Prelude (Oxford World's Classics)* by William Wordsworth (Author), Stephen Gill (Editor)

- *Seizing the Enigma: The Race to Break the German U-Boat Codes, 1933-1945* by David Kahn

- *Torpedo Junction: U-Boat War Off America's East Coast, 1942* by Homer Hickam

Popular Books Published in 1942:
    The Robe by Lloyd C. Douglas
    Calamity Town by Frederic Dannay

Popular Movies Released in 1942:
    Blondie Goes to College (Penny Singleton, Arthur Lake, Janet Blair)
    Captains of the Clouds (James Cagney, Dennis Morgan, Brenda Marshall)
    A Date with the Falcon (George Sanders, Wendy Barrie, Allen Jenkins)

Ash Wednesday February 18, 1942

The machinery for Catholicism functions on an eventful day; thousands received the accolade of ashes to remind them of their mortality, and the necessity for penance in preparation for passover. Five persons came to our prayer service. In Catholicism, if I understand aright, the ashes from the previous Palm Sunday's palms are used as a token of penance and the forgiveness of Christ. "Do not be seen of men to fast, but thy Father which seeth in secret, and thy Father which seeth in secret, shall reward thee openly" (*Matthew 6:18, paraphrased*)--this just came over the air from the evening service in London--perhaps it has some bearing on the case. Let us see. To go on--there is in Catholic theology, first the contritio cordis, contrition of the heart; second confessio oris, that is confession of the lips, as a sign of repentance; next, satisfactio operis, or penance, literally satisfaction of the works; and finally, absolutio sacerdotis, or absolution of the priest of God. Well lubricated machinery which operates en masse on Ash Wednesday.

Let's see how it is with us Protestants. First, we're not educated as children to anything of the sort, nor as adults either, consequently we have no machinery for forgiveness of sins---penance and absolution, confession, etc. This was obviated at the time of Luther as presumptive power on part of the pope and priest, and predicated on the assurance that Christ is the one true mediator between God and man. We might also question the sincerity of mass contrition--the Pharisaism of fasting, shall we say. Moreover, our ministers have no authority to forgive sins, even in the name of the Master. Hence, it is left strictly to the individual, following the dogma of the priesthood of all believers, with usual result--no priesthood and no believers! The remorse of the individual for sins committed is rare; if remorse, no wherewithal to change this contrition into forgiveness and faith, save through prayer on the part of a friend perhaps; no forgiveness voiced audibly nor assurance that one's sins are forgiven, except when the heart, "strangely warmed", such as the conversion experience of Wesley in London; no penance imposed, for the heart of the matter is that Christ did once and for all make a "full perfect and sufficient sacrifice for the sins of the whole world" at Golgotha, 2,000 years ago.

Now, all this is highly unsatisfactory to me as a minister. While I deplore mass penance, contrition, and confession, yet it seems to me that our church should make it possible for the individual worshipper to find his way to God with the help of the Church and not in spite of it! For there is still contrition in the hearts of men for sins committed against the most High--there ought to be opportunity for the worshipper to confess his sins in Church, privately or publicly--alone or to an understanding confessor; some worthy penance should be suggested in the way of good works for its salutary effect upon the soul; and finally the sinner and clergyman should pray together for the assurance of forgiveness, which Christ alone can offer to the willing soul. His "treasury of merit" is surely availing and available, but we have often blocked the way to its reception. The blood of our Lord which of the new covenant is shed for many for the remission of sins (*Matthew 26:28*)--the old Day of Atonement and the scapegoat give way to the willing sacrifice of the Son of God. And penance should not be a "giving up" of something but an "adding to" the enrichment of human life. The forgiven and shriven soul desires truly that his new faith should have the generating power of Christ for the more abundant life in the hearts of men. Perhaps we shall work out a formula someday for this new, yet old, conception of men working together with God for the establishment of his Kingdom. "...and purify unto Himself, a people for His own possession, zealous of good works" (*Titus 2:14*), is the way St. Paul describes it to Titus. That is something to hope for and something to work for. Then Ash Wednesday will attain real significance for Protestants as well as Catholics.

Suggested Daily Spiritual Reading:
Matthew 6:16-18
Titus: 2:1-15

Further Reading Related to Diary Entry:
- *Catechism of the Catholic Church: Second Edition* by U.S. Catholic Church

- *How the Catholic Church Built Western Civilization* by Thomas E. Woods

- *The Second Vatican Council - An Unwritten Story* by Professor Roberto deMattei (Author), Michael M. Miller (Editor)

- *Catholicism: A Journey to the Heart of the Faith* by Robert Barron

- *The Compact History of the Catholic Church: Revised Edition* by Schreck Ph.D., Alan

- *The Jesuit Guide to (Almost) Everything: A Spirituality for Real Life* by James Martin

- *The Age of Reason* by Thomas Paine

- *The Cloud of Unknowing and Other Works* (Penguin Classics) Reissue Edition by Anonymous (Author), A. C. Spearing (Translator)

Popular Books Published in 1942:
Chess Story by Stefan Zweig, Joel Rotenberg (Translator)

Go Down, Moses by William Faulkner

Popular Movies Released in 1942:
Eyes in the Night (Edward Arnold, Ann Harding, Donna Reed)
Flying Tigers (John Wayne, John Carroll, Anna Lee)
The Forest Rangers (Fred MacMurray, Susan Hayward, Paulette Goddard)

Good Friday April 5, 1942

"The spirit of the Lord is upon me, for he hath anointed me to preach the gospel to the poor, to heal the broken hearted; to preach deliverance to the captives, and the recovering of sight to the blind; to set at liberty them that are bruised; to preach the acceptable year of our Lord." (*Luke 4:18-19*) How I would like to have the facilities of a world-wide station like WRUL in Boston, for example, to preach these words to the captives and the bruised, of mind, body, and spirit, in Norway, Belgium, Holland, Germany, Czechoslovakia, Java, the Philippines, Hong Kong, where--by report, the captives are wasting away-- Greece, where they are dying, and in Japan, where Kagawa is in protective custody! Perhaps I could, with a little more gumption, or initiative, to use a more literary word. John Steinbeck has done it in a book, "The Moon is Down". Excellent--historical thesis is that the conquerers are conquered by the vanquished--a correct viewpoint, I believe, in the long run, but sometimes the run is too long! Witness the stability of the Roman empire. However, the book is fine--The flies have captured two hundred miles more of fly paper, and herd men win battles, free men win wars. Deliverance to the captives! Liberty to them that are bruised! It will be a day of Jubilee when the prisons are opened and the dead walk forth, and the hungry are fed, and the blind see again! May we live to see that great and wonderful day! But so much of life is compromised--the end of the last great war was an inglorious affair, which we looked upon with shame in its after-effects. The forces of idealism, so strong in waging a war, are spent with its conclusion, and practical (?) men dominate the scene, with second-rate diplomats hovering about solicitously.

Lacking the initiative to approach WRUL melodramatically and announce that I have news comforting and of world-wide import I will sublimate the emotion, and write it down instead. But in this I <u>am</u> confident, that the Day of Freedom will come again for all peoples. Even the Hundred Years War ended in toleration and peace at last. The only battlefield which is never stilled is in the human heart. A Chinese Christian recently said, pertinently, "Reform Thy world, O Lord,--beginning with me!"

Today, from 12-3, seven preachers united in bringing to the union service at St. Stephen's Episcopal Church, the seven last words of Christ from the cross. I had the seventh word, "Father into Thy hands I commend my spirit." (*Luke 23:46*) Jesus literally emptied himself for humanity--he gave his body, and his keen mind, in selfless service, and at the end he gave his life. All that was left to give was the inviolable core of His being--his soul, which he returned to the Father in these lovely words, "Greater love hath no man than this, that he lay down his life for his friends" (*John 15:13*)--that he put his whole life at the service of his friends. Here is precisely where we fail our religion. We give God everything--time, talents, money--except ourselves. That is the one supreme gift. General Bramwell Booth once said (*paraphrased*), If I have aided humanity it was because, once, I resolved that God should have all there was of me. (*Reference is to General William Bramwell Booth, Second General of the Salvation Army, 1912-1929*)

Of the Corinthians it is written, they gave their tithes with one accord, but first they gave <u>themselves</u> unto the Lord. (*Reference to Corinthians 8:5*) The first and greatest commandment is this, thou shalt love the Lord with all thy heart, mind, and strength. (*Reference to Matthew 22:37*) INTO Thy hands, O God...!

Darkness settles over the land, and over the world. It is in the dark and cold that the seed germinates. Out of death comes life. We hear the faint stirrings of the Hallelujah Chorus from Handel's Messiah. Handel, a German! Converts are called "resurrected people" by certain tribes in Africa. "Blessed be the God and Father of our Lord Jesus Christ, who through His abundant mercy, hath begotten us again unto a lively hope by the resurrection of His son. To an inheritance incorruptible, and undefiled, and that fadeth not away, reserved in heaven for you!" (*paraphrased from*) 1 Peter 1:3,4.

We had our first trial blackout Tuesday night in Lynn (*MA*), with 50 other communities. It was thrilling to see the lights go out all over the city, to hear the sirens wailing, and to find that such organized effort was possible. 171 street lights were extinguished by hand here, by use of the telephone fan-out system. I am one of the precinct wardens. The moon was hidden behind the clouds. There was no blackout of hope, however.

Same Day - *Good Friday April 5,1942* - Page 2
First we were told to expect the blackout between 8:30 pm and midnight. I surmised it would come about nine o'clock, because orders in Boston were given to begin extinguishing the lights at 8:45 pm. Sure enough, about that time the order came via phone to go ahead. So, I called up two persons to put out lights on their poles, then donned my simple equipment: an armband, a phosphorescent rosette in my lapel, my whistle, and flashlight (properly covered to give an aperture light of one-eighth inch). Then, I dashed down the street to the intersection. Already the streetlights and many of the home lights were out. I spoke to only four homeowners to quench their lights, and to one chap with a lighted cigarette. Then in a few minutes the sirens began to sound; first the Boston sirens, then our own, including the powerful General Electric horn. The city was soon in nearly complete darkness. The lights along the Lynn causeway continued to gleam until the blackout was nearly over, but were finally

extinguished. It was eerie and awe-inspiring. I met some of the other wardens patrolling, and we watched it together. Then the all-clear sounded. There was considerable hesitancy in turning the lights back on. The autos recovered first, then the street lights. Some house lights were turned on and then off again. After the blackout, we reported to our district headquarters, then home, and so to bed.

Last week, on Thursday, we entertained a dozen members of the mineral club. One of the members gave a talk on aluminum. It was good to see some of my old friends again, who had not attended recent meetings; notably, Mr. Lester Spear and Mr. Alden Jacob--both charter members. Our next meeting is in Melrose.

At the close of this Good Friday I should like to quote, and so preserve, the words of an anonymous writer about the significance of One Solitary Life:

> "Here is a man who was born in an obscure village, the child of a peasant woman. He grew up in another obscure village. He worked in a carpenter shop until he was thirty, and then for three years he was an itinerant preacher. He never owned a home. He never had a family of his own. He never went to college. He never travelled two hundred miles from the place where he was born. He never did one of the things that usually accompany greatness. He had no credentials but himself. He had nothing to do with this world except through the naked power of his divine manhood.
>
> While still a young man, the tide of public opinion turned against him. His friends ran away; one of them betrayed him. He was turned over to his enemies. He went through the mockery of a trial. He was nailed upon a cross between two thieves. His executioners gambled for the only piece of property he had on earth while he was dying, and that was his coat. When he was dead, he was taken down, and laid in a borrowed tomb, through the pity of a friend.
>
> I am far within the mark when I say that all the armies that ever marched, and all the navies that were ever built, and all the parliaments that ever sat, and all the kings that ever reigned, put together, have not affected the life

of man upon this earth as powerfully as that One Solitary Life." (*Attribution to James Allan Francis*)

What a beautiful tribute to Jesus! Factual, succinct, true. If only dictators could read and understand! But their eyes are blinded, and their hearts are hardened. But Napoleon understood, and Pliny understood, and the Cesars understood. King Agrippa sighed, "Almost thou persuadest me to be a Christian." It may be the Catacombs for a time, but it will be the Cathedrals forever!

Junior took Rover, the collie, over to the Lynn woods today, in company with two other boys. He reports that they had a fine time, and that the dog behaved very well, so well that they are taking him again. Janet has been downtown shopping for Easter things two times today. She became separated from Ann, in the store, but they found their way home all right. Easter is a time of quiet happiness for the children.

Janet and Rover, circa, 1943.

Suggested Daily Spiritual Reading:
Luke 4:18-19
1 Peter 1:3-12.

Further Reading Related to Diary Entry:
- *The Moon is Down* by John Steinbeck

- *Echoes and Memories* by Bramwell Booth

- *These Fifty Years* by Bramwell Booth

- *Jesus: A Pilgrimage* by James Martin

♦ *Beautiful Outlaw: Experiencing the Playful, Disruptive, Extravagant Personality of Jesus* by John Eldredge

♦ *Living Buddha, Living Christ: 20th Anniversary Edition* by Thich Nhat Hanh

Popular Books Published in 1942:
Capitalism, Socialism and Democracy by Joseph Schumpeter
The Case for Christianity by C.S. Lewis

Popular Movies Released in 1942:
George Washington Slept Here (Jack Benny, Ann Sheridan, Charles Coburn)
Holiday Inn (Bing Crosby, Fred Astaire, Marjorie Reynolds, Virginia Dale)
King's Row (Ann Sheridan, Ronald Reagan, Robert Cummings)

June 7, 1942

It is six months to (*since the attack on*) Pearl Harbour. Yesterday came news of the naval action off Midway, which needs a Pepys to do it justice, in terms of dramatic historical value (*I believe he is referring to Samuel Pepys—administrator of the navy of England in the 1600s*). Our planes wrought havoc with the Japanese task or invading force, destroying or damaging three or four aircraft carriers, two or three battleships, three transports, and three or four light cruisers, and possibly a hundred planes. Lives not considered! A soldier is a pawn, a number in the game of war; as are civilians if they happen to be caught in a raid, like Cologne, for example. But this naval battle, unlike the Macassar Straits and Coral Sea and Java Sea, was apparently decisive, and so we can sense its importance in historical perspective. As Admiral Nimitz of the U.S. Fleet quipped, "We are midway to our objective." It was thrilling to me, because I was copying code from Reuters, routinely, when the operator sent "Flash--Washington" and proceeded to give the exact number of ships in each category sunk or damaged, and followed this with the jubilant message of Nimitz to the American people. "The citizen can well rejoice in this momentous victory," he said, in part, and I think I am transgressing on no copyright of Reuters in quoting it; if fact I have misquoted the words somewhat but given the substance. But if an admiral of a fleet uses such diction, you may be sure he does so only after first ascertaining the validity of the victory. Not knowing the number of ships engaged, it is hard to evaluate its importance in the long run, but the Japanese navy has received a setback, unquestionably, which will give pause to the naval commanders of that impertinent little island.

Since writing last, emotionally I have gone through a cyclothymic swing of abnormal dimensions--not far, but still far enough--do to initiation on my part (*He is 40 years old*). Briefly, a committee in the Church, or certain members of it, rather, desired my removal and took steps toward that end. It made things a bit unpleasant for a time, and I resigned, but the Conference saw fit to return me to this charge, no other of suitable compensation being open, and 99% of the Church welcomed us back, giving us a little reception last week. It was an enlightening experience, and was based on personal feeling--since the members of the committee concerned were not consulted about our coming here, and, hence, had never accepted us in their minds. We have accomplished more in certain directions in the past two weeks than in the previous two years, and it was worth the disagreeableness to learn how widely we were liked in the parish. The pastor can ask for a transfer, the pastoral relations committee can recommend a transfer, but we are under orders, and the Bishop can send us where he pleases. I have never had such an experience before, and would not wish another. But like a thunderstorm, it clears the air, and I look forward confidently to a profitable year.

My good friend Lester Spear, obtained a job, in the meantime, as broiler cook at the New Ocean House in Swampscott, and I didn't expect to see him for a long time, since he has long hours of labour; hence, I was agreeably when he called up the other day and asked me to go golfing with him. I did so with great pleasure, and yesterday we went again. We were joined by Reverend Leonard Gray of the Vine Street Congregational Church (310 years old today) with whom I have become better acquainted, recently, since we are both much interested in Thoreau. In fact, Thoreau is an inspiration to me to try to record daily happenings, interesting people and places for the edification of others. He became successful by being himself, and following his own bent, rather than by emulating Emerson or other contemporaries. I would like to do the same.

My son has just completed a chemistry experiment in making CO_2. The bench here looks like a drugstore. He and a friend rode on bicycles to Howe and French's in Boston yesterday, and procured some zinc. Fifteen miles each way! He also received his second class badge in scouting last Monday night. Janet has interested herself in reading, and is reading quite a lengthy book. I am quite proud of my children. They give us relatively little trouble, and both are progressing well in school and social relations. May it ever be so!

Suggested Daily Spiritual Reading:
Ephesians 4:1-7
Psalm 7:1-5

Further Reading Related to Diary Entry:
- *Walking* by Henry David Thoreau

- *The Power of Jesus' Names* by Tony Evans

- *The Battle of Midway* by Craig L. Symonds

- *Pacific Crucible: War at Sea in the Pacific, 1941-1942* by Ian W. Toll

- *World War II at Sea: A Global History* by Craig L. Symonds

Popular Books Published in 1942:
The Art of Dramatic Writing: Its Basis in the Creative Interpretation of Human Motives by Lajos Egri
The Secret Life of Salvador Dalí by Salvador Dalí

Popular Movies Released in 1942:
- *The Magnificent Ambersons* (Joseph Cotten, Anne Baxter, Dolores Costello, Agnes Moorehead, Tim Holt)
- *The Man Who Came to Dinner* (Monty Woolley, Bette Davis, Ann Sheridan, Billie Burke)
- *Mrs. Miniver* (Greer Garson, Walter Pidgeon, Teresa Wright)

June 11, 1942

> We are not sure of sorrow;
> And joy was never sure;
> Today will die tomorrow;
> Time stoops to no man's lure;
> And Love, grown faint and fretful…
> And with eyes regretful, weeps that no loves endure.
> (Algernon Swineburne, "Garden of Proserpine")

I have but now returned (what a quaint expression) from a garden party at the home of one of the choir members, who is being joined in marriage to another choir member next week. There was an outdoor fireplace, with heated frankfurts as the specialty, together with soft drinks. Songs around the campfire, the sparks ascending in the night and matching the fireflies--the searchlight beacon swinging across the Big Dipper and the northern star--the evening and the dark--were lovely, yet all is missing when One is missing. My wife wasn't there, and so the party while fun, seemed more like a pageant. To have these things last one must be romantic and serious, and in deadly earnest--having that melancholy sense of the swift passage of time so prevalent in a sundial or in the slow wheeling of the stars where with Keats (or is it Byron?)

> "Alone on eternity's ocean I stand and think
> Till love and fame to nothingness do sink."

(*The actual quote from John Keats' poem "When I Have Fears that I May Cease to Be", is: "...Of the wide world I stand alone, and think Till Love and Fame to nothingness do sink." [From The Academy of American Poets. Available from poetry.org at* https://poets.org/poem/when-i-have-fears-i-may-cease-be *[January 23, 2021].*)

That is the weltanschauung of twenty; at forty it is just a good party, and the mosquitoes bite fiercely; the tonic is excellent, and the host very courteous and very patient with young people. We were given roses at the parting--the perfect ending. I wish these young people, about to be married, the best life has to offer, including its disciplines.

Mae and I visited the rose garden at the Pennybrook gate entrance of the Lynn Woods today. There were many varieties, including my favorite--the Talisman. My wife recalled that when Albert Earl was born, Aunt Christina (*his sister*) sent her a dozen Talisman roses via telegraph. One variety was called Dame Edith Louise, another Caledonia, still another Mrs. McNulty. There are still many buds, but most have bloomed into over-maturity. Just beyond the lovable stage, like a chicken of two months.

I have given up reading for a while. At least, I hope I have. Too much reading is as deleterious as too much drinking. I would like to break myself of the habit of reading two or three books a night, in order that I might write a page, at least, of my journal, and concentrate on copying code dispatches, particularly from Reuter news agency in London. The news I get tonight, for example, is seen in tomorrow's papers. I have narrated the thrill I experienced in copying the exact number of Japanese losses in the Midway battle; two nights ago I read of the odd will of John Barrymore, who authorized the inspection of his body by any interested person to make sure he was really dead; to avoid being buried alive. Perhaps he had gone through the four stages of inebriation--jocose, morose, bellicose, and comatose--so many times he did not desire to take the risk of being laid away while still alive but moribund. I have heard of folks who installed telephones in their mausoleums just in case. But morticians today make impossible such a possibility. Truly flesh and blood cannot inherit the kingdom of God, and when they are separated, the one from the other, there is little likelihood of their doing so.

And then last night I copied the news of the Nazi outrage at Lidice in Czechoslovakia, where all the men were shot, because of suspected complicity in the bombing of Reinhard Heydrich, Gauleiter of Praha. All the women carried to the concentration camps and all the children transported to "educational centers". The town was razed and the name expunged from the Nazi maps. But the name lives on as the symbol outraged freedom, and someday, by the grace of God, it will be inhabited by freed men. The Czechs will see to that after the war is won by the Allies.

There is a symbiosis in spiritual things, just as Cavalry lives, so will Lidice. The sacrifice of its inhabitants will not have been in vain.

It has been unusually warm today with the thermometer in the 90s. The sea was hazy and the summer is at hand. But the heat of summer feels good in the bones, after a long, cold spring. Nature luxuriates in heat.

<u>Suggested Daily Spiritual Reading:</u>
Lamentations 3:22-26
2 Esdras 9:14-17

<u>Further Reading Related to Diary Entry:</u>
♦ <u>*Complete Poems and Selected Letters of John Keats*</u> by John Keats

- *Roses: Placing Roses, Planting & Care, The Best Varieties* by Editors of Sunset Books

- *Lieber's Standard Telegraphic Code* by B. Franklin Lieber; Lieber Publishing Company, New York (1898). Available from Internet Archive at https://archive.org/details/liebersstandard02liebgoog/page/n5 [January 23, 2021].

- *Code Girls: The Untold Story of the American Women Code Breakers of World War II* by Liza Mundy

- *The Liberator: One World War II Soldier's 500-Day Odyssey from the Beaches of Sicily to the Gates of Dachau* by Alex Kershaw

- *A Little Village Called Lidice: The Story of the the Return of the Women and Children of Lidice* by Zdena Trinka

- *World War II Auschwitz: A History From Beginning to End* by Hourly History

Popular Books Published in 1942:
The Skin of Our Teeth by Thornton Wilder
Laura by Vera Caspary

Popular Movies Released in 1942:
My Favorite Blonde (Bob Hope, Madeleine Carroll, Gale Sondergaard, George Zucco)
A Night to Remember (Loretta Young, Brian Aherne)
The Old Chisholm Trail (Johnny Mack Brown, Tex Ritter, Jennifer Holt)

June 12, 1942

It has been an unconscionably warm day, and your correspondent played 18 holes of golf with Rev. Arthur Hopkinson of First Methodist Church at Sagamore in Lynnfield Center. I left my shirt off while playing and the result is that tonight my shoulders are sore with the first sunburn of the season. Had I had remained in the coolness of the basement where I am writing, it would have been all right, but I dressed to attend a committee meeting at the local YMCA; relative to Holy Week services next year. These services are for the general public and are held in the theater, which is generously donated for the cause.

The question of denominationalism came up and was decorously derided by the gentry present. I will admit its deplorability in dividing us, but the best Christian work has been done by and through the denominations. Let us not belittle their significance. As the states are to central government, so are the denominations (including Catholicism and the Salvation Army) to the Church. Weak states make for an arrogant government. I favor the dominance of the national government, but I can readily see that if our states were to surrender their prerogatives, we would be the losers thereby. The Constitution specifically states that whatever powers are not delegated to the executive or the congress, are reserved to the states and the people thereof.

I once took a course in constitutional law, and it has benefited me in better understanding our political system of government. On the other hand, a government like Weimar Republic, which nominally granted powers to the provinces, but was imposed from without, actually, easily succumbed to the machinations of the Nazis. The rock-ribbed Puritans who fled authority, and faced the perils of the wilderness to find a new authority within themselves, laid the ground work for our national system.

We are often exasperated in the governance of our Churches, to find streperous laymen, but in the final analysis I think such a Church under persecution would fare better than the oligarchical Churches. If one accepts the Lutheran dogma of the priesthood of all believers, one is confronted with an interesting paradox, unity within diversity, but out of the priesthood of believers have come our strong denominations, and out of our strong denominations will someday come the unified church, just as surely as out of the strong united nations will come the super-state; to which will be delegated powers of governance. Let us not belittle our denominations, which with all their faults, have many virtues, and which have been forged out of the lifeblood of many faithful followers of our Lord. In essentials, unity; in nonessentials, liberty; in all things, charity!

Bir Hachim, the southern outpost of the Free French, in the Libyan desert, has fallen to the Nazis. The Free French have withdrawn and the fortress taken. But for sixteen days it held out, and reminds one of the French outpost described by Percival Christopher Wren in "Beau Geste". In that story, the fortress was stormed by the Arabs, and the heroic defenders propped up the dead men, put guns in their hands at the loopholes and went on defending the fort, successfully. Only two men were left when the Arabs withdrew finally—one of these killed the sergeant and then slipped over the walls. When the fort was finally reached by the rescue party, none was left alive to tell the story.

The children went for a swim in the bay tonight for the first time this year. The water is still pretty cold, they report. This evening I took the family, including Rover, for a ride in the car around Lynnfield Triangle, and then finished with an ice cream, and so to bed.

My sister, Christina, who has had a month's vacation, leaves for New York tomorrow for a short visit at the Henry Street Settlement, before returning to her work as a nurse at the Trudeau Settlement at Saranac Lake, New York. She visited us for a couple of days, and we took her to various places of interest, the Lynn Woods, the ocean, etc, which she seemed to enjoy.

It was lovely at the lake today, where I took the dog for a walk. The rippling water, the sunshine, the gulls wheeling overhead, and a P40 high in the sky, lent beauty to the scene. *(Note: The Curtiss P-40 Warhawk/Tomahawk is an American single-engined, single-seat, all-metal fighter and ground-attack aircraft that first flew in 1938.)*

Suggested Daily Spiritual Reading:
Matthew 4:23-25
Ephesians 6: 10-20

Further Reading Related to Diary Entry:
- *Zen Golf: Mastering the Mental Game* by Dr. Joseph Parent

- *Yearbook of the Young Men's Christian Associations of North America (May 1, 1905 to April 30, 1906)*; published by the International Committee of Young Men's Christian Associations, New York, 1906. Available from Internet Archive at https://archive.org/details/ymcayearbookof1906younuoft/page/n51 [January 23, 2021].

- *The Social Sources of Denominationalism* by H. Richard Niebuhr; Living Age Books; published by Meridian Books, New York, 1922. Available from Internet

Archive at https://archive.org/details/in.ernet.dli.2015.462204 [January 23, 2021].

- *Beau Geste* by Percival Christopher Wren (1924). Available from The Project Gutenberg of Australia at http://gutenberg.net.au/ebooks06/0600231h.html [January 23, 2021].

- *Aircraft Pictorial No. 5 - P-40 Warhawk* by Dana Bell

- *P-40 Warhawk Aces of the MTO* by Carl Molesworth

Popular Books Published in 1942:
How to Cook a Wolf by M.F.K. Fisher
Pied Piper by Nevil Shute

Popular Movies Released in 1942:
Paris Calling (Basil Rathbone, Randolph Scott, Elisabeth Bergner)
The Pride of the Yankees (Gary Cooper, Teresa Wright, Walter Brennan, Babe Ruth)
Reap the Wild Wind (John Wayne, Paulette Goddard, Ray Milland)

June 15, 1942

This is one of the mediocre days when the routine things are done in the routine way, and life does not savor that poetic quality that enhances the dance of the hours in other and more exalted times.

As on every Monday, I paid my bills, as far as able—I am often reminded, in that connection, of Voltaire, was it, who said, "I have nothing; I owe much, the rest I leave to the poor," (*This is actually a quote from François Rabelais, paraphrased*), and of that other wise man who was dunned by a creditor until he exclaimed in exasperation, "Look here, I have a system. Each week I put all my bills in a basket. On pay day I take out five and pay them. Now if you persist in dunning, I won't even put yours in the basket!" (*Source of this quote is unknown*).

Then I visited my friend, Lester Spear, and found him troubled with his game leg, so that he couldn't go golfing with me. But he did give me a retort for Junior, which is an addition to his chemistry set.

Copied some code, some German, some Spanish, some numbers, and some English. Went golfing on a pretty little course called Cedar Glen in nearby Saugus this afternoon with my son. Did pretty well, and Albert Earl (*aka Junior*) had fun hitting the ball around with me. The course is aptly named, for there are many cedars and arbor vitae on the sides of the course. The roses are beautiful too, beside the homes, in their embankments.

Have written some letters tonight and taken the dog for a walk, but I do not feel particularly inspired about anything, least of all the war. The Germans seem to be making headway in Libya, and in Russia, Sevastopol has been under heavy siege. But if the Russians are not discouraged, there is no reason why we should be! And one of the traits of English character is that even in the midst of reverses they have something to be confident about! During the furious Battle of Britain, they not only took it uncomplainingly, but even found cause for rejoicing in the daily toll of German planes brought down. I wonder if the German character is as strong? Of course we hear only the propaganda, and do not know the real situation as regards morale in Germany, but it is significant that in Hamburg, yesterday, the people had revolvers with which they shot several Gestapo policemen—in Hamburg, where food riots were the beginning of the end in the last war. And I wonder if deep in his heart the German, including Herr Hitler, did not hear the distant tolling of the bells when their government declared war on the United States, which many of them know as the greatest productive nation on earth! It was our entrance into the last war which spelled finis for the German effort at Lebensraum and Deutschland uber alles! As was spoken tonight, Lidice and other towns are their own memorials, and will be remembered as willful atrocities. There are many ifs this time, however, and space enters into calculations. Japan in China could be a menace to Russia, and Germany in the Caucasus could obtain the necessary oil to wage a long war on the military front. And both are definite prospects.

How is one to argue against fatalism or try to convince one who proclaims himself a fatalist? The mother of my dentist, with who I had an interesting chat today, was in that pessimistic mood, which is often the precedent condition for a belief in fatalism, and it was hard to try and convince her that God is in His heaven and all is right with the world! Her son is going off to join the army, as a dentist, soon, which means that she must cope with many affairs in the conduct of his office, such as storing the furniture, etc. "The Moving Finger writes, and having writ moves on"—Omar Khayyam discovered long ago. But life has its freedom of will, and there is no chance. We have instead a choice of predetermined possibilities. I prefer to my stand on the premise that we can influence our actions, and sway the future. All history proclaims that fact, even Khayyam himself! Or would he say that it was predestined that he should write fatalistically concerning the soul of man? As I said in the beginning, the logic of fatalism makes it difficult to refute. But it needs refutation every day. Even Christ seemed to imply to Pilate that the latter had no choice in the matter, but rather was an instrument of destiny. And there is a definite element of fatalism in the whole of the passion story. But it is recorded that Christ set his face steadfastly toward Jerusalem!

Suggested Daily Spiritual Reading:
Proverbs 3:5
Mark 15:1-15

Further Reading Related to Diary Entry:
- *Candide* by Voltaire. Available from The Project Gutenberg at http://www.gutenberg.org/files/19942/19942-h/19942-h.htm [Accessed January 23, 2021].

- *The Moving Finger,* from the Rubaiyat of Omar Khayyam; a sermon by Reverend E.F. Dinsmore, Unity Church, Santa Barbara, CA. Available from Internet Archive at https://archive.org/stream/movingfingerofom00dinsrich/movingfingerofom00dinsrich_djvu.txt [Accessed January 23, 2021].

- *The Emperor's Codes: The Thrilling Story of the Allied Code Breakers Who Turned the Tide of World War II* by Michael Smith

- *A Higher Call: An Incredible True Story of Combat and Chivalry in the War-Torn Skies of World War II* by Adam Makos and Larry Alexander

♦ *Surviving Hitler: A Boy in the Nazi Death Camps* by Andrea Warren

Popular Books Published in 1942:
We Took to the Woods by Louise Dickinson Rich
Crazy Horse: The Strange Man of the Oglalas by Mari Sandoz

Popular Movies Released in 1942:
Reunion in France (Joan Crawford, John Wayne, Philip Dorn)
Sherlock Holmes and the Secret Weapon (Basil Rathbone, Nigel Bruce, Lionel Atwill)
The Talk of the Town (Cary Grant, Jean Arthur, Ronald Colman)

Vacation Diary - 1942 - Piermont, New Hampshire

(The Reverend uses the word "Dad" in this vacation diary to refer to his father-in-law—Ernie Brock. His own father, Solomon, was deceased [1932] by this time.)

Resume of First Vacation Week- 1942
August 2nd Sunday to August 9th

Highlights—Eagle perched on limb on bank of Connecticut (*River*). Visit to Bill Yetten with three-hour talk on minerals. Boat ride on Lake Morey with the children. Swimming at the river beach.

$19.75 (*Budget*) Sunday $2.00 Mon. $10.00 + $2.50 Wed. $4.50 Thurs. $0.75 (equals $19.75). Borrowed Fri. $1.50 dogwood plus Lake More Sat. Hayfork $2.00 (*total borrowed = $3.00*)

Sunday 2nd—nice ride up, no difficulty. Only about one-quarter traffic. Stopped at Massabesic and Franklin diner. When we arrived, Mother had lovely supper for us—chicken, coffee, veg., and ice cream.

Monday 3rd. Quiet restful day, as I recall. Ride to Bradford with children. Went to beach. Three dogs and three children my responsibility.

Tuesday 4th. Went up to see George and Bess (*his wife's aunt and uncle*) in afternoon. Stonewall visited.

Wednesday 5th. Got gas. Also haircut. Went up to Yetten's 2-6pm.

Thursday 6th. Road up the back road, route 10. Examined electric fence switches.

Friday 7th. Took children to Lake Morey this evening. Boating. With Dad a.m.

Saturday 8th. Haying for the first time in earnest. Broke hayfork. Saw Bald Eagle on river. Pure white on head and tail and big as a turkey. Do not know exact designation, but it was first time I had seen an eagle up in this country; very unusual and very patriotic. Also went up to see George and Bess again.

Haying time on the farm, circa 1940.

Sunday 9th. Raining. Went to creamery. Made plans this week to climb Mt. Moosilauke this next week. Chief difference is lack of traffic on roads. We have no extensive plans, as last year. Perhaps a short trip with Bill Yetten in search of minerals. Perhaps a game of golf with Stevenson, a little more haying on the lower meadow, but I for one appreciate the cool nights and the low pressure vacation system, where you just take each day as it comes. Yesterday morning, pitched hay back into the mow. Friday afternoon took Junior and Janet to the beach via the pool. Probably saw eagle then. Sonny was ill on Thursday, so he couldn't go swimming on Friday. We have had raspberries twice, also blackberry pie.

Worldwide News—Germans have advanced to Maikop oil fields, and towards Stalingrad. Nothing in North Africa. In India, Ghandi and all-India congress open Civil Disobedience Campaign. This morning it is announced that Ghandi and some of his followers are jailed. U.S. Has attacked Solomon Islands. Japs claim 22 ships sunk. Six saboteurs executed yesterday, and two given prison sentences. OWI (*U.S. Office of War Information*) reports our war effort below schedule in recent months. Systematic transfer of Dutch, three million, and others begun to Ukraine fields for cultivation. Eventful week for diagnosis. Watch the Caucusus and India particularly.

Brock Farm, circa 1942

Olive on the farm, circa 1942

Suggested Daily Spiritual Reading:
Romans 12:2
Ecclesiastes 3:1

Further Reading Related to Diary Entry:
- *Berlin Diary: The Journal of a Foreign Correspondent 1934-1941* by William L. Shirer

- *Radio Goes to War: The Cultural Politics of Propaganda during World War II* by Gerd Horten

- *Fighting in Ukraine: A Photographer at War* (Images of War series) by David Mitchelhill-Green

Popular Books Published in 1942:
    Now and on Earth by Jim Thompson
    The Works of Henry David Thoreau by Henry David Thoreau

Popular Movies Released in 1942:
    To the Shores of Tripoli (Maureen O'Hara, John Payne, Randolph Scott)
    Woman of the Year (Spencer Tracy, Katharine Hepburn, Reginald Owen)
    Wake Island (Brian Donlevy, Robert Preston)

Resume of Second Vacation Week-1942- Piermont, N.H.
August 10th - 15th

<u>Weather</u>: High humidity and good breeze

<u>Monday 10th</u> — Janet, Junior, and I went over to Oliverian looking for mineral specimens, also down to Haverhill-Piermont road. In the evening we went up to south Newbury (*VT*) and visited the old Drant place, built by one Moore and now owned by one Swift. There are inlaid floors, walls of stone, and all that sort of thing. Seven bedrooms, besides the servants' quarters—spooky. I liked the library best, with Plato, Schopenhauer, art catalogs (one Drant was an artist or art collector, it seems, and visited all the salons and auctions in Paris and New York)—fireplace, stuffed birds (excellent taxidermy), desk and easy chairs, and a very pleasant view, I assume, not having seen the same by reason of mist. Janet was haunted by the haunted house. I don't wonder. Years of labour and thousands of dollars spent on it, and for years an old lady occupied it alone, or nearly so, and slept with a revolver under her pillow. Seven bedrooms and no evidence children in the house, ever. Too austere for that!

<u>Tuesday 11th</u> — Back to the Oliverian with Janet today. Little boy found piece of graphite. Tonight Janet went home with Lloyd Bailey, her third cousin, jovial meat dealer. In Bradford, the rest of us had a cherry sundae (Mae remembers them from childhood, and they were just as good now as then).

<u>Wednesday 12th</u> — Haying, Flying Fortress went over river valley low. Army bomber. Bought beryl xl tonight, $0.50, size 6" x 6", from a Mrs. George Levoix of Haverhill. Brought to her porch by husband, from gravel pit somewhere. It is a broken xl, so split that the deep inner green of the xl is shown, while three faces of the hexagon are plainly seen. Biggest xl I have seen outside museums.

<u>Thursday 13th</u> — Hayed, went swimming. Blackout for state of Vermont, in which Piermont participated, 9:40-10:16 p.m.

<u>Friday 14th</u> — Albert, Janet, and I climbed Black Mt. In Benton this morning. Mountain is 2800 feet, and a good, sharp climb; comparable to Mt. Monadnock in southern New Hampshire. Many things of interest noted—ponies which followed us, a pair of Pintos; the pasture; the spruces; the rocks-mostly quartz and micaeous shist; and the tower on top—newly built by U.S.F.S. Harry Repair, ranger. He gave us luncheon of tea and crackers. Visited tilting, or balanced, rock. Mist over mountain. Rover went with us. Lovely blueberries on top. In evening, calibrated Mother Brock's radio (*Mae's mother*).

Saturday 15th -- Helped dig ditch in morning, then went swimming with children. We waded across the river, and Rover swam halfway across before I turned him back. First time he has done so, that is swim alone voluntarily over his depth. He then chased sticks. In evening rode to Newbury. Albert and I saw a woodchuck—front, grey, rear, dark brown—this evening on riverbank. Albert stalked him, but he got away at first shot! Hottest night we have had, thus far, this summer. Hard to sleep.

Mae made covers for studio couch this week.

Expenses: monbenson $4.00; cards $1.00; tire, gas $1.50; incidentals $1.00; beryl $1.50; incid. $0.38 = $9.38

Suggested Daily Spiritual Reading:
Psalm 118:24
Luke 11:1-4

Further Reading Related to Diary Entry:
- *Flying Fortress* by Edward Jablonski

- *Nature* by Ralph Waldo Emerson

Popular Books Published in 1942:
30 Days to a More Powerful Vocabulary by Wilfred Funk
The Life Divine by Sri Aurobindo

Popular Movies Released in 1942:
Thunderbirds (Gene Tierney, Preston Foster, John Sutton)
Sons of the Pioneers (Roy Rogers, George "Gabby" Hayes, Maris Wrixon)
Saboteur (Robert Cummings, Priscilla Lane, Norman Lloyd)

Resume of Third Vacation Week - 1942 - Piermont, N.H
August 16th - 23rd

Weather: humid and extremely warm during the day; cooler at night.

High points: digging ditch, haying, bowling, electric fence, Fred leaves.

Expenses: $5.00 borrowed and paid, $14.00 aside, $10.00 Dad—six spent and three for gas.

International situation: Marines take the Solomon Islands; Commando raid on Dieppe. B-17s on four raids—Rouen, Abbeville, etc; lost no planes, all returned. 11 B-17s met 25 Focke-Wulfs 190 — (147), newest plane of Germany, over channel and knocked out six without loss. Significant. In Russia, Germans drive to Krasnograd, within short distance, also, of Stalingrad; pushed beyond Maikop oil fields, threaten Caucasus.
Report of German committee claims Hitler has 15,000 planes capable of bombing East Coast—only lacks gas. Time will tell.

Monday 17th — Saw Lloyd butcher three hogs. Mae stayed at Aunt Bess'.

Tuesday 18th — Dug ditch to pump house, laid pipe—water clearer, better force. Enjoyed the digging, but not the filling in. In fact, we haven't thrown it all back yet. Cherry sundaes tonight. Sundaes on Tuesdays, one of the highlights of the week. Grandpa, Mother, Albert, Mae, Janet, and YT (YoursTruly).

Wednesday 19th — Went to Woodsville in morning, visiting Geraldine. Last of hay, afternoon.

Thursday 20th — Bowling this afternoon, at Bradford. Janet 63 plus 67. YT (yours truly) 96 plus 82. Fred and Albert and Dad did well. Ride to Aunt Bess' tonight.

Friday 21st — Went hunting for lost cow this morning, clear to back pasture, with Mae and Rover. Showed up herself tonight. Saw combine work on oats; brought up oats in truck. Borrowed bags from Fred Blaisdell. Swimming with Janet at Anderson's pool (*Janet remembers this as a pit that was dug and filled with water*).

Saturday 22nd — Put up 25 poles with Fred for electric fence, insulators. Afternoon, went to auction in Fairlee, VT. Finished fence and assembled Shoxtock. Worked fine—I got shocked 8 times! The cows none. Joyce came tonight (*Joyce is Mae's brother's, Carl's, daughter*). Fred finished work here.

<u>Sunday 23rd</u> — Cleaned out stables with the girls. Put Fred and his dog together. Helped Elmer fix a tire. Lovely day; cloudy, warm, yet good breeze. Dad brought home two chickens for dinner. Look forward to pleasant week. Mother has had some fine meals—blackberries in abundance, apple pies, good steaks, corn, new potatoes, beans, excellent coffee, plenty of milk and cream.

This is the day the Lord hath made; let us rejoice and be glad in it. (*Psalm 118:24*)

From the rising of the sun, until the going down of the same, the Lord's name is to be praised. And "...He will shew forth his loving kindness every morning, and his faithfulness every night." (*Psalm 92:2, paraphrased*)

"And Spirit with Spirit shall meet; Closer is He than breathing, and nearer than hands and feet." (*From "The Higher Pantheism" by Alfred Lord Tennyson*) Selah.

Suggested Daily Spiritual Reading:
Psalm 118:29
Luke 11:9-11

Further Reading Related to Diary Entry:
- *Mini Farming: Self-Sufficiency on 1/4 Acre* by Brett L. Markham

- *You Can Farm: The Entrepreneur's Guide to Start & Succeed in a Farming Enterprise* by Joel Salatin

- *Islands of Destiny: The Solomons Campaign and the Eclipse of the Rising Sun* by John Prados

Popular Books Published in 1942:
The Fall of Paris by Ilya Ehrenburg
Physics and Philosophy by James Hopwood Jeans

Popular Movies Released in 1942:
Once Upon a Honeymoon (Cary Grant, Ginger Rogers, Walter Slezak)
Maisie Gets Her Man (Ann Sothern, Red Skelton, Allen Jenkins)
The Major and the Minor (Ginger Rogers, Ray Milland, Rita Johnson)

Cows on the farm—Piermont, New Hampshire (circa 1942)

Resume of Fourth Vacation Week - 1942 - Piermont, N.H.
August 24th - 30th

Weather: Sunny and warm; cumulus clouds approaching

Predominant Mood: Quietness—cattle munching cuds under trees; humming of thousands of insects; little wind stirring; all people occupied. Green fields stretching to nearby horizons, the dooryard deserted for the nonce. "Be still and know that I am God." (*Psalm 46:10*) Sunday is different from other mornings, somehow. There is an aura of repose coupled with expectancy. How Rover will miss his comparative freedom. He and Albert are at the rabbit hutch. Mother is mixing something for dinner. The telephone rings—it is a 24 party line, so no matter. Patient Lucy blooms with cerise in washtub on stump in yard. The elms and maples loom thirty feet into the blue sky.

International Front: Stalingrad still holds; Milne Bay battle in New Guinea takes place with fighting still going on; Solomons now safely in hands of Marines; lull in Libya; Flying Fortresses yesterday completed eighth trip without a loss to themselves. Chinese recaptured Chusien airport with its 30 miles of runways, this week. British have bombed various points in occupied Europe.

Monday the 24th. Just a day on the farm. $1.00 spent.

Tuesday 25th — Albert with Lloyd Bailey. Janet at Aunt Bess'. Eclipse of moon 10:00 to 1:30 a.m. Clear and inspiring.

Wednesday 26th — We climbed Moosilauke today, our family and Joyce. Clear cool day, no wind to speak of on top. Saw Mt. Green in Maine; Presidentials, incl. Washington; the Green Mountains in Vermont; and the Adirondacks. Found Epidote xl on top. Found beryl xls in Glencliff. $2.50 High points—vegetable soup, wagon and horses on carriage road.

Thursday 27th — $0.25 gas, $2.00—children and I went swimming in Lake Morey tonight. Fun on diving board and slide. Children went to Indian pond pasture today, brought back first calf. Bull calf named Bobby.

Friday 28th — Bess and George down. Fixed wheelbarrow. $1.50 liniment, t.p., etc.

Saturday 29th — Searched lower pasture for black cow, which calved last night. Found her and calf, brown and white, Bessy, near house. Junior and I brought her to barn on improvised stretcher. Janet and Joyce visited friends in Haverhill today. $0.20 Janet $0.30 tonight, ride to Conicut and Bradford.

Fred left us last Sunday. Paul Hackett came over on Friday and secured hired man's job. He is to come Sunday night. 14 years old, not born when Pete Hackett began work here. Got in a load of edgings this afternoon from hurricane timber.

Sunday 30th — Look forward to nice Sunday dinner. Then will take the children to Lake Morey for boat ride and swim. Would like to go to Groton (*VT*), but distance is far; and Bill Boomhower's bumboats may not be available. Besides, "you can't go home again". There is only a melancholy satisfaction in revisiting old scenes; tout casse; tout passe; comme disent les Francaises. Autres temps, sutre mores. Better go to the new scenes, and gain new experiences.

The children are now playing "three old cat in yard".

SUNDAY AFTERNOON—CANOE RIDE LAKE MOREY WITH MAE AND ALBERT.

Signing off until vacation is over.

Suggested Daily Spiritual Reading:
Psalm 46:10
Psalm 23:2

Further Reading Related to Diary Entry:
- *Casey & the Flying Fortress* by Mark Farina

- *Deadly Sky: The American Combat Airman in World War II* by John C. McManus

- *Turning Point: The Battle for Milne Bay 1942 - Japan's first land defeat in World War II* by Michael Veitch

Popular Books Published in 1942:
The Screwtape Letters by C.S. Lewis
The Theory of Capitalist Development by Paul M. Sweezy

Popular Movies Released in 1942:
Life Begins at Eight-Thirty (Ida Lupino, Monty Woolley, Cornel Wilde)
Joe Smith, American (Robert Young, Marsha Hunt)
Eagle Squadron (Robert Stack, Diana Barrymore)

Resume of Fifth, and Final, Vacation Week-1942- Piermont, N.H
August 31st - September 3rd

<u>Monday August 31st</u>. Rode to Groton with Aunt Bess and George. The old coal kilns, which my grandfather operated, still stands, unaffected by time and the river of events, as do the stones along the borders of his fields. All else seems changed, and there is little in Groton to attract me now. Even the cemetery is uncared for, the caretaker having gone the way of all flesh, and joined his fellow dead. It just proves that "you can't go home again". But it was a lovely ride even though the mountains were hazy.

Went to North Haverhill for a load of shavings this afternoon with Dad, Paul Hackett-the new hired "man", Albert, and Mae. Went roller skating this evening with the children at Piermont town hall. Janet and Junior both did splendidly.

Expenses: $2.25 gas, $0.50 haircut, $0.65 skating, $2.00 glasses, $1.60 incidentals.

<u>Tuesday September 1st</u>.

```
"A haze on the far horizon,
  The infinite, tender sky—
The ripe rich tint of the cornfields,
  And the wild geese sailing high…"
```

(*From "Each in His Own Tongue" by William Herbert Carruth*)

Checked fence this morning; cows out last night—three times this week. Unloaded oats this afternoon. Took nice swim with children and Paul, this evening. Paul reminds me more and more of Pete, of whom I thought a great deal. Rode to Bradford with children and Dad for ice cream—$0.25 + $0.40. Mae and Dad saw flock of 25 wild geese headed south tonight, going between house and barn. Cold winter ahead?

<u>Wednesday September 2nd</u>:
Cows out again. Dad, Paul, and I extended electric fence to river, putting in a dozen poles. I tested it when finished. It worked all right! This was after dinner, and the cows did not get out tonight. This morning Mae, Mother (*Olive, Mae's mother*), and I rode to Wells River and Woodsville. Nice quiet ride—children with Dad on milk route. Tonight, swim, horseshoes, then to Bradford. $1.30 spent.

<u>Thursday September 3rd</u>:
Came home today, leaving at 9:15 a.m. Raining in Piermont, cleared in

Rumney. At dinner in Concord. Stopped at Massabesic. Went to Natick for supper. Home at 10 p.m., after 200-mile trip, without trouble of any kind. Rover a good boy. Things unpacked. Refreshed for fall work. One of the best vacations we have known, even if there were problems. Left with $40.00, returned with $100.

From all perils and dangers, O' Lord, though hast preserved us; with farm and field and friends thou hast refreshed our wearied souls; we give thee hearty thanks; thine be the honor and the power and the glory forever and ever. Amen. And so to bed.

Suggested Daily Spiritual Reading:
John 13:34
Jeremiah 4:23-27

Further Reading Related to Diary Entry:
- *Cruising New Hampshire History: A Guide to New Hampshire's Roadside Historical Markers* by Michael A Bruno

- *Two shakes of a lamb's tail, or, Rambles and bygones and from "Long Look Farm", New Hampshire* by Marjorie Whalen Smith

Popular Books Published in 1942:
The Wisdom of China and India by Lin Yutang (Editor)
Can Capitalism Survive? Creative Destruction and the Future of the Global Economy by Joseph Schumpeter

Popular Movies Released in 1942:
Dr. Kildare's Victory (Lew Ayres, Ann Ayars, Lionel Barrymore)
The Dawn Express (Michael Whalen, Anne Nagel, Constance Worth)
The Courtship of Andy Hardy (Lewis Stone, Mickey Rooney, Cecilia Parker, Donna Reed)

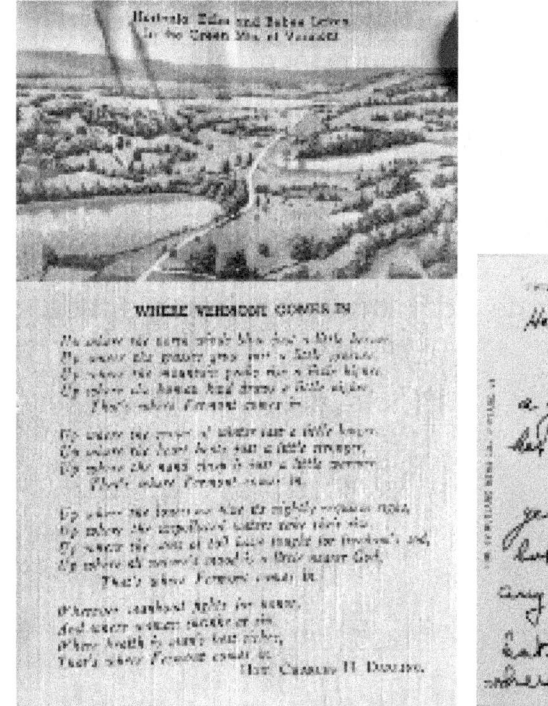
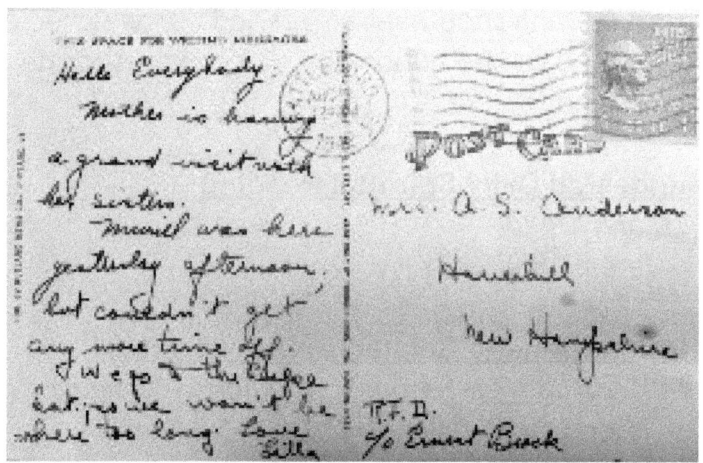

(Postcard, front and back, from the Reverend's sister Lilla. Postmarked Aug 12, 7:30 am, 1942)

Back Row: Olive ("Mother Brock"—Mae's mother and Reverend's mother-in-law), Aunt Bess (Ernie's sister-Mae's aunt), Carl (Mae's brother), Millie with cigar (Carl's wife), George (Bess' husband), Ernie with hat on stick ("Father Brock", Mae's father). Front row: Carl Jr. (Carl and Millie's son), Janet, Joyce (Carl' and Millie's daughter), Albert "Junior", and the Reverend. Circa 1937.

October 1st, 1942
Lynn, Mass.

I haven't the patience, nor narrative ability, to tell the story as Elmer told it, but unless I do tell it with the potential immorality of written words, and invest it with glamour of fiction, the world will be the loser thereby. Elmer needs to be remembered for the way he told that story. I understand from his contemporaries that he is a colossal liar, but he lies so authentically, and with straightforwardness so deceiving, that I will let you decide whether the story is true or not.

When it was rumored that Bacon wrote Shakespear (One of the 260 misspellings, by the way), someone remarked that if he hadn't, he had missed the greatest opportunity in his life.

Elmer's story has the rustle of angel's wings; it deserves to be true. I forgot to tell you that Elmer is, or was, at the time, a hired hand on the farm in the North country. He drove into the field one afternoon with a dump cart load of rubbish destined for the upper end of the field, where a gully eroded by the river needed considerable fill. The team of horses was as solid and dependable as Elmer; what an auctioneer would describe as "sound and true". I saw him from the cow stable and hailed him just beyond the bars. I wanted to ask him a question. He whooped the horses, spat out a quantity of tobacco juice, tilted back the shape-less brim of his hat, squinted sharply through his spectacles, and relaxed.

We chatted awhile, he telling me, among other things, that he was tired of his boss interfering with his work and was quitting. "He don't feed his cattle enough," he remarked. "Why last winter he came into the stable after I had fed corn fodder to the cattle, and began pulling out the corn and hay. It made me mad. I threw the fork on the floor and told him if he was going to start cheating the cows, he could do the feeding himself. I didn't feed 'em another forkful all winter." Here, Elmer worked himself into a mood of virtuousness that prefaced the real story he had to tell. "It's a shame to starve cattle, not only that, it's uneconomical. The cows don't give down so well, and what you save in feed you lose in milk." I agreed with him, and we talked generalities for a few minutes, then the talk switched to lumbering.

Elmer is a stout fellow. You wouldn't think so to look at him, but there's plenty of muscle there, beneath a modest exterior. Then the story came out, how one Saturday night found him in town, from the lumber camp, with a street carnival going on, and all the boys getting a little convivial with the drinks and all. He was on the main street where the carnival was, minding his own business, when he heard a little argument. A stocky chap, who had imbibed just enough to make him bellicose, was calling an old man all kinds of names. The old man replied, somewhat bitterly, "If I was ten years younger, you wouldn't get away with this."

The stocky gent cursed him some more, and Elmer, through some atavistic Lochinvar instinct, found himself propelled into the midst of the argument. "You don't have to stand for it," he told the old man. "If this man wasn't a bully and a coward he wouldn't say such things." Whereupon the troublemaker challenged Elmer to a fist fight. "I don't want that," Elmer told him, "I haven't got the money to pay a fine." The stocky chap cursed him. Elmer said, money or not, he wouldn't take that, and they adjourned to the other side of the street to have it out. "Now, put up or shut up," Elmer demanded. "If you want a fight, you can have it. You started it, now begin." And the man advanced, thinking he would knock him down with one blow. Elmer said, with a quiet seriousness that belied its dramatic quality, "I blocked his blow with one hand, and with the other, I socked him hard in the nose." He went down. When he arose, his nose was bleeding, but he came on. Elmer said, "I socked him again, and hit him in the jaw. I let him have it over the eye." He stayed down that time, and cried, "enough". The bully got to his feet slowly, and staggered down the street, looking for a doctor. The crowd dispersed. Elmer wandered around, taking in the sights. Some time later, the policeman, who was stationed down the street, and had seen the whole thing, came up to Elmer. "You were kinder rough with that guy, weren't you?" he queried. "I don't know, was I?" Elmer parried. "Well," remarked the policeman, "you gave him a cut over the eye, broke his nose, and fractured his jaw. But I don't blame you for what you did. He had it coming to him." Sic semper tyrannis!

Suggested Daily Spiritual Reading:
Matthew 5:38-39
Psalm 37:11

Further Reading Related to Diary Entry:
- *Shakespeare Beyond Doubt?: Exposing an Industry in Denial* by John M. Shahan (Author), Alexander Waugh (Editor)

- *Bacon, Shakespeare and the Rosicrucians* by William Francis C. Wigston

Popular Books Published in 1942:
The Puritan Family: Religion and Domestic Relations in Seventeenth-Century New England by Edmund S. Morgan
I Saw The Fall Of The Philippines by Carlos P. Romulo

Popular Movies Released in 1942:
Cairo (Jeanette MacDonald, Robert Young, Lionel Atwill)
The Bugle Sounds (Wallace Beery, Marjorie Main, Donna Reed)
The Big Street (Henry Fonda, Lucille Ball, Barton MacLane)

November 24, 1942
Janus on the War

History is always on the march. When these words are read again, they will be dated, and outdated. A factual statement is in order, however, in order to get an interpretation. By divorcing tremendous truths from their context they are made to live forever. The Lord is my shepherd is a simple statement of faith that can be made in any century. The tremendous truth that we wrest from the context of today's events is that the road to victory is rough but certain. But first the events—

As of this date, Russians have forced the Germans back on a fifty mile stretch north and south of Stalingrad, with casualties and prisoners totaling 50,000. They have captured or destroyed large quantities of planes, tanks, guns, and in one place have recrossed the Don River. This encircling maneuver threatens not only the Germans in Stalingrad, but also the German army in the Caucasus. Of course this diversionary movement may be limited in scope, but it underlines the failure of Hitler to capture Stalingrad, not to mention his failure to storm the passes of the Caucasian Mountains, which lead to the oil fields near Baku. This was his 1942 objective and the sands of time are running against him.

Yesterday it was announced that Dakar—strategic African base—had swung to the Allied nations at the behest of Admiral Darlan. In North Africa, the great American and British invasion the first of the month, consisting as it did of 500 transports and 350 warships, captured Algeria and Morocco with light casualties, and is sweeping on to Tunis and Bizerte. Romel's Afrika Korps is back at El Agheila, hotly pursued by General Montgomery's Eighth British Army. He may elect to stand at that point or retreat to Tripoli. In any case, the back of the German offensive in North Africa is broken, and cannot be repaired. Hitler was caught flatfooted.

Genoa and Turin, in Italy, have been incessantly pounded by the Royal Air Force. Genoa is out as a supply base for months to come. The Italians stand in doorways with umbrellas to protect them from shrapnel. Their dream of a Roman Empire is crumbling fast. German "tourists" are infiltrating the country. Reservists of the German army, of course. The United (not Allied) Nations will probably spend the winter cleaning up North Africa. Next year will witness an invasion of Europe, perhaps through the Balkans, possibly through Italy, possibly through France; perhaps simultaneously at many points. A long period of preparation lies ahead, but when dictatorships begin to lose they crack fast. In the last war, Germany sued for an armistice just one month after the peak of success for her.

In New Guinea, only Buna remains to the Japs. They are being attacked there constantly. On Guadalcanal, the situation is good—half of the 1500 Japs on the Island having been cleaned up. The recently naval battle of Guadalcanal sent 28 Jap warships to the bottom, including 8 transports.

The four turning points of the war to me have been—1st, Sept. 15, 1940, when 185 German planes were shot down over England, the RAF losing only 30 planes and but 15 pilots; 2nd, the Battle of Midway, which turned back a large Japanese fleet, and destroyed her hopes of attacking Hawaii again; 3rd, the defense of Stalingrad, which still holds out after 90 days, though part of the city was occupied; 4th, the utter rout of Rommel in Africa by the 8th British Army. September 15th, 1940, removed the threat of invasion of England; Midway told the Japs that the day of reckoning was coming; Stalingrad spelled no oil to Hitler; and Montgomery deprived the Germans of easy victory in Africa and Asia. The nations which hold out longest usually win a war. The imponderables, such as the human spirit, implemented with weapons, must be counted. Then too, it is necessary to be on God's side!

Suggested Daily Spiritual Reading:
Psalm 23
Leviticus 26:6

Further Reading Related to Diary Entry:
- *Patton, Montgomery, Rommel: Masters of War* by Terry Brighton

- *The Forgotten 500: The Untold Story of the Men Who Risked All for the Greatest Rescue Mission of World War II* by Gregory A. Freeman

- *Pacific Crucible: War at Sea in the Pacific, 1941-1942* by Ian W. Toll

- *Operation Drumbeat: The Dramatic True Story of Germany's First U-Boat Attacks Along the American Coast in World War II* by Michael Gannon

- *The 1942 Sears Christmas Book* (Paperback – Facsimile, September 18, 2019) by Sears Roebuck and Co.

Popular Books Published in 1942:
Admiral of the Ocean Sea: A Life of Christopher Columbus by Samuel Eliot Morison
Put Out More Flags by Evelyn Waugh

Popular Movies Released in 1942:
    Cadet Girl (Carole Landis, George Montgomery)
    Crossroads (William Powell, Hedy Lamarr, Claire Trevor)
    The Falcon's Brother (George Sanders, Tom Conway, Jane Randolph)

1943

Friday Night, January 1, 1943

(The Reverend is age 41 years old, his wife, Mae is 39 or 40 years old, Albert junior is 14 years old, and Janet is 12 years old.)

1942 has been the scene of a great and significant change in the international relationship. Midway Island, Stalingrad, and Romel's Retreat, are the high points in a year crowded with suspense, and including the occupation of North Africa by a joint armada of British and American troops, on 850 ships. The greatest change of all, however, is one of attitude. We are more confident of the ultimate outcome now that we can see Hitler on the defensive, at least on his most offensive points. Stalingrad, as has been pointed out, has great strategical possibilities, and the capture of it by Hitler's divisions, this fall or winter, would have guarded his flank for a drive into the Caucasus.

As it is, Stalingrad, still in Russian hands, is a definite threat to the troops now south of the Don (*River*), and it is intimated that the Nazis toward Stalingrad, and in that city, are hemmed in by two iron rings of troops. At any rate, Hitler failed intuitively, or otherwise, to scale the Caucassian Mountains, and without oil his panzers and planes are stymied. Meanwhile, the strength of the Allies is growing. Already our production of planes exceeds that of the Axis, and the preponderance makes itself felt on the airways of the world. Things are "shaping up", and things forecastable look promising. The blood, sweat, toil, and tears are bearing fruit. "He that goeth forth and weepeth, bearing precious seeds, shall doubtless come again, bringing his sheaves with him" (*Psalm 126:6*). There is a justice, a balance in the world. Be not deceived, God is not mocked. The mills of God grind slowly, but they grind exceedingly small!

On the home front, we are now without butter and bananas. Sugar and oil are rationed, and other commodities are rationed by the shopkeepers on a basis of supply. Coffee, too, is rationed, 1/2 lb per person, over 15, per week, but we still have four cups a day at that. Cars are obstreperous from a war standpoint, with many restrictions. But we still drive them, and thus far my tires have held out, I get enough gasoline, and have registered it for the coming year.

My wife's folks have sold their livestock on the farm. Dad Brock (Ernie) is working in an airplane factory in Hartford, Conn., and Mother Brock is staying for the winter in the home of a friend at Newbury, Vermont.

We have been transferred from the Lynn Church to the Methodist Church in

Hudson (*MA*). The Church, built in 1912, is thoroughly modern, with Elizabethan exterior, and oak paneling with episcopal chancel in the interior. White-robed senior and junior choirs, fine pulpit, cross and candles and lovely flowers, with a service flag in the background, make an excellent setting for a minister. Moreover, we have a unified service were Worship and Education walk hand in hand. Children and parents come at the same hour. Hudson is a busy town of 7,000, with several defense plants. It is in the country, and it is good to be out of the dim-out zone, for one thing, and near farms for another. Like Wordsworth, I am still a lover of the woods and fields, and desire to live from day to day in natural piety.

The parsonage has twelve rooms, with garage at hand, which same is nearly as big as our bungalow in Lynn. I have a fine, ample study, and good equipment. The house is heated by steam, and we have a fireplace as well. The people are well educated and well mannered, and I am sure I am going to enjoy our pastorate here. Furthermore, we are within 20 miles of our old friends in Cochituate, Lincoln, and Natick. We look forward to a happier year than we have had for many a calendar span. The salary is larger, too, which does not detract from the enhanced situation. There is more relative freedom on every hand, and it is good to be beyond the dim-out area with its multiple regulations. I have been invited to join the auxiliary police force here.

"A day in thy courts is better than a thousand. I would rather be a doorkeeper in the temple of my God than to dwell in the tents of wickedness." (Psalm 84:10) How lovely is thy dwelling-place!

Suggested Daily Spiritual Reading:
Job 37:23
Ecclesiastes 5:8

Further Reading Related to Diary Entry:
- *Grandma's Wartime Kitchen: World War II and the Way We Cooked* by Joanne Lamb Hayes and Jean Anderson

- *Grandma's Wartime Baking Book: World War II and the Way We Baked* by Joanne Lamb Hayes

- *Eggs or Anarchy: The remarkable story of the man tasked with the impossible: to feed a nation at war* by William Sitwell

- *The Winter Army: The World War II Odyssey of the 10th Mountain Division, America's Elite Alpine Warriors* by Maurice Isserman

Popular Books Published in 1943:
   Most Popular Books Published In 1943. Available from Goodreads.com at https://www.goodreads.com/book/popular_by_date/1943 [Accessed January 23, 2021].

Popular Movies Released in 1943:
   Action in the North Atlantic (Humphrey Bogart, Raymond Massey, Alan Hale Sr.)
   Edge of Darkness (Errol Flynn, Ann Sheridan, Walter Huston)
   The Gang's All Here (Alice Faye, Carmen Miranda)

April 25, 1943
Clouds

Clouds have a terminology of their own. Their names, which I quote from memory are as follows, depending upon their altitude.

Stratus—low-lying, level clouds. Include "scud" before a wind.
Nimbostratus—flat clouds with buildup of cloud at the end.
Cumulus—accumulation of cloud material. Several variations.
Stratocumulus—clouds twisted into strands like a rope. Or rather the strands of cloud material are twisted into the formation.
Nimbocumulus—the thunderhead, beautiful in the sun.
Fractocumulus—the broken accumulations of clouds.
Altocumulus—which remind one of a flock of sheep grazing.
Cirrocumulus—wavy, undulating clouds, herringbone pattern.
Altostratus and **Cirrostratus**—which seem to differ only in their height, the latter being higher by far.
Cirrus—frozen particles of ice, like feathers, 7,000 ft. Plus.

As can be readily seen in this classification, there are but three types of clouds, with variations thereof—**Stratus**, meaning flat or level; **Cumulus**, meaning a gathering or accumulation of cloud material; and **Cirrus**, meaning feather. Nimbus, of course, is Latin for cloud. It is interesting for me, since I am just beginning to try and classify the patterns. Some are easy, like the cirrus or cirrocumulus, and even stratocumulus, but some are confusing as they seem to be a combination of several types. I imagine this to be so.

The cumulonimbus is of course the most majestic—great thunderheads outlined in the sun, which precede a thunderstorm. There is fog, too, which is a cloud of sorts. I cannot understand why the cirrus formations should remain aloft if they are ice. It would seem to me they would be heavier than air, and would, therefore, fall, but perhaps they are diffused enough to be held up by high winds.

I could go on and develop the theme that clouds are vital to our life here on earth, as indeed they are, distributing the water from lakes and oceans inland, to the desert areas, but let us conclude with the observation that clouds have their aesthetic uses too. As the poet writes:

```
"I wandered lonely as a cloud
That floats on high o'er hill and vale…"
```
(From "I Wandered as Lonely as a Cloud" by William Wordsworth)

Or again:

> "Be still sad heart, and cease repining,
> Behind the clouds is the sun still shining…"
> *(From "The Rainy Day" by Henry Wadsworth Longfellow)*

Today is Easter Sunday, and a lovely one it has been, with beautiful flowers, and music with two choirs, and I acquitted myself creditably in the pulpit (so I am told) with a sermon on John 20:27, about Doubting Thomas, "Be not faithless, but believing." There were about three hundred present, including Mother Brock, who is visiting us. We had a sunrise service on Pope's Hill at six this morning, at the foot of the cross. Twenty-three young persons present.

On the battlefront, things are quiet in the Pacific and at the Russian fronts; in North Africa Rommel and Arnim's forces are confined to a relatively small area of Tunisia with about 10 divisions. Opposing are the allied forces with about 25 divisions and a definite superiority in airplanes. Last night I saw, at the Hudson theater, a showing of pictures taken by the U.S. Signal Corps in North Africa, in technicolor, of the unloading of tanks, their progress toward Tunis, air raids on Bone by the Germans, a tank battle at Tebourba, which the Americans and British won, a German raid on one of our airfields; the progress of the tanks over the foothills of the Atlas Mountains, the captured Italian and German prisoners, a destroyed Red Cross train; parade of the French Foreign Legion in Algiers, and other colorful shots of life in North Africa. Raids on Hitler's European fortress have been heavy lately, and much vital war material has been destroyed.

And the last enemy to be destroyed is death—the death of the soul. We must have faith, for this is the victory that overcometh the world.

Suggested Daily Spiritual Reading:
John 20:27
John 11:25

Further Reading Related to Diary Entry:
- *The Cloudspotter's Guide: The Science, History, and Culture of Clouds* by Gavin Pretor-Pinney

- *The Book of Clouds* by John A. Day

- *The Cloud Collector's Handbook* by Gavin Pretor-Pinney

- *National Audubon Society Field Guide to Weather: North America* (National Audubon Society Field Guides) by David Ludlum

- *Peterson First Guide to Clouds and Weather* by Vincent J. Schaefer

Popular Books Published in 1943:
    Being and Nothingness by Jean-Paul Sartre
    Johnny Tremain by Esther Forbes

Popular Movies Released in 1943:
    Above Suspicion (Joan Crawford, Fred MacMurray, Conrad Veidt)
    Five Graves to Cairo (Franchot Tone, Anne Baxter)
    Girl Crazy (Judy Garland and Mickey Rooney)

June 21, 1943
MALAISE

This is the beginning of summer, if memory serves me right. This is the day the Lord hath made, and I ought to rejoice in it, but I have cramps in my stomach, and in spite of the fact that it is my day off, and I have no engagements, I find no pleasure in it.

Malaise—ill at ease—describes it pretty well. The day seems like a chocolate which is tasteless to the palate.

My garden is coming well, and I have worked hard this morning cutting out sod to enlarge it. So far so good. We had a nice shower last night, which did the garden a lot of good. And the children and Mae gave me a nice box of chocolates last night for Father's Day. The card enclosed in the box pleased me even more—it read, "To the grandest dad in the world." Of course, that is gross flattery, but it made me feel fine nevertheless. It is the first day of summer, and the sun is shining, and the world is young. Why then malaise?

I have been playing chess with the doctor, and he won four games straight now, and I dislike that. I was winning two out of three or four for a time. What makes the discomfiture more complete is the fact that I have been playing over some of the championship matches in comparative chess. Steinetz, Lasker, Capablanca, and Morphy could really play. Also Alekhine. I have played a game from the 16th century—that of Count Giulio Polerio; one in the 17th, that of Philidor, the first great positional player; one in the 18th, M'Donnell, the son of a Belfast physician, vs. Bourdonaiss, wherein M'Donnell sacrifices his queen and wins with a knight's game; and Morphy versus the Duke of Brunswick, where brilliance predominates. Also, some of the hypermodern games. The doctor is good, and perhaps in trying to imitate the masters I have left myself open too much. I think that is the answer. Chaque a son chess! Says Emerson, "Never imitate. Your own qualities you can present with a whole life's concentration, but of the talents of another you have only an extemporaneous half-possession." (*Paraphrased from Ralph Waldo Emerson's essay "Self-Reliance"*) Henceforth, I think I'll stick to my own style of play. I like the Ruy Lopez (*chess opening*) pretty well and am fair at it, but the Indian defense doesn't go so well.

My garden has good soil, but is shady in the mornings. The beans, corn, and pumpkins are doing fine; but I have had to plant endive and spinach twice, and still it isn't doing so well. I have 34 tomato plants, which are coming along well. And peas, squash, and of course lettuce and spinach. Also carrots and swiss chard. As Robert Frost says, "Something must be left to God," and so I'll let him look after the growing things.

Took the Sunday school children to Little Pond, Saturday, where they had a good time swimming and playing games. Also, took my Boy Scouts to Curtis' Pond on Friday night—they also enjoyed themselves greatly. Mother (Brock) who has been staying with us a couple weeks since her return from Hartford, Conn., went back to New Hampshire this morning. Albert (*fourteen*) is hard at work on the soda fountain at Toohey's Drug Store, and Janet (*twelve*) is planning to attend the movies.

My hobbies, stamp collecting, shortwave, and minerals are static and quiescent at present. I have been putting my extra time in the garden, as that will yield us food in the way of green vegetables. And they taste good already. We have had lettuce and radishes nearly every day. My beets didn't come up, so I have planted them all over again too. The second crop hasn't shown up yet, but I have hopes.

One of our parishioners just called to say she will bring us a box of strawberries tonight. I am very fond of berries, and well remember eating my weight in berries from my grandfather's garden. I would like to step into his patch today, and pick and eat as many as I liked, with lots of cream of course. Man does not live by vegetables alone, but they do add a lot of the joie de vivre. Now that I have worked myself into a better mood, I will resume my gardening with pleasure and resignation, and perhaps chess will improve also.

Suggested Daily Spiritual Reading:
Genesis 2:8
Ecclesiastes 7:3

Further Reading Related to Diary Entry:
- *Bobby Fischer Teaches Chess* by Bobby Fischer, with Stuart Margulies, Don Mosenfelder

- *Logical Chess: Move By Move: Every Move Explained* by Irving Chernev

- *Chess: 5334 Problems, Combinations and Games* by László Polgár and Bruce Pandolfini

- *How to Reassess Your Chess: Chess Mastery Through Chess Imbalances* by Jeremy Silman

Popular Books Published in 1943:

The Greatest Gift by Philip Van Doren Stern
The Human Comedy by William Saroyan

Popular Movies Released in 1943:
This is the Army (George Murphy, Joan Leslie, Ronald Reagan)
Destination Tokyo (Cary Grant, John Garfield)
Watch on the Rhine (Bette Davis, Paul Lukas, Geraldine Fitzgerald)

July 27, 1943
The First Break

"He hath put down the mighty from their seats, and exalted them of low degree." (*Luke 1:52*)

It was announced Sunday night, by the Italian Broadcasting System, that the King Victor Immanuel III had accepted the resignation of Benito Mussolini as prime Minister and secretary of the Fascist party. "Ill health" is ascribed by the German press as the cause.

Every event lies in a chain of causation, both according to Buddhist doctrine and modern science.

Every institution is but the lengthened shadow of a man, according to Emerson.

God became weary with Napoleon, according to Victor Hugo.

The morning paper quotes dispatches from Bern to the effect that crowds demonstrated for peace in Milan, Rome, Naples, Bologna, Turin—all bombed heavily by the allied nations—and celebrated the overthrow of fascism. Talks are currently underway in the Vatican, leading to peace overtures. Berlin propagandists are stunned. It is the end of the beginning, at least as Churchill declaimed. I for one am delighted, for it will mean the saving of countless lives from needles slaughter. Would that Hitler seeing the handwriting on the wall might partially expiate his crimes by abdicating, and so save countless German lives.

The beginning of the beginning lay at Midway, El Alemain and Stalingrad—names that must live in history as the three turning points in the struggles between the rising fascisms and the decadent democracies. China has withstood the might of Japan for six years. Russia, for two and a half years, has withstood the whole weight of the German wehrmacht, and still holds like a rock, having regained ground lost in the summer offensive of 1943, and has Orel nearly surrounded at the present writing. The pattern of victory is on the table. Our superiority of production has outdistanced the Axis, and today our planes are masters of the air, or at least have a marked superiority. It remains for us to rollup the map in the Pacific, and liberate the Dutch East Indies, China, and to restore independence to the Philippines in 1945, according to our pledged word, but the days of real anxiety have passed, I believe.

Post-war problems will be great, but trifling compared to those days of our unpreparedness in 1939 and 1940, when only England seemed to stand between us and the domination of the world by the Axis. If Russia had fallen in three months, as was expected, if Rommel had taken the Middle East, and later Africa;

if Japan became entrenched in Australia, and if England went down because of the U-boats, then our isolation would have availed us nothing. Then only the dead would remain free—then the dark ages of barbarism and cruelty and ignorance would be ours—then the octopus grip of a heinous imperialism might have imperiled liberty for a thousand years in very truth. Thank God that our generation has been spared that terrible alternative! For this was a revolution against religion as well as against free governments. The minds, bodies, and souls of men would have been enslaved. We have passed through terrible trials and sloughs of despond, and the dawn of a new day is at hand, when even the Germans and Japanese can look for peace and righteousness in the earth.

May the new world be ordered in such a way that never again can a Mussolini or Hitler lay hold upon the gullibilities of a frustrated people to enchain it to work their collective wills. May there be no master races—for God is no respecter of persons, and he has made of one blood all nations of men to dwell upon the face of the earth.

> "Serene they live, nor note with pining,
> All the fever of some differing soul."
> (*Paraphrased from Matthew Arnold's poem "Self-Dependence"*
> <u>*The actual quote is*</u>:
> "For self-poised they live, nor pine with noting
> All the fever of some differing soul.")

Suggested Daily Spiritual Reading:
Luke 1:52
Deuteronomy 4:19
Numbers 6:26

Further Reading Related to Diary Entry:
- <u>*The Pope and Mussolini: The Secret History of Pius XI and the Rise of Fascism in Europe*</u> by David I. Kertzer

- <u>*My Rise And Fall*</u> by Benito Mussolini

- <u>*Bloodlands: Europe Between Hitler and Stalin*</u> by Timothy Snyder

- <u>*The Burning Shore: How Hitlers U-Boats Brought World War II to America*</u> by Ed Offley

- <u>*The Heart of the Buddha's Teaching: Transforming Suffering into Peace, Joy, and Liberation*</u> by Thich Nhat Hanh

- *Self Reliance* by Ralph Waldo Emerson. Available from The Project Gutenberg at http://www.gutenberg.org/files/16643/16643-h/16643-h.htm [Accessed January 23, 2021].

- *Notre-Dame of Paris* (The Hunchback of Notre Dame) by Victor Hugo

- *Les Miserables* by Victor Hugo

- *The Rape of Nanking: The Forgotten Holocaust of World War II* by Iris Chang

Popular Books Published in 1943:
Hungry Hill by Daphne du Maurier
Journey in the Dark by Martin Flavin

Popular Movies Released in 1943:
The Song of Bernadette (Jennifer Jones, William Eythe)
Whistling in Brooklyn (Red Skelton, Ann Rutherford, Jean Rogers)
Immortal Sergeant (Henry Fonda, Maureen O'Hara)

Wednesday September 29, 1943

In the course of my travels, I came across a woman whose granddaughter is married to an army flyer. He is listed as missing in action. She has a small son, and now has taken a job in a defense plant, and plans to bring him up by her own support if need be. Such courage and quiet heroism as women display! The husband was operating out of Burma, or near Burma, in a plane which landed in the sea, ten miles from land. The crew had on life jackets, and it is presumed that some, or all of them, reached land. But miles upon miles of uninhabited jungle might prevent them from reaching their base for days or weeks or even years. There is many a San Fernandez Island today with its Robinson Crusoes in the broad reaches of the Pacific. Not to know, not to hear, for weeks or years must be a heavy cross to bear. Work and children help, but even so there must be many prayers to God for strength to carry on. My Communion theme for Sunday is from II Thess. 3:5 "The Lord direct you into Love of God and the Patience of Christ."

The war as a whole needs patience. Even far from battle zones we are hedged about with increased costs of living, higher taxes, deprivation of essentials like butter, for example, and eggs. Potatoes, now plentiful, were scarce last spring, and even on the home front a great deal of patience is required. Patience to read of brutalities, like the despoliation of Naples, the ravaging of conquered countries, the sighing of the prisoners, the maimed and bruised, and above all patience for the satiation of the blood lust that must mark the retribution of unnumbered crimes before peace can come to a troubled and warring world. Sicily, Sardinia, and Corsica are now in Allied hands. Unrest is fomented in the Balkans, and Italy invaded as far as Naples. The Russians have retaken Orel, Bryansk, Belgorod, Mariupol, Smolensk, and have enveloped Kiev and Dnipropetrovsk. We are learning Russian geography! How far will the Russians go? They are nearing the Pripet Marshes where they suffered the defeat of Tannenberg in the last war. Will they stop at the borders of Poland, or advance into Germany? My own guess is that they will content themselves with throwing the invaders out of Russia, the Baltic countries, and such parts of Poland as they wish to take for themselves. The country of Holy Russia (since the Greek Orthodox Church has been reestablished) has saved the day for the allies by depleting German man-power, but it seems to me that post-war problems in Europe will be almost as great as the problems of conquest of Germany.

In August, a neighbor of ours, Mr. Merrill, invited my wife, Janet, and I to go with his daughter and himself to his camp on Lake JoSylvia in Contoocook, N.H. His camp, located at the northwest end of the lake, has all modern conveniences, and we enjoyed the five days we spent there greatly. We chopped wood, visited an old Indian fireplace, and went fishing. The first night under the stars we caught 63 hornpout. I enjoyed the fishing, especially in the morning when I rowed around the lake trolling. The lily beds, the mouth of the brook with heron, the white sandy beach at the other end of the lake, the sunken island, and the peninsular jutting out from land, where the turtles used to sun themselves on the logs thereof, are all memorable to me. As Masefield says, "Best trust the happy moments, what they gave—Makes men less fearful of the certain grave—And gives his work compassion and new eyes—The days that make us happy, make us wise." (*From John Masefield's poem "Biography"*).

On the last night at camp, Mr. Merrill caught 20 hornpout and almost brought an eel into the boat. I'm rather glad he left the hook. And be it recorded that Janet caught the largest pickerel of the trip on a bare hook at sunken island, among the lily pads; quite a fisherman.

> There's a sandy beach at Muertos, and it never stops to roar
> And it's there we came to anchor, and it's there we went ashore.
> (*Paraphrased from John Masefield's poem "Spanish Waters".*
> *The actual quote is:*
> *"…There's a surf break on Los Muertos,*
> *And it never stops to roar,*
> *And it's there we came to anchor,*
> *And it's there we went ashore.*)

Suggested Daily Spiritual Reading:
2 Thessalonians 3:5
1 Thessalonians 1:3

Further Reading Related to Diary Entry:
- *Robinson Crusoe* by Daniel Defoe

- *Sea Fever: Selected Poems of John Masefield* by John Masefield and Philip W. Errington

- *A Woman of No Importance: The Untold Story of the American Spy Who Helped Win World War* II by Sonia Purnell

- *Shot Down: The True Story of Pilot Howard Snyder and the Crew of the B-17 Susan Ruth* by Steve Snyder (Author), John Maling (Editor)

Popular Books Published in 1943:
The Doctrine of Awakening by Julius Evola

The Ship by C. S. Forester
Colonel Effingham's Raid by Berry Fleming

Popular Movies Released in 1943:
Air Force (John Garfield, John Ridgely, Gig Young)
Bombardier (Pat O'Brien, Randolph Scott, Anne Shirley, Eddie Albert)
China (Loretta Young, Alan Ladd, William Bendix)

Thursday November 4, 1943

One week from today comes the twenty-fifth anniversary of the signing of the Armistice from the first World War. It seems tragic, and ironic, that so much of suffering and anguish must be endured again to complete what was thought to be ended then. But all of us in our private lives have to learn to do things over again, when they fail to stay put the first time. We can only hope that the big powers will be able to implement in the peace that which is gained in war, namely the cessation of fighting. That has not been done hitherto, but the Moscow conference gives hope that the nations are on the right trail—namely an Imperium of nations united by bonds of common interests.

Four provisions of the compact are transient—namely the (1) opening of a second front, (2) unconditional surrender of the axis nations, Germany and Japan; Italy already having capitulated, (3) retribution for war criminals, and (4) restoration of Austria and Italy to a place in decent society. The fifth provision says that England, Russia, and the United States, plus China, will constitute a permanent imperium, after the war, to maintain peace and order. This is much preferable to a League of Nations, in my opinion, for in the league sovereignty is delegated only in part, where as in an imperium the contracting powers either assent or dissent fully. There is less opportunity for alibis and side-stepping. The cement for the imperium is only self-interest, to be sure, but it is an appeal to basic interests in the nations' welfare, and a united stand on that ground furnishes plenty of power, for we will possess overwhelming superiority in the air, at sea, and on land.

Indeed Germany's treatment of conquered nations gives us the clue to our procedure. Take away the factories that make the munitions, guns, planes, tanks, ships; render the country subservient industrially and agriculturally; and deprive it of access to materials of war, such as gasoline and rubber, natural or synthetic; and occupation is not necessary. Let Germany work out her destiny with a minimum of these essentials, allowing her plenty of food, and peacetime pursuits, but none for re-arming. There has been no armed revolt in any conquered country deprived of these essentials. Yugoslavia (*Kingdom of Yugoslavia*) has never been really subjugated, and in any case the resistance is not menacing to Germany. Allow Germany access to those materials necessary to building and maintaining her peacetime economy, but rigidly deny her access to iron or oil or other imports which would permit her to re-arm. Maintain strong establishments in the air, on the sea, and on the land, and I predict that Germany will not again menace the world for generations to come. As for the political re-education of a nation whose whole tradition has been martial, that is difficult. The only language such a people understand is force, and in this day and age the most powerful weapon is economics.

Let them have another Hitler if they choose, let them goose-step and train with wooden weapons, let them prate, "Ein reich, Ein volk, Ein fuhrer," but deprive them of the means to implement their warlike tendencies. We have the means and the power to do that—the vital question is, will the imperium maintain its cohesion and vigilance? We may drift far apart on other issues, but if at that common point of our self interest we hang together, and insist on immediate and thorough chastisement of any nation which in future seeks to fulfill its manifest destiny through arms and self-glorification, then lasting peace is not only possible, but probable. Lines of cleavage are many, but the USSR, China, The British Empire, and the United States have a common will in this direction—not to permit aggression to become strongly entrenched in any country, to the detriment of the big powers and the smaller nations. We seek no territorial aggrandizement, and it seem to me that Russia , England, and China too have enough land, and enough problems to keep them occupied for the rest of the century without desiring to encroach upon the peace and goodwill of their neighbors.

Suggested Daily Spiritual Reading:
Mark 9:23
2 Corinthians 4:8

Further Reading Related to Diary Entry:
- *Silent Night: The Story of the World War I Christmas Truce* by Stanley Weintraub

- *The Greatest Battle: Stalin, Hitler, and the Desperate Struggle for Moscow That Changed the Course of World War II* by Andrew Nagorski

- *The Drive on Moscow, 1941: Operation Taifun and Germany's First Great Crisis of World War II* by Anders Frankson (Author), Niklas Zetterling

- *The Kingdom of Yugoslavia: The Turbulent History of the Country's Formation and Occupation during World War I and World War II* by Charles River Editors

Popular Books Published in 1943:
They Also Ran by Irving Stone
Street Corner Society by William Foote Whyte
The Fountainhead by Ayn Rand

Popular Movies Released in 1943:
Coney Island (Betty Grable, George Montgomery, Cesar Romero, Phil Silvers)
Cosmo Jones, Crime Smasher (Richard Cromwell, Gale Storm)
The Desperadoes (Randolph Scott, Claire Trevor, Glenn Ford)

December 2, 1943
Minutiae

The charm of Pepys' diary (*The Diary of Samuel Pepys*), which I was reading the other evening, lies in its details. Written in cipher, and certainly not intended for the eyes of others, it yet reveals an inordinate vanity and pride in self, which cannot be hidden from any eyes. Why must we express ourselves and, so, try to make ourselves superior to our fellows? I suppose it is a biological trait, aggressiveness, we survive. According to the Lamarcki theory of use and disuse. The ideal of course, is not to advance at the expense of our fellows, but through their betterment. A newspaper correspondent gives his best to his readers, and is rewarded therefore. He risks his life for his readers. He propones himself, as it were, on their behalf. Any rewards his editor gives him are amply deserved. After the pattern and spirit of Jesus, who said, "He that finds his life shall lose it, and he that loses his life shall find it..." (*Paraphrased from Matthew 10:39*)

Pepys has not such motive in mind, and so his revelations of his minor vanities are readily accepted, not as ostentation, but as self-complimentary. But we are indebted to him for the larger picture, through detail—and is not a good painting always characterized by mastery of detail?—of an England under Cromwell, James II, and Charles II; of the war with Holland, and the victory of sea power; of the plague, and the great London fire; the doings at court; and the ups and downs of religious tolerance, as well as the contemporaneous of preachers and plays.

The larger canvas of the past is intriguing to those who like history or feel that it repeats itself—though it never does exactly. "Time goes, we stay, you say? Ah, no, time stays, we go!" (*Paraphrase of the poem "The Paradox Of Time" by Henry Austin Dobson*)

No two wars have been alike, though there are points of similarity; especially between the present conflict and World War I. No two lives are alike. No two events are alike, though many a Caesar has had his Brutus. And the larger canvas of the future is appealing the mind, which synthesize events, and predicts on the probables. The present seems mundane, innocuous, dull, boring. The day by day life of one man is a succession of petty habits, thoughts, and actions. Our present inventions and tools are not nearly as exciting as those to come. Radio is wonderful, but consider the possibilities of television, exempli gratia!

Yet, I have often felt that if someone could report faithfully on his day-by-day activities, patterns of thought and habit, his tools and paraphernalia of living, over a period of years, as Pepys did, a microcosm within the macrocosm as it were, the result would be invaluable for future generations. To say nothing of its entertainment value! Only Pepys has done this faithfully, to my knowledge; though, many have kept diaries for years, my grandfather included. Such diaries usually include the weather—I saw one recently, which put down the temperatures for the morning, afternoon, and evening throughout the whole years of 1881-82, I think it was; some sixty years ago, anyhow. It was very interesting. Occasionally, the diarist butchered a hog, or went to town for supplies, or hoed corn, or cut wood, but there was continuity in weather, superior even to the almanacs, for his observations were based on fact. To do this for other items, such as the war news or crime or social activities or problems within the home, all together would give a comprehensive account of one life at least. Thoreau does it grandly for his year at Walden. How devastating his criticism of so-called progress—"improved means to an unimproved end..." He was trying to find a life, not a living. Such a project of course—the detailed reporting of one's daily activities over a period of years, is beyond the scope of most of us. It would occupy a great deal of time and space, but I think it would be infinitely worthwhile, especially if the reporter was objective, like the personable Pepys.

Suggested Daily Spiritual Reading:
Matthew 10:39
Matthew 7:7

Further Reading Related to Diary Entry:
- *The Diary of Samuel Pepys* by Samuel Pepys. Available from The Project Gutenberg at http://www.gutenberg.org/files/4200/4200-h/4200-h.htm [Accessed January 23, 2021].

- *Walden* by Henry David Thoreau. Available from The Project Gutenberg at http://www.gutenberg.org/files/205/205-h/205-h.htm [Accessed January 23, 2021].

- *When Books Went to War: The Stories That Helped Us Win World War II* by Molly Manning

Popular Books Published in 1943:
The God of the Machine by Isabel Paterson
The Ministry of Fear by Graham Greene
The Abolition of Man by C. S. Lewis

Popular Movies Released in 1943:
The Fallen Sparrow (Maureen O'Hara, John Garfield, Walter Slezak)
For Whom the Bell Tolls (Gary Cooper, Ingrid Bergman, Arturo de Córdova)
Heaven Can Wait (Don Ameche, Gene Tierney)

1944

January 15, 1944
Matutinal Musings

Before I start work this day, I ought in praise to my maker, to pause and give unto Him the homage that is his due. I have tried to do just that by getting out for a walk on the lake—no Walden 'tis, and yet the whole of nature is represented there. It is frozen inches thick, with a light covering of snow, the sun shines through the overcast, and it is a mild mid-winter's day.

Two things I noted, yea three. Up at Merrill's Point, a birch tree bends gracefully over the water, and if you stand beyond it, seems to enfold half the pond in its graceful sweep. Farther along, I saw a weather-beaten old fir still standing after many bouts with wind and water; though, its companion beside it has broken near the base and given up the ghost, having toppled into the water and swum or swam or swimmed quite a ways out from shore. Or perhaps in its passivity the water floated it along. The fir is still standing, and it is thirty or forty feet in height, is denuded of branches except at the top, as firs often are—reaching upwards for sun and air—but at the top it curves into a graceful S, though not as pronounced in curves as the letter of course. I don't recall seeing anything quite like it in my travels. But then nature is filled with erratics, exotics, eccentrics, sports, which infinitely intrigue one's attention (perhaps we are such). Then on the way home, I came upon a footprint in the snow, wherein reposed a cluster of three tiny pine cones; simple, yet artistic. The interpretation of the meaning of 'artistic' occupies many schools of thought; yet, art is indigenous to the human spirit. "He that hath eyes to see, let him see," said one whose life was supremely artistic (*Believe quote to be paraphrased from Matthew 13:16*). So, I return to my labors in a contented mood.

How goes the war? Action in the Pacific is essentially a holding action, and minor gains on Cape Gloucester and in the Marshalls do not interest me greatly. In Burma, the Ledo Road to replace the Burma road is being built as fast as the army advances, which isn't very fast—I judge by lack of communiques. A month or so ago, the Chinese drove the Japanese from Chengteh and the rice bowl, after the annual depredations of the Nipponese on that important area. In Italy, the allies are nearing Cassino, slowly, and occasionally bomb Rome and Sofia. On the sea, the big recent naval action destroyed the Scharnhorst, pride of the German navy, off the Norwegian coast. The invasion from the West is talked about, but not started. The air war is proceeding, but costly. Berlin is half destroyed, and vital targets are attacked daily, but the Sweinfurt raid cost many bombers, and sixty were destroyed early this week in another raid on the assembly plants of the Me 110s near Berlin. Six hundred pilots and technicians lost. Despite fighter coverage, the Germans are taking a heavy toll on planes. But on the Russian front things are moving—Sarny, a rail junction in the middle of the Pripet Marshes, has been captured (remember Tannenberg in World War I?), and the German forces in the Dneiper Bend are in great danger of encirclement. Poland and Russia are negotiating boundary problems—what a reshuffling of frontiers if and when Germany finally collapses! The Russians have broken the German lines into areas, and are on the march. They are superb! We once thought they could not last six weeks. But they took the mightiest army in the world and brought it to a standstill before Stalingrad, and then forced it to retreat. The Germans in the Crimea are cut off. The retreat of the Germans from Rostov-on-Don after a week's occupation is classic. The Germans are now halfway to Berlin. I firmly believe the Russians have not only saved the USSR but the whole world from the domination of Nazism. They have my accolade, especially if they preach deliverance to the captives and set at liberty them that are bruised. Some of the finest minds of our times, Niemoeller, Kagawa, and their coworkers, are prisoners of totalitarianism.

Suggested Daily Spiritual Reading:
Psalm 30:12
1 Peter 4:11
Mark 8:18

Further Reading Related to Diary Entry:
- *The Lost Art of Reading Nature's Signs: Use Outdoor Clues to Find Your Way, Predict the Weather, Locate Water, Track Animals—and Other Forgotten Skills* by Tristan Gooley

- *Finding Your Way Without Map or Compass* by Harold Gatty

- *Then They Came for Me: Martin Niemöller, the Pastor Who Defied the Nazis* by Matthew D Hockenos

- *South From Corregidor* by Lt. Comdr. John Morrill, Pete Martin

- *The Saga of Pappy Gunn* by George C. Kenney

Popular Books Published in 1944:
Most Popular Books Published In 1944. Available from Goodreads.com: https://www.goodreads.com/book/popular_by_date/1944 [Accessed January 23, 2021].

Popular Movies Released in 1944:
    Double Indeminity (Fred MacMurray, Edward G. Robinson, Barbara Stanwyck)
    Going My Way (Bing Crosby and Barry Fitzgerald)
    Passage to Marseille (Humphrey Bogart, Claude Rains, Michèle Morgan)

Thursday February 3rd, 1944

This is an interim period between the past and the present. The care of the Church, which like St. Paul, comes upon me daily, doesn't begin again until after dinner; my letters are in order, and the morning is nearly done.

After breakfast, I went for a walk up the frozen surface of the pond, and plucked a specimen of pine branch from the large one blown off into the lake, and now embedded in the ice; enjoyed the warm rays of the sun, which mounts daily, higher in the heavens; and played with the dog, Rover, who forgets his ancestral fears sufficiently to chase the stick on the ice. I have recently read that a pack of wolves will not venture onto the ice, and can well believe it. For I have had to entice Rover, a shepherd/collie, with cookies (*dog biscuits?*) and thrown sticks to get him to venture upon the uncertain footing. Bruce's Pond, which is perhaps a quarter of a mile long, is frozen to a depth of many inches, except at the upper part where steam from Lamson's ice-making plant keeps the pond open most of the winter. It is a struggle between the forces of cold and the forces of heat.

Our unseasonably warm spell in January, when the thermometer was about ten degrees above average, daily, and the snowfall measured three instead of nineteen inches, as it should normally, gave way the first of this month to normally cold weather, and yesterday morning the temperature was reported from two to eight below.

What an endless topic the weather is! Last summer I came across a journal in Vermont that narrated the weather continuously for about a year, with entries morning, noon, and night for degrees of temperature and such interesting inclusions as daily work chopping wood or hoeing corn, or hitching up the horse for a trip to the village. And the year was 1868, if memory serves me right.

The family is well, and in spite of the fact that our standard of living is severely limited, with an income tax of around $180 this coming year, we managed to get along nicely. Our lovely church, and people, and a fireplace in the home, and congenial surroundings, make this past year one of the happiest we have ever known.

The war goes slowly, but well. Germany is retreating steadily from Russia, whose troops are already in Estonia, and Poland, and are making progress in the Dneiper bend; the situation in Italy being one where the Germans are flanked by a landing force at Nettuno and Anzio. At five each day on shortwave, I receive reports direct from U.S. headquarters in Algiers. They must have a powerful set there. In the Pacific our forces have just landed at the Marshall Islands from a covering force of hundreds of ships and planes. Kjawlein, or is it Kwajlein (?), and Rio and Motje, and other strange names, now swim into our ken. The Japs can see the pattern of defeat. Our submarines have sunk nearly four hundred ships. By closing off their sea lanes, and isolating Japan proper, I think we can pull them down, and in the not too distant future. The importance of sea power is recognized today. Hitler has lost the battle of the Atlantic, as he admits, to radar; and 1500 planes have been over the continent the past two days without encountering any air opposition. Unless unforeseen imponderables enter the picture, the defeat of Germany in the next year or so is mathematically certain. Then the world can concentrate on the Japanese.

I do not feel loaded down with wisdom this morning. To enjoy my lord the Sun, to do one's work, and to luxuriate in the bosom of the family—these are the largesses of life.

A book of outstanding importance, which I have read recently, is that of Lin Yutang, "Between Tears and Laughter". He narrates the humiliations the Chinese have received, and feels the great powers do not intend to allow China to develop a large air force; he speaks of karma, and how there is a cumulative force at work in the world resisting evil, as well as superintending the good, and says the real conflict in the post war world is between power politics and the forces of freedom. Imperialism versus democracy, and may the best idea win!

Suggested Daily Spiritual Reading:
Wisdom of Solomon 12:24-26
Matthew 5:8

Further Reading Related to Diary Entry:
- *The Marshall Islands 1944: Operation Flintlock, the capture of Kwajalein and Eniwetok (Campaign)* by Gordon L. Rottman and Howard Gerrard

- *Between Tears and Laughter* by Lin Yutang

- *War at Sea: A Naval History of World War II* by Nathan Miller

Popular Books Published in 1944:
A Bell for Adano by John Hersey
The Razor's Edge by William Somerset Maugham

Popular Movies Released in 1944:
The Fighting Seabees (John Wayne, Susan Hayward, Dennis O'Keefe)
The Fighting Sullivans (Anne Baxter, Thomas Mitchell, Selena Royle)
National Velvet (Mickey Rooney, Elizabeth Taylor, Donald Crisp)

April 20, 1944
If We Only Knew---

Pursuant to the purpose of this journal, which is that it shall be of some interest or help to others, beyond a mere compilations of recollections, the thought came to me today…"If I only knew, in this interesting era of world history (and every era is interesting, as is every place and person) just what the man or woman or child of 50, 500, or 5,000 years would be especially interested in, how eager I would be to tell them!"

Dramatic war news -- the newspapers are too transient, too near the scene; history books are too turgid, too replete with summary. Truk, the Japanese Pearl Harbor, was heavily attacked by a naval force some weeks ago, and proved a dud. That is the ships left the harbor—the Imperial Navy, I mean—before the task force arrived and haven't been seen since.

Some 200 planes were destroyed in the air and on the ground, and for two days our carriers (we have 50 in the Pacific) were busy pounding away at the installations. Later on our task force raided Ponope (*Pohnpei*) and Palau and other bastions of empire, heavily. At present, Nimitz is Admiral of the Ocean Sea, as far as he can see. There have been no challenge to our navy from units of the Imperial Japanese Navy, and probably won't be for some time to come. Today our bombers raided two points in the Dutch East Indies for the first time. We are reaching out toward the Philippines, and someday—a year hence?—they will be in American hands again.

In Europe, the forthcoming invasion takes the spotlight, with Italian fighting stalemated for months now at Cassino and Anzio.

Russia has driven the German invaders to the Balkans and is now cleaning up the Crimea, at the gates of Sevastopol. Russia held out eight heroic months there in 1941-42, or was it 1940? The commander of the garrison wrote, in his last letter, "It is but a step from discipline from heroism…"—a statement worthy of preservation and study. Fighting in Poland centers around Lwow. In the past year, Russia has won a thousand miles of Russian territory and re-taken the Ukraine.

I might write of daily life on the home front—our boys are on 53 war fronts around the world—and tell of rationing, which is not hard on us at all, for we have a sufficiency of all things, busy factories and busy people.

I might write of advances in medicines, the marvelous sulfa drugs, which are used widely for pneumonia, and many other things just now.

I might say, there are very few good books, since the male writers seem otherwise occupied, and the women writers tend to romanticize everything in light novel form.

I might say there are a few good movies, for the same reason, the good actors being away at war.

I might speak of scientific achievements, radar and jet propulsion planes, but these will be commonplace a few years hence. Our largest land transport plane, the Constellation, four motored and capable of carrying 57 passengers or 100 soldiers, has just crossed the country in less than eight hours, but 50 years hence, that will be of relatively little significance.

Instead, I shall speak of the good earth. I have been spading my garden today, and turning over the rich soil. Ready for the planting of beans, tomatoes, and whatever else I choose to plant. 50,000 years hence, that will be significant still, for I cannot imagine synthetic vegetables will ever take the place of the products raised in the soil by the farmer. My plot is small, but it is typical of a million others, now termed Victory gardens. A bit of soil, the riverbank, the trees, the birds, the good sun and the clouds above—these will be around for quite a while to come, and people will still be interested in them, I think. Some things I shall not bother with, since they did not do well last year, such as celery, squash, and pepper plants, but others will be fruitful, especially beans and tomatoes, and spinach, and carrots. These contain nourishing vitamins. I fancy soybeans will increase in food value. To work in the vineyard of the Lord is to feel at one with Him.

Suggested Daily Spiritual Reading:
Genesis 9:20
Leviticus 19:10

Further Reading Related to Diary Entry:
- *Brass Button Broadcasters: A Lighhearted Look at 50 Years of Military Broadcasting* by Trent Christman

- *D Day: June 6, 1944: The Climactic Battle of World War* II by Stephen E. Ambrose

- *Fighting for Life: American Military Medicine in World War II* by Albert E. Cowdrey

- *Facing the Abyss: American Literature and Culture in the 1940s* by George Hutchinson

Popular Books Published in 1944:
The Lost Weekend by Charles Jackson
Stick and Rudder: An Explanation of the Art of Flying by Wolfgang Langewiesche

Popular Movies Released in 1944:
   Andy Hardy's Blonde Trouble (Lewis Stone, Mickey Rooney, Fay Holden)
   Buffalo Bill (Joel McCrea, Maureen O'Hara, Linda Darnell, Anthony Quinn, Thomas Mitchell)
   The Canterville Ghost (Charles Laughton, Margaret O'Brien)

July 22, 1944
It Cometh Soon ----

This morning's informs us: (A) The Russians have crossed the Bug River on a 37-mile front. The Lublin Plains are filled with tanks and armored cars. They are headed for Warsaw and the Vistula. Four years ago the Germans headed for Moscow from the Bug River; military justice, this reversement. The Russians have eight armies on the march now, and German opposition is weakening. (B) Hitler, whose attempted assassination by Gen. Von Beck and others (I should say purported assassination), announced the liquidation of his enemies in another blood purge. There has been a wide spread plot by the army to unseat Hitler, which has apparently failed, but it shows the lines of cleavage and coming events —a probable civil war in the Reich. Hitler was burned about the face, and suffered a slight concussion from a time bomb which exploded two feet (?) from his chair, two or three nights ago. It gave Himmler's Geheimstaatspoligie (*Geheime Staats Politie or Geheime Staats Polizei or Geheim Staats Poligie*) free reign to liquidate their enemies from Runstedt—(*Walther von*) Brauchitsch to the lowest civilian. But destroying generals will not help the war effort. This is really the beginning of the breakup, in my humble opinion. (C) We have landed on Guam after days of fierce pounding by planes and ships. The Japanese cabinet of Tojo resigned en masse three days ago, confessing their inability to cope with a serious naval situation. A new cabinet has been formed. (D) The British are below Caen in Normandy, and the Allies have taken Livorno (Leghorn) in Italy. All is going well for the Allies, bad for the Axis. If, as a General Conference of the Methodist Church proclaimed, "God has a stake in this struggle", He must be pleased too.

(**Prenote:** *According to the Reverend's daughter Janet, the Reverend often took on odd jobs during the summer to help supplement the family income. In 1944 he was 42 years old.*)

The past three weeks have been interesting ones, yea, the past month. The first week and a half I worked in an apple orchard for Harold A. (Hap) Priest of Gleasondale (*MA*). He has three thousand trees. We thinned out the apples, atop 21-foot ladders, eight hours a day. Hard work, but enjoyable. Trees as far as one can see; beautiful in the mornings. Particularly, I remember a white birch tree and a windmill up against the woods. "How precious are Thy thoughts unto me, O God—How great is the sum of them. If I should count them, they are more in number that the sands of the seas. When I am awake I am still with Thee." (*Psalm 139:17-18*)

For the next week and a half, I worked in Fillmore's Ice Cream stand, keeping the girls supplied with cans of ice cream, helping Mr. Fillmore make it, ten gallons at a time, and about sixteen flavors; and learning how to wait on customers, make frappes, sundaes, etc. Very interesting indeed. With the money so earned Mae and I took the car, along with my sister Lilla, and a friend, Roberta, and Journeyed to Saranac Lake in the Adirondacks to visit my older sister Christina (Christina named for a famous Queen in Sweden). We went via the Mohawk Trail (*Route 2 in Massachusetts*)—Williamstown (*MA*), Glenn Falls (*NY*), Lake George, Loon Lake, Schroon Lake, Lake Placid, to Saranac lake.

Motor boat rides on Lake Placid and lower Saranac were enjoyed by us. The mountains, Whiteface, Marcy, and others were magnificent. Clear weather the first two days. The second day, last Monday, we went to Paul Smith's, visiting St. John's in the Wilderness, an Episcopal Church built by the famous Dr. Edward Livingstone Trudeau, who, in 1884, went to the Adirondacks to die of tuberculosis, and lived to build three Churches and the famous Trudeau Sanitorium just outside Saranac Lake Village. He lies buried with his family in the quiet Churchyard of St. John's in the Wilderness at Paul Smith's. Apollos (known as Paul) Smith is also buried there. He was a burly Vermonter who went to the place now bearing his name and built an inn. He became wealthy by buying up two or three power plants in adjacent communities. Trudeau stayed with him. Clifford Pettis, who began the conservation program of state forests in the Adirondacks, is also buried there. We saw the surviving son of Dr. Trudeau, also a doctor, on the streets of Saranac Village. His car number is 400. We visited Fish Creek camping ground another day. 500 fireplaces. Birches. Returned home yesterday via Lake Champlain and Fort Ticonderoga. And so to work.

Suggested Daily Spiritual Reading:
Psalm 139
Proverbs 16:3

Further Reading Related to Diary Entry:
- *Normandy '44: D-Day and the Epic 77-Day Battle for France* by James Holland

- *The Plot to Kill Hitler: Dietrich Bonhoeffer: Pastor, Spy, Unlikely Hero* by Patricia McCormick

- *D DAY Through German Eyes - The Hidden Story of June 6th 1944* by Holger Eckhertz (Books 1 and 2).

- *Cure Cottages of Saranac Lake: Architecture and History of a Pioneer Health Resort* by Philip L. Gallos

- *The Adirondacks: Season by Season* by Heilman II, Carl and Bill McKibben

- *Finding True North: A History of One Small Corner of the Adirondacks* by Fran

Yardley

Popular Books Published in 1944:
How to Stop Worrying and Start Living by Dale Carnegie
Fascism: What It Is and How to Fight It by Leon Trotsky

Popular Movies Released in 1944:
The Conspirators (Hedy Lamarr, Paul Henreid)
Gaslight (Charles Boyer, Ingrid Bergman, Angela Lansbury)
Hail the Conquering Hero (Eddie Bracken, Ella Raines, William Demarest)

Thursday August 24, 1944

Coming back from New York state and settling down to work at Fillmore's Ice Cream stand, helping to make ice cream and keeping the cabinets supplied with five gallon cans. We had assumed that vacation was over, but one night Fern and Helen Taylor came up and invited us to spend three or four days with them in Sprucehead, Maine. We did, going on a Tuesday morning and coming back on a Saturday. We found a lovely little cottage on Sprucehead Island right on the coast, about ten miles below Rockland. The wooded islands of the bays, the tide coming in mornings, and the boats moored nearby made a pretty picture.

Fern and I arose two mornings at five o'clock (awakened by full tide and the kree-ing of the seagulls, and went out lobster fishing with Sam Archer. It was a rare experience, giving us the opportunity to learn how the markets are supplied with lobsters; a real delicacy hereabouts.

Near the shore, but in deep water, is a weir, constructed of birch poles, where the herring are caught, and scooped up in nets for bait. The weirs were made by the Rackliffe clan, consisting of the father, who had been at it for 38 years, summer and winter, and his sons, and Sam, a son-in-law. All have built houses nearby. There is Bernard, Frank and Debo (for "Dear Boy"), and also a son in the service now. All have lobster launches. Each has a string of between one hundred and one hundred and fifty traps, with different colored buoys. Sam's were yellow and white, Frank's orange, and Pop Rackliffe had buoys of black and white.

Two pails of herring are taken along to put in the bait bags for the traps, and it was our humble office to keep these filled. It was interesting to see the lobstermen approach the buoy, haul up the bottle on the rope attached, apply the rope to the winch, and haul in the traps. He is busy every minute. Then while the launch "walks around" the area in a circle to the right, the trap is emptied. They may contain kelp, sea urchins, crabs, and various denizens of the deep in addition to lobsters. Lobsters must be three and one-eighth inches long, and not over three and three-quarter inches; in other words, between seven and twelve years old. Many are "shorts" and some are too long, being seed lobsters, or old fellows. He throws the shorts back, and keeps the others on a shelf until he can peg them, that is, place a wooden peg at the outside edge of the large mandible, so that the lobsters cannot harm anyone. Then he throws them in a barrel, and for a good day's catch the barrel is filled. He puts in a new bait bag, locks the trap with a wooden clasp, and hauls the trap to a new location or, if the catch was good, puts it back in the old one, and proceeds to the next buoy.

He goes near reefs with impunity, and even goes out in the fog. The traps are ingeniously constructed, with two compartments, each with a circular opening through which the lobster can venture, to the region of the bait. These are woven of fine rope, with a circular hoop for the opening. Because of hauling, the lobsters are usually found in the second compartment. A good day's catch is worth forty dollars. This (the catch) is taken to a pound, some miles south and sold.

The scenery on the open ocean is lovely. The sea, the rocks, the trees, the gulls and shags, the blue sky with clouds, make an unforgettable picture. Sam's hospitality included two big meals of lobsters for us—the first a lobster stew, of which I partook with gastronomic pleasure, consuming three dishes; plenty of lobster meat in milk and richly seasoned with butter. Sam was unusual in that he allowed me to pilot the boat on occasion, to "walk it around"; to approach the buoys, and even to steer it to the lobster pound. We shall not soon forget the hospitality of these kind folks in Maine, nor the beauty of Sprucehead. He took it for granted we would return next year and, God willing, we shall!

The life habits of the lobsters are interesting—they are born in the coves and work out to the open sea, being found miles offshore in the winter-time.

Yesterday, Paris was declared free by the patriots—today is still enchained—Rumania is out of the war. Much of France is in Allied hands. Good news from all fronts.

Suggested Daily Spiritual Reading:
Genesis 1:10
Luke 21:25

Further Reading Related to Diary Entry:
- T*he Secret Life of Lobsters: How Fishermen and Scientists Are Unraveling the Mysteries of Our Favorite Crustacean* by Trevor Corson

- *The Lobster Coast: Rebels, Rusticators, and the Struggle for a Forgotten Frontier* by Colin Woodard

- *The Bedford Boys: One American Town's Ultimate D-day Sacrifice* by Alex Kershaw

Popular Books Published in 1944:
The Ashley Book of Knots by Clifford W. Ashley
Can Do! The Story Of The Seabees by William Bradford Huie

Popular Movies Released in 1944:
The Hour Before the Dawn (Veronica Lake, Franchot Tone, Binnie Barnes)
The Keys of the Kingdom (Gregory Peck, Thomas Mitchell, Roddy McDowall)
Lifeboat (Tallulah Bankhead, William Bendix)

Wednesday, August 30, 1944

Having bought a new typewriter ribbon yesterday, I am anxious to try it out in this journal. An old ribbon makes recording anything laborious, but the light touch necessary with a new ribbon seems almost effortless. I can see the time where even the pushing of the keys will be done by a motor, if that day has not already arrived, and then the touch will be featherlight. Thoreau would say, bah, only an improved means to an unimproved end.

When a chap is made as comfortable as possible, he goes to sleep. To illustrate —I have some felled wood a neighbor gave me for my fireplace—in order to get it I must brave the poison ivy, then saw it, and in some instances cut it, not to mention carrying it for some distance. But that wood will be more appreciated this winter than some which by some unlikely eventuality might be donated to us. Let me hasten to mention that my good wife, Mae, actually helped me saw the wood with a crosscut saw. The saw loaned by the same neighbor, Walter Cain, who gave me the wood, is sharp and cuts easily. You can "loaf along" on most wood, but we ran into some fence posts of hard wood, which required a little assiduous application of kerosene to the saw, from time to time. Albert helped me last night too. Janet, who bought a new pair of shoes today, has been taking care of three babies in the neighborhood, and yet she helped me some this morning too, even using the bucksaw better than her brother.

We went for a short ride tonight in the car, around Sawyer Hill in Berlin; lovely sunset to the left of Wachusett (*Mountain*). People sitting on their porches somehow reminds me of woodchucks sitting up in their burrows. I have watched them many times in the evening on the farm, through a telescope. Their lives may be relatively short, but they seem to enjoy them. If the chief aim of life is "to know God and to enjoy Him forever," as the Westminster catechism puts it, then it seems to me that a woodchuck fills that aim. He seems to enjoy the quiet evening air, the scent of clover, the glint of sunset on the river, and the singing of birds. But I had better veer away from this intriguing subject, which borders on the eternal—this world of subjective idealism—and return to events of the objective realism, namely the war.

The German 7th army is done for, its equipment scattered on the West bank of the Seine. The 15th army is pulling back from the rocket coast, toward Belgium, it is reported. A German army retreating up the Rhone Valley has been cleverly trapped by the Americans, and their vehicles smashed. Forward elements of Patton's army are on the Aisne, having speeded through Chateau Thierry and Soissons. They are somewhere beyond Chalons-sur-Marne, about sixty miles from the Belgian frontier. German arms seem doomed in France. Russia hasn't recaptured Warsaw, but she has taken the Ploesti oil fields of Rumania and Constanta, the Black Sea port. The Balkans are falling apart and seething with unrest. Italy sees the Germans falling back, toward the Brenner Pass. Troyes seems to be the southern anchor of the Allied army tonight; some place near Rheims, the northern anchor. The British are pressing toward the Northeast to free the rocket coast of France, aided by the Canadians. Russian troops have planted a wedge between Warsaw and East Prussia, and have also driven a wedge into Esthonia. Where will the Germans hold, if they can hold? Another month will tell the story. In the Pacific, the Dutch East Indies and Halmahera have been bombed, also the Kuriles. We hold Saipan and Guam. We seem headed toward the Philippines. Our B-29s, or super-fortresses, have bombed industrial targets on Japan's home islands, and given a concentration of power, Japan itself will be bombed heavily. I think we may not occupy Japan, but isolate and quarantine her by sea power; and then spend many weary months driving her troops out of the Philippines, Dutch East Indies, and China. Even then she may be ahead by her policy of infiltration of civilians all over the Pacific. Time will tell. Are we headed for power politics?

Suggested Daily Spiritual Reading:
Deuteronomy 6:5
Ecclesiastes 9:11

Further Reading Related to Diary Entry:
- *Typewriters: Iconic Machines from the Golden Age of Mechanical Writing* by Anthony Casillo (Author), Bruce Curtis (Photographer)

- *Walden and Civil Disobedience* by Henry David Thoreau

- *The Unwomanly Face of War: An Oral History of Women in World War II* by Svetlana Alexievich

- *Spearhead: An American Tank Gunner, His Enemy, and a Collision of Lives in World War II* by Adam Makos

Popular Books Published in 1944:
The Life and Selected Writings of Thomas Jefferson by Thomas Jefferson
The Adventures of Sam Spade and Other Stories by Dashiell Hammett

Popular Movies Released in 1944:
Meet Me in St. Louis (Judy Garland, Margaret O'Brien, Mary Astor)
Thirty Seconds over Tokyo (Spencer Tracy, Van Johnson)
Rationing (Wallace Beery, Marjorie Main)

Wednesday, October 11, 1944

    The German city of Aachen (Aix-la-chapelle) is under assault tonight, with some two-hundred heavy guns pounding it, after a day's attack by Thunderbolts and other dive bombers. The Germans refused a 24-hour ultimatum to surrender, and in consequence the city is doomed to destruction. There are 1500 stormtroopers in the city. Already great clouds of black smoke billow high in the sky. This is a test—evidently the Germans tend to defend the Vaterland to the last, even if it means the destruction of Valhalla. After making an end run around the German forces in Normandy, the Allies advanced rapidly through Paris, and are now facing roughly - - Arnhem in Holland, where a gamble of 8,000 paratroopers was only partially successful; Aachen, Metz, Nancy, and the vicinity of the Belfort Gap. Not much good weather is left before the winter forces a stalemate on the Western front.
    Russia is still stalled before Warsaw, but has broken through to the Gulf of Riga, above Memel, thus trapping about 150,000 Germans in Latvia and Lithuania. They are only 40 miles from Budapest, and have occupied about half of that satellite, and much of Transylvania. The Germans are withdrawing from Greece, the British having taken Corinth without a struggle. In the far east, Islands near Japan itself have been attacked by one of our carrier task forces with a resultant loss of many ships and planes to the Sons of Heaven. We are consolidating our hold on the Palau group, and MacArthur's forces have advanced beyond New Guinea to Morotai. Raids in strength have been made on the Philippines by our naval planes, and it seems the navy is headed in that direction; strategically bearing, as it does, along all the sea lanes to the Dutch Indies, Siam, etc.
    It is still a big war, and a strike of 3,000 men in the local Bethlehem ship building plant in Quincy does not seem in keeping with the general purposes of it.

    The pond behind the house is a sight worth seeing tonight. The water is still and clear, and it reflects not only the houses on the farther bank, but also the vivid, varied colors of the autumn leaves still remaining on the trees. Each year about this time there is nostalgia in the lines of Bliss Carmen to remember:

> "There is something in the autumn that is native to my blood:
>   Touch of manner, hint of mood:
>   And my heart is like a rhyme,
> With the yellow and the purple and the crimson keeping time.
>
>   The scarlet of the maple can shake me like a cry
>   Of bugles passing by.
>   And my lonely spirit thrills

> To see the frosty asters like a smoke upon the hills.
>
> There is something in October sets the gypsy blood astir;
> We must rise and follow her,
> When from every hill of flame
> She calls and calls each vagabond by name!"

(From Bliss Carmen's poem "A Vagabond's Song")

The reds are more vivid this year than for some seasons past. The garden has gone by, and since I planted no corn and no pumpkins, I cannot recall James Whitcomb Riley's words, "The frost is on the punkin and the fodder's in the shock", very well, but suffice it to now that Nature is getting her plants and animals ready for winter, and we had best follow suit. I have cut about a cord of wood for the fireplace, have lots of kindling, and have laid in some coal, so I guess we are started, anyway.

For books, I have purchased recently, Roget's Thesaurus, Funk and Wagnall's College Standard Dictionary, Luccock's "In the Minister's Workshop", and others.

Suggested Daily Spiritual Reading:
Psalm 126:5
Leviticus 23:22

Further Reading Related to Diary Entry:
- For an in-depth history of Massachusetts' Bethlehem Shipbuilding Corporation, Ltd, (Formerly Fore River) naval yard, with pictures of many of the ships built, see the article, *A History of Shipbuilding at Fore River* by Anthony F. Sarcone and Lawrence S. Rines; available from the Thomas Crane Library, Quincy, Massachusetts at http://thomascranelibrary.org/shipbuildingheritage/history.htm [Accessed January 23, 2021].
  - The article contains a picture of the destroyer the Northampton before she was torpedoed and sunk near the Guadalcanal by the Japanese in 1942. The article also clarifies the origins of "Kilroy was here".

- *D-Day Girls: The Spies Who Armed the Resistance, Sabotaged the Nazis, and Helped Win World War II* by Sarah Rose

- *The Cretan Runner: His Story of the German Occupation* by George Pschoundakis

- *In the Minister's Workshop* by Halford Edward Luccock

♦ *The Complete Poetical Works of James Whitcomb Riley* by James Whitcomb Riley

♦ *World's Best Poetry: Poems of Nature (1904)* by Bliss Carmen

Popular Books Published in 1944:
An Essay on Man: An Introduction to a Philosophy of Human Culture by Ernst Cassirer
Story of a Secret State: My Report to the World by Jan Karski

Popular Movies Released in 1944:
Murder, My Sweet (Dick Powell, Claire Trevor)
Mr. Winkle Goes to War (Edward G. Robinson, Ruth Warrick)
The Miracle of Morgan's Creek (Eddie Bracken, Betty Hutton, William Demarest)

Friday, November 17, 1944

In the autumn of 1621, the Pilgrims had their first holiday season. The occasion is so important in our thinking that the passage from Mourt's "Relation" is given in full:

"Our harvest being gotten in, Our Governour sent foure men on fowling, that so we might after a more speciall manner, rejoyce together after we had gathered the fruit of our labours; they foure in one day killed as much fowle, as with a little helpe beside, served the Company almost a weeke, at which time amongst other Recreations, we exercised our Armes, many of the Indians coming amongst us, and amongst the rest their greatest King Massasoyt, with some ninetie men, whom for three dayes we entertained and feasted, and they went out and killed fine Deere, which they brought to the Plantation, and bestowed on our Governour, and upon the Captaine and others. And although it be not alwayes so plentifull, as it was at this time with us, yet by the goodness of God, we are so farre from want, that we often wish you partakers of our plentie."

This Thanksgiving we shall not have deer, nor turkey, nor any of that abundance which characterized the groaning tables of the Pilgrims, for we are at war. Due to the urgent paper shortage, our Governor, Leverett Saltonstall, lineal descendant of Sir Richard Saltonstall of Watertown, and recently elected United States Senator, announces temporary discontinuance of further proclamations. But he has issued one for Thanksgiving, and I desire to quote briefly from it.
Speaking of the Pilgrims, he says, "Sometimes their descendants fail to discern God's Providence at work among them. Even the devout frequently find it difficult to see God's holy purpose unfolding in a world marred by unholy division...Far from seeing in this hour of crisis any obscuring of God's provident care for us, I call upon our people particularly to thank God, in this predestined year for hearts, that no ill fortune could depress; for minds that grew in wisdom in the mire of war; for darkened ways that lead us into Light; for all God's guidance through our man-made woes."
The proclamation closes with this ancient plea, so pertinent to our present state, wherein so much racial hatred has been exhibited at home and abroad: "O God, The Father, do, Thou, make up the dissensions which divide us from each other, and bring us back into the unity of love, which to Thy Divine Nature may bear some likeness. As Thou art above all things, make us one by the unanimity of a good mind, that through the embrace of charity and the bonds of Godly affection, we may spiritually be as one, within ourselves and with each other, by that Peace of Thine which taketh all things peaceful...Amen."

It is unfortunate that with such an abundance of Comics and Sunday papers, which run nearly to a hundred pages, we must eschew such stately language. But the Governor sets a good example. We are not reduced to three grains of corn, as were the early Pilgrims, but an unauthorized truck strike has severely straitened our supplies, and we are limited in amounts. But we have much to be thankful for. "In every thing give thanks, for this is the will of God in Christ Jesus concerning you." (*1 Thessalonians 5:18*)

The war is going well. Six armies on the western front have opened an offensive. Russia is at the gates of Budapest and Warsaw, and has achieved control of the Baltic states, and Northern Finland. MacArthur has captured most of Leyte in the Philippines, and three forces of the Japanese fleet were routed and badly beaten in the recent classic naval battle of the Philippines. They have lost (by estimate) approximately half of their working fleet. Germany is bombed by day and by night. Hitler hasn't been heard from for a long time--a blessing in itself.

A chap who's business was destroyed in the San Francisco fire posted a sign: "I have lost everything but the things which matter most," he said, "my health and my family. Business as usual in the morning." That is our spirit in this year of our Lord, 1944, at Thanksgiving time.

Suggested Daily Spiritual Reading:
Psalm 100:4
Philippians 4:6

Further Reading Related to Diary Entry:
- *The Pilgrim's Progress* by John Bunyan

- *Pilgrim Theology: Core Doctrines for Christian Disciples* by Michael Horton

- *Mayflower: A Story of Courage, Community, and War* by Nathaniel Philbrick

- *Atlas of Indian Nations* by Anton Treuer

- *Mourt's Relation or Journal of the Plantation at Plymouth* with an Introduction and Notes by Henry Marten Dexter. Available from Internet Archive at https://archive.org/details/mourtsrelationo00dextgoog/page/n15 [Accessed January 23, 2021].
    - ***Note that the original text of Mourt's Relation is written in an older english style, for example an "s" looks like an "f" without the crossbar and a "v" looks like a "u".
    - A paraphrased edition, with the old english edited, is available through The

Plymouth Colony Archive Project at http://www.histarch.illinois.edu/plymouth/mourt1.html [Accessed January 23, 2021].

- *Pilgrim Theology: Core Doctrines for Christian Disciples* by Michael Horton

- *Mayflower: A Story of Courage, Community, and War* by Nathaniel Philbrick

- *Atlas of Indian Nations* by Anton Treuer

- *The Works of John Robinson, Pastor of the Pilgrim Fathers*, volume I, 1851; publisher John Snow, 35, Paternoster Row, London; Reed and Pardon, Printers, Lovell's Court, Paternoster Row, London. Available from Internet Archive at https://archive.org/details/worksofjohnrobin01robi/page/n3 [Accessed January 23, 2021].

- *Seuen treatises containing such direction as is gathered out of the Holie Scriptures, leading and guiding to true happines, both in this life, and in the life to come: and may be called the practise of Christianitie. Profitable for all such as heartily desire the same: in the which, more particularly true Christians may learne how to leade a godly and comfortable life euery day.* Penned by Richard Rogers, preacher of the word of God at Wethersfield in Essex by Rogers, Richard, 1550?-1618. At London: Imprinted by Felix Kyngston, for Thomas Man, and Robert Dexter, and are to be sold at the brasen Serpent in Pauls Churchyard, 1603. Available from the Text Creation Partnership, Early English Books Online; University of Michigan, Digital Collections, at https://quod.lib.umich.edu/cgi/t/text/text-idx?c=eebo;idno=A10945.0001.001 [Accessed January 23, 2021].

- *American Caesar: Douglas MacArthur 1880 - 1964* by William Manchester

- *The Admirals: Nimitz, Halsey, Leahy, and King--The Five-Star Admirals Who Won the War at Sea* by Walter R. Borneman

- *American Comic Book Chronicles: 1940-1944* by Kurt F. Mitchell (Author), Roy Thomas (Author), Keith Dallas (Editor), Jack Kirby (Artist), Joe Simon (Artist), Will Eisner (Artist), Irv Novick (Artist)

- *Take That, Adolf!: The Fighting Comic Books of the Second World War* by Jack Kirby (Author, Artist), Joe Simon (Author, Artist), Alex Schomburg (Author, Artist), Will Eisner (Author, Artist), Lou Fine (Author, Artist), Mark Fertig (Editor)

Popular Books Published in 1944:
    Brave Men by Ernie Pyle
    One Man's Meat by E.B. White

Popular Movies Released in 1944:
    Ministry of Fear (Ray Milland, Marjorie Reynolds, Carl Esmond)
    Lights of Old Santa Fe (Roy Rogers, Dale Evans)
    Laura (Gene Tierney, Dana Andrews, Clifton Webb, Vincent Price, Judith Anderson)

December 19, 1944
Journal

"The snow had begun in the gloaming, and busily all the night" (*Quote is from the poem "The First Snowfall" by James Russell Lowell*) is true of last night, for when I arose this morning there was a blanket of white, three or four inches deep, as I ascertained when I walked up the lake. It is still snowing lightly. I like a snowstorm, and as this is the first of the year, it is doubly welcome. It magically transforms the landscape; if it be ugly, it makes it picturesque; and if it be lovely to begin with, as a grove of pines for instance, it becomes positively beautiful under the blanket of snow...Christmas is like that.

We are just a week away from Christmas. We have the tree set up and decorated, and presents are around it already. Mae and I bought the tree, a lovely balsam, tall and symmetrical, up on Fosgate Road—cut it ourselves and brought it home. As a boy, I always use to go out and cut my own tree, somewhere deep in the woods. I remember going way back on the hills, almost to an old sugar house, and there finding, one winter, a small tree but perfectly shaped, and carting it home on my sled. We remember the tree sometimes long after the presents are gone. Living trees must be a fine thing to remember Christmas by.

In this fourth year of war, stores are filled with people shopping. They have plenty of money, seemingly, and prices are high. A measure of inflation. Toys are scarce. One woman in the nation eyed a fur coat priced at $4,000, and said casually, "I'll take that." But when she learned the luxury tax was $800 she changed her mind. She could afford the luxury, but not the tax—sad commentary on our war aims. For it costs money to run a global war, or so I've read...General von Runstedt's men, literally supplied with tanks, reserves, planes and V-bombs, have broken through the First Army's line, in the direction of Liege, for at least 18 miles...a rigid censorship now prevails, so we know not how much farther they have gone. Paratroopers have been used also. Whether this is a diversion to ease pressure on the Saar and Ruhr by the 7th, 9th, and 3rd armies, or a concerted effort really to drive the Americans back, and "reach Paris by Christmas" is something only the future can tell...We await the issue.

I have played so much chess with my next door neighbor, who beats me consistently, that I realize the value of imponderables. The outcome may be delayed, but not denied.

Albert is very busy with school work. He has just received two As in geometry. He knows which planet is nearest the sun. He has given me a year's subscription to the Reader's Digest for Christmas. He brought home two bushels of apples from the farm for our delectation. Janet is equally busy. Three persons desire her service in caring for children this afternoon, and she also has a play rehearsal at the Church. She has all her shopping done for Christmas. Lucky girl!

I have had four weddings and two funeral lately. The wedding which impressed me the most was that of Douglas Corbett, Petty Officer in the Royal Canadian Navy, who has been on ships, twice now, which were torpedoed, and Adele Bowlby, graduate nurse. A Church wedding, and lovely. The couple are very much absorbed in each other, and make a fine couple. At present, they have gone to Montreal to be with his folks over the holidays.

At Church, I have organized a Junior Youth Fellowship of 18 members, who have a religious service, study period, business meeting, games, and refreshments (in the gymnasium) on Sunday evenings. They are singing Christmas carols after the Christmas party and Tree next Sunday night. Then Men's Club will have its first meeting January 24th (I hope).

German prisoners in England say that Adolph Hitler visited the front a short time ago, and talked to the men, promising a nasty surprise to the Americans on December 16th. Well we received it, and the woman who failed to buy the fur coat, may wish the government had the $800 to buy more ammunition with. Soldiers may be had for nothing, but ammunition must be paid for. Sic transit gloria mundi.

Suggested Daily Spiritual Reading:
Matthew 2:1
John 3:6

Further Reading Related to Diary Entry:
- *A Christmas Carol* by Charles Dickens

- *The Battle for Christmas: A Social and Cultural History of Our Most Cherished Holiday* by Stephen Nissenbaum

- *The Origins of Christmas* by Joseph F. Kelly Ph.D.

- *Women Heroes of World War II: 26 Stories of Espionage, Sabotage, Resistance, and Rescue* by Kathryn J. Atwood

Popular Books Published in 1944:
Harvey by Mary Chase
No Exit by Jean-Paul Sartre

Popular Movies Released in 1944:
   Ladies Courageous (Loretta Young, Diana Barrymore, Anne Gwynne, Geraldine Fitzgerald)
   The Heavenly Body (William Powell, Hedy Lamarr)
   The Adventures of Mark Twain (Fredric March, Alexis Smith)

1945

February 2, 1945

Today is Candlemas Day. That is relatively unimportant. The sky is entirely clear, but the temperature is below freezing and a cold wind is blowing. The groundhog can see his shadow, which means eight more weeks of winter, if you accept him as a weather prophet. He guesses wrong more times than right, we hear.

But today is also the second anniversary of Stalingrad. The Russians, in two years, have advance 1300 miles, and stand at the gates of Berlin. They have reconquered all of Poland, except for a small strip in the Northwest corner and the two major cities of Poznan and Koenigsberg (in East Prussia), which are under siege. The 1st Ukranian army, under General Zukov, has driven a wedge into German territory, almost to the Oder River. Officially, according to Moscow, it is 63 land miles from Berlin, but according to German reports it is about forty miles away, and the glare of the big guns can be seen at night in the capital, which is being fortified for siege under the direct command of Goebbels, we are told. The Russians are in the vicinity of Kustrin. They have gone steadily forward since their offensive started on the Vistula beyond Warsaw on January 12th, and are not yet definitely checked anywhere. The armies number some three million men, we are told, and have already engulfed some 200,000 troops in East Prussia, the home of the Junkers. Work has stopped in the mines and factories of Silesia, Oppeln is captured, and Breslau besieged. It is a tremendous offensive, and dwarfs anything the world has yet seen. For it must be remembered that the German offensive in 1939 was that of a superbly equipped army against superior forces.

Strategically, work has stopped in Berlin factories; the industrial area of Silesia is denied them; the Ruhr and Saar are bombed frequently, railroad junctions bombed, and they are deprived of oil. They lost the war at Stalingrad two years ago, and have steadily given ground ever since. Their war potential is gone, and Germany has many enemies.

In the West, the Allies have won completely the Battle of the Bulge, and are now advancing over thinly contested ground. It is my considered opinion that the Germans will not put up much defense against the British and Americans from here on, preferring to surrender to their enemies from the West, who have fewer memories of German atrocities than the Russians.

In the Philippines, American troops under MacArthur are nearing Manila. There has been a third landing below Manila. The first, and highly successful, was at Lingayen Gulf, which has driven to within less than fifty miles of Manila.

The second was in the Subic bay area, which has sealed off the Bataan peninsula. The third cuts off effective Japanese help from the South. Night before last, a force of Rangers—some five hundred—aided by Filipino guerrillas, traveled 25 miles behind the Japanese lines and freed some five hundred prisoners held by the Japs since the days of Corregidor and Singapore. More than five hundred enemy troops were killed; we lost 27 men. Two prisoners died on their way to freedom. Deliverance to the captives; that is the thrilling news from the Pacific front.

On the day when all the concentration camps in Europe are opened and all the slave workers of Poland, France, and other countries, are freed, will be a day of profound rejoicing. That to me has been the tremendous tragedy of this, or any, war—that people should be restrained, confined, and in many cases tortured. Soldiers or civilians. No man has the moral right to dominate another or place his life in jeopardy. Of course, we are slaves to habits or to work or to ideas, but these are of our own making and not by compulsion from without. "To preach deliverance to the captives...to set at liberty them that are bruised..." (*Luke 4:18*) is the great task to which America is committed.

Suggested Daily Spiritual Reading:
Matthew 5:9
Luke 2:29-38

Further Reading Related to Diary Entry:
- *Ardennes 1944: The Battle of the Bulge* by Antony Beevor

- *A Train Near Magdeburg—The Holocaust, the survivors, and the American soldiers who saved them* by Matthew Rozell

- *MacArthur at War: World War II in the Pacific* by Walter R. Borneman

- *Ghost Soldiers: The Epic Account of World War II's Greatest Rescue Mission* by Hampton Sides

Popular Books Published in 1945:
Most Popular Books Published In 1945. Available from Goodreads.com: https://www.goodreads.com/book/popular_by_date/1945 [Accessed January 23, 2021].

Popular Movies Released in 1945:
Mildred Pierce (Joan Crawford, Jack Carson, Zachary Scott, Eve Arden
And Then There Were None (Barry Fitzgerald, Walter Huston, Louis Hayward, Roland Young)
State Fair (Jeanne Crain, Dana Andrews, Dick Haymes, Vivian Blaine)

February 22, 1945
THE CASE SYSTEM

    Having just returned from seeing Alan Ladd and Loretta Young acting their parts superbly in a motion picture adapted from Rachel Field's novel, "And Now Tomorrow", which story revolves around the cure of deafness from meningitis, I feel thoughtful and somewhat sad. Here is a young doctor (and it often transpires in real life) giving his whole time and attention to the curing of one person and one ailment. All the knowledge and techniques of medicine are at his disposal, and he succeeds in developing a serum which cures the wealthy and beautiful Miss Blair, who is a personality of integrity in her own right. He does this, in spite of her wealth and beauty, because it may help some other deaf person smitten with the same affliction. "If I can help some fainting robin unto his nest again, I shall not have lived in vain." (*Quote is paraphrased from Emily Dickinson's poem "If I Can Stop One Heart from Breaking"*) That makes me sad. How succinct and far reaching in its efficacy is the miracle of medicine! It is clearcut, precise, beneficial.

    In contrast, how often confused and lame and disappointing and futile is the work of a minister. Seldom does he "cure an immortal soul", even if he could find one that wanted curing. We hold hands with the sick, and make social calls, and preach sermons ineffective as buckshot scattered over the landscape—but seldom do we follow, or have a chance to follow, the example of the Great Physician in the case of a Zaccheus or a Magdalene or a Nicodemus.

    What a thrill it must have been to the man stricken with palsy to have someone say to him with assurance, "Son thy sins are forgiven thee; take up thy bed and walk." (*Quote is paraphrased from Matthew 9:5; Mark 2:9*) Jesus cured by faith, for faith is the basis of all cures; and He healed the soul, the psyche first, knowing that bodily and mental health are conditioned by spiritual well-being. We need the case system in the ministry. To be able to devote five months if necessary, as Dr. Merrick did to cure one person; aided by the unearned increment of knowledge and techniques in curing souls; this would give each minister satisfaction beyond measure!

    We have the case system in medicine; each patient is given exclusive attention and care—individual dosage as it were. We have the case system in law; each case is decided on its merits, aided by common or statute law laid down in similar cases. Why not a case system for the ministry? We need it. Christ used it—each of his "miracles" was given individual attention, excepting perhaps the feeding of the five thousand—and that began with a limited quantity—five loaves and two fishes! The insane man chained to the rocks over in the country of Gadarenes (or Gergasenes), on the eastern shore of Galilee, is a good case in point. He found him "torn apart" and left him integrated, "sitting and clothed and in his right mind". (*Mark 5:15, Luke 8:35*)

Many of our people must be similarly torn with conflict—not outwardly, but inwardly—in the welter and confusion of the times. Racial hatreds, war phobias, financial anxieties, personal worries must make for disturbed souls. God grant that we have the vision to see that these need to be treated individually, and that we have the strength of character, the wisdom, the patience and confidence so to treat them! It would make a revolution in our way of thinking if we could follow the pattern laid down by the Master, and treat each parishioner as worthy of our time and attention; our knowledge and techniques; for there are enough of these if we have the intelligence to see and use them. "Believest thou that I can do this?" (*paraphrased from Matthew 9:28*) is the basis for spiritual healing. "Thy sins are forgiven thee; go and sin no more" (*paraphrased from John 8:11*) the essential technique. "I am come that they might have Life and that they might have it more abundantly" (*John 10:10*) is the werden und zein of our calling. General principles are good, even as lectures in a medical school are good, but consequent upon principles are practices that will help to restore the individual to a fuller participation in all that life has to offer. The whole aim of a doctor is to heal—even if it be but one person. That too is the summun bonum of the ministry.

Suggested Daily Spiritual Reading:
Matthew 14:17-19
John 8:11

Further Reading Related to Diary Entry:
- *Holy Spirit And Power* by John Wesley
- *The Theology of John Wesley: Holy Love and the Shape of Grace* by Kenneth J. Collins
- *Dark Nights of the Soul: A Guide to Finding Your Way Through Life's Ordeals* by Thomas Moore
- *The Seven Storey Mountain* by Thomas Merton

Popular Books Published in 1945:
The Egg and I by Betty MacDonald
Animal Farm by George Orwell

Popular Movies Released in 1945:
And Now Tomorrow (Alan Ladd, Loretta Young)
They Were Expendable (Robert Montgomery, John Wayne, Donna Reed)
Anchors Aweigh (Frank Sinatra, Kathryn Grayson, Gene Kelly, José Iturbi)

April 14, 1945

"The past is a bucket of ashes," says Carl Sandburg, and I agree with him, but sometimes it makes interesting reading. Postquam haec olim meminisse juvabit. Later on it will be pleasing (and perhaps profitable) to have remembered these things.

Ten years ago today, according to my neighbor's diary, it was snowing in Hudson, Mass. U.S.A. Today it is around 80 (*Fahrenheit*), warm as a day late in May, and my lilacs are half in bloom. Yesterday was unconscionably hot.

Events are moving so rapidly that they seem out of control. The war in Germany is reaching its final stages, with the Allies on the Elbe and Oder rivers; nearly one half of Germany overrun, and a junction near (*seems to be a word he left out here*) between American and Russian forces. Out in the Pacific, 400 B 29- super-fortresses gave Tokyo a going over yesterday with bomb incendiaries, and our advance on Okinawa is slow but steady. We have 1400 Naval vessels in that invasion force alone, and perhaps 100,000 men. I wish I could have followed a Marine from Guadalcanal to Okinawa, or a GI Joe from Oran to Leipsig, and then perhaps I would know how the boys really live and feel and think.

History of past things has the calmness of a dead fish—I like my history to be up-to-date and moving. It certainly has been in the last few days. On Thursday at 6 p.m., as I was listening to the news, we heard of the dramatic and sudden demise of president Franklin Delano Roosevelt, 32nd President of these United States. I was immediately curious above all to know how he had died. It was after this manner. He was having sketches made at the Little White House on Pine Ridge, Warm Springs, GA—the infantile paralysis foundation which he started before becoming Governor of New York— when he suddenly complained of terrific pain in the back of his head. This was about 1:30 p.m. He fainted soon after, and the naval surgeon diagnosed his illness as massive cerebral hemorrhage. He died in about two hours without regaining consciousness or speaking further. He is our major casualty of the war. Harry S. Truman became President about 7 p.m., taking the oath of office in the presence of Supreme Court Justice Harlan S. Stone.

Mrs. Roosevelt said, on learning of her husband's death, "I feel more sorry for the people of the country and of the world than for us." Since then, the radio stations, omitting all routine commercials, have been giving time to only appropriate music and tributes to the late President, and speculations by commentators on its effect relative to the foreign policy of the country. His funeral this afternoon in the East Room of the White House is private, with interment tomorrow at Hyde Park.

All current animosities ceased with the passing of Mr. Roosevelt. De mortuis nihil nisi bonum. Actually, there has been remarkable unanimity of feeling in the country since the war began. We have been united in spirit and purpose, and he has led us. Of his many accomplishments, and his unquestioned place in history, I shall not here speak, but I do feel regret that his influence could not be personally felt at the San Francisco conference, which meets April 25, to formulate and set in motion plans and programs for the establishment of a World Security Council.

I suppose the people of Lincoln's day felt the same shock and uncertainty when their War President was suddenly taken from them. But the flag still waves and the government at Washington carries on. None are indispensable in democracy, but some are well nigh so. My children have never known another President. I can remember seeing campaign posters for Cleveland, and I worked a Bull Moose in my lapel in 1912 in honor of Theodore Roosevelt. It was my privilege to meet Coolidge when he was Vice President. But my children remember only FDR, as he was commonly known. Oddly enough, we shall have no Vice President for nearly four years, there being no provision in our Constitution for one when he takes over the duties of President. I wonder what would happen should the President-elect die on the eve of a Presidential election! We vote for electors to be sure. Would they meet and proceed to elect a President as outlined in the Constitution? Interesting to speculate upon.

"We have nothing to fear, but fear itself." FDR 1933. Memorare—

Suggested Daily Spiritual Reading:
Psalm 23:4
Psalm 48:14

Further Reading Related to Diary Entry:
- *FDR* by Jean Edward Smith

- *No Ordinary Time: Franklin and Eleanor Roosevelt: The Home Front in World War II* by Doris Kearns Goodwin

- *The Fall of Berlin 1945* by Antony Beevor

- *The Complete Poems of Carl Sandburg: Revised and Expanded Edition* by Carl Sandburg

Popular Books Published in 1945:
    Cannery Row by John Steinbeck
    The Black Rose by Thomas B. Costain

Popular Movies Released in 1945:
    The Clock (Judy Garland, Robert Walker, James Gleason)
    A Song to Remember (Paul Muni, Merle Oberon, Cornel Wilde)
    Story of G.I. Joe (Burgess Meredith, Robert Mitchum, Freddie Steele, Wally Cassell)

Sunday, July 8, 1945

"I being in the way, the Lord led me." (*Genesis 24:27*) So speaks the Bible. Paraphrased, I being in the mood, the Word moved me. And I am in the mood to catch up with my journal. The family—Janet, Junior (pardon me, it is Albert now [*Albert Jr. is approximately 16 and Janet is 14*]), Mae, and Mother Brock have just returned from Hanson's Beach on Lake Boone, where we have been swimming and boating. It is lovely there, especially when you take a row around the basin, and observe the clouds (altocumulus today, with some cumulus); the trees, including many pines against the sky; the expanse of water, with a light breeze; and the people—on their cottages painting, as I saw one man do; or on their porches, viewing the scenery; or down on the wharves sunning, like woodchucks out of their burrows; or in the boats, canoes, kayaks, et al., enjoying the water, as we were; or diving off the piers and diving boards. Everything, everybody, was serene, in tune with nature and infinite; quite in keeping with the day, for "this is the day the Lord hath made; let us rejoice and be glad in it" (*Psalm 18:24*), and I think you can worship Him "who opens His hand and satisfieth the desire of every living creature" (*paraphrased, Psalm 145:16*) fully as much in His natural environment as in temples made with hands. Perhaps more, seeing He dwelleth not in the temples made with hands (*paraphrased from Acts 17:24*), and that He giveth life and health and breath to every creature (*paraphrased from Acts 17:25*).

I am on vacation. I have been very busy at Fillmore's Ice Cream stand, working every evening except Monday. I worked four days last week making ice cream. I have been making it alone, too, much of the time. Friday, I made 477 gallons in the freezer, a day's record for me, using 22 1/2 jugs of mix (compounded of 12% butterfat milk, plus sugar and gelatin) and adding the different ingredients—such as coffee, or butterscotch, or strawberry plus the flavorings and colors. Fascinating work, but exacting and sometimes tiring, for the routine and rhythm must be learned to keep the machine going as long as possible without stopping. In hot weather, a lot of ice cream is consumed, nearly 750 gallons last weekend. We have made 10,000 gallons since May 1st. The hardening room, where the ice cream is kept, has a temperature averaging 10 below zero Fahrenheit. I find that to be best for consistency. It is enjoyable work and I am enjoying my vacation.

Last June 6th was VE day (*Victory in Europe day*), with the war over in Europe. It has been well reported in the papers. Goering surrendered, Hitler disappeared, the hated Himmler committed suicide, and the other high Nazi leaders have been caught one after the other. Nazism is dead as an active force, and done with, but probably not as an idea. It may plague the world for decades to come. We have captured the Philippines and Okinawa, and have 2200 planes in action from Guam, and the Mariannas, and Okinawa, Tokyo reports. With fire bombs—jellied gasoline—we have destroyed some 100 square miles of Japanese cities. The Japanese navy has been reduce to impotence. We are masters of the broad Pacific seas, and, save for the suicide planes of the Japanese—the Kamikaze—the skies. All that remains is the arduous talk of invasion of the homelands, Manchuria, China and the Dutch East Indies; although, the Australians have retaken Balikpapan in Borneo, which has some of the richest oil fields. Many of the boys in service have been discharged—I have recently met two who have been in China—and America is on the way to her larger destiny; what that may be, only the future can tell. It is hopeful in that the San Francisco conference is concluded and with it the signing of a new world charter for the United Nations. Its efficacy depends on the ability of the nations to work together in peace as they have in war. It is a magnificent start in the right direction. Problems, many; but let us remember, the Sun shines today also!

Suggested Daily Spiritual Reading:
Genesis 1
Genesis 24:27
John 1:1

Further Reading Related to Diary Entry:
- *Victory in Europe: D-Day to V-E Day* by Max Hastings

- *Michigan POW Camps in World War II* by Gregory D. Sumner

- *Savage Continent: Europe in the Aftermath of World War II* by Keith Lowe

- *Postwar: A History of Europe Since 1945* by Tony Judt

- *After the Reich: The Brutal History of the Allied Occupation* by Giles MacDonogh

Popular Books Published in 1945:
The Portable Walt Whitman by Walt Whitman
Pilates' Return to Life Through Contrology by Joseph H. Pilates

Popular Movies Released in 1945:
Confidential Agent (Charles Boyer, Lauren Bacall, Victor Francen, Wanda Hendrix)
The House on 92nd Street (William Eythe, Lloyd Nolan, Signe Hasso, Gene Lockhart)
Pursuit to Algiers (Basil Rathbone, Nigel Bruce, Marjorie Riordan, Rosalind Ivan)

August 9, 1945
Current Events

1. Albert and I visited New York July 26, 27, 28.
2. A B-25 bomber crashed into the Empire State building July 28th.
3. An atomic bomb struck Hiroshima day before yesterday. Yesterday another was launched on Nagasaki.
4. Russia declared war on Japan yesterday, August 8th, at 3 p.m.

Of great importance to the world of course is the atomic bomb, created by splitting the rare isotope Uranium—ordinary 238, rare 235—into radioactive atoms of barium by bombarding it with neutrons. One such atom was split in 1940, creating 200,000,000 electronic volts thereby, which was used to switch on the 50,000 watt transmitter of radio station WBZ in Hull, Massachusetts. The first atomic bomb, it is reported, destroyed 60% of Hiroshima, a city of 350,000 people. The second all but obliterated the port of Nagasaki. Many scientists contributed to its development at a cost of two billion dollars—said cost borne by this government. One who held the key to the secret, a Jewish scientist, Dr. Lize Meitner, with her associates, Dr. Otto Hahn and Dr. F. Strassman, were exiled from Germany, as non-Aryans, one of the ironies of history, for the Nazis with the atomic bomb might have defeated Russia and England and ruled the world.

Albert and I went to New York by train on Thursday, July 26. We arrived at Grand Central about four o'clock and stayed at Prince George Hotel, 14 East 28th St., for two nights. It was cloudy all the time we were in the city. The first night we visited Riverside Drive, on a 5th Avenue bus, then St. Patrick's cathedral, where a litany of Benediction and elevation of the cross was being enacted. We saw the Rockettes, orchestra, and "A Bell for Adano" at Radio City Music Hall. I enjoyed, particularly, the shower each morning at the hotel (*only a tub in the parsonage*). Friday, we visited the Statue of Liberty; the RCA building studios in Rockefeller Center; Central Park Zoo; the Museum of Natural History, with its famous exhibit of Carl Akeley's African Hall; and in the evening—the Hayden Planetarium. I particularly enjoyed seeing a replica of the Time Capsule, a copper shell buried in the fall of 1938 on the World Fair grounds. It contained ordinary articles for men and women, a doll and toy auto for children, microfilm of newspapers and magazines, metallurgical specimens, and a whole copy of the Bible and a book of the Lord's Prayer in 300 languages—-said capsule to be opened in 6939. I understand that a description of contents and location has been sent to the leading libraries of the world.

Saturday, a dull, drizzly day, we went to Coney Island at 8 a.m. Two bathers for three miles of beach—no amusements open. We visited the pier where men were fishing for flounders—flukes, they call them. Tonic in New York is soda; a frappe is made like a sundae. Coney Island without its teeming millions, bright lights and crowded beach; but we were glad to see it nevertheless.

On our return, we planned to go up in the Empire State Building, but a bomber's crash killing 13 persons prevented it. We could see the gaping holes and smoke pouring from the South side of the building, opposite that which the bomber hit. It was awe-inspiring. I talked with three who saw it immediately after the crash and explosion (*read more about this incident in this report from NPR: https://www.npr.org/templates/story/story.php?storyId=92987873 [Accessed January 23, 2021]*).

In the afternoon we visited the Bronx Park Zoo, a fascinating place, with its lions in the open on an island surrounded by a ditch 15 feet deep; and the giant pandas—gift of Madame Kai Shek. Albert particularly liked the reptile house, and later purchased Ditmar's book, "Reptiles of the World". We saw "The Arabian Nights" on Broadway, a modernized version of the story of Aladin, and very funny. After visiting a book store and restaurant, we came home on the midnight train, having covered the town to our mutual satisfaction.

Suggested Daily Spiritual Reading:
Isaiah 41:10
John 16:33

Further Reading Related to Diary Entry:
- *Hiroshima* by John Hersey

- *To Hell and Back: The Last Train from Hiroshima* by Charles Pellegrino

- *Coney Island: Lost and Found* by Charles Denson

- *The Historical Atlas of New York City, Third Edition: A Visual Celebration of 400 Years of New York City's History* by Eric Homberger

Popular Books Published in 1945:
The Adventures of Solar Pons by August Derleth
The Pearl by John Steinbeck

Popular Movies Released in 1945:
Lady on a Train (Deanna Durbin, Ralph Bellamy, Edward Everett Horton, Allen Jenkins)
Duffy's Tavern (Ed Gardner, Bing Crosby, Betty Hutton, Paulette Goddard)
Spellbound (Ingrid Bergman, Gregory Peck, Michael Chekhov, Leo G. Carroll)

Tuesday, August 14th, 1945

"He maketh wars to cease unto the ends of the earth..." Psalm 46:9

At 7 o'clock tonight, 2300 GMT, I heard Prime Minister Atlee pronounce the magic words—"Japan has surrendered." He then went on to say that the Emperor agrees to give the order to his troops to surrender, and to put himself under the orders of the Supreme Commander of the Allied Forces to carry out the terms of the Potsdam Declaration—a more satisfactory conclusion that we had dared to hope for. President Truman announced the same thing at a press conference in Washington. At 7:10, the whistles and bells began to ring in our town, and the children began to toot their horns. It is still going on. My neighbor listening to it, echoed my sentiments (for I was reading Psalm 46). "We ought to be praying," she said, "and thanking God." I do plan a service of thanksgiving tomorrow night at 8 o'clock, when things have quieted down a bit. I couldn't hear myself speaking tonight. Well, the American public deserves to let off steam. "Behold what desolations He maketh in the earth." (*Paraphrased, Psalm 46:8*)

Germany, Italy, and Japan have come to the same end—so relatively early for Japan it is stupefying; but the atomic bomb, and the entry of Russia into the war were the straw's that broke the camel's back, evidently. The Nipponesse have lost a great deal of face, but if they can save their dynasty and their emperor, it will mean much to them. Their people need not know he is subject to the will of foreign devils, though they may be occupying the main islands soon.

"Be still, and know that I am God; I will be exalted among the heathen, I will be exalted on the earth." (*Psalm 46:10*) The spirit of the Lord among His peoples has been under a cloud since 1939—six long war years; but it has emerged—the prisoners go free, and the little folks everywhere can lift their heads again, for after the storm and the earthquake and the fire, comes the still small voice of sanity and hope and a brave new world. Bless all who have suffered; and sanctify all who have died, that this new world might come into being.

The bells still ring, as they have for nearly and hour. They will be ringing in London, and Moscow, and Chungking (if they have bells in Chungking) for the Chinese have suffered longest of all.

How shall we begin to count the cost, the tragedy of it all? Only the Christ on His cross could do that. Should we say it has cost us $300,000,000,000—three hundred billion dollars, as it has? 25,000,000 millions of Russian lives, as it has? Or that a mother somewhere in America has lost two of her three sons, as she has? The long vigil to England ended "God knows we've earned it," a speaker on BBC just said.

The break in the line above represents a break in continuity. I went, at that point, to the Church where there were a handful of the faithful. Flowers on the alter and candles lighted. Before the benediction, I substituted two candles which had burned on the altar on V-E Day. Bless the faithful! They who remember in prayer and inchoate feelings the loved ones overseas.

After the service, I took Mae and Mother Brock through the main street of Hudson, and then of Marlboro. Lots of noise and paper strewn about, but no firecrackers, nor drunkenness—mostly young people of grammar and high school age standing around just waiting for something to happen. Albert went to the movies prior to seven o'clock. "The Picture of Dorian Gray" by Oscar Wilde is showing. Janet is in Lynn visiting her friend, Ann Holdsworth.

Suggested Daily Spiritual Reading:
Psalm 46:9-10
Philippians 4:4-9

Further Reading Related to Diary Entry:
- *Japan's Longest Day* by The Pacific War Research Society

- *The Fall of Japan: A Chronicle of the End of an Empire* by William Craig

- *If You Survive: From Normandy to the Battle of the Bulge to the End of World War II, One American Officer's Riveting True Story* by George Wilson

- *Potsdam: The End of World War II and the Remaking of Europe* by Michael Neiberg

Popular Books Published in 1945:
Brideshead Revisited: The Sacred and Profane Memories of Captain Charles Ryder by Evelyn Waugh
Stuart Little by E.B. White

Popular Movies Released in 1945:
The Picture of Dorian Gray (George Sanders, Hurd Hatfield, Donna Reed)
I Know Where I'm Going! (Wendy Hiller, Roger Livesey, George Carney, Walter Hudd)
Back to Bataan (John Wayne, Anthony Quinn, Beulah Bondi)

November 12, 1945

Feeling quite bored and having nothing to read except a story on surgery, which I bought the other night for my son. I am turning to expression to relieve that feeling of ennui, and to give my ego a sense of importance, for only so can we go on living, let alone advance. With the cessation of the war we seem to be simply "marking time". That gave purpose and direction to all our thinking and acting. Now that it is over, there is a terrific letdown. We did not do all that we could have done, and that bothers us. And yet, in a larger sense, the real work has just begun, for the spirit of the Cross must take up where the military leaves off. The guns have excised the excrescences of madness and false ambition from the Hitlers and the Hirohitos after the manner of a surgeon, and now the healing process must begin. Bridges of understanding must be built, and only a kingdom of love in Christ can really take into its sovereignty the children of men. It is the only true world state. Any other is subject to disintegration, through collusion and greed. I do not refer to state religions for they are more corrupt than none at all, since they are handmaidens or servants of the political state.

Even Japan subsidized Christianity to spread its propaganda of co-prosperity among the islands of the seas prior to Pearl Harbor, even though Shintoism is the state religion. The real City of God cuts across denominational lines as surely as it cuts across political ones. Tertullian's dogma, Extra ecclesiam nulla salus, outside the Church there is no salvation, was exorcised by Christ himself, who said of one who cast out devils in His name, though he was not listed in the distinguished company of the disciples, "He that is not against us is for us." (*Luke 9:50*)

Real religion even cuts across the boundaries of war itself, as witness the ministrations of Christian nurses to Japanese soldiers. As Edith Cavell said, "Patriotism is not enough. I must have no hatred in my heart for anyone." Not even for those who condemned her. There is no defense against love transcending. A world secure and free is a world dominated not by Maginot lines, but by positive affection. Jesus said, "The Kingdom of Heaven is entos humon" (*Luke 17:21*), and whether we interpret that to mean "within you" or "among you" (in the person of Himself)—if we accept and follow the dictum, the end result is the same; for then the corporate body of humanity becomes love incarnate. And the Word becomes flesh and dwells among us, and we behold His glory, the glory as of the only begotten of the Father, full of grace and truth. To achieve that end we must begin with ourselves. How does Emerson express it? Live so true to yourself that your private action will become world compulsion. Approximately. In short perfect love casts out fear an every other evil way.

There was a big Armistice Day parade in Boston today, with General Dwight D.

Eisenhower as the honored guest. I took Albert and Janet into town via Lake Street, and we saw the general, also several hundred marchers, mostly members of the State Guard. Eisenhower is just as affable as his pictures. He took off his hat to our segment of the crowd, twice. At the reviewing stand a girl from Watertown broke through the police lines and kissed him twice, whereupon he murmured, "Gee, thanks" as he wiped the lipstick from his cheek. Just a regular fellow! And yet his guiding genius brought to a successful conclusion the most devastating war in history.

This evening Mae and I went to the movies. We saw Edward Arnold enacting the role of a blind detective with excellent results, aided by his police dog, Friday (*"Eyes In The Night"*). The main feature was "The Princess and the Bellboy" (*actual title is "Her Highness and the Bellboy"*) with Robert Walker, June Allyson, and Hedy Lamarr taking the lead roles. It was humorous and yet serious too, proving that even a queen could abdicate a throne for the love of a man. Altogether an interesting day. And so to bed. Selah.

Suggested Daily Spiritual Reading:
Matthew 5:10
Numbers 15:26

Further Reading Related to Diary Entry:
- *As a Man Thinketh* by James Allen

- *Serving God and Country: United States Military Chaplains in World War II* by Lyle W. Dorsett

- *Pure Grit: How American World War II Nurses Survived Battle and Prison Camp in the Pacific* by Cronk Farrell, Mary

- *And If I Perish: Frontline U.S. Army Nurses in World War II* by Evelyn Monahan

- *Crusade in Europe* by Dwight D. Eisenhower

Popular Books Published in 1945:
Ross Poldark by Winston Graham
The Age of Reason by Jean-Paul Sartre

Popular Movies Released in 1945:
Eyes In The Night (Edward Arnold, Ann Harding, Dona Reed [released in 1942)
Her Highness and the Bellboy (Hedy Lamarr, Robert Walker, and June Allyson)
The Corn is Green (Bette Davis, John Dall, Nigel Bruce)

December 26, 1945
Christmas 1945

Another Christmas has come and gone, but it has left behind a feeling of satisfaction. One year ago our hearts were troubled by the setback of the Ardennes Offensive, the so-called Battle of the Bulge, and many war restrictions. This year the war is over, many of the soldiers have returned home, some nonexistent items like alarm clocks, for instance, have reappeared on the markets, and a real holiday spirit prevailed. In Hudson, the cross on the hill to the south of the town was relighted after four years, and a fine sight it is as it shines forth brilliantly each night.

On the international scene, the Big Three have had another conference, this time in Moscow, with Stalin, Truman, and Atlee present. The Nuremberg trials of Geering, Hess, Ribbentrop, Keitel, and company continue. The Pacific is relatively quiet, with Japan taking directives from MacArthur. In China, our policy is to aid the Nationalist government with supplies, but not with men; that is to take no active part in routing the Communists, who probably will be eventually included in a coalition government. In the Dutch East Indies, the British are committed to cleaning out extremist elements who they claim are sponsoring the Indonesian drive for Independence. At home, on the national scene, the Atomic age holds first place in discussions, though if there is to be a light in the sky it seems to me it should be the Star of Bethlehem.

We had a fine Christmas Sunday with a large attendance and many returned service men. I preached on the subject of gifts, quoting Emerson who said, "The only gift is a portion of thyself. Thou must bleed for me." And Acts 20:35, "Remember the words of the Lord Jesus, how he said, It is more blessed to give than to receive." A Christmas party for the Sunday School at five o'clock was well attended, with refreshments, tree, Dicken's "A Christmas Carol", a Santa Claus in the person of Elmer Gale, and presents for the Children.

Mae and I listened, via radio, to the midnight mass on Christmas Eve from St. Patrick's cathedral in New York, Francis Cardinal Spellman of Whitman, Mass. officiating, Rt. Rev. James Griffiths preaching the sermon. He is an artist in word pictures. We had a fine Christmas tree lighted and decorated. The children were up early, as usual, to enjoy their presents. Albert received an Eversharp pen and pencil set, Janet a white dressing gown, among other things. Mae found a Presto pressure cooker, which I was fortunate in obtaining the day before in Marlboro. I discovered a strong box for my "valuables" and a bathrobe, which I have long wanted.

Christmas Day we all went, as per custom, to Donnie Burgess' in Lincoln, where he showed us motion pictures of winter sports and a news reel of important events in 1945. Then to Mother Anderson's (his mother), where we partook of a fulsome turkey dinner with all the fixings, ending with plum pudding and ice cream, mirabile dietu! Another tree and presents. In the afternoon, Mae and the children visited the Townsends (*Marion and Henry*) and Auntie Fiske in Cochituate. More presents. We called our friends, the Fern Taylors in Cochituate before coming home.

Weather—light snow turning to rain, it rained half the night, and the rain was accompanied by a high wind. Today it is cloudy and warm, the snow has melted from the roofs, and Bruce Pond, in back of the house, is ice covered with water, leaving a rectangular ring, ironically, where the boys and girls laboriously shoveled away the deep snow a few days ago. It ought to be wonderful skating when the lake freezes over again. I heard a portion of Dicken's "A Christmas Carol" read again over the air by Lionel Barrymore. Tuned in just about in time to hear him repeat the words of Tiny Tim, which I echo here, "And may God bless us, every one!" (*Listen to Lionel Barrymore as Ebenezer Scrooge in the 1939 radio drama, "A Christmas Carol"; available on YouTube at* https://youtu.be/3gJ3jINcTR0 [*Accessed on January 23, 2021*])

Suggested Daily Spiritual Reading:
Acts 20:35
Matthew 2:11

Further Reading Related to Diary Entry:
- *Mission at Nuremberg: An American Army Chaplain and the Trial of the Nazis* by Tim Townsend

- *A Train Near Magdeburg—The Holocaust, the survivors, and the American soldiers who saved them* by Matthew Rozell

- *Unbroken: A World War II Story of Survival, Resilience, and Redemption* by Laura Hillenbrand

- *Mr. Dickens and His Carol* by Samantha Silva

- *The Man Who Invented Christmas: How Charles Dickens's A Christmas Carol Rescued His Career and Revived Our Holiday Spirits* by Les Standiford

Popular Books Published in 1945:
Arch of Triumph: A Novel of a Man Without a Country by Erich Maria Remarque
Christ Stopped at Eboli: The Story of a Year by Carlo Levi

Popular Movies Released in 1945:
- *The Bells of St. Mary's* (Bing Crosby, Ingrid Bergman, Henry Travers, William Gargan)
- *Christmas in Connecticut* (Barbara Stanwyck, Dennis Morgan, Sydney Greenstreet, Reginald Gardiner)
- *An Angel Comes to Brooklyn* (Barbara Perry, Charles Kemper)

1946

February 23, 1946

"Thou hast maddens to drink the wine of astonishment..." Ps. 60:30

Nearly every day something arises to interest, astonish, or amuse us. It may be something scientific, like the atomic bomb; the proximity fuse (with its own little radio set in the nose of a shell); loran (long range navigation), which enables a shipper at sea to check its bearings by triangulation; radar, which recently reached out to the moon, with a powerful four million watt wave, and was received back in 2.4 seconds as a blip on a fluorescent screen with voltage now something like one four millionth of a watt, and with slightly increased frequency in accordance with the Doppler effect.

Or it may be something long lost and familiar, such as the sound of a bird I heard off in the woods, somewhere, yesterday, as I was standing on the ice of the pond. It sounded like a Curlew, and may have been a winter bird, but to me it as the first voice of spring.

Or it may be the account of another human being, and the daily newspapers are filled with human interest accounts of the strange things people do and say. Man is perennially interesting to man. I have just been reading the life of Edgar Cayce of Kentucky, as related by Thomas Sugrue in a fascinating book entitled, "There is a River". Thomas Sugrue was the victim of a strange paralysis for which the doctor found no name, and he was treated and cured by Cayce; hence, the interest that led him to tell the story of Edgar Cayce. Cayce now has a hospital, or clinic rather, at Virginia Beach, Virginia; is about 65 years of age, and since childhood has been helping people physically and mentally by a most unusual method. That method is clairvoyance while in a self-imposed state of trance or autohypnosis. During this trance Cayce is able to give "readings" concerning anyone near or far, which diagnoses the ills of the body and suggests remedies for treatments. He has given some 10,000 of these readings.

It began in his boyhood, with his bible reading. He had a vision one day of a "lady with wings" who told him he had but to ask for anything he wanted, and he replied that he wanted to help people, especially little children. He has read the bible each year of his life. His first experience was with a spelling book. He fell asleep with it under his head, and when he awoke, he had literally the power to visualize it all. Edison could do that with a dictionary, it is reported. Glancing at a couple of pages for two minutes he could visualize it so well he could relate all the words on both pages. A photographic mind. Edgar did this with his other books, and the result was that he advanced rapidly in his studies; although, he had only nine grades of schooling, and no medical training. Later, he healed himself of a blow on the spine sustained when hit with a baseball, went into a trance and suggested the necessary remedies; he healed his wife of tuberculosis when she had been given up by the doctors; and years later his son's eyes were saved, after an explosion of flash powder in his photographic studio, by the same method. He received little encouragement from the doctors, but has helped hundreds of friends and neighbors. "The wine of astonishment..."

Suggested Daily Spiritual Reading:
Psalm 60:30
Matthew 9:35

Further Reading Related to Diary Entry:
- *Loran, Long Range Navigation: Massachusetts Institute of Technology, Radiation Laboratory Series, No. 4* by John Alvin Pierce (Editor), A. a. McKenzie (Editor), R. H. Woodward (Editor)

- *Celestial Navigation: Using the Sight Reduction Tables from "Pub. No 249"* by Dominique F. Prinet

- *There Is a River: Story of Edgar Cayce* by Thomas Sugrue

- *A Search for God (Books 1 & 2), 50th Anniversary Edition* by Edgar Cayce

Popular Books Published in 1946:
Most Popular Books Published In 1946. Available at Goodreads.com: https://www.goodreads.com/book/popular_by_date/1946 (accessed August 23, 2109).

Popular Movies Released in 1946:
The Big Sleep (Humphrey Bogart, Lauren Bacall)
The Yearling (Gregory Peck, Jane Wyman, Claude Jarman Jr.)
The Blue Dahlia (Alan Ladd, Veronica Lake, William Bendix)

February 23, 1946
(Continued)

One is convinced after reading the book that Edgar Cayce is no fake, and that he has made a genuine contribution to human progress, not only in the good that he has done, but in his frank revelation of the power of the subconscious mind in the interest of doing good. His technique is interesting in itself. Twice a day he unfastens his cufflinks, and shoelaces and lies down on a table. In a short while his respiration is deep and regular. Then he is told the name and address of the person—who may live in another country, even. He gives an anatomical diagnosis, and corresponding treatment. When he awakens claims to have no knowledge of what he has said. Of nine pregnant mothers in the town of Cayce, he divined correctly the sex of each unborn, as evidenced later when the children were born. He solved a murder case in another state. He wasn't able to find oil in the state of Texas for a company, which he headed, but perhaps the oil wasn't there.

But the book is filled with case histories of people whom he has helped, and it all bears the stamp of authenticity. His grandfather was psychic too, and could find water anywhere with a divining rod. Snakes loved him, though he hated them, and would follow him to the house, and curl around his hat brim. They caused him to give up farming and move to town.

Through his friend Lammers, Cayce becomes interested in metaphysical phenomena, such as the law of Karma, the ancient mysteries, and incarnation of souls, which he affirms by the way. This part of the book is dubious to me, as it smacks of pseudo-science, and dabbles in the fringes of that which is unknown and perhaps unknowable. It seems to validate astrology, life on other spheres before coming to this one, and the eight influences of the eight planets (what if a ninth is discovered?), and the fourth dimension. The other is astonishment enough. But he has given life "readings" for the total personality, and may have been genuinely interested and perhaps helped.

To me the outstanding interest is the fact that occasionally, just as there are mutations or "sports" in plants and animals, so do there seem to be in humans and human minds. "We are fearfully and wonderfully made," (*Psalm 139:14, paraphrased*) without a doubt. Zerah Colburn, of Peacham, Vermont, a hundred years ago in Boston, could and did, at 6, give the number of seconds that had elapsed since the time of Christ. His mathematical ability was phenomenal. In the realm of clairvoyance, a chap named Davis—Andrew Jackson Davis of Bloominggrove, Orange County, New York—underwent almost the same experiences as Cayce, save that he lay on his side after hypnosis instead of on his back. In the time of Mesmer there was a shepherd boy called Victor, who under the influence of hypnosis could also diagnose and heal. How Victor or Davis or

Cayce can "see" a person he has not previously known, and describe his surroundings, and prescribe remedies of which he is not even aware when conscious, does indeed pose many problems in the realm metaphysics, let alone such abstruse things as metempsychosis and numerology and lost continents, such as Atlantis and Lemuria.

It does fill us with "the wine of astonishment" for most of our lives are prosaic enough, and the hidden world of the soul or individuality or personality is remote from the average run of men. Just as there are diversities of gifts in physical strength and mental powers (and my neighbor beats me regularly at chess), so there seem to be wide divergencies in the spiritual realm. Cayce maintains, for example, that Christ was initiated into the Kabbalah, or hidden mysteries of the east, by the Essenes, and that Nicodemus, an elder in Israel, was probably aware of them. Even Wordsworth would write in "Intimations of Immortality", "Our birth is but a sleep and a forgetting..." The wine of astonishment is an excellent raison d'etre.

Suggested Daily Spiritual Reading:
Luke 9:11
Acts 10:38

Further Reading Related to Diary Entry:
- *Edgar Cayce's Story of Jesus* by Edgar Cayce

- *Essene Book of Everyday Virtues: Spiritual Wisdom From the Dead Sea Scrolls* by Kenneth Hanson, Ph.D.

- *The Principles of Nature, Her Divine Revelations and a Voice to Mankind: All Three Volumes* by Andrew Jackson Davis

- *Supernormal: Science, Yoga, and the Evidence for Extraordinary Psychic Abilities* by Dean Radin (Author

- *The Spiritual Brain: A Neuroscientist's Case for the Existence of the Soul* by Mario Beauregard and Denyse O'Leary

- *The Essential Kabbalah: The Heart of Jewish Mysticism* by Daniel C. Matt

- *Ode: Intimations of Immortality from Recollections of Early Childhood* by William Wordsworth

Popular Books Published in 1946:
Autobiography of a Yogi by Paramahansa Yogananda

Man's Search for Meaning by Viktor Frankl

Popular Movies Released in 1946:
 The Razor's Edge (Tyrone Power, Gene Tierney, John Payne)
 Till the Clouds Roll By (June Allyson, Lucille Bremer, Judy Garland, Kathryn Grayson, Van Heflin, Lena Horne, Van Johnson, Angela Lansbury)
 Blue Skies (Fred Astaire, Bing Crosby, Joan Caulfield)

July 16, 1946

"The happiest heart that ever lived
Was in some quiet breast
That found the common daylight sweet
And left to Heaven the rest."

(*Quote from the poem "The Happiest Heart" by John Vance Cheney. The Reverend listed Hermann Hagedorn as the author. Hagedorn was an English professor at Harvard University, where the Reverend attended divinity school.*)

We moved to Ludlow on June 7th (*Albert is 17 or 18 and Janet is 15*) to our new parishes at Ludlow and Bondsville (*MA*). Since then we have been too busy settling in our new home and carrying on with our work to relate anything, but I do desire to record that some of the countryside hereabouts is beautiful. Tonight we rode fifteen miles to the town of Hadley, where the highway meets the Connecticut River, at the foot of Mt. Holyoke, on top of which is kind of a hotel and lookout tower. The sun was nearly set when we arrived, and with the mountains in the distance, a motorboat on the river, and Mt. Holyoke rising in the North near at hand, the scenery was lovely beyond description. It took me back to the lower meadow on the farm, though the river (*still talking about the Connecticut River*) is only half as wide there. Tonight the river was shallow—in fact, the motorboat grounded in the middle of it—but signs on the road nearby indicated the height of the flood in 1927, at the time of the hurricane in 1938, and highest of all, the flood level at the time of the flood of 1936, March 19th, when the river must have inundated at least the lower floors of the houses all around that section.

1946—Albert (a.k.a. "Junior), 17 years old and Janet, 15 years old

Albert, Mae, and I went, and we witnessed the setting of the sun. It was very gratifying to see the Connecticut River again, for I have seen it all the way from Canaan (*NH*) and West Stewartstown (*NH*), near the Connecticut lakes, to its breadth near Saybrook (*CT*), where it debouches into the sea. It is always interesting, especially in view of the fact that dinosaurs in Triassic times roamed up and down the river, their fossil remains being left in the sandstone around Turner's Falls (*MA*), and other places along the Connecticut.

We like our parsonage, it being smaller with only eight rooms instead of fourteen, as in Hudson. It is well constructed, being insulated and having storm windows. The Church is not as large, but to compensate, there is the added parish of Bondsville. Quite a bit of extra work, but very interesting. The parish is wide, many families living in Springfield and neighboring towns. This is a section of Massachusetts new to us, and ought to furnish many interesting places to visit. We have already been to Frank Look Memorial Park in Northampton for a Church picnic, and are going again next Saturday. There are state parks in abundance hereabouts, also Westover Field, an army flying base. And of course in Easthampton there is a dealer in minerals, whom I intend to visit before long. It is good to be in the mountains again, and while Mount Tom and Mount Holyoke are not exactly in the same class with the Adirondacks or the White Mountains, still they are good sized peaks, and evoke the mood of the Psalmist, "I will lift up mine eyes unto the hills from whence cometh my help." (*Psalm 121:1*)

There are several ponds nearby, and I was thinking as we visited one the other evening, how large a measure of tolerance on finds in the out-of-doors, and especially at the pond. Some like to swim, and some to go boating, and some to fish, and each can do as he pleases within reasonable limits. The city is intolerant —one must keep moving so to speak, and keep off the grass, and obey a thousand taboos, but in the country, on a lake, one is free to indulge one's fancy. I imagine that is why Thoreau found Walden so congenial. He would play his flute while drifting in a boat, and even the fish would come up to listen (or so tis said). He wrote, "I desire a broad margin to my life," and that is something we should all search for. Jesus excelled all mankind in this. He was not bound by earthly possessions, and he urged us to free our souls from all encumbrances, and find a broad margin for our lives. The Lord is my shepherd...He restoreth my soul... Amen.

Suggested Daily Spiritual Reading:
Psalm 23
1 Peter 2:25

Further Reading Related to Diary Entry:
- *Dinosaur footprints in Connecticut and Massachusetts.* Available from the Joe Webb Peoples Museum & Collections, Earth & Environmental Sciences, Weselyan University at https://www.wesleyan.edu/ees/museum/footprints_CT_MA.html# [Accessed January 23, 2021].

- *Where Dinosaurs Walked: Eight of the Best Places to See Prehistoric Footprints* by Robin T. Reid. Available at Smithsonianmag.com (October 27, 2015): https://www.smithsonianmag.com/travel/where-dinosaurs-walked-8-places-prehistoric-footprints-180956982/ [Accessed January 23, 2021].

- *A History of the Connecticut River* by Wick Griswold

- *The Connecticut River from the Air: An Intimate Perspective of New England's Historic Waterway* by Jerry Roberts and Tom Walsh

Popular Books Published in 1946:
    All the King's Men by Robert Penn Warren
    Five Chimneys: A Woman Survivor's True Story of Auschwitz by Olga Lengyel

Popular Movies Released in 1946:
    Notorious (Cary Grant, Ingrid Bergman, Claude Rains, Louis Calhern)
    The Stranger (Orson Welles, Edward G. Robinson, Loretta Young, Philip Merivale)
    The Best Years of Our Lives (Myrna Loy, Dana Andrews, Fredric March, Teresa Wright)

Saturday, August 31, 1946

 This being the last day of my vacation period, I hasten to recount, in this journal, some of the highlights in it.

 Last Sunday we drove the car down the river (*Connecticut River*) to the sea; that is to say, we motored from here to Saybrook, Conn., where the waters of Long Island Sound join those of the Connecticut River. We (meaning my son, Albert, my wife, and I) partook of a good lunch at Saybrook Point, were a good view of the river and sound can be had. The tide was just receding, but it didn't go down very far compared with ocean beaches. There were salt water flats to see; motor and sail boats ascending and descending the river; white cirrus clouds overhead, shading into stratocumulus (this begins to sound like a weather report); and gulls—it was good to see them again, remembering them from Sprucehead, Maine —diving into the water for their lunch, and for aught I know, their breakfast too.

 My son and I took advantage of the opportunity to have a seaplane ride out over the sound; he going farther than I, out to the lightship. Looking down at the ocean everything seems to come to a stop—the water, the boats below, and even the plane itself. The water on the sunward side had ripples, which seemed frozen in their places; and from the other side of the plane looked exactly like dark icier winter. We could see Fisher's Island, Great Gull and Plum Islands, and others, which are part of the Long Island chain.

 On the way home we stopped at the Portland, Conn; pegmatite quarries, atop a mountain there. They are seemingly unused now, though mica was produced there during the war. There are two immense piles of grout, mostly quartz and feldspar. We found no unusual, or even good, specimens, though many have been taken from there. In 1879, twenty-one consecutive dinosaur tracks were uncovered. Speaking of dinosaur tracks, one of our greatest thrills this summer was in finding the many tracks—now preserved by the state—of dinosaurs at the foot of Mt. Tom. Later, at Murray's quarry in Holyoke, we found more, and uncovered one or two, in the sandstone shale, where also have been preserved raindrops from ancient times (mesozoic), ripple marks, and other vestige. As I reconstruct the picture from Dana's Geology, back in Triassic period, about 100,000,000 years ago, there were dinosaurs of various sizes ranging the Connecticut Valley—some small four- and five-toed varieties, and large three-toed ones called Anchisaurus pelorus Marsh, of which skeletons have been found (*Not sure why the Reverend typed "Anchisaurus pelorus Marsh", but links to the articles "The Tangled History of Connecticut's Anchisaurus" and "A revision of the problematic sauropodomorph dinosaurs from Manchester, Connecticut and the status of Anchisaurus Marsh", found under "Further Reading Related to Diary Entry" below, may lend a clue.*)

These were carnivorous, and were from eight to twelve feet long. They stood upright on hind legs, balanced by an enormous tail, and had two forefeet dwarfed in size, which they used for clinging to branches. The river flowed to the sea on the West side of Mt. Tom, and this side was evidently part of the ocean, judging by the hundreds of layers of sedimentary rocks deposited there. The dinosaurs lived on the leaves of the cycads (our modern rubber plants look like them), the conifers, and the gingko tree, which is the only tree surviving from those times. There is one here in the park in Ludlow (*MA*). They were preserved for centuries by the Buddhist priests in China and Japan. The trunk looks like a beech, but the tree leaves are exotic, and different from modern kinds. There was no grass in those times, it being a later development of such a distant age. What will the Connecticut Valley be like 150 million years from today, one wonders? Will man and all his works have perished as the dinosaur did, crushed by the weight of new glaciers from the north?

Suggested Daily Spiritual Reading:
Genesis 1:11-12
Psalm 96:12

Further Reading Related to Diary Entry:

- *Hidden History of Connecticut* by Wilson Faude

- *The Rise and Fall of the Dinosaurs: A New History of Their Lost World* by Steve Brusatte

- *Curious Footprints: Professor Hitchcock's Dinosaur Tracks & Other Natural History Treasures at Amherst College* by Nancy Pick, Frank Ward

- *The Tangled History of Connecticut's Anchisaurus* by Riley Black. Available from Smithsonianmag.com at https://www.smithsonianmag.com/science-nature/the-tangled-history-of-connecticuts-anchisaurus-91839935/ [Accessed January 23, 2021].

- *A revision of the problematic sauropodomorph dinosaurs from Manchester, Connecticut and the status of Anchisaurus Marsh* by Adam M. Yates. Available from *Palaeontology* (July 19, 2010, volume 53, issue 4, pages 739-752) through Wiley.com at https://onlinelibrary.wiley.com/doi/full/10.1111/j.1475-4983.2010.00952.x [Accessed January 23, 2021].

- *Not by Fire but by Ice: Discover What Killed the Dinosaurs...and Why It Could Soon Kill Us* by Robert W. Felix

- *Death from Space: What Killed the Dinosaurs* (Isaac Asimov's New Library of the Universe series) by Isaac Asimov and Greg Walz-Chojnacki

- *What Killed The Dinosaurs? Extinction Theories* by Dave Smith. Available from *Dino Buzz*, University of California-Berkley, Museum of Paleontology at https://ucmp.berkeley.edu/diapsids/extinctheory.html [Accessed January 23, 2021].

Popular Books Published in 1946:
Why I Write by George Orwell
The Fields by Conrad Richter

Popular Movies Released in 1946:
Terror by Night (Basil Rathbone, Nigel Bruce, Alan Mowbray, Dennis Hoey)
Cloak and Dagger (Gary Cooper, Robert Alda, Lilli Palmer, Vladimir Sokoloff)
Till the End of Time (Dorothy McGuire, Robert Mitchum, Guy Madison, Bill Williams)

August 31, 1946
(Continued)

The second Sunday of the month, we drove out through the lovely Berkshires to Lenox, where overlooking a lovely lake and the distant mountains were privileged to hear, at Tanglewood, the Boston Symphony Orchestra with chorus, under the direction of Serge Koussevitzky, play Beethoven's Ninth Symphony. It was a real treat for the whole family. They also played while a male chorus sang Thompson's "The Testament of Freedom". There was an estimated crowd of 12,000 music lovers. Half of them sat or stood on the grass outside the music shed.

On the first Sunday of vacation, we visited Westover Army Air Field, where we saw big transport planes, and visited the base hangar; and then we went to Easthampton where I purchased some minerals from Schortmann's. He has a marvelous collection of fluorescent minerals from Franklin, N.J., with the reds of the calcites mingling superbly with the violets of fluorite and the greens of willemite. I bought an amethyst specimen from Uruguay, staurolite from Fannin County, Georgia, and a rubellite crystal from Brazil. I have also visited the Westfield trap rock quarries, where I obtained good specimens of datolite, epidote, prehnite, and babingtonite. Several times we have visited the Museum of Natural History in Springfield, where I have made the acquaintance of Leo Otis, curator of minerals; and J. C. Colton, a retired mining engineer. It was he who told me how to get to Murray's quarry in Holyoke, where we found the dinosaur tracks.

I learned last night, to my sorrow, that Lester J. Spear, one of my old friends in Lynn (MA) has passed away. May he find a happy hunting ground for minerals in his travels to all eternity! We had many good field trips together; organized the Lynn Mineral Club at his home; and we have played golf many times. He was ever generous and helpful to me.

For reading I have been perusing Thoreau's Journals (I have traveled a great deal in Concord), and always find them interesting. He has the happy faculty of making you feel at home with him, whether he is chasing an escaped pig or is making friends with a woodchuck. His was the real wealth of this world, and he knew it. Expressions of despair do not emanate from those who have enjoyed the serenity of nature! He is fundamentally optimistic.

Our remaining Sunday was spent on Mt. Tom, where we visited Goat Peak; Northampton, where we visited Look Park and had our lunch, and saw an archery contest—one chap made a perfect score—all his arrows landed in the bull's eye, and someone said he was from Pennsylvania—thence to Laurel Park, and up route 5 to fertile tobacco farms. Late in the afternoon we visited the great Quabbin Reservoir, which houses 415 billion gallons of water for the needs of Boston. The manmade lake (*reservoir*) nestling between the mountains, makes a beautiful picture.

And so, my vacation is over, and I will soon lose myself in the routine of the daily round, "yet, having known, life will not press so close, and I shall always feel about me (because of it) the thin windy presence of eternity." (*Paraphrased from the poem "The Most-Sacred Mountain" by Eunice Tietjens*)

We did not get to the high mountains, but for a pleasant substitute we often drive to Granby and look upon the mountains, which constitute the Tom and Holyoke ranges, and the sunsets are beautiful.

Last night the crescent moon was above Jupiter and Venus, in a straight line. Lovely to behold. And the countryside itself is lovely, with its many farms, its herds of cattle and sheep and an occasional horse kicking up its heels and glad to be free to run again. Such a one we saw last evening, and it symbolizes life at its best, when for a little while can run free before the wind, and forestall the days and nights of patient endurance.

Joy and health I bequeath to you who read this.

Suggested Daily Spiritual Reading:
Galatians 5:22
1 Thessalonians 3:9

Further Reading Related to Diary Entry:
- *Harvey Penick's Little Red Book: Lessons And Teachings From A Lifetime In Golf* by Harvey Penick
- *Triassic-Jurassic of western Massachusetts: easily acessable geology field trips* by John F. Hubert
- *Quabbin: A History and Explorer's Guide* by Michael Tougias and Les Campbell
- *Henry David Thoreau: A Life* by Laura Dassow Walls

Popular Books Published in 1946:
King Jesus by Robert Graves
Gentleman's Agreement by Laura Z. Hobson

Popular Movies Released in 1946:
Night and Day (Cary Grant, Alexis Smith, Monty Woolley, Ginny Simms)
Humoresque (Joan Crawford, John Garfield, Oscar Levant, J. Carrol Naish)
The Show-Off (Red Skelton, Marilyn Maxwell, Marjorie Main, Virginia O'Brien)

Tuesday, October 29, 1946
Ennui?

"Tomorrow and tomorrow and tomorrow creeps on this petty pace from day to day," is a statement from Shakespeare, which my son was learning for an oral topic last evening. By the way, it should read, I understand—"creeps in this petty pace," etc. I like "on" better, so I will keep it and thus improve on the immortal bard.

Now it so happens that monotony is the lot of everyone, even an adventurer. Even adventure stales, and cafard sets in. Work becomes monotonous; even play and especially play. One can become bored even in pain—and the pleasure principle is no guarantee that ennui will not set in, if the mood be right. I read a book last evening that profoundly impressed me, entitled "The Spear in the Sand", by Faure. The author tells in vivid descriptive prose, with concomitant wide vocabulary, of a young man marooned, a la Crusoe, on an island in the far off seas below Australia. He lives there for thirty or forty years before dying, unrescued, and without meeting a single soul.

The outstanding impression one gathers is the terrific sense of monotony in the midst of superb variety of color and form that the islands afford. His mind roves over the past, dawdles over building and furnishing a hut, investigates all the known flora and fauna of the island, writes tomes and reads them—indulges his imagination endlessly—and yet he is bored, almost to madness. A unique book and a true one.

Crusoe seemed too busy to be bored. Besides, he found a track in the sand, and with it human companionship.

But Saure's young man has no one—he has entered the Great Calms. I venture to say that even in a great city—as Thomas Wolfe has revealed in his books—one can only be lonely and bored to distraction.

Which brings me to the point of my narrative this day. I have discovered a new and rich source of enjoyment this past month—namely, I have become a stargazer. Four visits to the planetarium in Springfield, and the perusal of a number of books, with guides to the constellations, and the aid of a good pair of binoculars, made in Germany for use in World War I, have led me out into a new and beautiful world. I have counted 22 constellations in an evening, and understand there are 88. I have seen the Great Nebula in Andromeda, an island universe separate from our own by an estimated 800,000 light years. I have counted numberless double stars, found a pretty northern crown of my own just below Algenib, or Marfak (as it is also called), in Perseus; seen Sirius the dog star rising in the south; and have read the fascinating legends of the constellations, such as that of Andromeda and Perseus. The earth in its annual course around the sun, passes through the constellations of the zodiac, as has been observed from time immemorial. They seem to come into view in a regular order, beginning with Aries in November.

I recommend the pursuit of astronomy to keep one from boredom, ennui, cafard, or whatever it is that puts us in the mournful mood and despairing mood of "Tomorrow and tomorrow creeps in this petty pace" ! Truly as the psalmist says, "The heavens declare the glory of God, and the firmament sheweth His handiwork." (*Psalm 19:1*) And again, "When I consider the heavens, the work of Thy hands; the moon and the stars which Thou hast ordained; what is Man, that Thou art mindful of him, and the Son of Man, that Thou visitest him?" (*Psalm 8:3-4, paraphrased*)

```
"The Ram and Bull lead off the line;
 Next Twins and Crab and Lion shine;
        The Virgin and the Scales.
    Scorpion, Archer, and He-goat—
  The Man that bears the watering pot,
      And Fish with glittering tails."
```

(*Quote is a paraphrase of that found on page 23 of the book "The Evolution of Man: His Religious Systems and Social Customs" by William Wright Hardwicke, published in1899*)

Suggested Daily Spiritual Reading:
Psalm 19:1
Psalm 8:3

Further Reading Related to Diary Entry:
- *The Spear in the Sand* by Raoul C. Faure

- *Majesty in Monotony: Everyday Things With A Cosmic Perspective* by Ariel Manzanares-Scisney

- *Stargazing For Dummies* by Steve Owens

- *God of the Big Bang: How Modern Science Affirms the Creator* by PhD Leslie Wickman

- The Witness of the Stars By The Rev. Ethelbert William Bullinger, D.D; published by the Author, London 1893. Available from Project Gutenberg at http://www.gutenberg.org/files/49018/49018-pdf.pdf [Accessed January 23, 2021].

- *The Evolution of Man: His Religious Systems and Social Customs* by William

Wright Hardwicke, M.D.; Watts and Company, publishers, 1899. Available from Internet Archive at https://archive.org/details/evolutionmanhis01hardgoog/page/n8 [Accessed January 23, 2021].

- *Through My Telescope; Astronomy For All* by Will T. Hay; published by John Murray, Albemarle Street, West; London (1935).

Popular Books Published in 1946:
Mr. Blandings Builds His Dream House by Eric Hodgins
Three Came Home by Agnes Newton Keith

Popular Movies Released in 1946:
A Stolen Life (Bette Davis, Glenn Ford, Dane Clark, Walter Brennan)
The Harvey Girls (Judy Garland, Ray Bolger, John Hodiak, Angela Lansbury)
The Dark Corner (Lucille Ball, Clifton Webb, William Bendix, Mark Stevens)

October 30, 1946
Things I have seen in the sky...

In the Big Dipper, or Ursa Major, Mizar and Alcor.

In the tail of Draco the Dragon, Thuban the North Star of the skies. When the Pyramids were abuilding, two shafts admitted the light of Thuban into the inner chambers of the great pyramid.

The ninth magnitude star, just above Polaris, as viewed in October. Just recognizable with the opera glasses.

Delta Cepheus, the first variable to be discovered and studied.

Arcturus in Bootes—the star which lighted the world's fair in Chicago—37 1/2 light years away from us.

The Corona Borealis, a circlet of six stars between Bootes and Hercules. Beautiful, but not lovelier, in my estimation, than the semi-circle of stars just below Algenib in Perseus, and which because I have never seen them named in any book on astronomy, I hereby name Corona Andersonis, in honor of my son, Albert, an amateur astronomer of note.

The double star above Vega in Lyra, which is a group of two doubles really, and the doubles in the parallelogram, which is attached to Vega. Vega is one of our brightest and will some 24,000 years hence be the Pole Star.

Only with the imagination can I see the ring nebula (like a smoke ring around a star) in this parallelogram, just as only in imagination can I see the great cluster of stars in the center of Hercules. The cameras bring these out clearly only after long exposure through big telescopes.

The Northern Cross, with Deneb at its top and Albireo at its bottom point. Significant to a minister of course, it is one of our loveliest constellations. To the ancients it represented Cygnus, a flying swan. Albireo is a double star, also. And there is a cluster near it in the direction of Aquila, which I hope to see.

The Milky Way, as it runs through Cygnus and down the sky to Perseus.

Altair in Aquila (The Eagle) a mighty sun, which is one of the three stars in the heavenly triangle; Vega and Deneb being the others.

The Water Jar in Aquarius, spilling its stars down into the mouth of Fomalhaut, the southern fish. Capricorn, the sea-goat, lies south between Aquarius and Aquila, but I have not seen it as yet.

The double cluster of stars between the mighty chair of Queen Cassiopeia and neighboring Perseus.

About 20 stars within the great square of Pegasus, the flying horse. Of course there are thousands in Pegasus, but I did well to see 20.

The Great Nebula in Andromeda, an island universe some 700,000 light years away. I have heard it called 900,000 light years away, but I am going to be conservative. The farthest object that can be seen with the naked eye (By the way, who ever heard of seeing anything with an eye that wasn't naked?). A diagonal line from upper to lower rungs of the chair in Cassiopeia will, if extended, reach the nebula. The chair is often upside down.

From the Pleiades through Taurus to Orion and Sirius is one of the most glorious regions in the heavens. One stands humble in the presence of such magnificence. Even with field glasses the view is breathtaking. Some 25 stars in the Pleiades. Aldebaran glowing red in Taurus the Bull, and the many doubles there. The rectangle of Orion, with Betelgeuse, a great giant star two or 300 times the diameter of our sun—Bellatrix, Saiph and Rigel enclosing the belt and dagger of Orion. The famous nebula of Orion is the next to last star in the dagger.

Star clusters in Auriga the charioteer, which figures like Bootes resembles a kite in the autumn skies. Capella the goat with three kids.

Suggested Daily Spiritual Reading:
Genesis 1:16
Psalm 136:9

Further Reading Related to Diary Entry:
- *National Geographic Pocket Guide to the Night Sky of North America* by Catherine Herbert Howell

- *Stargazing: Beginners Guide to Astronomy* by Royal Observatory Greenwich, Radmila Topalovic, Tom Kerss

- *National Geographic Backyard Guide to the Night Sky* by Howard Schneider and Sandy Wood

- *The Imperial magazine, or, Compendium of religious, moral, & philosophical knowledge*, volumes 1-12, 1819-1830. Available from the Hathi Trust Digital Library at https://catalog.hathitrust.org/Record/008696359 [Accessed January 23, 2021].

Popular Books Published in 1946:
The Tale of Beatrix Potter: A Biography by Margaret Lane
If You Ask Me by Eleanor Roosevelt

Popular Movies Released in 1946:
The Strange Love of Martha Ivers (Barbara Stanwyck, Van Heflin, Lizabeth Scott, Kirk Douglas)
Somewhere in the Night (John Hodiak, Nancy Guild, Lloyd Nolan, Richard Conte)
A Matter of Life and Death (David Niven, Kim Hunter, Robert Coote, Kathleen Byron)

October 30, 1946
Things I have seen in the sky...(cont.)

The Beehive Cluster in the constellation Cancer, or Crab. This is such a dim constellation that it was only by accident that I located it early this morning; one o'clock, as a matter of fact. I could see perhaps a dozen stars in the group, but they wavered in intensity. The planet Saturn is just below the group, as I believe, and it was while observing this "star", which seemed out of place, that I looked above it with the Feldglas 08 (Made in Gottingen for the German army of 1918 and now put to better use) and found the beehive. It is known technically as Praesepe. Galileo studied this group, Ptolemy records Jupiter passing over it, Herschel found over 200 stars in it, and Halley's comet was first seen near here in 1531.

Halley's Comet in 1910 was about 10 degrees above the western horizon and parallel with it, according to my observation as a child of 8 years. My mother awakened me to see the unique comet. What impressed me was the fact that it seemed to stand still while we watched it, though even then I knew it was moving rapidly.

An eclipse of the sun in 1932, which all the family, with the exception of Janet, still only a very little person (*1 years old*), cute but little, witnessed from a golf course in Bethlehem, N.H. in center of path of totality. Albert was only three, but I think the event was impressed upon his memory.

****

Things I have NOT seen in the Sky

The Southern Cross.

The Magellanic Clouds, composed of great nebulae of gases and stars. Named for the famous explorer, Magellan, and also I believe, discovered by him.

Alpha, and especially Proxima, Centauri, which is only four and one-half light years away. Nearest of all stars.

The Great Ship of the South, the stars comprising Carina (keel), Puppis (stern), and Vela (sails) of a group in the southern circumpolar sky.

Achernar in the Constellation Eridanus, or River Po; which beginning near Rigel in Orion, goes wandering all over the southern sky and ends up in latitude too far south for us to see at the star Achernar. I traced the northern part of it last night.

Capricorn, Sagittarius, and Virgo, which have thus far eluded me.

Leo the Lion and Scorpius are down over the horizon at present.

Frankly, there are many things of interest in the sky which we never shall see except as photographs from the observatories. "Or ever we be of the night, or we be lost among the stars..." We sigh for them wistfully (if one can sigh wistfully) but there is so much of interest even for the unaided eye that we can all be explorers as fine in our way (for we stand at the center our universe) as Ulysses in his. He said, in Homer—"And this my purpose, to sail beyond the sunset ere I die; Beyond the pathos all the western stars—To strive, to seek, to find, and not to yield!"

(The actual quote from Alfred Lord Tennyson's poem "Ulysses" is as follows:
"To sail beyond the sunset, and the baths
Of all the western stars, until I die.
It may be that the gulfs will wash us down:
It may be we shall touch the Happy Isles")

My favorite quotation with reference to astronomy is found as an epitaph for a famous astronomer (Who was he?), but it is applicable to all of life. And his wife was included in the reference. The quotation:

"WE HAVE LOVED THE STARS TOO FONDLY TO BE FEARFUL OF THE NIGHT."

(According to the The Arecibo Observatory [a facility of the National Science Foundation], the above quote is found as the last line in the poem, "The Old Astronomer to His Pupil" by Sarah Williams. [From "Best Loved Poems of the American People", Hazel Felleman, ed. Garden City Publishing Co., Garden City NY: 1936, pp. 613-614]

The Arecibo Observatory webpage containing the above information notes that the last line of the poem was used as an epitaph for an Astronomer-couple buried at Alleghany Observatory: https://www.naic.edu/~gibson/poems/swilliams1.html [Accessed January 23, 2021]).

Suggested Daily Spiritual Reading:
Psalm 148:3
Matthew 2:10

Further Reading Related to Diary Entry:
- *Star Finder! A Step-by-Step Guide to the Night Sky* by DK

- *100 Things to See in the Night Sky: From Planets and Satellites to Meteors and Constellations, Your Guide to Stargazing* by Dean Regas

- *National Geographic Backyard Guide to the Night Sky* by Howard Schneider and Sandy Wood

- *Astronomy, a Textbook, fourth edition* by John Charles Duncan, Ph.D. (Professor of Astronomy, Wellesley College. Harper and Brothers Publishers, New York and London, 1926, 1930, 1935, 1946. Available from Internet Archive at https://archive.org/details/in.ernet.dli.2015.176736/page/n1 [Accessed January 23, 2021].

- *Atoms, Stars, and Nebulae* by Leo Goldberg and Lawrence H. Aller. The Blakiston Company, Philadelphia, Publishers, 1943. Available from Internet Archive at https://archive.org/details/in.ernet.dli.2015.177391/page/n1 [Accessed January 23, 2021].

Popular Books Published in 1946:
Mister Roberts by Thomas Heggen
The Pianist: The Extraordinary Story of One Man's Survival in Warsaw, 1939–45 by Władysław Szpilman

Popular Movies Released in 1946:
It's a Wonderful Life (James Stewart, Donna Reed, Lionel Barrymore)
Duel in the Sun (Jennifer Jones, Joseph Cotten, Gregory Peck, Lionel Barrymore)
Lady in the Lake (Robert Montgomery, Audrey Totter, Lloyd Nolan, Tom Tully)
My Darling Clementine (Henry Fonda, Linda Darnell, Victor Mature, Cathy Downs)

1947

January 22nd, 1947
Happy Birthday…

This being my 45th birthday, it is in order to narrate a few family events. Albert received maximum honors in his senior year for the first half, as announced in January. He has put in his application for Dartmouth and has been interviewed by a committee of alumni in Springfield. He still works after school at Warner's Filling station on Boston Road, Springfield.

Janet hasn't achieved any meritorious distinction in her Sophomore school marks, but she leads in the personality field, having more young men interested in her than any young lady of her age has a right to expect. I hope her popularity continues throughout life.

The family went over to Natick for Thanksgiving to visit my mother and sister, Lilla. We had a sumptuous repast, and a fine time together. Lilla came to see us after Christmas for a weekend visit. For Christmas the family bought itself a record player, which we have greatly enjoyed. Albert purchased Beethoven's Ninth, I bought a few classical records, and we have borrowed a great many from the Springfield Library. They have a fine selection of classical records—the first in the country—and some are irreplaceable now. Currently we are enjoying Bizet's "Carmen"; Mascagni's Cavalleria Rusticana and Symphony No. 4 by Saint Saens. We had a very nice Christmas—everybody received something of the wrong size, but it was all straightened out soon afterwards.

Albert took part, two Sundays ago, in a program from radio station, WMAS in Springfield, entitled "Invitation to College", and sponsored by the Adaskim Furniture Company. Answering two questions of the five, he received a dollar in cash, and a certificate for a ball-bearing pen costing three-fifty.

We had a very nice Watch Night service at the Church to close the year. From 9 to 12. Games, music, comedy sketches by the young people, and refreshments preceded the service of worship, which was well attended.

The weather has been very unusual this winter. To date, we have had no heavy snowfall. It has been down to zero at times, but for the most part it has been quite comfortable. Today the wind is blowing, the temperature is only 4 (*Fahrenheit*) above, and it is typical January weather. However, on Monday, I think it was, we had rain, fog, sleet, snow, warm weather, and the next day the temperature rose to 63 outside.

In December I bought a 3 1/2 inch reflecting telescope, called "Skyscope", from the Skyscope Company, 475 Fifth Avenue, New York, and have been more than pleased with it. One evening last week, I saw the following: nebulae of Orion and Andromeda; clusters near Perseus, Cassiopeia, and Sirius, also the Beehive and Coma Berenices; and six double stars—Albireo 34" (*a quotation mark ["] denotes arcseconds*) of arc; Mizar 14"; Gamma Andromedae only 10" of arc; Cor Caroli, which I discovered to be a double and which no book I have read mentions as such; Pi Andromedae, magnitudes 4 and 8 about 1' (*an apostrophe ['] denotes arcminutes*) apart, and an unknown double in Canis Major.

I have also seen the double double on Epsilon Lyrae, but since it is only 3 seconds of arc, I cannot positively say I have seen them separated. Saturn with its rings and moon satellite Titan, is one of the most beautiful objects in the sky. I arose one morning at four o'clock and saw Jupiter with three of its moons plainly visible, and later saw the crescent of Venus for the first time. Arcturus in Bootes and Spica in Virgo were also on hand to give color to the spectacle. Seeing Leo the Lion for the first time last month was also a big treat, but I make out Gamma to be a double, though I know it to be one of the finest in the sky. All in all, watching the pageant of the stars, I feel like Balboa, "silent upon a peak in Darien." (*Quote is last line from the poem "On First Looking into Chapman's Homer" by John Keats*)

Suggested Daily Spiritual Reading:
Matthew 5:44
Colossians 3:14

Further Reading Related to Diary Entry:
- *1491: New Revelations of the Americas Before Columbus* by Charles C. Mann

- *The Night Sky: A Folding Pocket Guide to the Moon, Stars, Planets and Celestial Events* by James Kavanagh

- *Astrophysics for People in a Hurry* by deGrasse Tyson, Neil

- *Positions and Sizes of Cosmic Objects*. Space Book. Available from by Las Cumbres Observatory at https://lco.global/spacebook/sky/using-angles-describe-positions-and-apparent-sizes-objects/ [Accessed January 23, 2021].

- *The Story of the Cosmos: How the Heavens Declare the Glory of God* by Daniel Ray and Paul Gould

Popular Books Published in 1947:
Most Popular Books Published In 1947. Available from Goodreads.com at https://www.goodreads.com/book/popular_by_date/1947 [Accessed January 23, 2021].

Popular Movies Released in 1947:
 Gentleman's Agreement (Gregory Peck, John Garfield, Dorothy McGuire, Celeste Holm, Jane Wyatt)
 Song of the Thin Man (Myna Loy, William Powell)
 The Secret Life of Walter Mitty (Danny Kaye, Virginia Mayo, Boris Karloff)

Thursday, February 6, 1947
Canst thou bind the sweet influences of Pleiades?

Last night the Ludlow High School group put on a minstrel show, or perhaps I should say, to be grammatically correct, presented such a show. It was well done, with the usual stock routine. I find myself interested in the variations from the universal, the minutiae—in this case one of the end men pretending to drink from a goldfish bowl, and so deprive the fish of their livelihood, so to speak. This is true in all phases of life—others have seen minstrel shows, gone to dog fights, read books, worked at jobs, and loved, all through the ages; but each of us in these things may notice something different from anyone else. In evolution, it is an accumulation of minute variations that result in great changes in species. For want of a nail, the shoe was lost, et cetera. Edison noticed that a plate between two filaments, in his new lightbulb, enabled him to control the flow of currents, thus introducing the technology of electronics. Pepys' in literature is a classic example of what I refer to—multum in parvo. Hatpins of today become antiques and curiosities of tomorrow. This is today's lesson in philosophy. <u>The whole universe may be circumscribed from any given point</u>, from where you stand, in fact! Take thy shoes from off thy feet, for the place whereon thous staidest is holy ground. (*Paraphrased from Exodus 3:5*)

On the last night of January, Albert and I were invited to visit John Welch, 107 Beverly Hills, West Springfield, by Frank Korkosz, lecturer at the Seymour Planetarium in Springfield. Jack has a 10-inch reflecting telescope which he made and mounted himself. One stands on a little platform of three steps to look through it. It is equatorially mounted of course, and has a motor mechanism to drive it. It is about six feet long, octagonal in shape. We greatly enjoyed the privilege, for it brought out clearly many things I could just glimpse, or fail to see entirely, in my Skyscope (*3 1/2-inch reflecting telescope*). On Saturn, for example, we could see Cassini's Division, and the bands about the planet, and five of the nine moons. On our moon, with 160 power, we could get a closeup of the craters and other objects of interest. The nebula in Orion, with the trapezium, was clear and distinct. One of the stars, by the way, in Theta Orionis, as it is called, is only 4.3 seconds away from its primary, so I rejoice that I have seen that division in my telescope.

Jack split several doubles for us, particularly Castor, which interested me, as I cannot do it with my 3 1/2" reflector. I find my interest gravitating to doubles. The "New Handbook of the Heavens" (Bernhard, Bennett, and Rice) lists four pages of them, which should keep me busy for some time to come. They are of various colors. Albireo and Gamma in Andromeda are orange and blue. Beta in Libra is green, I have read; and others are "chalcedony, onyx, and beryl", which brings us right back to the department of mineralogy. And of course there are stars which are white, like Vega; red, like Aldebaran and Betelgeuse; and blue, like Orion's belt. O, B, A, F, G, K, and M are some of the classifications.

Another amateur astronomer, Rolland Lapelle of Longmeadow, was with us. He became interested in the stars through taking his son's dog for a walk each night. I am indebted to Frank Korkosz and five of his lectures in the planetarium for my extended interest. We had a most enjoyable evening, and were reluctant to leave.

This has been one of the oddest winters I have known. Cold is average, but we have not had as yet, two full inches of snow, and last week grass was greening on the ground bare. Temperature was down to zero this morning, however.

Suggested Daily Spiritual Reading:
Exodus 3:5
Deuteronomy 4:19

Further Reading Related to Diary Entry:
- *The Backyard Astronomer's Guide* by Terence Dickinson

- *Planetary Geology: An introduction, 2nd revised Edition* by Claudio Vita-Finzi, Dominic Fortes

- *Fundamental Planetary Science, Updated Edition: Physics, Chemistry and Habitability* by Jack J. Lissauer

- *New Handbook of the Heavens* by Bernhard Hubert H., Dorothy A. Bennett, Hugh S. Rice; Published by Whittlesey House / McGraw-Hill, New York;1941. Original and revised copies still available today—search online.

Popular Books Published in 1947:
The Diary of a Young Girl by Anne Frank
Miracles by C.S. Lewis

Popular Movies Released in 1947:
Road to Rio (Bob Hope, Bing Crosby, Dorothy Lamour)
Bommerang (Dana Andrews, Jane Wyatt, Lee J. Cobb)
Dead Reckoning (Humphrey Bogart, Lizabeth Scott, Morris Carnovsky)

February 21, 1947

I desire to make a list of some of the double stars from the "Handbook of the Heavens" (Bernhard, Bennett, & Rice) for future reference, but first let me state that we have had a big snowstorm during the night. About eight inches have fallen on the level, and it has drifted to two feet in places, such as my backyard, in front of the garage. Inasmuch as I have to get my car out for a wedding tomorrow in Bondsville, it is hard shoveling.

I had a wedding the other day of interest. The bridegroom was Portuguese and the bride French—having just come from Moselle, France. She knew hardly any English, and so I conversed a bit with her in French, having studied that language four years. We got along nicely and she was duly married, for love speaks a universal language.

And now for the double stars. I am negotiating with John Welch for the purchase of his six-inch reflecting telescope, but my results have been quite good with my Skyscope. Following, are the most likely doubles for observation, with distances apart, called the arc of separation, position angles, colors, etc.

Feb. 21, 1947

I desire to make a list of some of the double stars from the "Handbook of the Heavens" (Barnard, Bennett & Rice) for future reference, but first let me state that we have had a big snowstorm during the night. About eight inches have fallen on the level, and it has drifted to two feet in places, such as my back yard in front of the garage. Inasmuch as I have to get my car out for a wedding tomorrow in Bondsville, it is hard shovelling. I had a wedding the other day of interest. The bridegroom was Portugese and the bride French, having just come from Moselle, France. She knew hardly any English, and so I conversed a bit with her in French, having studied that language four years. We got along nicely and she was duly married, for love speaks a universal language.

And now for the double stars. I am negotiating with John Welch for the purchase of his six inch reflecting telescope, but my results have been quite good with my Skyscope. Following are the most likely doubles for observation, with distances apart, called the arc of separation, position angles, colors, etc.

Name	Magnitudes	Position Angle	Distance	Colors	
Nu Draconis	4.6/4.6	312 degrees	62"	yellow, white	o
Gamma Leporis	5/8	351	85"	pale yellow, garnet	o
Alpha Cassaopeia	3/9	281	63"	yellow, blue	
Eta "	4/8	279	9"	yellow, purple	
Polaris (North Star)	2/9	217	18"		oJW
Gamma Andromedae	3/5	63	10"	yellow, blue	o
Tau Leonis	5/7	170	90"	blue, white	
Eta Persei	4/8.5	301	28"	yellow, blue	o
Epsilon Persei	3/8	?	9"	green, blue	
Pi Andromedae	4/8		36"		
Omicron Aurigae	5/8	355	5.8	green, blue	
Beta Cephei	3/8	250	13.7	green, blue	
Sigma Cephei (Struve)	6/7	197	20"	green, blue	
Delta Cephei	4/8	192	41"	blue, ashen	
Omicron Cephei	5/8	205	3"	yellow, blue	
Middle Regions					
14 Aurigae	5/7	225	14.5	green, blue	
Rigel	1/8	202	9.4"	yellow, orange	oJW
Gamma Arietis	4/4	0	8.4	white, white	o
Zeta Lyrae	4/5	150	43"	yellow, green	
Beta Lyrae	3/7/9/9		46/70	Four stars plus	
Albireo	3/5	55	34"	yellow, blue	o
Theta Sagittae	6/7/9		11/79/45		
Chi Bootis	5/7	11	5"	yellow, red	
Zeta Coronae	4/5	304	6"	green, white	
Alpha Herculis	3/6	110	4.8"	yellow, blue	
Delta Herculis	3/8	206	11"	green, white	
Delta Orionis	2/7	0	53"	green, white	o
Theta Orionis			4.3"	Four stars, Trapezium	
Alpha Geminorum	2/4/9	213	4.6"	green, white (Castor)	
Kappa Geminorum	4/9	236	6.8	yellow, white	
Iota Cancri	5/7	307	31½ 176"	blue, white yellow	
Alpha Leonis	2/8	307	176"	blue, white (Regulus)	o

(*Note: quotation ["] symbol refers to arcseconds*)

Suggested Daily Spiritual Reading:
Genesis 1:1
Psalm 8:3

Further Reading Related to Diary Entry:
- *The Glass Universe: How the Ladies of the Harvard Observatory Took the Measure of the Stars* by Dava Sobel

- *New Handbook of the Heavens* by Bernhard Hubert H., Dorothy A. Bennett, Hugh S. Rice; Published by Whittlesey House / McGraw-Hill, New York; 1941. Original and revised copies still available today—search online.

- *An Introduction to Modern Astrophysics, 2nd Edition* by Bradley W. Carroll

- *Introduction to Cosmology, 2nd Edition* by Barbara Ryden

Popular Books Published in 1947:
Survival in Auschwitz by Primo Levi
Tales of the South Pacific by James A. Michener

Popular Movies Released in 1947:
My Favorite Brunette (Bon Hope, Dorothy Lamour, Peter Lorre, Lon Chaney Jr.)
The Farmer's Daughter (Loretta Young, Joseph Cotten, Ethel Barrymore)
Angel and the Badman (John Wayne, Gail Russell, Harry Carey)

March 11, 1947

Early this morning, three o'clock to be exact, I took my telescope out of doors with the dog, and had the pleasure of seeing Jupiter with its four moons, for the first time in a dozen years. It looked like this, as nearly as I can picture it:

. . O . .

It was very clear, and I could detect, also, (or thought I could, for the eye sometimes deceives us) two parallel lines on the surface of the planet. I felt a kinship with Galileo who first saw the moons some 400 years ago. His telescope magnified 33 diameters, mine 60—or nearly double. I also saw, again, the craters on our own moon, which was nearby and which is waning, the terminator lying along the northwestern edge. I also found a double star, which I had not seen before, and did not recognize, with about 7 seconds of arc separation, right ascension about 345 degrees, declination about 30 degrees.

It is very restful in the quiet of early morning, the temperature being mild, to gaze upon these distant stars and planets. It restoreth the soul of man. The sky soon clouded over, however, preventing further observation. I did not see Venus, which must have retroceded in the direction of the sun.

Last evening, while Albert was attending his first lecture as a naval reservist in one of the high schools of Springfield, my wife and I attended a lecture, or address, at the Auditorium, given by Bishop G. Bromley Oxnam, of New York, on "The Future of Protestantism". He quoted a number of statistics, which I should like to preserve. They are 1944 figures, but give the relative strength of the religious bodies in this country.

Protestants	212,336 Churches	41,943,104 members
Roman Catholic	14,791 Churches	23,419,701 members
Jews	3,728 Synagogues	4,641,000 members
Eastern Orthodox	834 Churches	686,000 members

The Methodist Church gained 1,021,000 members last year, making a total of some 9 million members. It has 124 colleges, worth 400 million.

Total membership in all other Churches 72,492,669 or 52.5% of population in 1946.

Comparison of gains membership in relation to population growth is also interesting:

In colonial times, 5% of population were members.
In 1890, 22.5%.
In 1946, 52.5%

Our Church membership growth in recent years is nearly twice that of population growth. In the past ten years, the population growth has been 14.3%. Protestant growth is 23.8%; Roman Catholic growth is 23.3%.

Does this also represent a growth of corresponding proportions in the grace and knowledge and love of God? That is the important consideration. Church membership means little of itself—the religious life of the members is the important factor. What we need is not bigger Churches, but bigger souls in the Churches we have. As Bishop Oxnam said, what we need most is not to be big, but to be good. But it is an encouraging sign that people are willing to subscribe to the doctrines of the Church and to pledge to support with "their presence, their prayers, their gifts, and their service." He spoke of the formation of a World Council of Churches, which meets next year for the first time, and which will include the Eastern Orthodox branch of the Church of Christ.

The weather has moderated; the ground is bare, and springs at hand. Perhaps "winter's rains and ruins are over" for another season.

Suggested Daily Spiritual Reading:
Psalm 26:12
1 Chronicles 6:32

Further Reading Related to Diary Entry:

- *NightWatch: A Practical Guide to Viewing the Universe*-Revised 4th Edition by Terence Dickinson (Author); Adolf Schaller (Illustrator)

- *Church Membership: How the World Knows Who Represents Jesus* by Jonathan Leeman

- *What Is a Healthy Church Member?* by Thabiti M. Anyabwile

- *Words of Counsel: For All Leaders, Teachers, and Evangelists* by Charles H. Spurgeon

- *Testimony of Bishop G. Bromley Oxnam, Hearing before the Committee on Un-American Activities*, House of Representatives, Eighty-third Congress, First Session, July 21, 1953. (*Bishop Oxfam defends himself against the accusations of communist activity*) Available from Internet Archive at https://archive.org/stream/

testimonyofbisho00unit/testimonyofbisho00unit_djvu.txt [Accessed January 23, 2021].

- *A Testament of Faith* by G. Bromley Oxnam; published by Little, Brown, and Company; Boston and Toronto. 1958. Available from Internet Archive at https://archive.org/details/testamentoffaith027498mbp/page/n7 [Accessed January 23, 2021].

- *Preaching in a Revolutionary Age* by Garfield Bromley Oxnam, published by Books for Libraries Press, Freeport, NY. 1944, reprint 1971. Available from Internet Archive at https://archive.org/details/preachinginrevol00oxna/page/n7 [Accessed January 23, 2021].

Popular Books Published in 1947:
Exercises in Style by Raymond Queneau
Company Commander: The Classic Infantry Memoir of World War II by Charles B. MacDonald

Popular Movies Released in 1947:
The Bachelor and the Bobby-Soxer (Cary Grant, Myrna Loy, Shirley Temple)
Apache Rose (Roy Rogers, Dale Evans)
Her Husband's Affairs (Lucille Ball, Franchot Tone, Edward Everett Horton)

March 17, 1947

A typical March day, clear, sunny, cold, and windy. The ground here is entirely bare of snow, though to the north of here, I understand, there is snow in abundance. A heavy fall of it this winter for northern New England—ten to twelve feet in places. I can well remember as a boy digging tunnels in big drifts of snow. Man can adapt himself to almost any climate, if the range of temperature is not too severe. Scotty has a castle in Death Valley and Esquimaux live above the Circle. Man is an adaptable creature, and with reasonable luck should outlive the dinosaurs, whose survival period was about 100 million years. We have only about 99 million years to go. A relatively short time in the geological history of our little planet.

Night before last, Albert Jr. and I purchased, jointly, a six-inch reflecting telescope, expertly made by Jack Welch of West Springfield. It is equatorially mounted and has a ten power telescope finder with cross hairs. Eyepiece powers we use are 48 and 96. Focal length of the parabolic mirror is f8 so the length is 48 inches, or four feet. An eye piece of one-inch in diameter gives a magnifying power ratio, therefore, of 48; the half inch, 96.

We set it up last night and had a glorious time surveying the stars. It was so good to be able to split many of the doubles which had baffled me with my Skyscope, which afterall has its limitations. Castor with 4.6" of arc separation; gamma Leonis, gamma Virginis, eta Cassiopeia, and several other well known doubles came under my scrutiny, well resolved. The double double of eta Lyrae, however, would not resolve for me. That is but 3" of arc, so is, apparently, the lower limit of my new telescope. For other features, we saw M13, the cluster in Hercules, and the Ring Nebula in Lyra, and two of the planets—Saturn and Jupiter. Four moons of Saturn, the dark line of Cassini's Division, and the bands of Jupiter were revealed. The Trapezium in Orion—Theta Orionis—stood out plainly. The ninth magnitude companion of Polaris could be plainly seen.

Let me state that the unaided eye can see up to the sixth magnitude. Each magnitude is 2 1/2 times fainter than the preceding magnitude, so that a ninth magnitude star is faint even in a telescope.

Vega is a typical star of first magnitude. Sirius, our brightest star, in Canis Major (or the Big Dog) is a minus magnitude of 1.58. Mira Ceti, the wonder star, goes in eleven months from first or second magnitude to eighth or ninth magnitude. It is a giant powerhouse of light, which increases and diminishes in intensity over a long period of time.

We look forward with pleasure to the use of our new acquisition, whose cost was seventy-five dollars (*around $875 in 2020*), but whose worth cannot be measured in terms of money. The quiet pleasure of observing at leisure the rings of Saturn, or the round orange and blue dots which represent two giant suns in gamma Andromedae, or contemplating the richness of the infinite in the fossil light of the great nebula in Andromeda is without parallel in my mundane experience. Only a poet could do justice to the beauty and grandeur revealed. The best tribute of all, I think, is a reverent silence. It is a kind of worship. The cosmos is greater than we know. We are like children, as Newton aptly said, on the shores of an illimitable ocean of truth, picking up a few brightly colored pebbles here and there. But it is a decided pleasure to pick up pebbles, especially the colorful ones!

Suggested Daily Spiritual Reading:
Psalm 8:1
Ecclesiastes 3:1

Further Reading Related to Diary Entry:
- *The Wizard and the Prophet: Two Remarkable Scientists and Their Dueling Visions to Shape Tomorrow's World* by Charles C. Mann

- *Growing Food in a Hotter, Drier Land: Lessons from Desert Farmers on Adapting to Climate Uncertainty* by Gary Paul Nabhan

- *50 Things To See With A Small Telescope* by John A Read

- *Introduction to Astronomy: A Guide for Night Watchers* by G.B. Sidgwick (Member of the Société Astronomique de France and of the British Astronomical Association); published by Philosophical Library Inc., 1944. Available from Internet Archive at https://archive.org/details/in.ernet.dli.2015.211991/page/n1 [Accessed January 23, 2021].

- Foundations of Astronomy by W.M. Smart (formerly professor of astronomy in the University of Glasgow); published by Longmans, Green, and Company, Ltd. Published in 1942, 1944, 1946, 1947, 1953, 1958, 1962. Available from Internet Archive at https://archive.org/details/in.ernet.dli.2015.84617/page/n5 [Accessed January 23, 2021].

Popular Books Published in 1947:
Gravity and Grace by Simone Weil
The Treasured Writings of Kahlil Gibran by Kahlil Gibran

Popular Movies Released in 1947:
The Hucksters (Clark Gable, Deborah Kerr, Sydney Greenstreet, etc.)
Magic Town (James Stewart, Jane Wyman)
The Perils of Pauline (Betty Hutton, John Lund)

April 1, 1947

      The day is warm, the air is sunny
      I'd like to travel but have no munny
      I have to work and that ain't funny
          So what to do?

Well, the thing to do obviously is to fool your mind into thinking that you have immense leisure time in which to loaf and invite your soul. I think prayer is sometimes like that. Spring fever is really an opportunity to roll up the desk and get out of doors and enjoy the lavish awakening of nature. How wonderful it is when the earth shrugs off its mantle of cold and sluggishness, and begins to bloom again. The sky is blue, the sparkling waters run to the sea in the sun, the birds sing, the buds grow. The crysalis unfolds its hidden treasure.

      "Who knows whither the clouds have fled?
     In the unscarred heavens they leave no wake—
    And the eyes forget the tears they have shed,
      The heart forgets its sorrow and ache."
(Quote is from the poem "The Vision of Sir Launfal" by James Russell Lowell)

Speaking of unscarred heavens reminds me of the typographical error of that editor in the south who wished to pay tribute to a soldier, who unfortunately was also a heavy drinker. He intended to call him a "battle-scarred veteran", but his typesetter made and error and the paper labelled him "a bottle-scarred veteran". Called upon to amend the label, he tried again, and this time it came out the man in questions a "battle-scared veteran".

And, I like this old cliche:
      "In the world's broad field of battle,
        In the bivouac of life,
    You will find the Christian soldier
      Represented by his wife."
(A play on words from the poem "A Psalm of Life" by Henry Wadsworth Longfellow)

Enough of this nonsense, even though this is the day for it. Speaking of unscarred heavens again, it was my wish to record that last evening was a perfect evening for astronomical observation. From early to late there was unfolded the pageantry of the heavens in all its glory, and I took full advantage of it. All the constellations for this time of year were visible. It was like the unfolding of a giant map of the heavens. The Pleiades, Orion, Taurus, Leo the Lion, Canis Major, Auriga, The Big Dipper, Cassiopeia, Perseus, Bootes, Hercules,

Virgo, Lyra—all answered present to the roll call, as did many double stars; and the planets were well represented. Our moon was just a little over half full; Saturn showed five of its moons to me; Jupiter four with three on one side; and even Uranus could be seen between the horns of Taurus. I found a new double in the latter location also—magnitudes 5 and 5 about 6 seconds apart. Albert showed me the Ring Nebula in Lyra, just a hazy wisp of light, and I was enabled to split, to my own satisfaction, for the first time the double double in Epsilon Lyrae. I looked at all the "stock" doubles, including Polaris, and found great enjoyment in contemplating them leisurely. The infinite meadows of heaven bloomed with many a flower of rare beauty. The heavenly lodge is a true and perfect dwelling.

Suggested Daily Spiritual Reading:
   2 Thessalonians 3:1
   Matthew 5:44

Further Reading Related to Diary Entry:
- *Astronomy*. Available from Smith College at https://www.smith.edu/academics/astronomy [Accessed January 23, 2021].

- *Seymour Planetarium*, Springfield, MA. Available from Springfield Museums at https://springfieldmuseums.org/about/springfield-science-museum/seymour-planetarium/ [Accessed January 23, 2021].

- *Poems* by W.H. Auden. 1937.

- *Poems of Gerard Manley Hopkins* edited with notes by Robert Bridges. 1918.

Popular Books Published in 1947:
   War as I Knew It by George S. Patton Jr.
   Little Pilgrim's Progress: From John Bunyan's Classic by Helen L. Taylor

Popular Movies Released in 1947:
   The Return of Rin Tin Tin (Donald Woods, Claudia Drake, Rin Tin Tin)
   Merton of the Movies (Red Skelton, Virginia O'Brien, Gloria Grahame)
   Living in a Big Way (Gene Kelly, Marie McDonald, Charles Winninger)

June 25, 1947

    Last night I read an interesting book, which I have not finished as yet, entitled "The Story of Mrs. Murphy" by Natalie Anderson Scott. It is the story of a man's periodic submission to alcoholic sprees, and gets its title from the fact that someone said to the "hero", or central character of the story, one James Murphy, "Booze is your wife."

    It reminds one of "Studs Lonigan" by James T. Farrell, but unlike Farell's sociological treatise, (*Scott*) approaches the subject of sex a little more delicately. Less stress is laid on the anatomical features of the subjects concerned, as would be natural, perhaps, with a woman writer, though "Rags" Murphy is more direct, more objective in his dealings with women than Studs, and both are frankly pagan, or amoral if you will. However, with regard to their own sisters, it is interesting to note, in both cases, that they are willing and ready to beat up any chap who even looks at them for even too long a time. This dualism, or ambivalence, extends to drink in the case of Murphy. It is a prolonged emotional debauch for him, but his fastidiousness extends to the point where he will not go home to his mother in that condition.

    Both are interesting psychological types—so called "black sheep"—in fine Irish Catholic families, each likable and liked by all, each obviously spoiled by their mothers. Studs of course is not an alcoholic, does not run away from reality except in day-dreaming. Both have fine qualities when sober and working. Murphy is especially generous to a fault. If his energies had been channeled in the right direction, he could have been a good husband and father, and at the same time a good son. Both Sue and his mother pray for him, though both are partly to blame for his dereliction by spoiling him, and giving in to his whims.

    A bishop of the early Church said to Monica, the mother of Augustine, who apparently was an analogous case, but who turned out exceedingly well, "It is not possible that a son of so many prayers can be ultimately lost."

    I am interested in the outcome of the story. Weaknesses in human nature are universal. There is something of Rags Murphy or Studs Lonigan in every man. We can say thoughtfully, there but for the grace of God go I!

    Night before last I saw the teapot-shaped constellation of Sagittarius for the first time, and the magnificent field of nebulae and clusters, which surrounds it, with my telescope. I could recognize M8 (cluster and nebula), M22 (cluster), M17 (the Omega nebula and cluster), but I missed M6, M7, M24 (clusters), and M20 (the Trifid nebula). I shall try for them another time, now I know their locations better. But this southern portion of the milky way, the great star cloud in Sagittarius, is the center of our galaxy, and is rich indeed in astronomical delights. The trees had hidden it from my view, previously, but I found a spot near the street where it could be clearly viewed. West northwest of Albireo I also found an uncharted nebula, about 10 degrees away.

Suggested Daily Spiritual Reading:
Psalm 107
Jeremiah 17:14

Further Reading Related to Diary Entry:
- *The Story of Mrs. Murphy* by Natalie Anderson Scott

- *Studs Lonigan* by James T. Farrell

- *Alcoholics Anonymous, The Big Book* by Bill Wilson, Dr. Bob Smith

- *Astronomy for Beginners*. Available from *Sky & Telescope* at https://www.skyandtelescope.com/astronomy-information/ [Accessed January 23, 2021].

Popular Books Published in 1947:
Nuremberg Diary by Gustave Mark Gilbert
The Chequer Board by Nevil Shute

Popular Movies Released in 1947:
It Happened in Brooklyn (Frank Sinatra, Kathryn Grayson, Peter Lawford, Jimmy Durante)
Hollywood Barn Dance (Ernest Tubb, Helen Boyce)
The Ghost and Mrs. Muir (Gene Tierney, Rex Harrison)

October 5, 1947

Were there a little more regularity and a little less lethargy in compiling this journal, the work would be easier. Three months have gone by, and perhaps I can only record the highlights of the summer months.

As for this fall, the highlight to record is that Albert has matriculated at Dartmouth College. He has been awarded a scholarship to cover his tuition; he is to work at the Dartmouth Dining Association for his board, and his room is at 412 Wheeler Hall. I roomed at Wheeler Hall during my senior year. He has as a roommate a young man named John Marshall of Billerica. His subjects of study are chemistry, with two hours of laboratory work on Wednesdays; English, Math, Psychology, and French, plus, of course, Hygiene and compulsory athletics.

Since both Daniel Webster and myself attended Dartmouth it has achieved quite a reputation (sic!)

For three weeks previous to college entrance, Albert was at the Dartmouth Ravine Camp in Warren, N.H., where he helped to construct needed culverts in the road, climb Mt. Moosilauke, and met various interesting members the Dartmouth Outing Club, as well as the football team, and even some professors—a fitting prelude to college days. No one who has ever been associated with the Dartmouth Outing Club will forget the good times spent under its aegis—at Happy Hill, Moose Mountain, and elsewhere, along the chain of cabins extending to Mount Washington. It is associated with the Appalachian Mountain Club.

Albert—high school graduation, circa 1947.

Albert with grandmother Olive.

The events of the summer can be briefly told.
On June 30 I saw the shadow of one of Jupiter's moons cross the planet.
On July 9th, I saw the Dumbbell, Omega, and Whirlpool nebulae.
July 20th we saw a sunspot, without telescopic aid, from Wilbraham Mountain.

August 5th we visited relatives in Brattleboro (*VT*).

On August 10th my mother, sister Lilla, wife, and I visited the Quabbin reservoir and tower. Had a picnic in Crystal Lake in Bondsville (*the lake is actually located in nearby Palmer, MA*).

Albert and Robert Wareham returned from their trip to Mt. Greylock. That night, observation with the telescope was well-nigh perfect. I saw the Trifid nebula (M17) and M15 above Pegasus, also M8, M22, M20, and M24, clusters or nebulae in Sagittarius.

August 12-13-14 Mae and I were in New York. We visited the Staue of Liberty, Metropolitan Museum of Art, Bronx Park Zoo, Coney Island, and several other places. It was so warm one night, we had to go over to Staten Island to cool off. Stayed at Hotel Latham, on 28th street.

On August 30 and 31, I took Albert, and Ernest (his father-in-law), and Richard Lang out to the Berkshires where we visited a cave at Pettibone Falls in the town of Farnums, above Pittsfield. (*The falls and cave, located in Cheshire, MA [near Farnum Rd], are now considered to be part of privately owned property with no public access*). The next morning we climbed Mt. Everett near Great Barrington.

For outstanding motion pictures lately, we have seen "Life with Father", on September 10th in Springfield; and "The Yearling" on September 23rd in Ludlow. There was a fine motion picture here last night, seen by my wife and myself, entitled "Winter Wonderland", showing skiing in Sun Valley (*CA*).

Altogether, it was a pleasant summer. Only one wish went unfulfilled—to climb Mt. Monadnock again, but I have climbed it many times, and only the other day I saw a picture, or painting, in the Springfield museum, which I am sure showed the brook at the foot of the mountain where the Red Cross Trail begins. It was nostalgic, and I am grateful to the painter thereof.

This past week has been profitable spiritually, for we have had a Worldwide (Ecumenical) Methodist Conference in Springfield. I met people from many parts of the world.

Suggested Daily Spiritual Reading:
Psalm 91:11
Joshua 1:9

Further Reading Related to Diary Entry:
- *The History of Dartmouth College* by Baxter Perry Smith; Houghton, Osgood, and Company, Boston; The Riverside Press, Cambridge (1878) Available from The Project Gutenberg at https://www.gutenberg.org/ebooks/28641 [Accessed

January 23, 2021].

- *Explore Solar System and Beyond*. Available from NASA at https://www.nasa.gov/topics/solarsystem/index.html [Accessed January 23, 2021].

- *Wesley and the People Called Methodists: Second Edition*, by Richard P. Heitzenrater

- *The Reformation* by Diarmaid MacCulloch

Popular Books Published in 1947:
    Battle for Leyte Gulf by C. Vann Woodward
    How I Raised Myself From Failure to Success in Selling by Frank Bettger

Popular Movies Released in 1947:
    The Yearling (Gregory Peck, Jane Wyman, Claude Jarman Jr.)
    Life with Father (William Powell, Irene Dunne, Elizabeth Taylor)
    Winter Wonderland (Lynne Roberts, Charles Drake, Eric Blore)

Monday, October 13, 1947

Last night, I had the pleasure of looking for, and finding, the nebula Triangulum, which is the nearest galaxy, or universe

(The Triangulum Galaxy, also known as Messier 33 or M33, is about 3 million light years from earth [a light year is the equivalent of approximately 6 million miles]).

It lies about halfway between Alpha of Triangulum and Beta of Andromeda; perhaps, a couple of degrees to the South. Through my six-inch there was no mistaking it, for it looked like a diffused glow of light without a central focus, such as you find in the great nebula of Andromeda—another island universe, which is visible even to the naked eye. Andromeda, however, even in the photographs of it taken at Mount Wilson through the hundred-inch telescope, is an oval of light, whereas Triangulum looks more like a whirlpool with arms streaming away from the central mass like a child's wind toy on the end of a stick.

Andromeda is 850,000 light years away, Triangulum somewhat nearer (*we now know Andromeda is actually about 2.537 million light years from earth, and that Triangulum is somewhat farther, as noted above*). Just imagine a circular patch of faint light without definition at the circumference, and you will understand without prior knowledge or optical aid just how Triangulum looked to me. I found it twice just to make sure. There are some 150 million other island universes, it is estimated, but I was anxious to see the nearest one, and my wish was granted after considerable searching. (*"Island universes" are now referred to as galaxies, and there are believed to be over 100 billion galaxies with each containing 100 billion stars and numerous planets. Information on island universes is available from astrophysics professor Brian Koberlein's website at* https://archive.briankoberlein.com/2014/09/17/island-universe/index.html *[Accessed January 23, 2021]*).

Last night the atmosphere was not too damp nor cold, and the sky was brilliantly clear, with Pleiades and Auriga rising. Using my 200 power eyepiece, I was able to separate the double stars in Zeta Aquarii (3" arc); new to my observations, and also my old friends—Albireo in the northern cross and the "double-double" in Lyra.

Columbus found a new continent; last night—I found a new universe, that is, new to me. It would take nearly ten thousand lifetimes, of one hundred years each, to reach it at the speed of light. A million lifetimes to return to the age of the dinosaurs, and twenty times as long to go back to the estimated beginning of our earth. Time and space are colossal to conjecture and yet the mind of man can at least compute their immensities.

On the world scene, India has been granted independence and has divided into India and Pakhistan, the Moslem State. Britain has withdrawn, as she plans to do from Palestine. The United States has given its support, in principle, to the partition of Palestine into two independent states, Jewish and Moslem, though the Mohammedans are opposed to this, desiring, I suppose, dominion over the whole country. Russia accuses the United States of imperialist aims through the columns of Pravada, and Vishingki recently attacked the economic imperialists from the rostrum of the United Nations, at Lake Success, New York. China is still beset by civil war—food is scarce and prices are high in this country, due to our policy of feeding Europe, and so everything is normal again.

Albert witnessed his first football game at college yesterday, Saturday, when Penn defeated Dartmouth, in Hanover, 32-0. Friday night there was a big football rally, and Dartmouth Night observed, with President Dickey speaking to the students.

The autumn foliage is at its peak of beauty now, with the yellows, greens, and scarlet of the maples mingled with the dull brown the oaks. Like a cloak of many colors is the mantle of autumn in New England.

Suggested Daily Spiritual Reading:
Psalms 23:6
Isaiah 40:30-31

Further Reading Related to Diary Entry:
- *From Our Galaxy to Island Universes*. Available from the Center for History of Physics, a Division of the American Institute of Physics at https://history.aip.org/history/exhibits/cosmology/ideas/island.htm [Accessed January 23, 2021].

- *"Island universes"* are now referred to as galaxies, and there are believed to be over 100 billion galaxies with each containing 100 billion stars and numerous planets. Information on island universes is available from astrophysics professor Brian Koberlein's website at https://archive.briankoberlein.com/2014/09/17/island-universe/index.html [Accessed January 23, 2021].

- *Messier 33 (The Triangulum Galaxy)*; February 20, 2019 (Last Updated: Oct 22, 2019; Editor: Rob Garner). Available from NASA at https://www.nasa.gov/feature/goddard/2019/messier-33-the-triangulum-galaxy [Accessed January 29, 2021].

- *Astrophysics through Computation: With Mathematica® Support* by Brian

Koberlein and David Meisel

- *Mohandas K. Gandhi, Autobiography: The Story of My Experiments with Truth* by Mohandas Karamchand Gandhi and Mahatma Gandhi

- *Midnight's Furies: The Deadly Legacy of India's Partition* by Nisid Hajari

Popular Books Published in 1947:
The Wayward Bus by John Steinbeck
Selections from the Prison Notebooks by Antonio Gramsci,

Popular Movies Released in 1947:
Blondie in the Dough (Penny Singleton, Arthur Lake)
Captain from Castile (Tyrone Power, Jean Peters, Cesar Romero)
Buffalo Bill Rides Again (Richard Arlen, Jennifer Holt)

December 2, 1947
Thanksgiving 1947

Albert Earl came home from Dartmouth for Thanksgiving, and it was good to see him again. We had a turkey weighing twelve pounds with all the fixings, and it has lasted until today. Snow covered the ground Saturday, and Lilla also came over from Natick to visit us. Janet has been doing splendidly in her (*high*) school work. It was a very pleasant Thanksgiving.

I gave the address at the Union Thanksgiving service this year, held in the Union Congregational Church, a week ago Sunday night. Quoted liberally from Mourt's Relation, which I read in full for the first time this year, thanks to a book I found in the Springfield Public Library.

I am teaching a class of eight girls in Girl Scouts the material for their course in Astronomy, and last night being fine, they had the privilege of seeing, for the first time, through my six-inch refelcting telescope some of the constellations, which they have been studying about. Also, the craters on the moon, and several doubles.

I wish that young people everywhere might have the same privilege. Carlyle exclaimed, on one occasion, "Oh why hasn't someone told me about the constellations, which I only half know to this day!"

(*Actual Quote by Thomas Carlyle was: "Why did not somebody teach me the constellations, and make me at home in the starry heavens, which are always overhead, and which I don't half know to this day?"*)

It is truly an interesting hobby. I wish that I had access to a larger telescope, but I have seen a great deal with the ones I have. I hope to take the group over to the Springfield Planetarium some night, after they have learned more about the stars.

It is a busy week, which lies ahead—Tomorrow night, a turkey supper and Christmas fair at our Church in Bondsville. On Thursday night, a family gathering at the Church here in Ludlow, with Rev. Donald Paige, Methodist minister in Easthampton, a former chaplain in the Air Forces, as speaker; Friday night the men's club will practice dart ball in preparation for a coming competition with a group from Ludlow Center; and Sunday a busy day with Holy Communion, and Every Member Canvass scheduled for the morning; and installation officers of the Methodist Youth Fellowship at Bondsville in the evening. Together with calling, which is always with us preachers!

On the world scene, Congress has voted several billions for relief in Europe, and will next tackle the problem of rising prices at home. The United Nations have granted the partition of Palestine, at which the Arab world is much incensed, threatening talk a Holy War or Jihad, but I don't think it will amount to more than talk. There will be incidents, of course, but there is much friction among their leaders. There is a conference of foreign ministers in London, dealing with the problem of Germany's frontiers (deferred); a peace treaty (doubtful); the Marshall Plan (problematical); the unity of occupation of Germany (which Russia wishes to continue for many years); and sundry other items of world import, which probably will be left hanging in the balance for want of amity in solution.

The ground is bare again, and Nature seems to be in a state waiting until such time as it really gets cold here in this Northern clime. There is snow to the north of us, of course.

In the realm of literature, I haven't read anything outstanding for a long time. We did see the motion picture "The Egg and I" last Friday evening, and it had many scenes of humor; although, it doesn't follow the book too closely.

There are no grains of wisdom lurking in my skull at this moment, so will bring this un-spritely narrative to a close. Facta non verba for today.

Suggested Daily Spiritual Reading:
John 12:25
2 Corinthians 4:15

Further Reading Related to Diary Entry:
- *Mourt's Relation or Journal of the Pilgrims at Plymouth*. Contributor Names: Bradford, William, 1590-1657. Winslow, Edward, 1595-1655. Dexter, Henry Martyn, 1821-1890, ed. Created / Published by J. K. Wiggin, 1865, Boston, Massachusetts. Available from the Department of Anthropology, University of Chicago, at Urbana-Champaign, Illinois (by Patricia Scott Deetz and Christopher Fennell) at http://www.histarch.illinois.edu/plymouth/mourt1.html [Accessed January 23, 2021].

- *The communion of sainctes A treatise of the fellowship that the faithful have with God, and his angels, and one with an other; in this present life. Gathered out of the holy Scriptures*, by Henry Ainsworth, 1571-1622(?). Imprinted at Amsterdam by Giles Thorp, 1607. Available from the Text Creation Partnership, Early English Books Online; University of Michigan, Digital Collections, at https://

quod.lib.umich.edu/cgi/t/text/text-idx?c=eebo;idno=A12475.0001.001 [Accessed January 23, 2021].

- *Indian Nations of North America by National Geographic* by Rick Hill, Teri Frazier

- *500 Nations: An Illustrated History of North American Indians* by Alvin M. Josephy Jr.

- *Astronomy 101*. Available from the Physics and Astronomy Department, Western Washington University at http://www.wwu.edu/planetarium/a101/astronomy101.shtml [Accessed January 23, 2021].

Popular Books Published in 1947:
The Psychology of Intelligence by Jean Piaget
One, Two, Three...Infinity: Facts and Speculations of Science by George Gamow

Popular Movies Released in 1947:
The Egg and I (Claudette Colbert, Fred MacMurray, Marjorie Main, Percy Kilbride)
It Happened on Fifth Avenue (Don DeFore, Ann Harding, Charles Ruggles)
The Guilt of Janet Ames (Rosalind Russell, Melvyn Douglas)
The Fabulous Dorseys (Tommy Dorsey, Jimmy Dorsey, Janet Blair)

December 30, 1947

Last night I read André Gidé's Journals 1893-1913. They are interesting, but not too informative to the average reader, because of their many obscure literary references. His descriptive accounts of the country and of his travels are best. His travels in Spain and other places reflects his interest therein. At home he is bored and fatigued, but travel seems to awaken his joie de vivre. I think that is true of many writers, from my cursory experience. If imagination and description could only translate themselves to the pages without the boring, grueling, mechanical process of writing them down or typing them, the world of literature would be filled with bigger and better books.

Many of us ordinary mortals even hate to write personal letters. But if we could really set forth in felicitous prose and in detail the sensuous pleasure of even a trip to the garden, it would be a masterpiece. Or the unfolding of one day's thoughts, good and bad, in the life of one individual—a stream of consciousness as it were, for "I myself am Heaven and Hell" (*Omar Khayyam*)—what a book it would make! Joyce has written Ulysses of course, but I doubt even a literary Dubliner would have had in 1906 such erudite and obtuse cogitations as appears therein.

Outside my study window long icicles suspend from the eaves and glisten in the morning sun. The trees, especially the evergreens, are a fairyland with their weight of snow. The buntings and sparrows look anxiously for their food, which a Kindly Heavenly Father seems to have withheld from them for the nonce. The trees are bare.

A comet, 1947N, may be seen in the Southwest from 4:30 to 5:30 p.m, with binoculars or low power telescope. It is twenty-million miles long, travels 30 miles a second, and was seen to break into two parts by observers in Texas. I haven't seen it as yet.

The filling station across the way is servicing cars, among them the red car of the fire chief of the Ludlow Fire Department. The theater down the street is showing "Stallion Road". The Church bulletin board and stop sign are in range of view. But having enumerated all these things there is much still missing in a simple description of what I can see from my two study windows, which face south and west, respectively. And so it is with life. We only get or give disjecta membra—broken fragments of our experiences. Even newspaper accounts of great events give only one man's point of view, and that a limited one. No one sees the whole picture. Each individual must see life for himself. His frame of reference is limited, of course, but it is valid and more satisfying than the extemporaneous half-possession of another's viewpoint. One good look at the nebula of Orion and the Trapezium through a telescope is worth a hundred descriptions by the best astronomers. If we are to savor life to the full, we must open every door of our senses and absorb life by sensation, as it were. Art, music, literature lead us to the door and bid us enter but only we can experience pragmatically the essential treasure trove of existence. And even then there is a veil past which we cannot see, which can only be pierced by interpretation and understanding. We can blot out the sun with our fingertips. We get a kaleidoscope of impressions usually out of any experience, which must be sorted out and subject to mental ordering to be understood. What is a rainbow? Different frequencies in the wave spectrum of light. But to the artist and lover it is a thing of beauty and a joy forever. Christmas has been like that for me this year. And for all of us with the family together, well and happy. "Beauty is truth, truth beauty—that is all ye know...and all ye need to know!" said Keats, and he speaks with authority. Of the Infant Christ, Christina Rossetti writes, "But His mother only, in her maiden bliss, Worshipped the Beloved with a kiss." That is the true spirit of Christmas.

Suggested Daily Spiritual Reading:
Matthew 2
Psalm 18:46

Further Reading Related to Diary Entry:
- *The Journals of André Gide: Volume I 1889-1913* by André Gide, Justin O'Brien (translator)

- *The Moving Finger,* from the Rubaiyat of Omar Khayyam; a sermon by Reverend E.F. Dinsmore, Unity Church, Santa Barbara, CA. Available from Internet Archive at https://archive.org/stream/movingfingerofom00dinsrich/movingfingerofom00dinsrich_djvu.txt [Accessed January 23, 2021].

- *Ulysses* by James Joyce

- *The Complete Poems* by Christina Rossetti,

Popular Books Published in 1947:
Rocket Ship Galileo Robert A. Heinlein
With Folded Hands by Jack Williamson

Popular Movies Released in 1947:
Stallion Road (Ronald Reagan, Alexis Smith, Zachary Scott)
Miracle on 34th Street (Edmund Gwenn, Maureen O'Hara, John Payne)
The Bishop's Wife (Cary Grant, Loretta Young, David Niven)
Christmas Eve (George Raft, Randolph Scott, George Brent, Joan Blondell)

1948

January 20, 1948
WINTER

We have about two feet of snow upon the level, and much more in drifts, of course. We have had approximately three storms, not of severe intensity, but I have never seen as much snow before in this state in the past twenty-four years. And it has been severely cold also, unofficial temperatures being reported as high as 45 below (Fahrenheit) from Ware, a town nearby. My wife reports 13 below. We have been feeding the sparrows in our backyard, and they have enjoyed bread, canary seed, cracked corn, and oats. A small evergreen nearby is almost bowed down with the weight of the snow, and the birds make a pretty picture as they sit upon it.

Man and civilization may go down under the strain and stress of atomic wars and revert to semi-barbarism (though statements of this sort always seem alarmist to an unreasonable degree to me), but I like to think the birds will be around for millions of years to come to sing their Maker's praise. Who made God, you say? Well, answer me this one—how could the sweet vitality of a living bird be evolved from inanimate, if not inert, elements? Not to mention such a minor matter as the works of Shakespeare, which were in all probability the works of that mastermind, Francis Bacon. If you question the latter statement, consult the volume entitled "The Great Cryptogram" by Ignatius Donnelly, published in 1930. He has deciphered the code to be found on the pages of Richard 11 and other plays. Just two items of interest. Why was the 23 year-old daughter of Shakespeare an illiterate person? Why was Shakespeare buried 17 feet deep? Bacon had the intellectual brilliance to write the plays, and Donnelly shows many parallelisms and identifies between his works and that of the plays of Shakespeare. He is also presumed to have written the works of Marlowe, Montaigne, and even the "Anatomy of Melancholy". Why did he conceal his authorship of the plays? Stage plays were beneath the dignity of gentlemen, for one thing, in those days; and again "Richard II" aroused the wrath of Queen Elizabeth who would surely have killed the author, could she have discovered him for seditious sentiments therein. Again, it may have pleased his vanity.

Last night I read the new book of the month club entitled "Raintree County" by Ross Lockridge Jr., a teacher at Simmons College. It comprised 1,060 pages, and like Joyce's "Ulysses", which he imitates, consists of flashbacks showing the events one day (July 4, 1892) in the life of one Richard Shawnessy. Its panorama covers the whole history of the country. I find techniques used by Dos Passos,

Thomas Wolfe, Joyce, and other writers, but it is well done. I enjoy a historical novel, and the philosophical dissertations are very good. I am wrong about the name of the hero—it is John Wickliff Shawnessy (*not Richard*).

Albert writes from Dartmouth that Stefansson has been helping the members of the Outing Club to construct an igloo on the campus in connection with the annual Winter Carnival. The ice statue on the campus is to be fifteen feet high, at least. I remember with pleasure the Winter Carnivals I witnessed; especially the ski jumping and the skating. He also gave us tickets to hear Jose Iturbi at the Springfield Auditorium last Thursday night. Besides a splendid program, Iturbi played as encores the "Nocturne in E Flat", "Claire de Lune", and "Liebestraum". Besides being a great pianist, Iturbi is a well known conductor of orchestras, having led most of the famous ones in this country.

Two days hence is my 46th birthday. It seems that I am getting along in years, but I have many interests and enjoy each day that passes. Sunday night I saw Saturn, Theta Orionis, the Alpine Valley on the moon, and the "split" Gamma Arietis with my telescope. I greatly enjoy the avocation of astronomy.

Janet attained the maximum at school this semester—five As in her studies. Well done!

Suggested Daily Spiritual Reading:
Matthew 6:25-34
Psalm 25:5

Further Reading Related to Diary Entry:
- *The Great Cryptogram: Francis Bacon's Cipher in the So-Called Shakespeare Plays* by Ignatius Donnelly

- *Anatomy of Melancholy* by Democritus Junior (Robert Burton's pseudonym). Available from The Project Gutenberg at https://www.gutenberg.org/files/10800/10800-h/10800-h.htm [Accessed January 23, 2021].

- *The Complete Works of William Shakespeare*. Available from a Massachusetts Institute of Technology (MIT) website created by Jeremy Hylton and operated by *The Tech* (MIT's newspaper) at http://shakespeare.mit.edu/index.html [Accessed January 23, 2021].

- *Raintree County* by Ross Lockridge Jr.

- *Ulysses* by James Joyce

- *Finnegans Wake* by James Joyce

- *Dubliners* by James Joyce

- *Jose Iturbi: Life and Piano Technique* by Dagmar Uythethofken

Popular Books Published in 1948:
Most Popular Books Published In 1948. Available from Goodreads.com at https://www.goodreads.com/book/popular_by_date/1948 [Accessed January 23, 2021].
The Seven Storey Mountain by Thomas Merton
Raintree County by Ross Lockridge Jr.

Popular Movies Released in 1948:
Bicycle Thieves (Lamberto Maggiorani, Enzo Staiola, Lianella Carell)
Oliver Twist (Robert Newton, Alec Guinness, Kay Walsh)
Albuquerque (Randolph Scott, Barbara Britton, George "Gabby" Hayes)

March 22, 1948
SPRING

Though I haven't seen any Robins as yet, Spring has undoubtedly come, for I am writing this in my shirtsleeves, nay even more, I have removed my shirt! The temperature is 70 (*Fahrenheit*) outside, and it is unseeingly warm. The ground is bare of snow, and we have been having rains for the past two days. Spring has been called the season which is shortest, but longest remembered. We have had a long, cold winter with record snows, and so the change is the more appreciated.

On February 15 I looked at Mars at the time of its "unfavorable opposition," some 63 million miles away, and with the 200 power on my six-inch telescope was able to see the northern polar cap clearly. It was interesting to me, especially since I have been reading quite a bit about it. Astronomer Gerard Kuiper at MacDonald Observatory in Texas, using an infrared spectrometer, developed during World War II, attests two facts: (1) the polar caps are readily ice and snow like our own; (2) no true vegetation exists on Mars, like trees or plants. The vegetation observed there may be moss or lichens. Oxygen is scarce on Mars, being 1/100 of one percent of the amount here. Photographs of the canals have never been taken. It is possible of course that they were dug eons ago, and that the Martian race has died out long since for lack of oxygen, but we have no way of knowing definitely. Independent observers, however, have confirmed visually the observations Schiaparelli taken in 1881-1882. These include Professor Lowell who made extensive surveys at Flagstaff, Arizona in 1915 and following years. Thus in all probability, men did tap the water supply from the poles to irrigate the desserts of Mars, and in all probability the work ceased long since. So, we are alone in our solar system—sports of an unfeeling universe. I hope with Whitman, however, who said (*paraphrased*), "The whole of earth and all the stars are subjects of religion" that ours will be proved a friendly universe. I feel it so. I also saw Cassini's division in Saturn the night of the 15th, and Gamma Leonis. Last Sunday night among other thingsI saw Epsilon in Bootes with only 2.7" of arc separation. About the best I can do with my equipment.

(Walt Whitman's quote from his poem "The Soul" was actually, "I say the whole earth and all the stars in the sky are for religion's sake.")

This week on the national scene the speech of president Truman to the Congress took first place. He recommended immediate aid to Europe, furtherance of national defense, and passage of legislation for universal military training. Russia took over Czechoslovakia in February, and now interest centers on Italy, where the national elections take place April 18th. We are aiding Greece with arms. The UN is considering placing Palestine under a trusteeship. The Arabs call for demilitarization of Haganah, the Jewish force of troops. The pattern emerges. The prize is Western Europe. Already, some countries, like England, France, and the Netherlands, and Belgium have banded together for economic and military cooperation. It is disturbing to find distrust between the united States and Russia so pronounced, but Russia has consistently failed to cooperate in writing treaties of peace and in supporting United Nations plans to build a lasting peace among the nations. The use of the veto has been the principle stumbling block, though there have been others. I would like to see lines of demarcation laid down between the powers of east and west, and then have them adhered to, but power politics do not operate so felicitously.

Albert Earl came home on a surprise visit Feb. 27th for the weekend, and on that same night Janet received a call to work for Mrs. James at Booth's drugstore. She has been working there since, and Mae has occasionally taken her place at taking care of children. Albert is coming home for the Easter recess on Saturday.

I have been quite busy with Church work, and sometimes feel like St. Paul, on whom fell the burden of the Churches daily. But it is all to the glory of God. "I am swept up to Thee by Thy Beauty!" (*Saint Augustin*)

Suggested Daily Spiritual Reading:
Genesis 1:15
1 Peter 3:3-4

Further Reading Related to Diary Entry:
- *Astronomy in the Old Testament* by Giovanni Virginio Schiaparelli

- *Death on Mars: The Discovery of a Planetary Nuclear Massacre* by John E. Brandenburg, PhD

- *The Future of Humanity: Terraforming Mars, Interstellar Travel, Immortality, and Our Destiny Beyond Earth* by Michio Kaku

- *Walt Whitman: Poetry and Prose* by Walt Whitman and Justin Kaplan

- *Walt Whitman (The Camden Sage) as Religious and Moral Teacher: A Study* by William Norman Guthrie

- *Iron Curtain: The Crushing of Eastern Europe, 1944-1956* by Anne Applebaum

♦ *Saint Augustin: Top Biography Collections* by Louis Bertrand

Popular Books Published in 1948:
   Cheaper by the Dozen by Ernestine Gilbreth Carey
   The White Goddess by Robert Graves

Popular Movies Released in 1948:
   Red River (John Wayne, Montgomery Clift, Joanne Dru)
   Easter Parade (Judy Garland, Fred Astaire, Peter Lawford)
   Blondie's Secret (Penny Singleton, Arthur Lake)

May 13, 1948
THINGS SATISFYING

The only things truly satisfying are the eternal...

This morning I heard the birds singing in the rain, in fact a truly heavy shower. It is a nice morning in May—the ground is wet with rain; though the sun is not shining the trees are burgeoning forth with leaves, the purple and white lilacs are in bloom, and the apple blossoms give forth a pleasant smell. Crocus and jonquils are at hand, and even tulips are out with variegated colors. The air is chill, but the great mysterious work of the Creator goes on, and the world expresses His unfailing fruitfulness. We had a strawberry supper at the Church last night, strawberries being served in the form of shortcake, steeped in satisfying juice. From a material standpoint, Spring evokes a land of promise of good things—"how good is man's life, the mere living, how fit to employ all the heart and the soul and the senses forever in joy!" (*Quote is from Robert Browning's poem "David Singing before Saul".*)

Janet (*17 years of age*) is busy with her (*high*) school work, being engaged in a number of examinations at present, and also with her work at Booth's drugstore. Albert Earl, at Dartmouth, is also close to his examinations and will be home again next month. He sent home a thesis on early Greek astronomers, which was concise and well annotated. Their chief emphasis was on deductive analysis rather than induction, and since they were severely handicapped in use of instruments, of necessity were limited to reasoning about the universe. My six-inch telescope would seem a marvelous instrument to them.

On the state of the nation, we have just averted a serious rail strike through use of a federal injunction; prices have risen steadily—coke (*fuel similar to coal*), for example, will cost me four dollars a ton more next winter than last—universal military training is being debated in and out of congress; and finally the Soviet Union has indicated its willingness to talk over differences existing between east and west. This is a hopeful sign, but contrary to Soviet procedure in the past.

Mae and I are interested in crossword puzzles, working out one each day from the morning paper. The theory is that if we cannot solve big problems, perhaps we can solve the little ones. And we have had good success the past two weeks. We run across some interesting words—e.g. "Alan", for wolfhound; "orle", for shield-bearing; "att" for Siamese coin; "Enid", for wife of Geraint, "unau" for two-toed and "ai" for three-toed sloth; and "orlop" for the lowest deck of a ship—where the anchor chain is stored. Not of any practical use that I can see, but it is interesting to build up the words nevertheless.

The stars continue wheeling about the firmament, and the moon is waxing again, but bad weather has made observation difficult for a long time, and I haven't had my big telescope out for about three weeks. The magnificent display of winter's skies has given way to more somber groups of Virgo, Bootes, and Lyra. The three planets are still visible—Venus in crescent form in the West, Mars and Saturn overhead with the invisible Pluto between and to the north of them. I have missed Jupiter this winter.

I have been reading a Greek anthology, including the work of the poets, the historians Herodotus and Thucydides, and of course Plato's account of the cave and the doings of Socrates. He told his judges, "No evil can come to a good man in this life or the next"—walked barefoot through the snow, and stood for a day, and a night in deep thought. Then he thanked his God and went his way.

Suggested Daily Spiritual Reading:
   Matthew 13:31-32
   Psalm 118:6

Further Reading Related to Diary Entry:
- *The History of the Crossword: The World's Most Famous Word Puzzle* by John Halpern

- *The Night Sky Observer's Guide: Autumn & Winter: 1* by George Robert Kepple, Glen W. Sanner

- *The Greek Anthology, Volume I*: Book 1: Christian Epigrams. Book 2: Description of the Statues in the Gymnasium of Zeuxippus. Book 3: Epigrams in the ... 5: Erotic Epigrams (Loeb Classical Library) by Michael A. Tueller (Editor), W. R. Paton (Translator)

Popular Books Published in 1948:
   The Heart of the Matter by Graham Greene
   The Plague and I by Betty MacDonald

Popular Movies Released in 1948:
   The Treasure of the Sierra Madre (Humphrey Bogart, Walter Huston, Tim Holt)
   Fort Apache (John Wayne, Henry Fonda, Shirley Temple)
   The Bride Goes Wild (June Allyson, Van Johnson)

May 31, 1948
MESNE MEASURE

A cycle has ended. I have completed twenty years in the ministry (*age 46*), and begin another twenty. Forty years is the customary stint with genteel poverty at the end of it, if one is lucky enough to survive that long. There are exceptions of course. I heard of a minister who is now 100 years old who preached 21 years after he had retired, and gave a half-hour sermon on his 100th birthday! Another has bought and sold houses and so stands at last possessor of a house and competence of his own. John L. Lewis recently procured for the coal miners a pension equal to four times that of a Methodist minister in this conference. They deserve it, of course, but it will increase my coal bill by four dollars a ton this coming winter—not simply the pension of course, but the scarcity of coke caused by the strike. Oh well, we get our compensations in other ways. Acquaintance with the great and near great—freedom to move and associate freely on all cultural and financial levels—freedom to read and study anything under the sun (all is grist for the minister's mill)—friendships in a score of places instead of one. Denied a material dwelling and earthly competence, we must fashion a spiritual one at home in the universe, and our coin is trust in the Heavenly Father. And of course in spite of reverses and disappointments, the humblest minister accomplishes some good in cultivating his particular corner of God's vineyard. "Bane and blessing, pain and pleasure, by the cross are sanctified—Peace is there that knows no measure—joys that through all time abide!" May the peace of God, which passeth all understanding dwell in the hearts of all who read these words! (*Quote above is from line 4 of the hymn "In the cross of Christ I glory, Towering o'er the wrecks of time" by John Bowring, 1825.*)

Today was observed as Memorial Day in Massachusetts. At the bridge crossing the Chicopee River I gave the prayer for the men who died in the service of their country on the high seas. "Deep calleth unto deep at the noise of Thy waterspouts. All Thy waves and Thy billows have gone over me, yet the Lord will command His loving-kindness in the daytime, and in the night His song shall be with me, a prayer unto the God of my life." (*Psalm 42:7-8*) The Girl Scouts cast flowers over the rail into the turbulent waters, where perchance the currents will carry some part of them to the mighty ocean via the Connecticut River. Three volleys were fired, taps was played, and their souls commended to their Maker. I had the pleasure of meeting and conversing with the new Portuguese priest, a Father Rocha, who has studied philosophy at Rome and Louvain and was formerly director of work for Catholic youth in the Azores.

In a window on Boylston Street in Boston last Wednesday night, I saw a Ferris wheel complete with gondolas made of 17,000 toothpicks glued together—the handiwork of an inmate of the state prison in Thomaston, Maine. More than two hundred hours of labor went into the project, which is powered by a small motor so that it runs and simulates its bigger brothers.

On Friday night the sky was wholly clear for observation. With my six-inch telescope using different lenses I saw the planets Venus—a thin crescent; Mars—with the reduced polar cap mostly imagined, though I did see it well and clearly last winter; Saturn—with its rings and Cassini's division; and Jupiter—with its four moons in line, two on each side of the planet. Quite an unusual spectacle for one evening! I also found the Ring Nebula in Lyra, the great cluster in Hercules; the extragalactic nebula M 80 in Scorpius (lying between Antares and B Scorpii) and other objects of interest. It is good to rest one's soul in the infinite meadows of heaven! How lovely is Thy dwelling place, my King and my God!

Suggested Daily Spiritual Reading:
Romans 12:4-5
1 Peter 4:11

Further Reading Related to Diary Entry:
- *The Vulnerable Pastor: How Human Limitations Empower Our Ministry* by Mandy Smith

- *Friends' Review: A Religious, Literary, and Miscellaneous Journal*, volumes 1-48 (1847-1894). Editors: Sept. 1847- Enoch Lewis. Samuel Rhoads. Publisher, Josiah Tatum, Philadelphia. Available from the Hathi Trust Digital Library at https://catalog.hathitrust.org/Record/000545855 [Accessed January 23, 2021].

- *Canoeing the Mountains: Christian Leadership in Uncharted Territory* by Tod Bolsinger

- *The Saturn System Through The Eyes Of Cassini* by NASA

Popular Books Published in 1948:
Cry, the Beloved Country by Alan Paton
No Highway by Nevil Shute

Popular Movies Released in 1948:
A Foreign Affair (Jean Arthur, Marlene Dietrich, John Lund)
State of the Union (Spencer Tracy, Katharine Hepburn, Van Johnson)
The Fuller Brush Man (Red Skelton, Janet Blair, Hillary Brooke, Adele Jergens)

September 23, 1948
MOTIF NO. 1

About the middle of August I was invited to go deep sea fishing with some friends in Church and Lodge (*men's club*); eight of us comprising the party. We road down (*up*) to Rockport in the night, and before the break of dawn were standing on the town wharf in Rockport, Mass. I immediately recognized, in the darkness, the old fishing shack just across the channel, which had been painted by hundreds of artists and has come to be known as motif number one. Later on in the daylight, the faded red paint, lobster markers, and large gulls (gannets?) atop the roof made it quite recognizable. And the little boats in the harbor, with their tall swaying masts, were an unforgettable sight. There were some beautiful, private yachts in the harbor too, which has a breakwater of stone at the entrance. One of the yachts was equipped for tuna fishing, with its leather chair and stout fishing rod at the stern—altogether a sleek craft.

The dawn broke cloudy and with wind from the Northeast, which made the sea rough, but we went out with our host nevertheless, past Thatcher's twin lights to the fishing grounds. We saw a sunken Liberty ship with hull standing out of the water, and a large rocky island our left inhabited only by many gulls, some of which followed us out to partake of the tasty tidbits, which were thrown to them as the lines were baited.

The sea was rough, and one wave broke clear over the cabin dousing the men sitting in the stern. Let me say in passing that only two of us out of the eight were free from seasickness, and of course mine host who went out to his lobster pots every day. Only two other boats joined us during the time we were there. There was a cross-tide and a riptide to enliven things, and the boat and waves were never still. We let out our lines to a depth of 180 feet and soon one of the men caught a good sized pollock, which were our main catch that morning. They averaged a little over two feet long, and from 9 to 27 pounds.

One of the men caught a small cod, and later on hitched on to a sand shark, which I saw and which weighed perhaps 125 pounds. We never found out, for he slipped the hook while being gaffed. My line was entangled with the others three times, and so I only caught two pollock, as compared to eight for one chap. But I enjoyed watching the sea, and a trawler heading for Gloucester with its nets attached to the masts.

It was hard to anchor the boat. We were only out three hours. On the way in we saw a small tuna leaping out of the water after a small school of menhaden or mackerel, and I was interested also in seeing for the first time, to my knowledge, the small birds known as Mother Carey's chickens. So many of the men were sick that the skipper deemed it best to come in. We had a good mess of fish, and a pleasant memory of a beautiful harbor and the sea running free. The depth of the ocean nearer shore was 400 feet.

Early in August I went to New York City for the seventh visit. Highlights for me were the obelisk of Cleopatra in Central Park; a walk across the park; and visit to the Museum of Natural History where I saw Tyrannosaurus Rex and the splendid mineral collection, including the largest star ruby in the world. I also visited several bookstores, and met a number of casual acquaintances—one in Time Square who told me his war service was spent in the Aleutians; a bus driver on Fifth Avenue whose war service was in the South Pacific, including Okinawa; and a chap I met on the ferry boat coming back from Staten Island to whom I pointed out Jupiter, Antares, and some of the constellations. On Staten Island I visited Midland Beach. Ich habe genossen das erdische Gluck—ich habe gelebt und geliebet—Schiller.

Suggested Daily Spiritual Reading:
Matthew 4:19
Mathew 13:467

Further Reading Related to Diary Entry:
- *Saltwater Fishing Made Easy* by Martin Pollizotto

- *Going Fishing: The Story of the Deep-Sea Fishermen of New England* by Wesley George Pierce

- *Crunch & Des: Classic Stories of Saltwater Fishing* by Philip Wylie (Author), Karen Wylie Pryor (Editor)

- *Friedrich Schiller Poet of Freedom Volume I* by Friedrich Schiller (Author), William F. Wertz (Translator), John Sigerson (Translator), Helga Zepp-LaRouche (Preface)

Popular Books Published in 1948:
The Celestial Plot by Adolfo Bioy Casares
Catalina by W. Somerset Maugham

Popular Movies Released in 1948:
Good Sam (Gary Cooper, Ann Sheridan, Edmund Lowe)
Homecoming (Clark Gable, Lana Turner, Anne Baxter)
The Iron Curtain (Dana Andrews, Gene Tierney, June Havoc)

December 29, 1948

Since my last entry a lot of water has flowed over the dam, but not the dam of time. I am convinced that this is but a convenient abstraction—and denotes the relative position of things space. Indeed, the very clocks we use in the house are patterned after the rotation of the earth in relation to the sun, let us say. I do not need to convince anyone of this, I know—that time is not real, though it seems terribly real at times (positions). Chess is a game of positions with skill in reaching the same, and the time element is a very elastic one, so elastic as to be virtually absent. Metaphysically, a chess game can be said to be without beginning (since positions are arbitrarily assumed at the start of the game) and without end, since it is mutually agreed upon that the end consists of a position (or positions) in which one proponent finds himself unable to move his king without capture. We postulate a beginning or end to ourselves, the earth, or the universe, but these may be only changed positions of relatively insignificant matter in the mind of the Prime Mover. "Time goes, we stay, you say? Ah no! Time stays—we go." (*Henry Austin Dobson*)

It does my psyche a great deal of good to set down with some philosophical speculation, like the above. When I think of all the books I might have written (and who doesn't?) I stand at the edge of the ocean of illimitable thought "and Time and Fame to nothingness do sink." (*Keats*) Fortunately for us we are geared to everyday living and other people and common principles (and herein lies the negation of Existentialism, Kierkegaard, and Sartre to the contrary not withstanding), which saves us from a great deal of melancholy and futility. Much study is a weariness of the flesh, and of making many books there is no end.

We have had a lovely Christmas season, all the way from the first snow, the arrival of Albert Earl on the 18th and the setting up of the Christmas tree, to the opening of the presents on Christmas morning. I received a shirt, a pocketbook, a sweater and sundry items; Albert Earl—a Schick shaving outfit; Janet—a coat, shoes, et cetera; and Mae—the money for a new hairdo. Janet gave us an enlarged, colored, framed picture of herself. Receiving some sixty dollars from parishioners, we purchased a Columbia long-playing record attachment and several records, among them Brahms symphonies one and two, Prokofiev's Fifth, Tchaikovsky's Fifth, Beethoven's Violin Concerto, and Mendelssohn's Midsummer Night's Dream. Albert Earl is learning to play the piano with Robert Wareham. Janet had a party prior to Christmas with four couples present. There were well-attended services in both Ludlow and Bondsville Churches. In short, we had a nice Christmas, and its influence will extend throughout the year ahead.

New rings and pistons installed in the car by Francis Naddo at Steve's filling station, on December 3rd, have resulted in a much more smoothly running motor, for which I am pleased. We have had two tons of coke put into the cellar and the heating system is working well. Today a light rain is falling, and the cold atmosphere causes the streets to be in a slippery condition. I have a touch of laryngitis, which is unpleasant.

On the international scene, the Communists have surrounded Peiping in China and are advancing toward Nanking. The United States refuses to lend aid, on the theory that Chiang Kai Shek is incompetent, and much of the supplies would fall into the hands of the Communists. Th United Nations has ordered Holland to cease fighting in Indonesia, but most of her objectives have been attained there anyway.

Suggested Daily Spiritual Reading:
Ecclesiastes 3
John 1

Further Reading Related to Diary Entry:
- *The Order of Time* by Carlo Rovelli

- *The Fabric of the Cosmos: Space, Time, and the Texture of Reality* by Brian Greene

- *A Brief History of Time* by Stephen Hawking

- *Communism: A History* by Richard Pipes

- *Essays in Musical Analysis* (Volume VI) by Donald Francis Tovey; published by Oxford University Press, London. Available from The Internet Archive at https://archive.org/details/in.ernet.dli.2015.28890/page/n3 [Accessed January 23, 2021].

Popular Books Published in 1948:
City Boy: The Adventures of Herbie Bookbinder by Herman Wouk
Last of the Conquerors by William Gardner Smith

Popular Movies Released in 1948:
Joan of Arc (Ingrid Bergman, José Ferrer)
June Bride (Bette Davis, Robert Montgomery)
The Miracle of the Bells (Alida Valli, Fred MacMurray, Frank Sinatra)
Apartment for Peggy (Jeanne Crain, William Holden, Edmund Gwenn

1949

February 9, 1949
EVEN KEEL

Life seems to be running along an even keel at the present moment—no crises at hand, to my knowledge, no emotional strains. I like to write and think dispassionately, but most of our horizons are emotionally colored, and that a great deal of time. Even the most learned mathematician may err when his stomach begins to rumble with hunger, or the most exact robot calculator may go "on the blink" when a drop of oil is lacking. It is hard to be utterly dispassionate either in thinking or in judgement. Besides, it is the height or depth of the cyclothymic swing which is longest remembered by ourselves and our contemporaries. Lincoln and Ann Rutledge. Churchill and the invasion of France —"I find it rather inspiring!" Jesus on the cross.

Albert Earl is in his second year at Dartmouth and has just finished his mid-year exams. He has invited Mary Ann Fillmore to be his guest at Carnival. Ice sculpture, the Dartmouth Players, the ski meet, skating races on Occam Pond, outdoor skiing in person on the golf links or at Balch Hill, and as a climax the ball in the gymnasium with its colored crystal ball suspended above the dance floor, made of triangles of glass mirrors, no doubt, but reflecting the lights and colors of dancers and gym decorations alike—all these combine to make an unforgettable weekend.

Janet Elizabeth takes in the finale of the Senior show two nights this week at the high school auditorium. Five or six couples in evening gowns and tuxedoes dance to the tune "When I Grow too Old to Dream". She has been doing very well in her studies the past two years, being on Honors. She has sent in her application to the Deaconess Hospital in Boston to study nursing.

My birthday came on January 22nd as usual—47 years old. Mae and Janet gave me a pair of lined gloves for my birthday. Lilla (*his younger sister*) sent me some money, to which I added a little and bought a record (Vinylite long-playing) of Beethoven's Seventh Symphony—my favorite—as played by the Philadelphia orchestra under the conductorship of Eugene Ormandy. How I would like to have a recording of the same by Koussevitsky and the Boston Orchestra! But they do not record for Columbia. However, thanks to Albert's generosity in getting us tickets, Mae, Janet, and I enjoyed the Boston Symphony in an evening's entertainment at the Springfield Auditorium on or about January 11th. Their final number was Beethoven's Seventh, and it was superbly done!

The weather has been unusually mild this winter, as contrasted with last, particularly. We have had no real snowstorm all, and only on two or three occasions storms of two or three inches. Hardly enough to shovel, and as a matter of fact, I have not had to shovel out the driveway to the garage this winter.

Astronomically, I have learned only two facts recently, viz-Sirius is in the same group with Ursa Major; and the dwarf companion of Procyon weighs 200 tons to the cubic inch, as compared with the dwarf companion to Sirius, which weighs only one ton (sic!) to the cubic inch. Scientific query—are protons, neutrons, and electrons the ultimate irreducible building blocks of the universe?

Suggested Daily Spiritual Reading:
Matthew 28:18
Isaiah 40:29

Further Reading Related to Diary Entry:
- *Beethoven: Anguish and Triumph* by Jan Swafford

- *The Soul of Ann Rutledge Abraham Lincoln's Romance* by Bernie Babcock

- *Cosmology: A Very Short Introduction* by Peter Coles

- *The Physics of God: Unifying Quantum Physics, Consciousness, M-Theory, Heaven, Neuroscience and Transcendence* by Joseph Selbie

Popular Books Published in 1949:
Most Popular Books Published In 1949. Available from Goodreads.com at https://www.goodreads.com/book/popular_by_date/1949 [Accessed January 23, 2021].
1984 by George Orwell
Jesus and the Disinherited by Howard Thurman

Popular Movies Released in 1949:
The Secret Garden (Margaret O'Brien, Herbert Marshall, Dean Stockwell)
Come to the Stable (Loretta Young, Celeste Holm, Hugh Marlowe)
A Connecticut Yankee in King Arthur's Court (Bing Crosby, Rhonda Fleming, Cedric Hardwicke)

April 20, 1949

Today, Spring comes in through the windows. The room is uncomfortably warm—perhaps because I hadn't turned off the radiator. The sun is bright, nearly at its meridian height, the birds have been singing, a soft breeze is blowing. In the spring a young man's fancy lightly turns to thoughts of love, but what does a middle-aged man's fancy turn to thoughts of? I cannot answer for others, but I have passing twinges of regret that I am not rich and famous—well, at least rich, for fame is a chimera, "that last infirmity of a noble mind", as McDougall aptly phrased it. (*Note: "that last infirmity of a noble mind" is from the poem Lycidas by John Milton*) But rich like Horace, the poet of old, with his villa in the countryside, where I could loaf and take mine ease beneath my vine and fig tree. A brook flowing near the house—the gurgle of the waters is conducive to relaxation (one flowed near the birthplace of my wife, one near mine—and still do, I imagine, in the slow-changing hills of Vermont). A library of a million volumes—diverse in content and continually replenished. A fine astronomical observatory. A collection of minerals. A good stamp collection. Time to read and think. Good children about me and loving wife, and a dog to take for a walk in the hills nearby.

But what am I saying? I have all these things now—except for the big bank account. How achieve that? Why, by writing a historical novel or an existential one, let us say; or one of realism; or refined pornography, as popular now as ever. Having read Ellis in toto, and Stekel and Kraft-Ebbing, and Freud, and Joyce, as well as Dos Passos, and Thomas Wolfe (my favorite prose writer by the way), I believe any modern doctor or clergyman could write a novel that would singe the eyebrows of the experts and the craniums of the critics. But we are inhibited by a thousand conventions, one being that of St. Paul written especially for ministers it seems: "And having food and drink, let us be therewith content." (*Paraphrased, 1 Timothy 6:8*)

So, we confine ourselves to journals, which are distinctly not profitable, as Thoreau found out long ago, when out of a thousand copies printed, he had to carry home more than nine hundred. One basis for such a novel might be this: the combined lives and intermingling of such diverse persons as a Protestant Republican; a Portugese Catholic; a Jew, not orthodox, from Russia; a former communist; a Hindu; a South African; a New Zealander; and so on. Of course, there must be an Englishman, meeting on a ship at sea, or in Paris or Chicago, or shipwrecked, or on a bus for that matter. A discussion of mores, politics, and religions would naturally follow. Perhaps two or three kinds of love stories thrown in for good measure. A heterogenous cosmopolitan group united by some common thread of thought or action. Following out some of Dale Carnegie's principles: 1. Act as if it were impossible to fail. 2. Remember the other fellow may be more timid than yourself. 3. Live opulently. Day dreams!

I have been reading lately, with deep interest, Willard's account of the buried cities of Yucatan-Chichen-Itza, Uxmal, and Mayapan. First under the enlightened rule of Itzamna, they were without bloody sacrifices and worshipped a monotheistic God who was neither pictured nor sculptured. Then conquered by Kukulcan the Toltec, they were forced to institute brutal sacrifices in the temples and at the sacred well. Then, subject to internecine wars and overwhelmed by the Spaniards, this magnificent civilization of perhaps several million people disintegrated, and the cities they built reverted to the jungle. They developed the art of astronomy, having a superb calendar for some five thousand years, the art of working metals like copper, and the art of painting, and architecture—their temples and palaces withstanding the assaults of time and savagery. It is strange to think of these cities flourishing when North America was a wilderness. Perhaps our own some day...?

Suggested Daily Spiritual Reading:
1 Peter 5:7
Psalm 138:3

Further Reading Related to Diary Entry:
- *Look Homeward, Angel* by Thomas Wolfe

- *Of Time and the River: A Legend of Man's Hunger in His Youth* by Thomas Wolfe

- *The Depths of the Soul: Psycho-Analytic Studies* by Wilhelm Stekel

- *City of the Sacred Well* by T.A. Willard. Available from Internet Archive at https://archive.org/details/cityofsacredwell00will/page/n7 [Accessed January 23, 2021].

Popular Books Published in 1949:
The Sheltering Sky by Paul Bowles
The Crow Comes Last by Italo Calvino

Popular Movies Released in 1949:
Sands of Iwo Jima (John Wayne, John Agar, Adele Mara)
On the Town (Gene Kelly, Frank Sinatra, Betty Garrett)
I Was a Male War Bride (Cary Grant, Ann Sheridan, Marion Marshall)

Festive occasion with family gathered. Janet's high school graduation, circa 1949.

Janet, Mae, and the Reverend ready for commencement.

Janet, officially a high school graduate.

The Reverend giving Janet a congratulatory kiss, with Mae smiling in the background, Albert Jr. Looking on.

The party begins. Back Row: Henry and Marion Townsend (good friends and former neighbors), the Reverend, Albert Jr. Middle: Olive (Mae's mother). Front row: Lilla (Reverend's younger sister) and Mae (Reverend's wife).

Olive, Mae, Marion, Janet, Lilla.

Lilla and the Reverend.

Janet, Olive, the Reverend, Mae, Albert Jr.

August 2, 1949
FISHING TRIP

Now that I am on vacation for the month of August, let me relate in detail the deep sea fishing trip we took a week ago, yesterday, from Rockport, Mass. My son, Albert Earl, and I, went with seven other men from Ludlow and Granby, arriving at the Town Wharf about four o'clock in the morning. We went out about five-thirty in Captain Nelson's lobster boat, a new one which he built last winter. It is thirty-eight feet long with marine engine and small, open cabin; like so many others in the harbor. It is called "Girlie", no doubt after the bride he took a week previously.

Albert Jr and the Reverend, circa 1949.

We anchored about eight miles off shore, and began to fish. There were two other boats anchored nearby. In two hours we had garnered a half ton of fish, mostly pollock, with a few cod, haddock, and an ugly-looking catfish. The sea was smooth as glass, and no one was seasick (10 on board), as compared with a rather rough sea last year, when all were seasick—with the minor exception of another fellow and myself.

While fishing ardently, we were pleasantly surprised to see a whale go by, about a hundred yards away. Probably a whalebone or finback whale. It was estimated to be forty or fifty feet long. It was the first I had ever seen, and so I was thrilled by the sight. I could see the back fin and blowhole clearly. He blew, or spouted, eight times in my sight, and I heard him spout the ninth time. He sounded just like the exhaust from a steam laundry. He kept a straight course and was soon out of sight.

There were only a few swells to the sea, and the smoothness of it was a revelation to me. The ocean was about 200 feet deep at that spot—has probably been a fishing ground for centuries. The tide began to run out about eleven o'clock, carrying out lines with it, and so went our fishing luck.

Albert Earl caught an 18 pound pollock, and was one up on me on the total number caught. Altogether, ten men pulled in 87 fish, the captain helping us. Though there were plenty of gulls and especially later when the captain cleaned the fish, nevertheless I missed seeing Mother Carey's chickens. Last year also we saw a shark, which Bill MacFarlane pulled up to the boat, and I saw a small tuna leaping clear out of the water to pursue a small school of mackerel.

The horizon was empty—devoid of even a freighter—and over an arc of 300 degrees from Thatcher's Island lights to the point of Cape Ann I saw nothing but open water, not even a painted ship upon the painted ocean. But it was very impressive, and for once in my life I saw enough of the open sea. We pulled up the lines about noon, ate our lunch and lifted anchor. The Captain asked Albert Earl to pilot the boat while he cleaned the fish, and Albert Earl did so, steering to the left of Guano Rocks, where hundreds of gulls nested, until we reached the harbor. Last year the waves were breaking over the top of the rocks, and the wind was blowing, and that was impressive too. On the way in I saw a four-masted schooner in the distance. The small sailing boats in the sheltered harbor of Rockport were lovely as ever in their different colored hulls, but they were not swaying gently in the breeze, as they did a year ago—making an unforgettable picture. Motif Number One was still on hand, waiting patiently for its portrait by a handful of painters gathered on the dock. The fishing smack, a seiner, anchored there last year about this time, was missing. Each year and each day presents a new scene. Only the gulls and the sea are permanent. We gave the fish we had caught to our friends.

Suggested Daily Spiritual Reading:
1 Thessalonians 5:16-18
Corinthians 13:13
Genesis 1:28

Further Reading Related to Diary Entry:
- *Castaways: The Penikese Island Experiment* by George Cadwalader

- *The Ocean of Life: The Fate of Man and the Sea* by Callum Roberts

- *The World Is Blue: How Our Fate and the Ocean's Are One* by Sylvia A. Earle

- *The Sea Around Us* by Rachel Carson

Popular Books Published in 1949:
    The Hero with a Thousand Face by Joseph Campbell
    Death of a Salesman by Arthur Miller

Popular Movies Released in 1949:
    Twelve O'Clock High (Gregory Peck, Hugh Marlowe, Gary Merrill)
    She Wore a Yellow Ribbon (John Wayne, Joanne Dru, John Agar)
    Ma and Pa Kettle (Marjorie Main, Percy Kilbride)

October 22, 1949
MEMOIR

Yesterday was Albert Earl's 20th birthday. I sent him five dollars and his mother sent him candy and other things, but that hardly begins to express our appreciation for him. I well remember the night he was born with his grandmothers and I waiting anxiously for news concerning him. It came at last and we could say, thankfully, his mother and I, "Unto us a son is born, unto us a child is given..." (*Isaiah 9:6*) He has been a blessing from that day to this, as has his little sister who came along a couple of years later. Life holds no greater cause for thankfulness than a devoted wife and two fine children. The vicissitudes pale into insignificance as one contemplates these precious jewels. Superior to the most precious jade or even star rubies. May their luster ever be undimmed!

Janet has departed to take up her work in training to become a child nurse. She is studying and working at the Peabody Home for Crippled Children at Newton Center, Mass. She reports that she was awakened in the middle of the night of her arrival to find a mouse trying to climb out of the wastebasket. She is rooming with a girl from New Hampshire. Her cot is hard, her hours long, but if I know my daughter these will be discounted in her eagerness to help little children who are unfortunately unable to help themselves. "And I say to you verily, whosoever shall give a cup of cold water only to one of these little ones shall in no wise lose his reward." (*Matthew 10:42, paraphrased*)

We are left alone except for our eight year old collie, Rover, and I am not sure that he is such a comfort, because of his unnecessary (so it seems to us) barking. He is nearly blind, and I suppose in his zeal to protect the place, he thinks he is doing his duty. I remember how at first meeting he would chew away at my fingers with his little teeth. He was very lovable then and for that I forgive him much.

Albert Earl is taking his exams today, seeking entrance to Dartmouth Medical School. I hope he makes it, since his heart is set on being a doctor. He is working very hard at college, doing two hours work each day at the dining hall, and peddling sandwiches and milk for two hours each night to the dormitories and fraternity buildings. His studies are also well advanced but with all, he has time to listen to classical music, since he has a record player, and so also have some of his friends.

Speaking of music, I too have been listening via shortwave to balalaika music from Moscow; recordings of classics from Leopoldville in the Belgian Congo; music box Nachtmusik from Switzerland; and I have also heard Hilversum, Holland, and Buenos Aires lately. I have the little set, that Scotty sold me up at the farm a long time ago, on my reading stand, and it gives a lot of comfort and pleasure at night while Mae is caring for the children of Tilly Monette, who runs a store nearby.

"Pleasant words are as an honeycomb, sweet to the soul, and health to the bones" (Prov. 16:24). And even so is the renewal of old friendships and acquaintances. I had the pleasure of talking with Leo Otis in the minerals room of the Museum of Natural History in Springfield Thursday. We discussed the many interesting specimens and agreed that a thing of beauty (amethyst e.g.) is a joy forever.

Suggested Daily Spiritual Reading:
John 4:18
Psalm 107:1

Further Reading Related to Diary Entry:
- *1934 Official Short Wave Radio Manual* by Hugo and H. Winfield Secor Gernsback; published by Short Wave Craft, New York, 1934.

- *The Empty Nest Chronicles: How to Have Fun (and Stop Annoying Your Spouse) After the Kids Move Out* by Jerry Zezima

Popular Books Published in 1949:
Death Be Not Proud by John Gunther
A Sand County Almanac: And Sketches Here and There by Aldo Leopold
The Art of Readable Writing by Rudolf Flesch

Popular Movies Released in 1949:
The Life of Riley (William Bendix, Rosemary DeCamp)
The Third Man (Orson Welles, Joseph Cotten, Alida Valli)
Riders of the Whistling Pines (Gene Autry, Patricia Barry)

December 28, 1949
CHRISTMAS

We have had a wonderful Christmas. Best of all it was to have the children home—Albert Earl for two weeks and Janet for one full day, the 21st, and two nights. Besides our usual gifts for each other, and from our relatives, the parishioners were most generous. Just to list their many gifts is a pleasure. We received over a hundred Christmas cards, for one thing, and over eighty dollars in money. Robert Holmes gave us two chickens; Otto Merkel gave us a box of chocolates and half a bushel of Florida oranges; Ted Muzinski—three quarts of ice cream; Vernon Monette—four ice cream patties; Frank Burr—two free theater tickets.

We have purchased seven long-playing microgroove records with a part of the money given—Beethoven's Fourth, his Quartet #14; Franck's Symphony in D Minor; Schubert's Seventh Symphony; Hayden's Symphony #101 (The Clock Symphony); Ezio Pinza's arias from the operas of Mozart; and South Pacific, a collection of songs from the stage show. We have enjoyed the Christmas tree greatly. A fine tree cut in Vermont; it has been gaily decorated with tinsel, lights, and ornaments. Christmas is gone, but the magic lingers. It is clear and sunny outside with a light wind, and a temperature of about forty degrees. We have been having record warm temperatures, one day it being 64 degrees above zero. No snow on the ground. And now we are wishing each other a Happy New Year.

On the newsstands today, in a man's magazine—"True"—is an article by Donald Keyhoe, summarizing the story of the Flying Saucers. He states that there are three types—a small disc, pilotless for television or the sending of impulses; a large disc, 250 feet in diameter, for close observation of earth (the type pursued by Lt. Mantell, whose plane disintegrated at 20,000 feet); and a cigar-shaped dirigible—or spaceship without wings. Exhaust is an amber color, thirty or forty feet behind the saucers. He claims they may come from a planet located near Wolf 539, say. The astronomers state there are 26 stars nearby which might have planets suitable for the development of life. He does not intimate that they may come from Mars or Venus. To come from space, 8 light years away, even at a thousand miles an hour would require several generations. He makes out a good case, but not a convincing one.

The government, today, announced the discontinuance of the Flying Saucer project, saying that it had investigated 239 cases, and that all these fell into two classes: (a) hallucination or hoax, and (b) misinterpretation of familiar objects—like observation balloons, planets, or meteorites.

Keyhoe intimates that earth observations have been going on for 175 years and that a permanent base or satellite space ship is established just within our orbit. This makes for interesting conjecture, and might be the course that earth men will follow in exploring other planets, but I should guess it will be a long time indeed before we get around to visiting Wolf 539 or any other star. A mild mass hysteria in the age of atomic energy fed by Well's "War of the Worlds", Jules Verne, and Buck Rogers make our credulity considerable.

Venus has been an object of great beauty in the western sky of late. It must be near maximum recession from the sun having long since passed Jupiter. This has been a season of happiness and contentment. May it long continue. Gloria in excelsis Deo!

Suggested Daily Spiritual Reading:
Jeremiah 29:11
Lamentations 3:22-23

Further Reading Related to Diary Entry:
- *The Flying Saucers are Real* by Donald Keyhoe

- *The Report On Unidentified Flying Objects* by Edward J. Ruppelt

- *Buck Rogers In The 25th Century: The Complete Newspaper Dailies, Vol. 5, 1935-1936* by John F. Dille

- *The War of the Worlds* by H.G. Wells

- *From the Earth to the Moon and Around the Moon* by Jules Verne

- *It's a Wonderful Christmas: The Best of the Holidays 1940-1965* by Susan Waggoner

Popular Books Published in 1949:
The Historian's Craft by Marc Bloch
To Hell and Back by Audie Murphy

Popular Movies Released in 1949:
My Friend Irma (Dean Martin, Jerry Lewis)
Blondie Hits the Jackpot (Penny Singleton, Arthur Lake)
Outpost in Morocco (George Raft, Marie Windsor)

The Reverend, winter in Ludlow, MA, circa 1950.

EPILOGUE—EXTRA MEMORIES

Below are memories from the Reverend's 1983-1984 diaries that offer additional information/memories, which add further insight to those found in this book. Enjoy!

Childhood Memories

Tuesday October 11, 1983

(*The Reverend is 81 years of age.*)

Here are a list of things I saw or did in Vermont as a boy. Some have been mentioned elsewhere in my Journals, but I recall them again here for old times sake! Forsan et haec olim meminisse juvabit (And perchance it will be pleasing to remember these former things). So, here goes...

1. Visiting a cave-in at a talc mine. This other boy and I ventured in a ways, and then retreated, no one being about. Talc is used mainly for powder.

2. Watching ice cutting on pond with large saws. Cakes (*of ice*) then stored in sawdust.

3. Seeing Mae's dad (*Ernie Brock*) hauling logs with horse and chain—used for firewood. I helped him with the circular saw, piling the chunks for him.

4. Seeing a huge snow roller (barrels with two men seated on top) drawn by four horses conquer the drifts at our home in Groton. Snow stayed packed down until July. Not suitable for cars (there were none) but for horses and men.

5. Seeing my first car, owned by my uncle Hosmer, who was garbed in linen outer, light cap and goggles; for dusty roads. Not later than 1910. He was married to my Aunt Lilla (*his mother Etta's half-sister*), who died in childbirth.

6. Going by buggy with her (*his Aunt Lilla*) to her little one-room school house in West Groton. She wore rimless glasses, had her hair in a bun, and wore a gold watch on her white shirtwaist. The watch had a snap cover. At the Wayside Inn in Sudbury, Mass. there is a one-room school house remarkably similar—it came from Sterling (*MA*) originally—Mary's lamb followed a girl to school there.

7. Watching my father carve names in granite with hammer and chisel. He also carved the pillars on the original First Church of Christ, Scientist, Boston, while working in Hardwick, Mass.

8. My mother and sisters cleaning Kerosene lamps, making molasses candy, and decorating our Christmas tree with popcorn and paper chains, pasted together.

9. Seeing my neighboring farmer butcher hogs, run a cream separator, pitching hay, mending fences, milking cows by hand (no milking machines then), and driving his team to town for supplies (I went with him sometimes).

10. Jumping in the hay from the high beams—climbing mountains—building and launching a raft on a little pond in Waterbury. (Tom Sawyer did the same.)

11. Visiting a cider mill one Sunday afternoon, in Duxbury, after a long walk down the tracks—all we could drink! Tramping two miles through the deep snow to a maple sugar shed deep in the woods. Here we had doughnuts to dunk in the syrup congealed on the snow outside the shed (This in Waterbury).

12. Watching "Lady" Jones churning butter—then making delicious cookies for me. In the parlor she had a black horsehair sofa—and underground a cellar for canned jars of fruit, vegetables, butter, and cream. Her husband had cream and berries, in season, on his Grapenuts. This was in Groton also.

13. Visiting a glacial erratic standing on edge, deep in the woods in Waterbury. It was called Stitt Rock. I have seen similar erratics on Black Mountain in Haverhill, N.H. (You could rock them slightly), and on Moosilauke.

14. Going out with my Botany class in high school (We didn't learn much, but it was nice being out in the open air). Also, berrying in Glencliff, Groton Pond, and atop Mt. Monadnock in Rindge, New Hampshire. Thoreau climbed the latter named, and presumably ate the blueberries there also. Janet, our daughter, found beautiful, small, red garnets in a rock near the Halfway House, where we stayed overnight one summer.

15. Seeing old Mose Whitehill going out with his sledge and a pair of oxen to Whicher Mountain in Groton to get a load of wood—carrying a switch in one hand, and shouting, "Git along that" and "Wo-hoosh" or "Gee" and "Haw". His son became Editor of the Waterbury Record, a weekly newspaper for which I worked in high school. Through his influence I also obtained a scholarship at Dartmouth, which launched me on my illustrious career!

✞ ✞ ✞

Thanksgiving Day November 24, 1983

...My grandfather (*Albert S. Clark*) in Groton, Vermont kept diaries also. I have the one for 1902 (*sadly this was lost—no one knows what happened to it*) where on January 22 he wrote "Etta (my mother) had a fat boy born this morning." Alas, there is no further mention of me in the diary! But he was perceptive and shrewd--when I was five or six years old, I laid about with my little rake and killed three or four pullets. My folks (parents) were puzzled, and wondered if they had died of some disease, but my grandfather took me aside and soon learned the truth—so we had chicken to eat after all! My sister, Christina, stayed up on the farm with him and my grandmother, more than she stayed at home, and she tells of picking strawberries from his field at three cents a quart—a quart sold for eighteen cents—and making vanilla ice cream on the back porch, then blending it with fresh strawberries for dessert. Yum! Yum! Yum!

Thursday December 8, 1983

...Today I am writing about games played. The first I remember, perhaps known as mumbletypeg was introduced by my cousin, about a year younger, but who lived in a big city, Montpelier, the capital of the state of Vermont, population 12,000. That made him more sophisticated than I. You whittled a short stick to a point at both ends, placed it over another stick, or a rock, then hit the point with another stick. This threw it into the air, where upon you whacked it again as hard as you could, sending it some distance. The one who sent it the farthest won the point!

Later on, in Waterbury I played Duck-on-the-Rock with other boys. Each holds a stone in his hand, and a bigger stone is placed on a boulder (there are plenty there due to glacial action). The object is to knock off the bigger stone, and while the goalie is scrambling for it, you run to "first base" and back. If he can tag you before you get "home" it is your turn to act as goalie. This was in the area near the railroad tracks to the west of town, not far from the home of the first settler, named Marsh, whose children met a bear while crossing the river, on ice, near Bolton.

Other games I played included cricket, which we improvised with old cans, bats and balls; and croquet—on the lawn with regular equipment. Of course we also played hide-and-seek, pump-pump-pullaway, and a war game called Capture the Flag—you established a line with players on both sides and defended a handkerchief on a stick. If you could sneak over the line when the foe was busy and snatch the handkerchief, you won. If not, you went to "prison". To get out of prison involved one of your teammates crossing enemy lines and tagging you.

For card games we played Flinch, Hearts, and Authors (I still remember the picture of Rudyard Kipling), and later with our parents a game called 500, though I have no idea why. Once or twice we children tried poker, using dried beans for chips, but that was too much like work!

✞ ✞ ✞

Sunday October 30, 1983

...If I were in Groton (my birthplace) on Sunday afternoon as a boy, I would climb the hill to look for beechnuts, or visit the brook to swim, or pick strawberries, or visit Ricker farm to jump in the hay and watch them bring in the cows for milking. The hired man gave me a pail once so that I could give it a try, but though he explained all the right moves, I never did milk more than a pint! But it was a pleasure to watch him do it, effortlessly!

If I were in Waterbury some of us boys on a Sunday afternoon would go down the railroad tracks, to the west of town, to play duck-on-a-rock, visit the cider mill, and gather eating apples, or (as we did in 1917) watch National Guard keeping law and order at the railroad bridge across the river (Winooski). I'll never forget the click of the rifle when one of the young men of the village started to cross the river and the guard said, "Halt!", and pointed his gun in the general direction of the young man. He came back! Would he have shot the young man? I'm sure he would, perhaps in the leg, but there was no fooling around at the beginning of World War I. Our Marines in Beirut carry empty rifles (or did before 229 Marines were blown up at their barracks near the airport) since they are a peace-keeping force, but at the outset of World War I it was serious business guarding bridges and such!

If I were in college on a Sunday afternoon, some of us would go for a long walk up around a lovely pond in Hanover (N.H.) Center, and talk about everything under the sun. On one of these hikes I met a very pleasant young man from Sweden, who was studying in this country. Of Sunday afternoons let it be said, "This is the day the Lord hath made; let us rejoice and be glad in it—from dawn to dusk, the Lord's name is to be praised!"

✞ ✞ ✞

Sunday January 22, 1984

...I went to school one winter morning in Waterbury, Vermont when it was 40 below there (*Fahrenheit*), and there was no school, since the radiators (*heaters*) had frozen! I remember finding some frozen Macintosh apples on a tree and trying to eat them—it was hard going! In my first home, in Groton, Vermont, we had inside running water, but an outdoor privy, next to the barn. We did not linger long at the "jakes", as James Joyce called it in "Ulysses"....

✝ ✝ ✝

Vermont

Tuesday November 8, 1983

This is about Lake Champlain, which borders Vermont and New York. It is 100 miles long and thirty miles wide. It is a fresh water lake, which was once salt. The ocean came in the St. Lawrence River and went out by way of the Hudson. As proof, the skeleton of a whale was found on the banks of the lake and was exhibited at the State House of Vermont in Montpelier (where my uncle William Reid, was Sergeant-at-arms for a time). On the other hand, the Great Salt Lake in Utah was once fresh water that had no outlet and so became salt!

Lake Champlain is named for the French explorer, Sieur Samuel de la Champlain, who sailed into its waters via the Richelieu River which unites the lake with the St. Lawrence, and so was the first white man to see the Green Mountains (Verd Mont) and the Adirondacks (how did they get that name?). To the best of my recollection, he also met some Iroquois Indians near the foot of the lake and scared the daylights out of them with his blunderbuss, and that is how they came to team up with the British!

My first contact with the lake came as a little boy when my father, in Groton, Vermont, showed me the skeleton head of a large fish, called a muskellunge, which he had caught on a line in Lake Champlain, and which weighed 21 pounds (The largest I ever saw him catch was about 9 pounds, trolling). Years later, while living in Waterbury, during grammar and high school days, we went to Burlington nearly ever summer for a couple of day's fishing, which included Shelburne and Mallet's Bays, and South Hero on Grand Isle. (Ethan Allen bought a place there with his brother, though not in my time.) We did see, in prohibition days, an icehouse near our cottage at South Hero where smugglers from Canada hid their liquor en route to Boston and New York. After we were married, Mae and I took a trip, one time, over the Sandbar Bridge to Grand Isle, and hence to Rouse's Point, then back home via Ticonderoga and Whitehall. (I crossed at

Rouse's Point in 1922 when there was a ferry in operation instead of a bridge. There was a man aboard who wrote the lines, "De wind she blows on Lac St. Pierre—Bimeby she blows some more..." A French Canadian ditty which I heard previously.)...

☦ ☦ ☦

Wedding Memories

Sunday October 2, 1983

I have been trying to remember the details of our wedding day, on August 7th 1928. Some are fuzzy and some are clear cut, and even with Mae's (*his wife's*) clairvoyance we can't remember them all. But in the main, this is how it went.

We (my father and mother, and sister Lilla) had come up from Watertown, Mass. the day before, in my old car, a Nash, and enjoyed the peace and quiet of Mae's father's farm in Piermont, N.H. At the wedding, next day, besides Mae's folks, including her brother Carl and his wife Mildred, there were present Mae's Aunt Bess and husband, George Martin, and the man and woman living upstairs (on the farm) at the time (She brought us a jar of homemade pickles for a wedding present—the only one I remember!). There were two clergymen—one Methodist and one Congregational—as I recall, attending with the reason being jurisdiction or something.

Everything went well—the house was tastefully decorated with greens and flowers—the wedding march and Träumerei (by Schumann) were played, the appropriate vows taken, and we were married! A wedding breakfast followed, then Mae and I prepared to go on our honeymoon. Like a damn fool I told the hired man where we were going (into the White Mountain region) and he promptly relayed the information to Carl, who followed us quite a ways in his car, tooting his horn frequently and loud! But he finally left us and turned back.

I do not remember our route, but we ended up on Sugar Hill where we spent the night—it is a wonderful lookout to the west of Franconia, and we should have seen the Washington range, but as I recall they were shrouded in mist. The next morning, before going home, I discovered we had a flat tire on the car (I made the lame remark to Mae that it was better to have a flat tire <u>on</u> the car than <u>in</u> one, but she didn't find that remark especially funny!) At any rate, we changed tires, and had the flat fixed at the first available garage, then went back to Piermont.

Mae tells me that on our way to Massachusetts we stayed overnight with my aunts in Bellows Falls (*VT*), but I don not recall any of that.

Arriving home we soon went to my first parish, to which I had been assigned—the Methodist Church in West Quincy, Mass. West Quincy still has the old railroad tracks in a small park, marking the first railroad in America—used to haul granite from the quarries to the ocean, whence the granite was conveyed by ship to Boston to build the state house and also the Charlestown revolutionary monument (Remember the battle of Bunker Hill?). The bodies of John Adams and Quincy Adams (2nd and 6th presidents) are buried in crypts in the old granite Church in Quincy Square. The inscription over the resting place of our second president reads, "Here lies all that is mortal of John Adams."

Mae and I remember West Quincy best for the short Irish butcher who took pity on us, and gave us marvelous cuts of sirloin and other steaks at an absurdly low price—blessed be his memory everlasting!

Albert Earl (*a.k.a "Junior"*) was born the following year, in 1929, and we are still <u>very</u> proud of him! Dr. Deon delivered him at Quincy City Hospital and only charged me only twenty-five dollars!

(*Note: Mae gave up her senior year at the University of Vermont to marry the Reverend and move with him to West Quincy.*)

✞ ✞ ✞

Albert Earl and Janet

Tuesday October 4, 1983

While Albert Earl was still a baby, we were living in South Hamilton, Mass. It was 1931. I made a little sandbox then drove my old Ford to Crane's Beach in Ipswich to get him some sand. I filled the rear compartment with white, white beach sand, and brought it home. Crane's Beach is named for the family which made the plumbing supplies, including bathtubs, and their estate was there, facing the broad Atlantic with rolling surf, dunes, beach grass, breeze constant, blue sky, fleecy clouds, and warm sun—truly a lovely place to be in summer!

Ipswich itself has the oldest stone bridge in America. There are now 75 deer in the Crane's Beach sanctuary, and it is proposed to open the herd to hunters, and kill off two-thirds of them! Is there no consideration for these lovely creatures?

Our son enjoyed his little playpen. While in South Hamilton we met the Leathes, "Auntie" Durkee, and also the Burgesses. Once when my car was being repaired she, Becky, let me borrow her car, a smooth running Chrysler. I appreciate her trust and thoughtfulness!

Our daughter Janet was born in Beverly Hospital in 1931, and I remember buying Mae a washing machine. Who took care of Albert Earl those two weeks I do not remember. Perhaps my wife can tell me?

...South Hamilton has the Myopia Hunt Club where polo is played. It was alleged by an eye witness that general Patton, who played there, became enraged at a workman one day, and hit him over the head with a polo mallet. So, I wasn't too surprised to hear later that he had slapped a wounded soldier in a hospital in Italy, accusing him of malingering (*This happened during World War II. Read more about this incident from the Encyclopedia Britannica at* https://www.britannica.com/biography/George-Smith-Patton/Controversies-and-appraisal *[Accessed on February 11, 2021]*). Also, there one night in the town hall, in a reception for Norman Vaughn—town boy who had charge of the sled dogs on Byrd's polar expedition to Antarctica, I met the Governor of the Commonwealth, Leverett Saltonstall—a fine aristocrat.

I had a small parish in East Hamilton and a young people's group. This parish bought an abandoned schoolhouse for five dollars! I persuaded the mayor of Salem to give us a bell and we were in business. The church women baked pies for sale by the cartload, and held socials and suppers to raise supplementary funds to pay our bills. They were devoted and loyal and I remember them with real affection.

Albert Earl had a real champion in our neighbor "Auntie" (Elizabeth) Durkee. If she heard him crying she would come over and say to Mae, "What are you doing to my boy?" She also brought him cookies and anent life she would remark, "God never closes one door without opening another." It is people like her who restore your faith in humanity!

☦ ☦ ☦

Life Before Electricity

Monday October 3, 1983

...Mae lived on a small farm in Newbury, Vermont, and helped clean the kerosene lamps and lanterns until they moved to a larger farm in Orford, New Hampshire.

We lived out in the country oil Groton, Vermont, and had the same lighting, until one day my grandfather, Albert Sturtevant Clark (*a.k.a. "Moody Clark"*), who lived two miles out of the village, had lights installed, and I remember turning the black button on the round, white porcelain and seeing the dining room light come on, like magic! I was around five years old then, but still recall the thrill...we had a wall telephone in Groton, and once when my mother was talking I climbed up on a stool and pulled down on the hook which held the receiver! My mother said to her caller—"We've been cut off!" I had released the hook by then and she never knew what happened. Best mother in the world, but easily fooled—one time I took her for a ride and she asked, "What place is this?" There was a sign up ahead, so when we reached it, I glanced at it and told her, "Horses Crossing!" She had no washing machine or refrigerator until late in life. I have seen long-johns stiff as a board on the clothesline in January, and other garments as well. Meats were kept frozen in the cellar until needed.

✞ ✞ ✞

High School 1920

Thursday October 6, 1983

...The teacher in my high school geometry class in 1920 in Waterbury, Vermont gave us this theorem by Euclid; said it was college caliber, and said we could try to solve it if we wished. I worked on it at intervals for three months, and finally solved it to my satisfaction by proportion. I submitted it to the teacher, but he had to leave school before passing on his opinion. I never did learn whether I had solved it or not! The theorem is this: "the bisectors of the exterior angles of a parallelogram form a square, the sum of the sides of which is equal to the sum of the sides of the parallelogram." Very neat and Euclid was very smart—incidentally I received a 100 mark on my final geometry exam. The teacher, a fine man named Reimer, was dismissed because he was of German parentage, and feelings ran high, even thought the war (*WWI*) had been over several years. There was another fine teacher, named Aldrich, who enlisted as an air force observer (*WWI*), and whose plane was shot down over France, killing him. He was our first war casualty, and I remember a picture of him in uniform, hanging on the school corridor wall. He had a field of beans near the school that I helped him cultivate the previous summer, with horse and plow, so his loss was a personal thing.

One of the boys in chemistry class manufactured some H_2S (hydrogen sulfide) one day, which caused the whole building to be evacuated. A skunk's scent is pleasant in comparison! We were a lively bunch. There were 28 in my graduating class. I was salutatorian (not valedictorian) and my paper was entitled, "Overcoming the Impossible". The Queen said to Alice (in Wonderland)— Don't say things are impossible. Why, I do six impossible things every morning before breakfast! Graduating from grammar school, my subject was "The Mineral Resources of Vermont". Why couldn't I be sensible and practical in my high school peroration? Oh well, nobody commented on it one way or another, and we did get graduated. Mae tells me there were 7 in her graduating class in Newbury High School in 1925.

✝ ✝ ✝

Dartmouth College & Harvard Divinity School

Friday December 9, 1983

...Fred Howland, retired president of the National Life Insurance Company of Montpelier, Vermont. Now it was Mr. Howland, a Dartmouth trustee, who secured a four-year scholarship for me, while I lived in Waterbury. I worked at the Waterbury Record as an errand boy at first, and later as a printer, setting type by hand and running the cylinder presses—which vocational training later enabled me to pay all of my college expenses, or nearly all. I had $344 in the bank when I started, and borrowed $60 from my sister Christina, along the way.

The editor of the country weekly was Harry C. Whitehill, a shrewd business man. (HE paid me a $1.75 a week while in high school—after hours during the week and ten hours on Saturdays.) But he did take enough interest in me to ask Mr. Howland, who he knew, to aid me, and for that I am truly grateful. Also for the printing experience, which enabled me to go to college in the first place. As a printer's devil, I learned early on what type lice are. The printer takes a tray (called a stick) filled with handset or linotype lines, pours in a little water in a convenient gap, and asks you to bend down a little closer to see them. He then slams the type together, and you see them all right! At the college print shop I earned only 50 cents an hour, and worked half the night, from 10 p.m. to 4 a.m., printing 2,300 copies (two sides, four sheets) of the Daily Dartmouth, but I lived comfortably (except for the hard work involved) and was offered a raise to 75 cents and hour when I quit in my senior year! But I declined.

✝ ✝ ✝

Friday November 4, 1983

On the ecclesiastical side I have read the Bible, the Koran (*Quran*), the Vedas, and something of the Zen masters—who are indeed cryptic in their teaching. Someone has said that Zen is like the sound of one hand clapping. At Harvard I also read the lovely prose writings of Rabindranath Tagore, entitled "Gitanjali". Very moving to the human spirit. And I have reveled in and have been depressed by the Rubaiyat of Omar Khayyam! (The Moving Finger writes, and having writ moves on—nor all your piety nor wit can cancel half a line, nor all your tears wash out a word of it!)

Incidentally, speaking of Tagore, I met a young man from India studying at

Harvard Divinity School while I was there, who was a pupil of Tagore, and who had met Gandhi. Gandhi, you will recall, took his principles of nonviolence from reading Henry Thoreau's account of his resistance to being taxed for unjust war, and who in consequence spent the night in jail in Concord, being bailed out the next morning by his aunt! It took Gandhi considerably longer, but he finally persuaded the mighty British Empire to grant independence to his country! Such is the power of human thought!

Red Russia has embarked upon a conquest of the free world to the maxims of Marxism, Leninism, Stalinism—thus repressing one brutal dictatorship (Czarism) with another more brutal still (Communism). We as American are fighting a rearguard action in this hemisphere to combat it, with indifferent success, as witness Nicaragua, Cuba, and Libya. We have freed Grenada, which was to spearhead the advance into other countries of America, and that has blunted the edge of their conspiracy, but wouldn't it have been much more effective to have stopped it at its source, and won over Lenin or Castro or Khadafy with our own principles of freedom and democracy, in which we firmly believe?

✝ ✝ ✝

Wednesday November 16, 1983

...Speaking of prisons, while at Harvard I took a course in sociology, and as part of that course one day we visited the Charlestown State Prison, and saw the prisoners at work. The guard told us that one beetle-browed man was a lifer, was now well behaved, and wore a different necktie for each day of the year. His name was Pomeroy. We also visited Death Row near the Cherry Hill section of the prison (no inmates there at the time), and were shown the electric chair, which was ordinary, with straps attached. Of course, we had to try it, and I was the last to do so. I sat there wondering what it would be like if it were the real thing, and concluded I couldn't do other than speculate. Without knowing it, all the students had left, leaving me there alone. I would be there still if the guard hadn't shouted, "Anybody else in here?" I got out in a hurry! It was an old stone building, isolated from the other structures.

Another time, at Dartmouth, I took a course in Newspaper Work, in which we went to Manchester, N.H. to the paper there, and I set up the headings for the news stories. We saw an old boiler-type fire engine drawn by horses and belching smoke go down the street. At the police station I was finger printed and given the prints to keep. Probably just as well!

✝ ✝ ✝

Shortwave Radio

Wednesday November 9, 1983

...On another occasion during World War II, I was listening to a soldier stationed in Rabat, Morocco, who was also transmitting. What I remember best is that while doing so, he was trying to light a cigarette, and ever all the miles (3,000 at least), I could hear the rasping of his cigarette lighter, which he must have spun a half a dozen times without getting a light!

I had five hobbies all together during my ministry—stamps, stones, stars, shortwave, and symphony—and enjoyed them all, especially shortwave listening. When Byrd was at the South Pole sending news to the New York Times, I couldn't hear Little America directly, but I could hear the relay station at the tip of South America passing on his messages! I cut my teeth, so to speak, copying code sent out by the American Relay League from Hartford, Connecticut. I think everyone should have a hobby—it is like mental tonic, and is educational besides!

✞ ✞ ✞

Automobiles

Thursday December 29, 1983

...Speaking of cars, I would like to record my experience with them. My first was a Nash (called an ash can by my friends), which broke down with me while crossing the bridge from Boston to Cambridge. I sold it for junk for $20! I had purchased it one afternoon in 1928 on Commonwealth Avenue, second-hand, and passed my driving test at the Commonwealth Armory on Mass. Ave.; driving it home to Watertown at five o'clock.

Next, I had two Model T Fords, each costing about fifty dollars (I resold one a year later for twenty-five), and these gave good service. (I once used a house shingle to bring to life a dead battery while we were on the farm!) Once going to the farm in 1930 we heated Albert Earl's bottle for nursing on the running-board with a can of Sterno!

Next, I had a Henry J. (Kaiser), which was a good little car, even though the brake fell off the first time I drove it—this was on Route 5 in Holyoke.

Next, I had a series of Fords and Chevrolets—all second-hand, but serving us well.

✞ ✞ ✞

ALL OF THE SUGGESTED DAILY SPIRITUAL READINGS LISTED THE BOOK

(1) **Suggested Daily Spiritual Reading:**
   Luke 2:8-15
   Matthew 5:44

(2) **Suggested Daily Spiritual Reading:**
   Matthew 6:26
   Timothy 4:9-15

(3) **Suggested Daily Spiritual Reading:**
   Jeremiah 17:5-8
   Genesis 1:26-31

(4) **Suggested Daily Spiritual Reading:**
   Zechariah 8:5
   Ecclesiastes 2:21-24

(5) **Suggested Daily Spiritual Reading:**
   Titus 3:4-6
   James 1:3-4

(6) **Suggested Daily Spiritual Reading:**
   Ephesians 6:1-4
   Ezekiel 47:9-10

(7) **Suggested Daily Spiritual Reading:**
   Ephesians 2:18-22
   Colossians 3:13-17

(8) **Suggested Daily Spiritual Reading:**
   Psalm 121
   Psalm 104:5-6

(9) **Suggested Daily Spiritual Reading:**
   Isaiah 43:2
   Ezekiel 47:9

(10) **Suggested Daily Spiritual Reading:**
1 Peter: 11
John 14:6

(11) **Suggested Daily Spiritual Reading:**
Psalms 118:24
Romans 12:9-15

(12) **Suggested Daily Spiritual Reading:**
1 Timothy 3:2-8
Proverbs 17:17

(13) **Suggested Daily Spiritual Reading:**
Philippians 4:13
Romans 15:13

(14) **Suggested Daily Spiritual Reading:**
Exodus 20:8-11
John 14:6

(15) **Suggested Daily Spiritual Reading:**
Psalm 121
1 Peter 5:8

(16) **Suggested Daily Spiritual Reading:**
Ephesians 6:10-11
Philippians 4:4

(17) **Suggested Daily Spiritual Reading:**
Ephesians 6:23
Colossians 3:15-17

(18) **Suggested Daily Spiritual Reading:**
Proverbs 3:3
Matthew 7:1

(19) **Suggested Daily Spiritual Reading:**
Jude 1:17-21
3 John 1:11

(20) **Suggested Daily Spiritual Reading:**
Titus 3:3-6
James 2:14

(21) **Suggested Daily Spiritual Reading:**
Luke 13:29-30
Proverbs 17:28

(22) **Suggested Daily Spiritual Reading:**
Ruth 1:16
Psalm 25:1-2

(23) **Suggested Daily Spiritual Reading:**
Genesis 1:1-26
Philippians 4:4-7

(24) **Suggested Daily Spiritual Reading:**
Galatians 3:26
Job 42:10

(25) **Suggested Daily Spiritual Reading:**
Obadiah 1:3-4
Luke 4:8

(26) **Suggested Daily Spiritual Reading:**
Psalm 57:1
1 John 1:1-7

(27) **Suggested Daily Spiritual Reading:**
John 3:16
1 John 2:15
Matthew 19:13-15

(28) **Suggested Daily Spiritual Reading:**
Romans 8:31
Micah 7:8

(29) **Suggested Daily Spiritual Reading:**
John 15:13
Mark 14:22-24

(30) **Suggested Daily Spiritual Reading:**
Genesis 3:19
2 Timothy 2:4

(31) **Suggested Daily Spiritual Reading:**
John 20:19-22
Luke 8:5-8

(32) **Suggested Daily Spiritual Reading:**
1 John 3:8
2 John 1:7

(33) **Suggested Daily Spiritual Reading:**
Romans 12:21
2 Peter 1:4

(34) **Suggested Daily Spiritual Reading:**
1 John 4:3
Proverbs 3:25

(35) **Suggested Daily Spiritual Reading:**
Revelations 21:19-20
1 Corinthians 15:41

(36) **Suggested Daily Spiritual Reading:**
Matthew 17:7
Luke 6:28

(37) **Suggested Daily Spiritual Reading:**
Ecclesiastes 1:7
Genesis 1:6-10

(38) **Suggested Daily Spiritual Reading:**
Jonah 1:17
Proverbs 3:5

(39) **Suggested Daily Spiritual Reading:**
John 7:7
John 3:17-18
Genesis 1:16

(40) **Suggested Daily Spiritual Reading:**
Philippians 1:29
Mark 4:37-41

(41) **Suggested Daily Spiritual Reading:**
John 6:16-20
Luke 20:46

(42) **Suggested Daily Spiritual Reading:**
Psalm 27:1
Matthew 18:33

(43) **Suggested Daily Spiritual Reading:**
Psalm 18:49
Ecclesiasticus 29:21-23

(44) **Suggested Daily Spiritual Reading:**
Ecclesiasticus 29:10
Mark 3:7

(45) **Suggested Daily Spiritual Reading:**
Luke 6:20-23
Hebrews 11:1-3

(46) **Suggested Daily Spiritual Reading:**
Matthew 15:35-38
1 John 3:16

(47) **Suggested Daily Spiritual Reading:**
Matthew 14:27
Hebrews 10:22

(48) **Suggested Daily Spiritual Reading:**
James 5:1-6
Matthew 6:28

(49) **Suggested Daily Spiritual Reading:**
John 18:36
Acts 18:9-10

(50) **Suggested Daily Spiritual Reading:**
Psalm 36:1-3
Proverbs 16:2

(51) **Suggested Daily Spiritual Reading:**
Deuteronomy 11:1
Samuel 22:32-33

(52) **Suggested Daily Spiritual Reading:**
Luke 6:37-38
Romans 16:20

(53) **Suggested Daily Spiritual Reading:**
Psalm 42:11
Wisdom of Solomon 9:15

(54) **Suggested Daily Spiritual Reading:**
Psalm 42:1-2
Matthew 5:6

(53) **Suggested Daily Spiritual Reading:**
Colossians 1:25
1 Timothy 3:16

(54) **Suggested Daily Spiritual Reading:**
Acts 15:18
Romans 1:16

(55) **Suggested Daily Spiritual Reading:**
Revelations 22:21
Matthew 3:1-3

(56) **Suggested Daily Spiritual Reading:**
Wisdom of Solomon 12:22
Colossians 2:6

(57) **Suggested Daily Spiritual Reading:**
Psalm 56
John 3:3

(58) **Suggested Daily Spiritual Reading:**
Matthew 6:16-18
Titus: 2:1-15

(59) **Suggested Daily Spiritual Reading:**
Luke 4:18-19
1 Peter 1:3-12.

(60) **Suggested Daily Spiritual Reading:**
Ephesians 4:1-7
Psalm 7:1-5

(61) **Suggested Daily Spiritual Reading:**
Lamentations 3:22-26
2 Esdras 9:14-17

(62) **Suggested Daily Spiritual Reading:**
Matthew 4:23-25
Ephesians 6: 10-20

(63) **Suggested Daily Spiritual Reading:**
Proverbs 3:5
Mark 15:1-15

(64) **Suggested Daily Spiritual Reading:**
Romans 12:2
Ecclesiastes 3:1

(65) **Suggested Daily Spiritual Reading:**
Psalm 118:24
Luke 11:1-4

(66) **Suggested Daily Spiritual Reading:**
Psalm 118:29
Luke 11:9-11

(67) **Suggested Daily Spiritual Reading:**
Psalm 46:10
Psalm 23:2

(68) **Suggested Daily Spiritual Reading:**
John 13:34
Jeremiah 4:23-27

(69) **Suggested Daily Spiritual Reading:**
Matthew 5:38-39
Psalm 37:11

(70) **Suggested Daily Spiritual Reading:**
Psalm 23
Leviticus 26:6

(71) **Suggested Daily Spiritual Reading:**
Job 37:23
Ecclesiastes 5:8

(72) **Suggested Daily Spiritual Reading:**
John 20:27
John 11:25

(73) **Suggested Daily Spiritual Reading:**
Genesis 2:8
Ecclesiastes 7:3

(74) **Suggested Daily Spiritual Reading:**
Luke 1:52
Deuteronomy 4:19
Numbers 6:26

(75) **Suggested Daily Spiritual Reading:**
2 Thessalonians 3:5
1 Thessalonians 1:3

(76) **Suggested Daily Spiritual Reading:**
Mark 9:23
2 Corinthians 4:8

(77) **Suggested Daily Spiritual Reading:**
Matthew 10:39
Matthew 7:7

(78) **Suggested Daily Spiritual Reading:**
Psalm 30:12
1 Peter 4:11
Mark 8:18

(79) **Suggested Daily Spiritual Reading:**
Wisdom of Solomon 12:24-26
Matthew 5:8

(80) **Suggested Daily Spiritual Reading:**
Genesis 9:20
Leviticus 19:10

(81) **Suggested Daily Spiritual Reading:**
Psalm 139
Proverbs 16:3

(82) **Suggested Daily Spiritual Reading:**
Genesis 1:10
Luke 21:25

(83) **Suggested Daily Spiritual Reading:**
Deuteronomy 6:5
Ecclesiastes 9:11

(84) **Suggested Daily Spiritual Reading:**
Psalm 126:5
Leviticus 23:22

(85) **Suggested Daily Spiritual Reading:**
Psalm 100:4
Philippians 4:6

(86) **Suggested Daily Spiritual Reading:**
Matthew 2:1
John 3:6

(87) **Suggested Daily Spiritual Reading:**
Matthew 5:9
Luke 2:29-38

(88) **Suggested Daily Spiritual Reading:**
   Matthew 14:17-19
   John 8:11

(89) **Suggested Daily Spiritual Reading:**
   Psalm 23:4
   Psalm 48:14

(90) **Suggested Daily Spiritual Reading:**
   Genesis 1
   Genesis 24:27
   John 1:1

(91) **Suggested Daily Spiritual Reading:**
   Isaiah 41:10
   John 16:33

(92) **Suggested Daily Spiritual Reading:**
   Psalm 46:9-10
   Philippians 4:4-9

(93) **Suggested Daily Spiritual Reading:**
   Matthew 5:10
   Numbers 15:26

(94) **Suggested Daily Spiritual Reading:**
   Acts 20:35
   Matthew 2:11

(95) **Suggested Daily Spiritual Reading:**
   Psalm 60:30
   Matthew 9:35

(96) **Suggested Daily Spiritual Reading:**
   Luke 9:11
   Acts 10:38

(97) **Suggested Daily Spiritual Reading:**
   Psalm 23
   1 Peter 2:25

(98) **Suggested Daily Spiritual Reading:**
Genesis 1:11-12
Psalm 96:12

(99) **Suggested Daily Spiritual Reading:**
Galatians 5:22
1 Thessalonians 3:9

(100) **Suggested Daily Spiritual Reading:**
Psalm 19:1
Psalm 8:3

(101) **Suggested Daily Spiritual Reading:**
Genesis 1:16
Psalm 136:9

(102) **Suggested Daily Spiritual Reading:**
Psalm 148:3
Matthew 2:10

(103) **Suggested Daily Spiritual Reading:**
Matthew 5:44
Colossians 3:14

(104) **Suggested Daily Spiritual Reading:**
Exodus 3:5
Deuteronomy 4:19

(105) **Suggested Daily Spiritual Reading:**
Genesis 1:1
Psalm 8:3

(106) **Suggested Daily Spiritual Reading:**
Psalm 26:12
1 Chronicles 6:32

(107) **Suggested Daily Spiritual Reading:**
Psalm 8:1
Ecclesiastes 3:1

(108) **Suggested Daily Spiritual Reading:**
2 Thessalonians 3:1
Matthew 5:44

(109) **Suggested Daily Spiritual Reading:**
Psalm 107
Jeremiah 17:14

(110) **Suggested Daily Spiritual Reading:**
Psalm 91:11
Joshua 1:9

(111) **Suggested Daily Spiritual Reading:**
Psalms 23:6
Isaiah 40:30-31

(112) **Suggested Daily Spiritual Reading:**
John 12:25
2 Corinthians 4:15

(114) **Suggested Daily Spiritual Reading:**
Matthew 2
Psalm 18:46

(115) **Suggested Daily Spiritual Reading:**
Matthew 6:25-34
Psalm 25:5

(116) **Suggested Daily Spiritual Reading:**
Genesis 1:15
1 Peter 3:3-4

(117) **Suggested Daily Spiritual Reading:**
Matthew 13:31-32
Psalm 118:6

(118) **Suggested Daily Spiritual Reading:**
Romans 12:4-5
1 Peter 4:11

(119) **Suggested Daily Spiritual Reading:**
Matthew 4:19
Mathew 13:467

(120) **Suggested Daily Spiritual Reading:**
Ecclesiastes 3
John 1

(121) **Suggested Daily Spiritual Reading:**
Matthew 28:18
Isaiah 40:29

(122) **Suggested Daily Spiritual Reading:**
1 Peter 5:7
Psalm 138:3

(123) **Suggested Daily Spiritual Reading:**
1 Thessalonians 5:16-18
Corinthians 13:13
Genesis 1:28

(124) **Suggested Daily Spiritual Reading:**
John 4:18
Psalm 107:1

(125) **Suggested Daily Spiritual Reading:**
Jeremiah 29:11
Lamentations 3:22-23

ALL OF THE SUGGESTED FURTHER READINGS RELATED TO DIARY ENTRIES

November 11, 1936
Further Reading Related to Diary Entry:
- *For the Fallen* by Robert Laurence Binyon. Available at *The Great War (1914-1918)*: http://www.greatwar.co.uk/poems/laurence-binyon-for-the-fallen.htm [Accessed January 22, 2021].

- *The Guns of August* by Barbara W. Tuchman

- *White Banners* by Lloyd C. Douglas. Available at Project Gutenberg of Australia: http://gutenberg.net.au/ebooks06/0608861h.html [Accessed January 22, 2021].

November 13, 1936
Further Reading Related to Diary Entry:
- *Above, when mentioning the character "Poker-Stover, the Reverend is referring to a series of three books that were part of the Mexican War Series written by Edward Stratemeyer* [sometimes under the pseudonym, "Captain Ralph Bonehill"]: 1) *For The Liberty Of Texas*, 2) *With Taylor On The Rio Grande*, and 3) *Under Scott In Mexico*. Although the books in the *Mexican War Series* can still be purchased and found online for free, you can read the third book in the series, *Under Scott In Mexico,* from the Library of Congress at http://lcweb2.loc.gov/service/gdc/scd0001/2007/20070516002un/20070516002un.pdf [Accessed January 22, 2021].

- *You can read more about Stratemeyer* (creator of the "Rover Boys", "Nancy Drew" and the "Hardy Boys" series) and his syndicate of writers at http://stratemeyer.org/edward-stratemeyer/ [Accessed January 22, 2021].

- *The Pennsylvania Railroad: 1940s-1950s* by Ball Jr., Don

November 14, 1936
Further Reading Related to Diary Entry:
- *Vermont History*. Available from The Vermont Historical Society at https://vermonthistory.org [Accessed January 22, 2021].

- *Moses Robinson and the Founding* of Vermont by Robert A. Mello

- *Black Beauty* by Anna Sewell

November 15, 1936
Further Reading Related to Diary Entry:
- *200 Years of Soot and Sweat* by Victor R. Rolando (1992). Available from the Vermont Archeological Society: https://www.vtarchaeology.org/publications/200-years-soot-sweat/ [Accessed January 22, 2021].
  - {**Note**: The Reverend's grandfather Albert S. Clark is mentioned in Chapter 6 of this book on page 172.} Also, a lecture film was created based on the book (11-28-2006): *Beyond 200 Years of Soot and Sweat: 19th Century VT iron, charcoal and limestone industries* by RETN, as part of the Harold Meeks Memorial Lecture Series, RETNVT, RETN, Victor Rolando, Brownell Library Events, Archaeology, Brownell Library: https://www.retn.org/show/beyond-200-years-soot-and-sweat-19th-century-vt-iron-charcoal-and-limestone-industries

- *Making Charcoal and Biochar: A Comprehensive Guide* by Rebecca Oaks

November 16, 1936
Further Reading Related to Diary Entry:
- *Bishop Chase's Reminiscences: an Autobiography*. Comprising a history of the principal events in the author's life to A.D. 1847. Seventy-first Psalm:17,18. Volume 1, second edition by Philander Chase. James B. Dow, Boston. Available at the Internet Archive:
  - Volume 1: https://archive.org/details/bishopchasesremi01chas/page/n10 [Accessed January 22, 2021].
  - Volume 2: https://archive.org/details/bishopchasesremi02chas/page/n8 [Accessed January 22, 2021].

- *The Story of Groton's Historical Sleeping Sentinel. His Memory Lives On* by Marilyn Hatch-Ruiter. Available at http://www.grotonvt.com/AboutGroton/Groton%20Sleeping%20Sentinel.htm [Accessed January 22, 2021].

November 16, 1936
(Continued)
Further Reading Related to Diary Entry:
- *Ricker Pond State Park*. Available from the VT Dept. of Forests, Parks and Recreation: https://vtstateparks.com/ricker.html [Accessed January 22, 2021].

- *Ricker Pond*. Available from the Vermont Campground Association: https://campvermont.com/campground.html?site=423 [Accessed January 22, 2021].

- *The Forest Service and The Civilian Conservation Corps: 1933-42*. Chapter 10: Region 7—The Eastern Region; Region 9—The North-Central Region (Last Updated, January 7, 2008). Available from the U.S. National Park Service (NPS): https://www.nps.gov/parkhistory/online_books/ccc/ccc/chap10.htm [Accessed January 22, 2021].

November 17, 1936
Further Reading Related to Diary Entry:
- *Zadock Thompson and The Story of Vermont* by Kevin Graffagnino. Available from the Vermont Historical Society: https://vermonthistory.org/journal/misc/ZadockThompsonVermont.pdf [Accessed January 22, 2021].

- *History of Vermont, Natural, Civil, and Statistical, in three parts, with an Appendix* (1853) by Zadock Thompson. Available at the Internet Archive: https://archive.org/details/historyofvermo00thom/page/n10 [Accessed January 22, 2021].

November 18, 1936
Further Reading Related to Diary Entry:
- *History of Vermont, Natural, Civil, and Statistical, in three parts, with an Appendix* (1853) by Zadock Thompson. Available at the Internet Archive: https://archive.org/details/historyofvermo00thom/page/n10 [Accessed January 22, 2021].

- *Vermont Prose: A Miscellany* by Arthur Wallace Peach (Editor), Harold Goddard Rugg (Editor)

- *Roads Taken: Contemporary Vermont Poetry* by Sydney Lea (Editor), Chard deNiord (Editor)

November 23, 1936
Further Reading Related to Diary Entry:
- *Zadock Thompson and The Story of Vermont* by Kevin Graffagnino. Available from the Vermont Historical Society: https://vermonthistory.org/journal/misc/ZadockThompsonVermont.pdf [Accessed January 22, 2021].

- *History of Vermont, Natural, Civil, and Statistical, in three parts, with an Appendix* (1853) by Zadock Thompson. Available at the Internet Archive: https://archive.org/details/historyofvermo00thom/page/n10 [Accessed January 22, 2021].

January 4, 1937

Further Reading Related to Diary Entry:

- *Religio Medici: The Religion of a Doctor*. Available at the Sir Thomas Browne website, University of Chicago: https://penelope.uchicago.edu/relmed/relmed.html [Accessed January 22, 2021].

- *Magnificent Obsession* by Lloyd Douglas. Available at the Internet Archive: https://archive.org/details/magnificentobses00byll [Accessed January 22, 2021].

- *In His Steps* by Charles M. Sheldon. Available at Project Gutenberg: https://www.gutenberg.org/ebooks/4540 [Accessed January 22, 2021].

January 6, 1937

Further Reading Related to Diary Entry:

- *History of the 1927 Flood*, from the University of Vermont, Land Change Program: https://www.uvm.edu/landscape/1927_flood/about_1927_flood.htm [Accessed January 22, 2021].

- *History of Waterbury, Vermont, 1763-1915*; edited by Theodore Graham Lewis; Published by Harry C. Whitehill (1915); The Record Print, Waterbury, Vermont. Available at the Internet Archive: https://archive.org/details/HOW_vtrbms [Accessed January 22, 2021].

Page 15 - No Date - 1937

Further Reading Related to Diary Entry:

- *The Moving Finger*, from the Rubaiyat of Omar Khayyam; a sermon by Reverend E.F. Dinsmore, Unity Church, Santa Barbara, CA. Available at the Internet Archive: https://archive.org/stream/movingfingerofom00dinsrich/movingfingerofom00dinsrich_djvu.txt [Accessed January 22, 2021].

- *John Bunny* biography. Available at imdb https://www.imdb.com/name/nm0120544/bio [Accessed January 22, 2021].

Page 16 - No Date - 1937

Further Reading Related to Diary Entry:

- *World War I: Camp Vail, 1916*, from the Vermont Historical Society: https://vermonthistory.org/world-war-i-camp-vail-1916 [Accessed January 22, 2021].

- *Waterbury Village Historic District*. Available from the U.S. National Park Service, Department of the Interior: https://www.nps.gov/nr/travel/centralvermont/cv8.htm [Accessed January 22, 2021]

Page 17 - No Date -1937
Further Reading Related to Diary Entry:
- *Roots (1736–1816), John and Charles Wesley and the Evangelical Revival in England*. Available from the United Methodist Church: http://www.umc.org/who-we-are/roots [Accessed January 22, 2021].

- *The Boy Scout and Other Stories for Boys* by Richard Harding Davis; copyright, 1891, 1903, 1912, 1914, 1917, by Charles Scribner's Sons. Available at Project Gutenberg: https://www.gutenberg.org/ebooks/30953 [Accessed January 22, 2021].

- *The History of the Radio Industry in the United States to 1940*. Available from the Economic History Association: https://eh.net/encyclopedia/the-history-of-the-radio-industry-in-the-united-states-to-1940/ [Accessed January 22, 2021].

Page 18 - No Date -1937
Further Reading Related to Diary Entry:
- *Nobscot Scout Reservation*. Available from the Sudbury Valley Trustees at https://www.svtweb.org/properties/page/nobscot-scout-reservation-conservation-restriction-sudbury [Accessed January 22, 2021].

- *Hiking Overview*. *Available from the* Vermont Department of Forests, Parks, and Recreation at https://vtstateparks.com/hiking.html *[Accessed January 22, 2021].*

- *A 1940s Monadnock Childhood* by Tom Shultz

Page 19 - No Date -1937
Further Reading Related to Diary Entry:
- *Lakes and Ponds*. Available from the State of Vermont, Department of Environmental Conservation at https://dec.vermont.gov/watershed/lakes-ponds [Accessed January 22, 2021].

- *Lake Champlain History*. Available from the Lake Champlain Maritime Museum at https://www.lcmm.org/explore/lake-champlain-history/ [Accessed January 21, 2021].

- *Benedict Arnold's Navy: The Ragtag Fleet That Lost the Battle of Lake Champlain but Won the American Revolution* by James L. Nelson

- *Lake Champlain Islands* by Tara Liloia

- *The Battle of Lake Champlain: A "Brilliant and Extraordinary Victory"* by John H. Schroeder

Page 20 - September 28, 1937
Further Reading Related to Diary Entry:
- *History of Waterbury, Vermont, 1763-1915*; edited by Theodore Graham Lewis; Published by Harry C. Whitehill (1915); The Record Print, Waterbury, Vermont. Available at the Internet Archive: https://archive.org/details/HOW_vtrbms [Accessed January 22, 2021].

- *The Printing Trades* by Frank L. Shaw. Copyright 1916 by The Survey Committee of the Cleveland Foundation (Charles E. Adams, Chairman). Published by WM. F. Fell Co. Printers, Philadelphia. Available at the Internet Archives: https://archive.org/details/printingtrades00shawrich/page/n7/mode/2up [Accessed January 22, 2021].

- *American Dictionary of Printing and Bookmaking*. A History Of These Arts In Europe And America, With Definitions And Technical TermsAnd Biographical Sketches. By Wesley Washington Pasko. Howard Lockwood and Company Publishers, New York, 1894.

- *Gallegher and Other Stories* by Richard Harding Davis (Copyright, 1891, By Charles Scribner's Sons). Available at Project Gutenberg: https://www.gutenberg.org/ebooks/5956 [Accessed January 22, 2021].

- *The Club of Queer Trades* by G. K. Chesterton

Page 21 - No Date - 1937
Further Reading Related to Diary Entry:
- *The Theologian's Tale; The Legend Beautiful* by Henry Wadsworth Longfellow. Henry Wadsworth Longfellow. Available through the Maine Historical Society at https://www.hwlongfellow.org/poems_poem.php?pid=2064 [Accessed January 22, 2021].

- *The Vision of Sir Launfal* by James Russell Lowell (1848). Available fromThe Camelot Project; A Robbins Library Digital Project, University of Rochester, at: https://d.lib.rochester.edu/camelot/text/lowell-vision-of-sir-launfal [Accessed January 22, 2021].

- *An Evening with Longfellow* by Henry Wadsworth Longfellow; publisher: Sherwin Cody School of English, 1907. Available at the Internet Archive: https://

archive.org/details/aneveningwithlo00longgoog/page/n6 [Accessed January 22, 2021].

- *For the Record. A look at the Waterbury newspaper's past and future* by Monica Mead (January 25, 2007; updated July 10, 2013). Availale from Stowe Today at https://www.stowetoday.com/waterbury/archives/for-the-record/article_557e6e08-4a99-5df7-8c2d-efa695f3bf2a.html [Accessed January 22, 2021].

- *1918 Influenza: the Mother of All Pandemics* by Jeffery K. Taubenberge and David M. Morens. Emerging Infectious Diseases; vol.12 (1), January 2006. Available from the Centers for Disease Control and Prevention (CDC) at https://wwwnc.cdc.gov/eid/article/12/1/05-0979_article [Accessed January 22, 2021].

- *History of Waterbury, Vermont, 1763-1915*; edited by Theodore Graham Lewis; Published by Harry C. Whitehill (1915); The Record Print, Waterbury, Vermont. Available at the Internet Archive: https://archive.org/details/HOW_vtrbms [Accessed January 22, 2021].

Page 22 - No Date -1937
Further Reading Related to Diary Entry:
- *The History of Printing in America, with a Biography of Printers, and an Account of Newspapers* by Thomas, Isaiah and Thomas, Benjamin Franklin (publication date: 1874); publisher: Albany, N. Y., J. Munsell, printer. Available at the Internet Archive: https://archive.org/details/aey4217.0005.001.umich.edu/page/IV [Accessed January 22, 2021].

- *The Vermont Historical Gazetteer: A Magazine, Embracing a History of Each: Civil, Ecclesiastical, Biographical, and Military*; edited by Abby Maria Hemenway. Available at the Internet Archive: https://archive.org/details/vermonthistorica01heme/page/n12 [Accessed January 22, 2021].

Page 23 - No Date -1938
(Sometime After September 1937, But Before 1939)
Further Reading Related to Diary Entry:
- *John Ledyard Departs Down the Connecticut River* by Jim Collins. Available from Dartmouth College: https://250.dartmouth.edu/highlights/john-ledyard-departs-down-connecticut-river [Accessed January 22, 2021].

- *Dartmouth Undying: A Celebration of Place and Possibility*, edited by David Shribman and Jim Collins

- *American Traveler: The Life and Adventures of John Ledyard, the Man Who Dreamed of Walking The World* by James Zug

- *Memoirs of the Rev. Eleazar Wheelock, D.D., Founder and President of Dartmouth College and Moor's Charity School* by David McClure, D.D and Elijah Parish, D.D. Published by Edward Little and Company, 1811. Available at the Internet Archive: https://archive.org/details/memoirsreveleaz00parigoog/page/n8 [Accessed January 22, 2021].

- *History and Traditions*, Dartmouth College. Available from Dartmouth College at https://home.dartmouth.edu/life-community/explore-green/history-traditions [Accessed January 22, 2021].

Page 24 - No Date -1938
Further Reading Related to Diary Entry:
- *The Storied History of Dartmouth* by Aziz G. Sayigh, Boris V. Babson, A.S. Erickson, Charles S. Dameron, Adam I.W. Schwartzman, and Nicholas P. Desatnick. Available from The Dartmouth Review at http://dartreview.com/history-of-dartmouth/ [Accessed January 22, 2021].

- *Papers of Jerome Davis*, 1912-1965. Available from the Franklin D. Roosevelt Presidential Library and Museum, National Archives, Marist College at http://www.fdrlibrary.marist.edu/archives/pdfs/findingaids/findingaid_davis_jerome.pdf [Accessed January 22, 2021].

Page 25 - No Date -1938
Further Reading Related to Diary Entry:
- *A Dartmouth History Lesson for Freshman* by Francis Lane Childs. The Dartmouth Alumni Magazine, December 1957. Available from the Dartmouth College Library at https://www.dartmouth.edu/~library/rauner/dartmouth/dartmouth_history.html [Accessed January 22, 2021].

- *A History of Hazing* by Michael J. Perkins (October 24, 2016). Available from The Dartmouth Review at http://dartreview.com/a-history-of-hazing/ [Accessed January 22, 2021].

Page 26 - No Date -1938
Further Reading Related to Diary Entry:
- *The "Pony" Press and the Patent Model Collection* by the National Museum of American History (NMAH), Smithsonian Institution, January 4, 2013. Available

from the NMAH at https://americanhistory.si.edu/blog/2013/01/the-pony-press-and-the-patent-model-collection.html [Accessed January 22, 2021].

- *The History of Dartmouth College* by Baxter Perry Smith; Houghton, Osgood, and Company, Boston; The Riverside Press, Cambridge (1878). Available from Project Gutenberg at https://www.gutenberg.org/ebooks/28641 [Accessed January 22, 2021].

- *The Dartmouth*. America's Oldest College Newspaper; founded in 1799. Available from Dartmouth College at https://www.thedartmouth.com [Accessed January 22, 2021].

- *A Sociological Interpretation of the Russian Revolution* by Jerome Davis (Political Science Quarterly; Published Jan 1, 1922). Available from the Internet Archive: https://archive.org/details/jstor-2142509/page/n1 [Accessed January 22, 2021].

- *Lost Songs of Old Dartmouth*. Available from The Dartmouth Review at http://dartreview.com/lost-songs-of-older-dartmouth/ [Accessed January 22, 2021].

Page 27 - No Date - 1939
Further Reading Related to Diary Entry:

- *The Writing and Speeches of Daniel Webster* edited by Fletcher Webster. Volume Two. National Edition. Available from the Internet Archive: https://archive.org/details/cu31924092900590/page/n16 [Accessed January 22, 2021].

- The Dartmouth Alumni Magazine, issues from 1924, available at http://archive.dartmouthalumnimagazine.com/issues/1924 [Accessed January 22, 2021].

- *Autobiography of Benjamin Franklin* by Benjamin Franklin; Frank Woodworth Pine (editor); E. Boyd Smith (illustrator). Henry Holt and Company, New York (1916). Available from Project Gutenberg - [EBook #20203 {release date, December 28, 2006}]: http://www.gutenberg.org/files/20203/20203-h/20203-h.htm [Accessed January 22, 2021].

- *The American Political Science Review*; Vol. 18, No. 4, Nov., 1924. Published by the American Political Science Association: https://www.jstor.org/stable/i306617 [Accessed January 22, 2021].

Page 28 - No Date - 1939
Further Reading Related to Diary Entry:
- *Boston in the 1920s*. Available from the Marion Ringwood Scrapbook Digital Library, Simmons College : https://slis.simmons.edu/mringwood/exhibits/show/life-and-times/boston-in-the-1920s [Accessed January 22, 2021].

- *Elsie Venner* by Oliver Wendell Holmes. 1859. Available from Project Gutenberg at https://www.gutenberg.org/files/2696/2696-h/2696-h.htm [Accessed January 22, 2021].

- *The City-State of Boston: The Rise and Fall of an Atlantic Power, 1630-1865* by Mark Peterson.

- *A City So Grand: The Rise of an American Metropolis, Boston 1850-1900* by Stephen Puleo.

- *Censorship of the Theatre in Boston* by Daniel M. Doherty. Available from Boston University at https://open.bu.edu/handle/2144/4569 [Accessed January 22, 2021].

- *The Telephone Gambit: Chasing Alexander Graham Bell's Secret* by Seth Shulman.

Page 29 - No Date - 1939
Further Reading Related to Diary Entry:
- *The Telephone: A Description of the Bell System with Some Facts Concerning the So-Called Independent Movement* by New England Telephone and Telegraph Company (1906)

- *The Innovators: How a Group of Hackers, Geniuses, and Geeks Created the Digital Revolution* by Walter Isaacson

- *The Autocrat of the Breakfast-Table* by Oliver Wendell Holmes. James R. Osgood and Company, Boston, 1873. Available from Project Gutenberg at https://www.gutenberg.org/ebooks/751 [Accessed January 22, 2021].

- *The Consolations of God: Great Sermons of Phillips Brooks* by Phillips Brooks

- *Twenty Sermons* by Phillips Brooks, Rector of Trinity Church, Boston. Fourth Series. E.P. Dutton and Company, New York, 1887.

Page 30 - July 23, 1940

Further Reading Related to Diary Entry:

- *History and Mission*, Harvard Divinity School, available at: https://hds.harvard.edu/about/history-and-mission [Accessed January 23, 2021).

- *Methodist Church* (last updated 7–12-2011). Available from the BBC at https://www.bbc.co.uk/religion/religions/christianity/subdivisions/methodist_1.shtml [Accessed January 23, 2021).

- *Wesley and the People Called Methodists*, 2nd Edition by Richard P. Heitzenrater

Page 31 - July 23, 1940
(Continued)

Further Reading Related to Diary Entry:

- *The Star Book for Ministers, Third Revised Edition, 1814-1901* by Edward T. Hiscox. Available from the Internet Archive at https://archive.org/stream/starbookforminis00hisc/starbookforminis00hisc_djvu.txt [Accessed January 23, 2021].

- *Nelson's Minister's Manual, NKJV Edition* by Thomas Nelson

First Page Following Last Dated Page (7/23/40)

Further Reading Related to Diary Entry:

- *Boston Holds a Water Celebration in 1848* (chronicles the use of Lake Cochituate to supply water for Boston). Available from the New England Historical Society at http://www.newenglandhistoricalsociety.com/flashback-photo-boston-holds-a-water-celebration-in-1848/ [Accessed January 23, 2021].

- *Magna Carta*. Available from the U.S. National Archives and Records Administration at https://www.archives.gov/exhibits/featured-documents/magna-carta [Accessed January 23, 2021].

Second Page Following Last Dated Page (7/23/40)

Further Reading Related to Diary Entry:

- *Fishing in Maine: Best Places to Catch Fish*. Available from *Wilderness Today* at https://www.wildernesstoday.com/fishing-maine/ [Accessed January 23, 2021].

- *Introduction to Portland's Waterfront*. Available from the City of Portland in the State of Maine at https://www.portlandmaine.gov/1281/Introduction-to-Portlands-Waterfront [Accessed January 23, 2021].

- *Places to Fish*. Available from the Maine Department of Inland Fisheries and Wildlife at https://www.maine.gov/ifw/fishing-boating/fishing/fishing-resources/maine-fishing-guide/regions/index.html [Accessed January 23, 2021].

- *Moosehead Lake*. Available from the Maine Office of Tourism at https://visitmaine.com/things-to-do/parks-natural-attractions/moosehead-lake [Accessed January 23, 2021].

Third Page Following Last Dated Page (7/23/40)
Further Reading Related to Diary Entry:

- *The Great New England Hurricane of 1938*. Available from the U.S. Department of Commerce, National Oceanic and Atmospheric Administration, National Weather Service at https://www.weather.gov/okx/1938HurricaneHome [Accessed January 23, 2021].

- *Timeline of Events (1933-1938)*, the holocaust. Available from the United States Holocaust Memorial Museum at https://www.ushmm.org/learn/timeline-of-events/1933-1938 [Accessed January 23, 2021].

- *Foreign relations of the United States diplomatic papers, 1938, Volume I*; U.S. Government Printing Office, 1938; United States Department of State, Washington, D.C. Available from the University of Wisconsin, Digital Collections at http://digital.library.wisc.edu/1711.dl/FRUS.FRUS1938v01 [Accessed January 23, 2021].

- *Appeasement: Chamberlain, Hitler, Churchill, and the Road to War* by Tim Bouverie

- *Fair Labor Standards Act of 1938: Maximum Struggle for a Minimum Wage* by Jonathan Grossman. Available from the U.S. Department of Labor at https://www.dol.gov/general/aboutdol/history/flsa1938 [Accessed January 23, 2021].

- *Fourth Annual Report of the Archivist of the United States, 1937-1938*. Available fromThe National Archives at https://www.archives.gov/files/about/history/sources/reports/1938-annual-report.pdf [Accessed January 23, 2021].

Fourth Page Following Last Dated Page (7/23/40)
(First Handwritten Page - Dated December 28, 1938; Cochituate, MA)

Further Reading Related to Diary Entry:
- *Lines composed a few miles above Tintern Abbey* by William Wordsworth (1770–1850). Nicholson & Lee, eds. The Oxford Book of English Mystical Verse 1917. Available fom bartleby.com at https://www.bartleby.com/236/67.html [Accessed January 23, 2021].

- *The Most-Sacred Mountain* by Eunice Tietjens. Jessie B. Rittenhouse, ed. (1869–1948). The Second Book of Modern Verse. 1922. Available from bartleby.com at https://www.bartleby.com/271/83.html [Accessed January 23, 2021].

September 6, 1939
Further Reading Related to Diary Entry:
- *A Battle Song of Failure* by Amelia Josephine Burr. The Literary Digest, Volume 45, October 19, 1912, page 691.

- *The Battle-Field* by William Cullen Bryant (1794–1878); Thomas R. Lounsbury, ed.; Yale Book of American Verse. 1912. Available from bartleby.com at https://www.bartleby.com/102/23.html [Accessed January 23, 2021].

- *The Works of John Bunyan, Volume 1: Experimental, Doctrinal, and Practical* by John Bunyan, edited by George Offor, Esq. (1855)

- *The Complete Works of Thomas Brooks, Volume 4—The Crown and Glory of Christianity* by Thomas Brooks (1662)

- *1939: Germany invades Poland*. On This Day. Available from the BBC at http://news.bbc.co.uk/onthisday/hi/dates/stories/september/1/newsid_3506000/3506335.stm [Accessed January 23, 2021].

- *The Coming of the Third Reich* (Book 1 in a series) by Richard J. Evans

- *World War II: The Definitive Visual History from Blitzkrieg to the Atom Bomb* by DK (part of Penguin Random House)

First Page Following Last Dated Page (9/6/39)
Further Reading Related to Diary Entry:
- *National Audubon Society Field Guide to Rocks and Minerals: North America* (National Audubon Society Field Guides) by National Audubon Society

- *Thirty Years that Shook Physics: The Story of Quantum Theory, Revised Edition* by George Gamow

- *Every Stamp Tells a Story: The National Philatelic Collection* (Smithsonian Contribution to Knowledge) by Cheryl Ganz (Editor), Richard R. John (Foreword), M. T. Sheahan (Contributor).

- *The World Encyclopedia of Stamps & Stamp Collecting: The Ultimate Illustrated Reference To Over 3000 Of The World's Best Stamps, And A Professional Guide to Starting and Perfecting Perfecting A Spectacular Collection* by James Mackay.

Second Page Following Last Dated Page (9/6/39)
Further Reading Related to Diary Entry:
- *International Morse Code (Instructions)* by U.S. Department of Defense; Departments of the Army and the Air Force, September 1957. Available from the Internet Archive at https://archive.org/details/Tm11-4591957 [Accessed January 23, 2021].

- *Compendium of Automatic Morse Code* by Ed Goss

- *Ham and Shortwave Radio for the Electronics Hobbyist* by Stan Gibilisco

- *On the Short Waves, 1923-1945: Broadcast Listening in the Pioneer Days of Radio* by Jerome S. Berg.

- *The Short Wave Magazine* (April 1939, Volume III, Number 2); published by the Short Wave Magazine Ltd., London. Available from WorldRadioHistory.com at https://worldradiohistory.com/UK/Short-Wave-UK/30s/SWM-1939-04.pdf [Accessed January 23, 2021].

- *Hammarlund Short Wave Manual, 1938, 4th edition*. Published by the Hammarlund Manufacturing Co. Inc., New York. Available from WorldRadioHistory.com at https://worldradiohistory.com/Archive-Early-Radio-Assorted/Hammarlund/Hammarlund_SW_Manual-1938.CV01.pdf [Accessed January 23, 2021].

October 31, 1939

Further Reading Related to Diary Entry:

- *Sysladobsis Lake, Lower*--a map; Maine Department of Inland Fisheries and Wildlife. Availble from The State of Maine at https://www.maine.gov/ifw/docs/lake-survey-maps/washington/sysladobsis_lake_lower.pdf [Accessed January 23, 2021].

- *Chickens, Gin, and a Maine Friendship: The Correspondence of E.B. White and Edmund Ware Smith* by E.B. White (Author), Edmund Ware Smith (Author), Martha White (Introduction)

- *American Paper Mills, 1690–1832: A Directory of the Paper Trade with Notes on Products, Watermarks, Distribution Methods, and Manufacturing Techniques* by John Bidwell

- *Henry S. Dennison papers*. Available from the Baker Library Special Collections, Harvard Business School, Harvard University at https://hollisarchives.lib.harvard.edu/repositories/11/resources/621 [Accessed January 23, 2021].

- *Dennison, Henry Sturgis* (March 4, 1877– February 29, 1952) by Daniel Nelson. Available from the American National Biography at https://doi.org/10.1093/anb/9780198606697.article.1000406 [Accessed January 23, 2021].

First Page Following October 31, 1939

Further Reading Related to Diary Entry:

- *Upper Sysladobsis Lake*; Lakeville, Penobscot, Maine. Available from the LakesOfMaine.org (a product of Lake Stewards of Maine, in collaboration with state and federal agencies and nonprofits) at https://www.lakesofmaine.org/lake-overview.html?m=4688 [Accessed January 23, 2021].

- *A Tomato Can Chronicle: And Other Stories of Fishing and Shooting* by Edmund Ware Smith (Author), Ralph L. Boyer (Illustrator).

- *The Sense of Beauty: Being the Outline of Aesthetic Theory* by George Santayana.

- *Early Labor Economics: Its Debt to the Management Practice of Henry S. Dennison*. History of Political Economy, 2007 by Kyle Bruce. Available from Academia.edu at https://www.academia.edu/31731484/

Early_Labor_Economics_Its_Debt_to_the_Management_Practice_of_Henry_S._Dennison [Accessed January 23, 2021].

- *Native American Tribes of Maine*. Available from the Native Languages of the Americas website at http://www.native-languages.org/maine.htm [Accessed January 23, 2021].

- *Maine Native Studies Resources*. Available from the Maine Department of Education at https://www.maine.gov/doe/learning/content/socialstudies/resources/mainenativestudies/resources [Accessed January 23, 2021].

Second Page Following October 31, 1939

Further Reading Related to Diary Entry:

- *Explorer's Guide Maine, Including the Coast and Islands* by Nancy English and Christina Tree

- *Cape Cod* by Henry David Thoreau

- *The Outermost House: A Year of Life On The Great Beach of Cape Cod* by Henry Beston

January 22, 1940

Further Reading Related to Diary Entry:

- *Dana's Textbook of Minerology (With an Extended Treatise on Chrystallography and Physical Mineralogy)* by Edward Salisbury Dana and William E. Ford Publisher: John Wiley & Sons, Inc.; 4th edition (January 1, 1932)

- *Dana's Manual Of Mineralogy For The Student Of Elementary Mineralogy, The Mining Engineer, The Geologist, The Prospector, The Collector, Etc* by James Dwight Dana and William Ebenezer Ford

- *The Weather Machine: A Journey Inside the Forecast* by Andrew Blum

- *Reality Is Not What It Seems: The Journey to Quantum Gravity* by Carlo Rovelli

March 4, 1940

Further Reading Related to Diary Entry:

- *Finland at War: The Continuation and Lapland Wars 1941–45* by Vesa Nenye, Peter Munter, Toni Wirtanen, Chris Birks

- *Frozen Hell: The Russo-Finnish Winter War of 1939-1940* by William Trotter

July 24, 1940
Further Reading Related to Diary Entry:
- *Jesus Through Middle Eastern Eyes: Cultural Studies in the Gospels* by Kenneth E. Bailey

- *Simply Jesus: A New Vision of Who He Was, What He Did, and Why He Matters* by N. T. Wright

- *Three Simple Rules: A Wesleyan Way of Living* by Rueben P. Job

- *Five Means of Grace: Experience God's Love the Wesleyan Way* (Wesley Discipleship Path Series) by Elaine A. Heath

- *Spurgeon on Prayer & Spiritual Warfare* (anthology of six of Spurgeon's classic books on prayer: *The Power in Prayer, Praying Successfully, The Golden Key of Prayer, Finding Peace in Life's Storms, Spurgeon on Praise, Satan: A Defeated Foe*) by Charles H Spurgeon.

July 30, 1940
Further Reading Related to Diary Entry:
- *History of Lynn* by Alonso Lewis. Available from the Internet Archive at https://archive.org/details/historyoflynn02lewi/page/n10 [Accessed on January 23, 2021].

- *The Legend of Dungeon Rock and the Pirate Treasure It Holds* (updated in 2020). Available from the New England Historical Society at https://www.newenglandhistoricalsociety.com/legend-dungeon-rock-pirate-treasure/ [Accessed on January 23, 2021].

- *Dungeon Rock, Lynn Woods*. Available from the Swampscott Public Library, Swampscott, Mass. at https://digitalheritage.noblenet.org/swampscott/items/show/277 [Accessed on January 23, 2021].

- *Lynn Woods Reservation*. Available from the City of Lynn at http://www.lynnma.gov/departments/lynnwoods.shtml [Accessed on January 23, 2021].

- *The Book of Roses* by Francis Parkman. Published in 1871 by J. E. Tilton And Company, Boston. Available from The Project Gutenberg at http://www.gutenberg.org/files/47232/47232-h/47232-h.htm [Accessed on January 23, 2021].

- *France and England in North America*, volumes 1-8 by Francis Parkman.
  - *A Half-Century of Conflict*. *France and England in North America, part 6*. Published by Little, Brown, and Company, Boston in 1910. Available from Internet Archive at https://archive.org/details/franceandenglan06parkgoog/page/n11 [Accessed on January 23, 2021].

August 7, 1940
Further Reading Related to Diary Entry:
- *The Last of the Hill Farms: Echoes of Vermont's Past* by Richard W. Brown

- *Historic Photos of Vermont* by Ginger Gellman

Page 2 of August 7, 1940
Further Reading Related to Diary Entry:
- *Smithsonian Handbooks: Rocks & Minerals* by Chris Pellant

- *National Geographic Pocket Guide to Rocks and Minerals of North America* (Pocket Guides) by Sarah Garlick

- *Geophysics for the Mineral Exploration Geoscientist*, 1st Edition by Michael Dentith and Stephen T. Mudge

- *Growing Up: Farm Life & Basketball in the 1940s & '50s* by Harold L. Schoen

August 26, 1940
Further Reading Related to Diary Entry:
- *Ordinary Church: A Long and Loving Look* by Joseph S Beach

- *At Home in Mitford* by Jan Karon

- *Home to Harmony* by Philip Gulley

- *World War II Map* by DK and Smithsonian Institution

Second Page of August 26, 1940
Further Reading Related to Diary Entry:
- *AMC's Best Day Hikes in Vermont: Four-Season Guide To 60 Of The Best Trails In The Green Mountain State* by Jen Lamphere Roberts

- *White Mountain Guide: AMC's Comprehensive Guide to Hiking Trails in the White Mountain National Forest* by Steven D. Smith (Editor)

- *David Harum: A Story of American Life* by Edward Noyes Westcott. Published by D. Appleton & Company in 1898.

Friday September 13th, 1940
Further Reading Related to Diary Entry:
- *The Ghost Army of World War II: How One Top-Secret Unit Deceived the Enemy with Inflatable Tanks, Sound Effects, and Other Audacious Fakery* by Rick Beyer and Elizabeth Sayles

- *Double Crossed: The Missionaries Who Spied for the United States During the Second World War* by Matthew Avery Sutton

Saturday January 23, 1941
Further Reading Related to Diary Entry:
- *The Artist's Way* by Julia Cameron

- *On Writing Well: The Classic Guide to Writing Nonfiction* by William Zinsser

- Writing About Your Life: A Journey into the Past by William Zinsser

- *The Liberator: One World War II Soldier's 500-Day Odyssey from the Beaches of Sicily to the Gates of Dachau* by Alex Kershaw

Page 2 of Saturday January 23, 1941
Further Reading Related to Diary Entry:
- *No Cross, No Crown. A discourse, shewing the nature and discipline of the Holy Cross of Christ* by William Penn. A New Edition Revised, 1842; Harvey and Darton publishers, London.
  - Available from Project Gutenberg at http://www.gutenberg.org/ebooks/44895 [Accessed on January 23, 2021].

- *Living the Quaker Way: Discover the Hidden Happiness in the Simple Life* by Philip Gulley

- *A History of Fascism, 1914–1945* by Stanley G. Payne

- *Exile in the Fatherland: Martin Niemöller's Letters from Moabit Prison* by Martin Niemöller (Author), Hubert G. Locke (Editor)

February 17, 1941
Further Reading Related to Diary Entry:
- *Evangelism's First Modern Media Star: Reverend Bill Stidger* by Jack Hyland

- *The Time Machine* by H.G. Wells

- *Earth (Second Edition): The Definitive Visual Guide* by Douglas Palmer, Robert Dinwiddie, John Farndon, Michael Allaby, David Burnie, Clint Twist, Martin Walters, and Tony Waltham

- *In Six Days: Why Fifty Scientists Choose to Believe in Creation* by John F. Ashton

- *Temperance and Education*: *The relation of the social drinking customs to the educational interests of the nation*, by Mark Hopkins, D.D. Published by the National Temperance Society, New York, 1876. Available from University of Michigan, Making of America Books at https://quod.lib.umich.edu/cgi/t/text/text-idx?c=moa;idno=AAW8208 [Accessed January 23, 2021].

- *Lectures on Moral Science* by Mark Hopkins, D.D. Available from the University of Michigan, Making of America Books at https://quod.lib.umich.edu/cgi/t/text/text-idx?c=moa;idno=AJF1419 [Accessed January 23, 2021].

- *Online Books by Mark Hopkins* (Hopkins, Mark, 1802-1887). Available from The Online Books Page, University of Pennsylvania at http://onlinebooks.library.upenn.edu/webbin/book/lookupname?key=Hopkins%2C%20Mark%2C%201802-1887 [Accessed January 23, 2021].

April 22, 1941
Further Reading Related to Diary Entry:
- *The Quantum of Explanation*—*Science, logic, and ethics, from a Whiteheadian Pragmatist perspective (go figure)* by Gary L. Herstein. Available from garyherstein.com at https://garyherstein.com/2017/11/01/reading-between-the-texts/ [Accessed January 23, 2021].

- *Alfred North Whitehead* by Andrew Irvine and Ronny Desmet (first published May 21, 1996; substantive revision Sep 4, 2018). Available from the Stanford Encyclopedia of Philosophy, Stanford University at https://plato.stanford.edu/entries/whitehead/ [Accessed January 23, 2021].

- *The Diary of Samuel Pepys* by Samuel Pepys. Available from The Gutenberg Project at http://www.gutenberg.org/files/4200/4200-h/4200-h.htm [Accessed January 23, 2021].

- *Emerson and the Art of the Diary* by Lawrence Rosenwald

- *Journals of Ralph Waldo Emerson with Annotations* by Ralph Waldo Emerson, edited by Edward Waldo Emerson and Waldo Emerson Forbes. Published by Houghton Mifflin Company, Boston, 1909. Available from Internet Archive at https://archive.org/details/journalsofralphw02emeruoft/page/n12 [Accessed January 23, 2021].

August 30, 1941
Further Reading Related to Diary Entry:

- *Henry David Thoreau : A Week on the Concord and Merrimack Rivers / Walden; Or, Life in the Woods / The Maine Woods / Cape Cod (Library of America)* by Henry David Thoreau

- *Walden; or, Life in the Woods* by Henry David Thoreau. Available from Lit2Go, University of South Florida at https://etc.usf.edu/lit2go/90/walden-or-life-in-the-woods/ [Accessed January 23, 2021].

- *A History of Vermont* by Edward Day Collins, Ph.D.; Ginn and Company Publishers, Boston, The Athenaeum Press, 1903. Available from the Internet Archive at https://archive.org/details/historyofvermont00co [Accessed January 23, 2021].

- *Fort Ticonderoga*. Infoirmation available from the Council of the Arts, New York State at https://www.fortticonderoga.org [Accessed January 23, 2021].

- *Battles - Fort Ticonderoga*. Available from the American Battlefield Trust at https://www.battlefields.org/learn/revolutionary-war/battles/fort-ticonderoga [Accessed January 23, 2021].

August, 30, 1941 - Page Two
Further Reading Related to Diary Entry:

- *Fodor's New England: with the Best Fall Foliage Drives & Scenic Road Trips* by Fodor's Travel Guides

- *Lonely Planet New England's Best Trips - 32 Amazing Road Trips* by Lonely Planet, Gregor Clark, Carolyn Bain, Mara Vorhees, Benedict Walker

- *To Lose a Battle: France 1940* by Alistair Horne

- *Russia's War: A History of the Soviet Effort: 1941-1945* by Richard Overy

- *The 40s: The Story of a Decade. The New Yorker.* By The New Yorker Magazine (Author), Henry Finder (Editor), David Remnick (Introduction), W. H. Auden (Contributor), Elizabeth Bishop (Contributor)

September 4, 1941
Further Reading Related to Diary Entry:

- *Ben Hogan's Five Lessons: The Modern Fundamentals of Golf* by Ben Hogan (Author), Herbert Warren Wind (Author), Anthony Ravielli (Illustrator)

- *Look Homeward Angel* (1929) by Thomas Wolfe

- *Of Time and the River* (1935) by Thomas Wolfe

- *The Journey Down* (1938) by Thomas Wolfe

- *You Can't Go Home Again* (1940) by Thomas Wolfe. Available from The Project Gutenberg - Australia at http://gutenberg.net.au/ebooks07/0700231h.html [Accessed January 23, 2021].

- *Yanks in the RAF: The Story of Maverick Pilots and American Volunteers Who Joined Britain's Fight in WWII* by David Alan Johnson

September 25, 1941
Further Reading Related to Diary Entry:

- *Citizens of London: The Americans Who Stood with Britain in Its Darkest, Finest Hour* by Lynne Olson

- *The Secret History of World War II: Spies, Code Breakers, and Covert Operations* by Neil Kagan and Stephen G. Hyslop

- *Foxhole Radio: the ubiquitous razor blade radio of WWII* by Brian Carusella

- *Crystal Set Projects: 14 Radio Projects You Can Build* by Patricia M Anderson and Members of Xtal Set Society

- *The Voice of the Crystal* by H. Peter Friedrichs

October 14, 1941
Further Reading Related to Diary Entry:
- *Gemstone Tumbling, Cutting, Drilling & Cabochon Making: A Simple Guide to Finishing Rough Stones* by James Magnuson

- *Handbook for the Amateur Lapidary* by James Harry Howard

- *Amateur Gemstone Faceting Volume 1: The Essentials* by Tom Herbst

- *The Mantle of Command: FDR at War, 1941–1942* by Nigel Hamilton

December 9, 1941
Further Reading Related to Diary Entry:
- *All the Gallant Men: An American Sailor's Firsthand Account of Pearl Harbor* by Donald Stratton

- *Brothers Down: Pearl Harbor and the Fate of the Many Brothers Aboard the USS Arizona* by Walter R. Borneman

- *Day Of Deceit: The Truth About FDR and Pearl Harbor* by Robert Stinnett

- *Churchill's Ministry of Ungentlemanly Warfare: The Mavericks Who Plotted Hitler's Defeat* by Giles Milton

- *A Handbook for Air Raid Wardens* prepared by Training Section, Office of Civilian Defense, revised edition. U.S. Government Printing Office, April 1942, Washington D.C. Available from the Illinois Digital Archives; Illinois State Library at http://www.idaillinois.org/cdm/ref/collection/isl3/id/10981 [Accessed January 23, 2021].

- *The Jewelled Trail* by Louis Kornitzer. Available from Online Books by Louis Kornitzer, The Online Books Page, University of Pennsylvania at http://onlinebooks.library.upenn.edu/webbin/book/lookupname?key=Kornitzer%2C%20Louis [Accessed January 23, 2021].

Saturday Morning, January 24, 1942
130 Bellevue Road, Lynn, MA
Further Reading Related to Diary Entry:
- *The Diary of Samuel Pepys* by Samuel Pepys. Available from The Project Gutenberg at http://www.gutenberg.org/files/4200/4200-h/4200-h.htm [January 23, 2021].

- *Boy Scouts Handbook: The First Edition, 1911* by Boy Scouts of America (Author). Available from The Project Gutenberg at http://www.gutenberg.org/files/29558/29558-h/29558-h.htm [January 23, 2021].

- *Girl Scouts Handbook: The Original 1913 Edition* by W. J. Hoxie

- *Scouting for Girls*. Official Handbook of the Girl Scouts, 1925 (Sixth Reprint) by Girl Scouts, Inc; editor: Josephine Daskam Bacon. Release Date: April 4, 2009. Available from The Project Gutenberg at https://www.gutenberg.org/files/28490/28490-h/28490-h.htm [January 23, 2021].

- *The Secret of Sherwood Forest* by Guy Woodward

- *Building for War: The Epic Saga of the Civilian Contractors and Marines of Wake Island in World War II* by Bonita Gilbert

- *The Aleutian Islands Campaign: The History of Japan's Invasion of Alaska during World War II* by Charles River Editors

- *Spearhead: An American Tank Gunner, His Enemy, and a Collision of Lives in World War II* by Adam Makos

January 31, 1942
Further Reading Related to Diary Entry:
- *No Death, No Fear: Comforting Wisdom for Life* by Thich Nhat Hanh

- *William Wordsworth - The Major Works: including The Prelude (Oxford World's Classics)* by William Wordsworth (Author), Stephen Gill (Editor)

- *Seizing the Enigma: The Race to Break the German U-Boat Codes, 1933-1945* by David Kahn

- *Torpedo Junction: U-Boat War Off America's East Coast, 1942* by Homer Hickam

Ash Wednesday February 18, 1942
Further Reading Related to Diary Entry:
- *Catechism of the Catholic Church: Second Edition* by U.S. Catholic Church

- *How the Catholic Church Built Western Civilization* by Thomas E. Woods

- *The Second Vatican Council - An Unwritten Story* by Professor Roberto deMattei (Author), Michael M. Miller (Editor)

- *Catholicism: A Journey to the Heart of the Faith* by Robert Barron

- *The Compact History of the Catholic Church: Revised Edition* by Schreck Ph.D., Alan

- *The Jesuit Guide to (Almost) Everything: A Spirituality for Real Life* by James Martin

- *The Age of Reason* by Thomas Paine

- *The Cloud of Unknowing and Other Works* (Penguin Classics) Reissue Edition by Anonymous (Author), A. C. Spearing (Translator)

Good Friday April 5, 1942

Further Reading Related to Diary Entry:

- *The Moon is Down* by John Steinbeck

- *Echoes and Memories* by Bramwell Booth

- *These Fifty Years* by Bramwell Booth

- *Jesus: A Pilgrimage* by James Martin

- *Beautiful Outlaw: Experiencing the Playful, Disruptive, Extravagant Personality of Jesus* by John Eldredge

- *Living Buddha, Living Christ: 20th Anniversary Edition* by Thich Nhat Hanh

June 7, 1942

Further Reading Related to Diary Entry:

- *Walking* by Henry David Thoreau

- *The Power of Jesus' Names* by Tony Evans

- *The Battle of Midway* by Craig L. Symonds

- *Pacific Crucible: War at Sea in the Pacific, 1941-1942* by Ian W. Toll

- *World War II at Sea: A Global History* by Craig L. Symonds

June 11, 1942

Further Reading Related to Diary Entry:

- *Complete Poems and Selected Letters of John Keats* by John Keats

- *Roses: Placing Roses, Planting & Care, The Best Varieties* by Editors of Sunset Books

- *Lieber's Standard Telegraphic Code* by B. Franklin Lieber; Lieber Publishing Company, New York (1898). Available from Internet Archive at https://archive.org/details/liebersstandard02liebgoog/page/n5 [January 23, 2021].

- *Code Girls: The Untold Story of the American Women Code Breakers of World War II* by Liza Mundy

- *The Liberator: One World War II Soldier's 500-Day Odyssey from the Beaches of Sicily to the Gates of Dachau* by Alex Kershaw

- *A Little Village Called Lidice: The Story of the the Return of the Women and Children of Lidice* by Zdena Trinka

- *World War II Auschwitz: A History From Beginning to End* by Hourly History

June 12, 1942

Further Reading Related to Diary Entry:

- *Zen Golf: Mastering the Mental Game* by Dr. Joseph Parent

- *Yearbook of the Young Men's Christian Associations of North America (May 1, 1905 to April 30, 1906)*; published by the International Committee of Young Men's Christian Associations, New York, 1906. Available from Internet Archive at https://archive.org/details/ymcayearbookof1906younuoft/page/n51 [January 23, 2021].

- *The Social Sources of Denominationalism* by H. Richard Niebuhr; Living Age Books; published by Meridian Books, New York, 1922. Available from Internet Archive at https://archive.org/details/in.ernet.dli.2015.462204 [January 23, 2021].

- *Beau Geste* by Percival Christopher Wren (1924). Available from The Project Gutenberg of Australia at http://gutenberg.net.au/ebooks06/0600231h.html [January 23, 2021].

- *Aircraft Pictorial No. 5 - P-40 Warhawk* by Dana Bell

- *P-40 Warhawk Aces of the MTO* by Carl Molesworth

June 15, 1942

Further Reading Related to Diary Entry:

- *Candide* by Voltaire. Available from The Project Gutenberg at http://www.gutenberg.org/files/19942/19942-h/19942-h.htm [Accessed January 23, 2021].

- *The Moving Finger,* from the Rubaiyat of Omar Khayyam; a sermon by Reverend E.F. Dinsmore, Unity Church, Santa Barbara, CA. Available from Internet Archive at https://archive.org/stream/movingfingerofom00dinsrich/movingfingerofom00dinsrich_djvu.txt [Accessed January 23, 2021].

- *The Emperor's Codes: The Thrilling Story of the Allied Code Breakers Who Turned the Tide of World War* II by Michael Smith

- *A Higher Call: An Incredible True Story of Combat and Chivalry in the War-Torn Skies of World War II* by Adam Makos and Larry Alexander

- *Surviving Hitler: A Boy in the Nazi Death Camps* by Andrea Warren

Vacation Diary - 1942 - Piermont, New Hampshire

Resume of First Vacation Week- 1942
August 2nd Sunday to August 9th

Further Reading Related to Diary Entry:

- *Berlin Diary: The Journal of a Foreign Correspondent 1934-1941* by William L. Shirer

- *Radio Goes to War: The Cultural Politics of Propaganda during World War II* by Gerd Horten

- *Fighting in Ukraine: A Photographer at War* (Images of War series) by David Mitchelhill-Green

Resume of Second Vacation Week-1942- Piermont, N.H.
August 10th - 15th

Further Reading Related to Diary Entry:
- *Flying Fortress* by Edward Jablonski

- *Nature* by Ralph Waldo Emerson

Resume of Third Vacation Week-1942- Piermont, N.H.
August 16th - 23rd

Further Reading Related to Diary Entry:
- *Mini Farming: Self-Sufficiency on 1/4 Acre* by Brett L. Markham

- *You Can Farm: The Entrepreneur's Guide to Start & Succeed in a Farming Enterprise* by Joel Salatin

- *Islands of Destiny: The Solomons Campaign and the Eclipse of the Rising Sun* by John Prados

Resume of Fourth Vacation Week-1942- Piermont, N.H.
August 24th - 30th

Further Reading Related to Diary Entry:
- *Casey & the Flying Fortress* by Mark Farina

- *Deadly Sky: The American Combat Airman in World War II* by John C. McManus

- *Turning Point: The Battle for Milne Bay 1942 - Japan's first land defeat in World War II* by Michael Veitch

Resume of Fifth, and Final, Vacation Week-1942- Piermont, N.H
August 24th - 30th

Further Reading Related to Diary Entry:
- *Cruising New Hampshire History: A Guide to New Hampshire's Roadside Historical Markers* by Michael A Bruno

- *Two shakes of a lamb's tail, or, Rambles and bygones and from "Long Look Farm", New Hampshire* by Marjorie Whalen Smith

October 1st, 1942--Lynn, Mass.
Further Reading Related to Diary Entry:
- *Shakespeare Beyond Doubt?: Exposing an Industry in Denial* by John M. Shahan (Author), Alexander Waugh (Editor)

- *Bacon, Shakespeare and the Rosicrucians* by William Francis C. Wigston

November 24, 1942 Janus on the War
Further Reading Related to Diary Entry:
- *Patton, Montgomery, Rommel: Masters of War* by Terry Brighton

- *The Forgotten 500: The Untold Story of the Men Who Risked All for the Greatest Rescue Mission of World War II* by Gregory A. Freeman

- *Pacific Crucible: War at Sea in the Pacific, 1941-1942* by Ian W. Toll

- *Operation Drumbeat: The Dramatic True Story of Germany's First U-Boat Attacks Along the American Coast in World War II* by Michael Gannon

- *The 1942 Sears Christmas Book* (Paperback – Facsimile, September 18, 2019) by Sears Roebuck and Co.

Friday Night, January 1, 1943
Further Reading Related to Diary Entry:
- *Grandma's Wartime Kitchen: World War II and the Way We Cooked* by Joanne Lamb Hayes and Jean Anderson

- *Grandma's Wartime Baking Book: World War II and the Way We Baked* by Joanne Lamb Hayes

- *Eggs or Anarchy: The remarkable story of the man tasked with the impossible: to feed a nation at war* by William Sitwell

- *The Winter Army: The World War II Odyssey of the 10th Mountain Division, America's Elite Alpine Warriors* by Maurice Isserman

April 25, 1943
Further Reading Related to Diary Entry:
- *The Cloudspotter's Guide: The Science, History, and Culture of Clouds* by Gavin Pretor-Pinney

- *The Book of Clouds* by John A. Day

- *The Cloud Collector's Handbook* by Gavin Pretor-Pinney

- *National Audubon Society Field Guide to Weather: North America* (National Audubon Society Field Guides) by David Ludlum

- *Peterson First Guide to Clouds and Weather* by Vincent J. Schaefer

June 21, 1943

Further Reading Related to Diary Entry:

- *Bobby Fischer Teaches Chess* by Bobby Fischer, with Stuart Margulies, Don Mosenfelder

- *Logical Chess: Move By Move: Every Move Explained* by Irving Chernev

- *Chess: 5334 Problems, Combinations and Games* by László Polgár and Bruce Pandolfini

- *How to Reassess Your Chess: Chess Mastery Through Chess Imbalances* by Jeremy Silman

July 27, 1943

Further Reading Related to Diary Entry:

- *The Pope and Mussolini: The Secret History of Pius XI and the Rise of Fascism in Europe* by David I. Kertzer

- *My Rise And Fall* by Benito Mussolini

- *Bloodlands: Europe Between Hitler and Stalin* by Timothy Snyder

- *The Burning Shore: How Hitlers U-Boats Brought World War II to America* by Ed Offley

- *The Heart of the Buddha's Teaching: Transforming Suffering into Peace, Joy, and Liberation* by Thich Nhat Hanh

- *Self Reliance* by Ralph Waldo Emerson. Available from The Project Gutenberg at http://www.gutenberg.org/files/16643/16643-h/16643-h.htm [Accessed January 23, 2021].

- *Notre-Dame of Paris* (The Hunchback of Notre Dame) by Victor Hugo

- *Les Miserables* by Victor Hugo

- *The Rape of Nanking: The Forgotten Holocaust of World War II* by Iris Chang

Wednesday September 29, 1943
Further Reading Related to Diary Entry:
- *Robinson Crusoe* by Daniel Defoe

- *Sea Fever: Selected Poems of John Masefield* by John Masefield and Philip W. Errington

- *A Woman of No Importance: The Untold Story of the American Spy Who Helped Win World War II* by Sonia Purnell

- *Shot Down: The True Story of Pilot Howard Snyder and the Crew of the B-17 Susan Ruth* by Steve Snyder (Author), John Maling (Editor)

Thursday November 4, 1943
Further Reading Related to Diary Entry:
- *Silent Night: The Story of the World War I Christmas Truce* by Stanley Weintraub

- *The Greatest Battle: Stalin, Hitler, and the Desperate Struggle for Moscow That Changed the Course of World War II* by Andrew Nagorski

- *The Drive on Moscow, 1941: Operation Taifun and Germany's First Great Crisis of World War II* by Anders Frankson (Author), Niklas Zetterling

- *The Kingdom of Yugoslavia: The Turbulent History of the Country's Formation and Occupation during World War I and World War II* by Charles River Editors

December 2, 1943
Further Reading Related to Diary Entry:
- *The Diary of Samuel Pepys* by Samuel Pepys. Available from The Project Gutenberg at http://www.gutenberg.org/files/4200/4200-h/4200-h.htm [Accessed January 23, 2021].

- *Walden* by Henry David Thoreau. Available from The Project Gutenberg at http://www.gutenberg.org/files/205/205-h/205-h.htm [Accessed January 23, 2021].

- *When Books Went to War: The Stories That Helped Us Win World War II* by Molly Manning

January 15, 1944

Further Reading Related to Diary Entry:

- *The Lost Art of Reading Nature's Signs: Use Outdoor Clues to Find Your Way, Predict the Weather, Locate Water, Track Animals—and Other Forgotten Skills* by Tristan Gooley

- *Finding Your Way Without Map or Compass* by Harold Gatty

- *Then They Came for Me: Martin Niemöller, the Pastor Who Defied the Nazis* by Matthew D Hockenos

- *South From Corregidor* by Lt. Comdr. John Morrill, Pete Martin

- *The Saga of Pappy Gunn* by George C. Kenney

Thursday February 3rd, 1944

Further Reading Related to Diary Entry:

- *The Marshall Islands 1944: Operation Flintlock, the capture of Kwajalein and Eniwetok (Campaign)* by Gordon L. Rottman and Howard Gerrard

- *Between Tears and Laughter* by Lin Yutang

- *War at Sea: A Naval History of World War II* by Nathan Miller

April 20, 1944

Further Reading Related to Diary Entry:

- *Brass Button Broadcasters: A Lighhearted Look at 50 Years of Military Broadcasting* by Trent Christman

- *D Day: June 6, 1944: The Climactic Battle of World War II* by Stephen E. Ambrose
- *Fighting for Life: American Military Medicine in World War II* by Albert E. Cowdrey

- *Facing the Abyss: American Literature and Culture in the 1940s* by George Hutchinson

July 22, 1944
Further Reading Related to Diary Entry:
- *Normandy '44: D-Day and the Epic 77-Day Battle for France* by James Holland

- *The Plot to Kill Hitler: Dietrich Bonhoeffer: Pastor, Spy, Unlikely Hero* by Patricia McCormick

- *D DAY Through German Eyes - The Hidden Story of June 6th 1944* by Holger Eckhertz (Books 1 and 2).

- *Cure Cottages of Saranac Lake: Architecture and History of a Pioneer Health Resort* by Philip L. Gallos

- *The Adirondacks: Season by Season* by Heilman II, Carl and Bill McKibben

- *Finding True North: A History of One Small Corner of the Adirondacks* by Fran Yardley

Thursday August 24, 1944
Further Reading Related to Diary Entry:
- *The Bedford Boys: One American Town's Ultimate D-day Sacrifice* by Alex Kershaw

- *The Secret Life of Lobsters: How Fishermen and Scientists Are Unraveling the Mysteries of Our Favorite Crustacean* by Trevor Corson

- *The Lobster Coast: Rebels, Rusticators, and the Struggle for a Forgotten Frontier* by Colin Woodard

Wednesday, August 30, 1944
Further Reading Related to Diary Entry:
- *Typewriters: Iconic Machines from the Golden Age of Mechanical Writing* by Anthony Casillo (Author), Bruce Curtis (Photographer)

- *Walden and Civil Disobedience* by Henry David Thoreau

- *The Unwomanly Face of War: An Oral History of Women in World War II* by Svetlana Alexievich

- *Spearhead: An American Tank Gunner, His Enemy, and a Collision of Lives in World War II* by Adam Makos

Wednesday, October 11, 1944
Further Reading Related to Diary Entry:

- For an in-depth history of Massachusetts' Bethlehem Shipbuilding Corporation, Ltd, (Formerly Fore River) naval yard, with pictures of many of the ships built, see the article, *A History of Shipbuilding at Fore River* by Anthony F. Sarcone and Lawrence S. Rines; available from the Thomas Crane Library, Quincy, Massachusetts at http://thomascranelibrary.org/shipbuildingheritage/history.htm [Accessed January 23, 2021].
  - The article contains a picture of the destroyer the Northampton before she was torpedoed and sunk near the Guadalcanal by the Japanese in 1942. The article also clarifies the origins of "Kilroy was here".

- *D-Day Girls: The Spies Who Armed the Resistance, Sabotaged the Nazis, and Helped Win World War II* by Sarah Rose

- *The Cretan Runner: His Story of the German Occupation* by George Pschoundakis

- *In the Minister's Workshop* by Halford Edward Luccock

- *The Complete Poetical Works of James Whitcomb Riley* by James Whitcomb Riley

- *World's Best Poetry: Poems of Nature (1904)* by Bliss Carmen

Friday, November 17, 1944
Further Reading Related to Diary Entry:

- *The Pilgrim's Progress* by John Bunyan

- *Pilgrim Theology: Core Doctrines for Christian Disciples* by Michael Horton

- *Mayflower: A Story of Courage, Community, and War* by Nathaniel Philbrick

- *Atlas of Indian Nations* by Anton Treuer

- *Mourt's Relation or Journal of the Plantation at Plymouth* with an Introduction and Notes by Henry Marten Dexter. Available from Internet Archive at https://archive.org/details/mourtsrelatiomo00dextgoog/page/n15 [Accessed January 23, 2021].
    - ***Note that the original text of Mourt's Relation is written in an older english style, for example an "s" looks like an "f" without the crossbar and a "v" looks like a "u".
    - A paraphrased edition, with the old english edited, is available through The Plymouth Colony Archive Project at http://www.histarch.illinois.edu/plymouth/mourt1.html [Accessed January 23, 2021].

- *Pilgrim Theology: Core Doctrines for Christian Disciples* by Michael Horton

- *Mayflower: A Story of Courage, Community, and War* by Nathaniel Philbrick

- *Atlas of Indian Nations* by Anton Treuer

- *The Works of John Robinson, Pastor of the Pilgrim Fathers*, volume I, 1851; publisher John Snow, 35, Paternoster Row, London; Reed and Pardon, Printers, Lovell's Court, Paternoster Row, London. Available from Internet Archive at https://archive.org/details/worksofjohnrobin01robi/page/n3 [Accessed January 23, 2021].

- *Seuen treatises containing such direction as is gathered out of the Holie Scriptures, leading and guiding to true happines, both in this life, and in the life to come: and may be called the practise of Christianitie. Profitable for all such as heartily desire the same: in the which, more particularly true Christians may learne how to leade a godly and comfortable life euery day.* Penned by Richard Rogers, preacher of the word of God at Wethersfield in Essex by Rogers, Richard, 1550?-1618. At London: Imprinted by Felix Kyngston, for Thomas Man, and Robert Dexter, and are to be sold at the brasen Serpent in Pauls Churchyard, 1603. Available from the Text Creation Partnership, Early English Books Online; University of Michigan, Digital Collections, at https://quod.lib.umich.edu/cgi/t/text/text-idx?c=eebo;idno=A10945.0001.001 [Accessed January 23, 2021].

- *American Caesar: Douglas MacArthur 1880 - 1964* by William Manchester

- *The Admirals: Nimitz, Halsey, Leahy, and King--The Five-Star Admirals Who Won the War at Sea* by Walter R. Borneman

- *American Comic Book Chronicles: 1940-1944* by Kurt F. Mitchell (Author), Roy Thomas (Author), Keith Dallas (Editor), Jack Kirby (Artist), Joe Simon (Artist), Will Eisner (Artist), Irv Novick (Artist)

- *Take That, Adolf!: The Fighting Comic Books of the Second World War* by Jack Kirby (Author, Artist), Joe Simon (Author, Artist), Alex Schomburg (Author, Artist), Will Eisner (Author, Artist), Lou Fine (Author, Artist), Mark Fertig (Editor)

December 19, 1944
Further Reading Related to Diary Entry:
- *A Christmas Carol* by Charles Dickens

- *Holiday* by Stephen Nissenbaum

- *The Origins of Christmas* by Joseph F. Kelly PhD

- *Women Heroes of World War II: 26 Stories of Espionage, Sabotage, Resistance, and Rescue* by Kathryn J. Atwood

February 2, 1945
Further Reading Related to Diary Entry:
- *Ardennes 1944: The Battle of the Bulge* by Antony Beevor

- *A Train Near Magdeburg—The Holocaust, the survivors, and the American soldiers who saved them* by Matthew Rozell

- *MacArthur at War: World War II in the Pacific* by Walter R. Borneman

- *Ghost Soldiers: The Epic Account of World War II's Greatest Rescue Mission* by Hampton Sides

February 22, 1945
Further Reading Related to Diary Entry:
- *Holy Spirit And Power* by John Wesley

- *The Theology of John Wesley: Holy Love and the Shape of Grace* by Kenneth J. Collins

- *Dark Nights of the Soul: A Guide to Finding Your Way Through Life's Ordeals* by Thomas Moore

- *The Seven Storey Mountain* by Thomas Merton

April 14, 1945
Further Reading Related to Diary Entry:
- *FDR* by Jean Edward Smith

- *No Ordinary Time: Franklin and Eleanor Roosevelt: The Home Front in World War II* by Doris Kearns Goodwin

- *The Fall of Berlin 1945* by Antony Beevor

- *The Complete Poems of Carl Sandburg: Revised and Expanded Edition* by Carl Sandburg

Sunday, July 8, 1945
Further Reading Related to Diary Entry:
- *Victory in Europe: D-Day to V-E Day* by Max Hastings

- *Michigan POW Camps in World War II* by Gregory D. Sumner

- *Savage Continent: Europe in the Aftermath of World War II* by Keith Lowe

- *Postwar: A History of Europe Since 1945* by Tony Judt

- *After the Reich: The Brutal History of the Allied Occupation* by Giles MacDonogh

August 9, 1945
Further Reading Related to Diary Entry:
- *Hiroshima* by John Hersey

- *To Hell and Back: The Last Train from Hiroshima* by Charles Pellegrino

- *Coney Island: Lost and Found* by Charles Denson

- *The Historical Atlas of New York City, Third Edition: A Visual Celebration of 400 Years of New York City's History* by Eric Homberger

Tuesday, August 14th, 1945
Further Reading Related to Diary Entry:
- *Japan's Longest Day* by The Pacific War Research Society

- *The Fall of Japan: A Chronicle of the End of an Empire* by William Craig

- *If You Survive: From Normandy to the Battle of the Bulge to the End of World War II, One American Officer's Riveting True Story* by George Wilson

- *Potsdam: The End of World War II and the Remaking of Europe* by Michael Neiberg

November 12, 1945
Further Reading Related to Diary Entry:
- *As a Man Thinketh* by James Allen

- *Serving God and Country: United States Military Chaplains in World War II* by Lyle W. Dorsett

- *Pure Grit: How American World War II Nurses Survived Battle and Prison Camp in the Pacific* by Cronk Farrell, Mary

- *And If I Perish: Frontline U.S. Army Nurses in World War II* by Evelyn Monahan

- *Crusade in Europe* by Dwight D. Eisenhower

December 25, 1945
Further Reading Related to Diary Entry:
- *Mission at Nuremberg: An American Army Chaplain and the Trial of the Nazis* by Tim Townsend

- *A Train Near Magdeburg—The Holocaust, the survivors, and the American soldiers who saved them* by Matthew Rozell

- *Unbroken: A World War II Story of Survival, Resilience, and Redemption* by Laura Hillenbrand

- *Mr. Dickens and His Carol* by Samantha Silva

- *The Man Who Invented Christmas: How Charles Dickens's A Christmas Carol Rescued His Career and Revived Our Holiday Spirits* by Les Standiford

February 23, 1946

Further Reading Related to Diary Entry:

- *Story of Edgar Cayce: There Is a River* by Thomas Sugrue

- *A Search for God (Books 1 & 2), 50th Anniversary Edition* by Edgar Cayce

- *Loran, Long Range Navigation: Massachusetts Institute of Technology, Radiation Laboratory Series, No. 4* by John Alvin Pierce (Editor), A. a. McKenzie (Editor), R. H. Woodward (Editor)

- *Celestial Navigation: Using the Sight Reduction Tables from "Pub. No 249"* by Dominique F. Prinet

February 23, 1946
(Continued)

Further Reading Related to Diary Entry:

- *Edgar Cayce's Story of Jesus* by Edgar Cayce

- *Essene Book of Everyday Virtues: Spiritual Wisdom From the Dead Sea Scrolls* by Kenneth Hanson, PhD

- *The Principles of Nature, Her Divine Revelations and a Voice to Mankind: All Three Volumes* by Andrew Jackson Davis

- *Supernormal: Science, Yoga, and the Evidence for Extraordinary Psychic Abilities* by Dean Radin (Author

- *The Spiritual Brain: A Neuroscientist's Case for the Existence of the Soul* by Mario Beauregard and Denyse O'Leary

- *The Essential Kabbalah: The Heart of Jewish Mysticism* by Daniel C. Matt

- *Ode: Intimations of Immortality from Recollections of Early Childhood* by William Wordsworth

July 16, 1946

Further Reading Related to Diary Entry:

- *Dinosaur footprints in Connecticut and Massachusetts.* Available from the Joe Webb Peoples Museum & Collections, Earth & Environmental Sciences, Weselyan University at https://www.wesleyan.edu/ees/museum/footprints_CT_MA.html# [Accessed January 23, 2021].

- *Where Dinosaurs Walked: Eight of the Best Places to See Prehistoric Footprints* by Robin T. Reid. Available at Smithsonianmag.com (October 27, 2015): https://www.smithsonianmag.com/travel/where-dinosaurs-walked-8-places-prehistoric-footprints-180956982/ [Accessed January 23, 2021].

- *A History of the Connecticut River* by Wick Griswold

- *The Connecticut River from the Air: An Intimate Perspective of New England's Historic Waterway* by Jerry Roberts and Tom Walsh

Saturday, August 31, 1946

Further Reading Related to Diary Entry:

- *Hidden History of Connecticut* by Wilson Faude

- *The Rise and Fall of the Dinosaurs: A New History of Their Lost World* by Steve Brusatte

- *Curious Footprints: Professor Hitchcock's Dinosaur Tracks & Other Natural History Treasures at Amherst College* by Nancy Pick, Frank Ward

- *The Tangled History of Connecticut's Anchisaurus* by Riley Black. Available from Smithsonianmag.com at https://www.smithsonianmag.com/science-nature/the-tangled-history-of-connecticuts-anchisaurus-91839935/ [Accessed January 23, 2021].

- *A revision of the problematic sauropodomorph dinosaurs from Manchester, Connecticut and the status of Anchisaurus Marsh* by Adam M. Yates. Available from *Palaeontology* (July 19, 2010, volume 53, issue 4, pages 739-752) through Wiley.com at https://onlinelibrary.wiley.com/doi/full/10.1111/j.1475-4983.2010.00952.x [Accessed January 23, 2021].

- *Not by Fire but by Ice: Discover What Killed the Dinosaurs...and Why It Could Soon Kill Us* by Robert W. Felix

- *Death from Space: What Killed the Dinosaurs* (Isaac Asimov's New Library of the Universe series) by Isaac Asimov and Greg Walz-Chojnacki

- *What Killed The Dinosaurs? Extinction Theories* by Dave Smith. Available from *Dino Buzz*, University of California-Berkley, Museum of Paleontology at https://ucmp.berkeley.edu/diapsids/extinctheory.html [Accessed January 23, 2021].

August 31, 1946
(Continued)
Further Reading Related to Diary Entry:
- *Harvey Penick's Little Red Book: Lessons And Teachings From A Lifetime In Golf* by Harvey Penick

- *Triassic-Jurassic of western Massachusetts: easily acessable geology field trips* by John F. Hubert

- *Quabbin: A History and Explorer's Guide* by Michael Tougias and Les Campbell

- *Henry David Thoreau: A Life* by Laura Dassow Walls

Tuesday, October 29, 1946
Further Reading Related to Diary Entry:
- *The Spear in the Sand* by Raoul C. Faure

- *Majesty in Monotony: Everyday Things With A Cosmic Perspective* by Ariel Manzanares-Scisney

- *Stargazing For Dummies* by Steve Owens

- *God of the Big Bang: How Modern Science Affirms the Creator* by PhD Leslie Wickman

- The Witness of the Stars By The Rev. Ethelbert William Bullinger, D.D; published by the Author, London 1893. Available from Project Gutenberg at http://www.gutenberg.org/files/49018/49018-pdf.pdf [Accessed January 23, 2021].

- *The Evolution of Man: His Religious Systems and Social Customs* by William Wright Hardwicke, M.D.; Watts and Company, publishers, 1899. Available from Internet Archive at https://archive.org/details/evolutionmanhis01hardgoog/page/n8 [Accessed January 23, 2021].

- *Through My Telescope; Astronomy For All* by Will T. Hay; published by John Murray, Albemarle Street, West; London (1935). Available from Internet Archive at https://archive.org/details/ThroughMyTelescope/page/n1/mode/1up [Accessed January 23, 2021].

October 30, 1946

Further Reading Related to Diary Entry:

- *National Geographic Pocket Guide to the Night Sky of North America* by Catherine Herbert Howell

- *Stargazing: Beginners Guide to Astronomy* by Royal Observatory Greenwich, Radmila Topalovic, Tom Kerss

- *National Geographic Backyard Guide to the Night Sky* by Howard Schneider and Sandy Wood

- *The Imperial magazine, or, Compendium of religious, moral, & philosophical knowledge*, volumes 1-12, 1819-1830. Available from the Hathi Trust Digital Library at https://catalog.hathitrust.org/Record/008696359 [Accessed January 23, 2021].

October 30, 1946
(Continued)

Further Reading Related to Diary Entry:

- *Star Finder! A Step-by-Step Guide to the Night Sky* by DK

- *100 Things to See in the Night Sky: From Planets and Satellites to Meteors and Constellations, Your Guide to Stargazing* by Dean Regas

- *National Geographic Backyard Guide to the Night Sky* by Howard Schneider and Sandy Wood

- *Astronomy, a Textbook, fourth edition* by John Charles Duncan, Ph.D. (Professor of Astronomy, Wellesley College. Harper and Brothers Publishers, New York and London, 1926, 1930, 1935, 1946. Available from Internet Archive at https://archive.org/details/in.ernet.dli.2015.176736/page/n1 [Accessed January 23, 2021].

- *Atoms, Stars, and Nebulae* by Leo Goldberg and Lawrence H. Aller. The Blakiston Company, Philadelphia, Publishers, 1943. Available from Internet Archive at https://archive.org/details/in.ernet.dli.2015.177391/page/n1 [Accessed January 23, 2021].

January 22nd, 1947

Further Reading Related to Diary Entry:

- *1491: New Revelations of the Americas Before Columbus* by Charles C. Mann

- *The Night Sky: A Folding Pocket Guide to the Moon, Stars, Planets and Celestial Events* by James Kavanagh

- *Astrophysics for People in a Hurry* by deGrasse Tyson, Neil

- *Positions and Sizes of Cosmic Objects*. *Space Book.* Available from by Las Cumbres Observatory at https://lco.global/spacebook/sky/using-angles-describe-positions-and-apparent-sizes-objects/ [Accessed January 23, 2021].

- *The Story of the Cosmos: How the Heavens Declare the Glory of God* by Daniel Ray and Paul Gould

Thursday, February 6, 1947

Further Reading Related to Diary Entry:

- *The Backyard Astronomer's Guide* by Terence Dickinson

- *Planetary Geology: An introduction, 2nd revised Edition* by Claudio Vita-Finzi, Dominic Fortes

- *Fundamental Planetary Science, Updated Edition: Physics, Chemistry and Habitability* by Jack J. Lissauer

- *New Handbook of the Heavens* by Bernhard Hubert H., Dorothy A. Bennett, Hugh S. Rice; Published by Whittlesey House / McGraw-Hill, New York;1941. Original and revised copies still available today—search online.

February 21, 1947

Further Reading Related to Diary Entry:

- *The Glass Universe: How the Ladies of the Harvard Observatory Took the Measure of the Stars* by Dava Sobel

- *New Handbook of the Heavens* by Bernhard Hubert H., Dorothy A. Bennett, Hugh S. Rice; Published by Whittlesey House / McGraw-Hill, New York;1941. Original and revised copies still available today—search online.

- *An Introduction to Modern Astrophysics, 2nd Edition* by Bradley W. Carroll

- *Introduction to Cosmology, 2nd Edition* by Barbara Ryden

March 11, 1947
Further Reading Related to Diary Entry:
- *NightWatch: A Practical Guide to Viewing the Universe*-Revised 4th Edition by Terence Dickinson (Author); Adolf Schaller (Illustrator)

- *Church Membership: How the World Knows Who Represents Jesus* by Jonathan Leeman

- *What Is a Healthy Church Member?* by Thabiti M. Anyabwile

- *Words of Counsel: For All Leaders, Teachers, and Evangelists* by Charles H. Spurgeon

- *Testimony of Bishop G. Bromley Oxnam, Hearing before the Committee on Un-American Activities*, House of Representatives, Eighty-third Congress, First Session, July 21, 1953. (*Bishop Oxfam defends himself against the accusations of communist activity*) Available from Internet Archive at https://archive.org/stream/testimonyofbisho00unit/testimonyofbisho00unit_djvu.txt [Accessed January 23, 2021].

- *A Testament of Faith* by G. Bromley Oxnam; published by Little, Brown, and Company; Boston and Toronto. 1958. Available from Internet Archive at https://archive.org/details/testamentoffaith027498mbp/page/n7 [Accessed January 23, 2021].

- *Preaching in a Revolutionary Age* by Garfield Bromley Oxnam, published by Books for Libraries Press, Freeport, NY. 1944, reprint 1971. Available from Internet Archive at https://archive.org/details/preachinginrevol00oxna/page/n7 [Accessed January 23, 2021].

March 17, 1947
Further Reading Related to Diary Entry:
- *The Wizard and the Prophet: Two Remarkable Scientists and Their Dueling Visions to Shape Tomorrow's World* by Charles C. Mann

- *Growing Food in a Hotter, Drier Land: Lessons from Desert Farmers on Adapting to Climate Uncertainty* by Gary Paul Nabhan

- *50 Things To See With A Small Telescope* by John A Read

- *Introduction to Astronomy: A Guide for Night Watchers* by G.B. Sidgwick (Member of the Société Astronomique de France and of the British Astronomical Association); published by Philosophical Library Inc., 1944. Available from Internet Archive at https://archive.org/details/in.ernet.dli.2015.211991/page/n1 [Accessed January 23, 2021].

- Foundations of Astronomy by W.M. Smart (formerly professor of astronomy in the University of Glasgow); published by Longmans, Green, and Company, Ltd. Published in 1942, 1944, 1946, 1947, 1953, 1958, 1962. Available from Internet Archive at https://archive.org/details/in.ernet.dli.2015.84617/page/n5 [Accessed January 23, 2021].

April 1, 1947
Further Reading Related to Diary Entry:
- *Astronomy*. Available from Smith College at https://www.smith.edu/academics/astronomy [Accessed January 23, 2021].

- *Seymour Planetarium*, Springfield, MA. Available from Springfield Museums at https://springfieldmuseums.org/about/springfield-science-museum/seymour-planetarium/ [Accessed January 23, 2021].

- *Poems* by W.H. Auden. 1937.

- *Poems of Gerard Manley Hopkins* edited with notes by Robert Bridges. 1918.

June 25, 1947
Further Reading Related to Diary Entry:
- *The Story of Mrs. Murphy* by Natalie Anderson Scott

- *Studs Lonigan* by James T. Farrell

- *Alcoholics Anonymous, The Big Book* by Bill Wilson, Dr. Bob Smith

- *Astronomy for Beginners*. Available from *Sky & Telescope* at https://www.skyandtelescope.com/astronomy-information/ [Accessed January 23, 2021].

October 5, 1947
Further Reading Related to Diary Entry:
- *The History of Dartmouth College* by Baxter Perry Smith; Houghton, Osgood, and Company, Boston; The Riverside Press, Cambridge (1878) Available from

The Project Gutenberg at https://www.gutenberg.org/ebooks/28641 [Accessed January 23, 2021].

- *Explore Solar System and Beyond*. Available from NASA at https://www.nasa.gov/topics/solarsystem/index.html [Accessed January 23, 2021].

- *Wesley and the People Called Methodists: Second Edition*, by Richard P. Heitzenrater

- *The Reformation* by Diarmaid MacCulloch

Monday, October 13, 1947
Further Reading Related to Diary Entry:
- *From Our Galaxy to Island Universes*. Available from the Center for History of Physics, a Division of the American Institute of Physics at https://history.aip.org/history/exhibits/cosmology/ideas/island.htm [Accessed January 23, 2021].

- *"Island universes"* are now referred to as galaxies, and there are believed to be over 100 billion galaxies with each containing 100 billion stars and numerous planets. Information on island universes is available from astrophysics professor Brian Koberlein's website at https://archive.briankoberlein.com/2014/09/17/island-universe/index.html [Accessed January 23, 2021].

- *Messier 33 (The Triangulum Galaxy)*; February 20, 2019 (Last Updated: Oct 22, 2019; Editor: Rob Garner). Available from NASA at https://www.nasa.gov/feature/goddard/2019/messier-33-the-triangulum-galaxy [Accessed January 29, 2021].

- *Astrophysics through Computation: With Mathematica® Support* by Brian Koberlein and David Meisel

- *Mohandas K. Gandhi, Autobiography: The Story of My Experiments with Truth* by Mohandas Karamchand Gandhi and Mahatma Gandhi

- *Midnight's Furies: The Deadly Legacy of India's Partition* by Nisid Hajari

December 2, 1947
Further Reading Related to Diary Entry:
- *Mourt's Relation or Journal of the Pilgrims at Plymouth*. Contributor Names: Bradford, William, 1590-1657. Winslow, Edward, 1595-1655. Dexter, Henry Martyn, 1821-1890, ed. Created / Published by J. K. Wiggin, 1865, Boston,

Massachusetts. Available from the Department of Anthropology, University of Chicago, at Urbana-Champaign, Illinois (by Patricia Scott Deetz and Christopher Fennell) at http://www.histarch.illinois.edu/plymouth/mourt1.html [Accessed January 23, 2021].

- *The communion of saincts A treatise of the fellowship that the faithful have with God, and his angels, and one with an other; in this present life. Gathered out of the holy Scriptures*, by Henry Ainsworth, 1571-1622(?). Imprinted at Amsterdam by Giles Thorp, 1607. Available from the Text Creation Partnership, Early English Books Online; University of Michigan, Digital Collections, at https://quod.lib.umich.edu/cgi/t/text/text-idx?c=eebo;idno=A12475.0001.001 [Accessed January 23, 2021].

- *Indian Nations of North America by National Geographic* by Rick Hill, Teri Frazier

- *500 Nations: An Illustrated History of North American Indians* by Alvin M. Josephy Jr.

- *Astronomy 101*. Available from the Physics and Astronomy Department, Western Washington University at http://www.wwu.edu/planetarium/a101/astronomy101.shtml [Accessed January 23, 2021].

December 30, 1947

Further Reading Related to Diary Entry:

- *The Journals of André Gide: Volume I 1889-1913* by André Gide, Justin O'Brien (translator)

- *The Moving Finger,* from the Rubaiyat of Omar Khayyam; a sermon by Reverend E.F. Dinsmore, Unity Church, Santa Barbara, CA. Available from Internet Archive at https://archive.org/stream/movingfingerofom00dinsrich/movingfingerofom00dinsrich_djvu.txt [Accessed January 23, 2021].

- *Ulysses* by James Joyce

- *The Complete Poems* by Christina Rossetti

January 20, 1948

Further Reading Related to Diary Entry:

- *The Great Cryptogram: Francis Bacon's Cipher in the So-Called Shakespeare Plays* by Ignatius Donnelly

- *Anatomy of Melancholy* by Democritus Junior (Robert Burton's pseudonym). Available from The Project Gutenberg at https://www.gutenberg.org/files/10800/10800-h/10800-h.htm [Accessed January 23, 2021].

- *The Complete Works of William Shakespeare*. Available from a Massachusetts Institute of Technology (MIT) website created by Jeremy Hylton and operated by *The Tech* (MIT's newspaper) at http://shakespeare.mit.edu/index.html [Accessed January 23, 2021].

- *Raintree County* by Ross Lockridge Jr.

- *Ulysses* by James Joyce

- *Finnegans Wake* by James Joyce

- *Dubliners* by James Joyce

- *Jose Iturbi: Life and Piano Technique* by Dagmar Uythethofken

March 22, 1948

Further Reading Related to Diary Entry:

- *Astronomy in the Old Testament* by Giovanni Virginio Schiaparelli

- *Death on Mars: The Discovery of a Planetary Nuclear Massacre* by John E. Brandenburg, PhD

- *The Future of Humanity: Terraforming Mars, Interstellar Travel, Immortality, and Our Destiny Beyond Earth* by Michio Kaku

- *Walt Whitman: Poetry and Prose* by Walt Whitman and Justin Kaplan

- *Walt Whitman (The Camden Sage) as Religious and Moral Teacher: A Study* by William Norman Guthrie

- *Iron Curtain: The Crushing of Eastern Europe, 1944-1956* by Anne Applebaum

- *Saint Augustin: Top Biography Collections* by Louis Bertrand

May 13, 1948

Further Reading Related to Diary Entry:

- *The History of the Crossword: The World's Most Famous Word Puzzle* by John Halpern

- *The Night Sky Observer's Guide: Autumn & Winter: 1* by George Robert Kepple, Glen W. Sanner

- *The Greek Anthology, Volume I*: Book 1: Christian Epigrams. Book 2: Description of the Statues in the Gymnasium of Zeuxippus. Book 3: Epigrams in the ... 5: Erotic Epigrams (Loeb Classical Library) by Michael A. Tueller (Editor), W. R. Paton (Translator)

May 31, 1948

Further Reading Related to Diary Entry:

- *The Vulnerable Pastor: How Human Limitations Empower Our Ministry* by Mandy Smith

- *Friends' Review: A Religious, Literary, and Miscellaneous Journal*, volumes 1-48 (1847-1894). Editors: Sept. 1847- Enoch Lewis. Samuel Rhoads. Publisher, Josiah Tatum, Philadelphia. Available from the Hathi Trust Digital Library at https://catalog.hathitrust.org/Record/000545855 [Accessed January 23, 2021].

- *Canoeing the Mountains: Christian Leadership in Uncharted Territory* by Tod Bolsinger

- *The Saturn System Through The Eyes Of Cassini* by NASA

September 23, 1948

Further Reading Related to Diary Entry:

- *Saltwater Fishing Made Easy* by Martin Pollizotto

- *Going Fishing: The Story of the Deep-Sea Fishermen of New England* by Wesley George Pierce

- *Crunch & Des: Classic Stories of Saltwater Fishing* by Philip Wylie (Author), Karen Wylie Pryor (Editor)

- *Friedrich Schiller Poet of Freedom Volume I* by Friedrich Schiller (Author), William F. Wertz (Translator), John Sigerson (Translator), Helga Zepp-LaRouche (Preface)

December 29, 1948
Further Reading Related to Diary Entry:
- *The Order of Time* by Carlo Rovelli

- *The Fabric of the Cosmos: Space, Time, and the Texture of Reality* by Brian Greene

- *A Brief History of Time* by Stephen Hawking

- *Communism: A History* by Richard Pipes

- *Essays in Musical Analysis* (Volume VI) by Donald Francis Tovey; published by Oxford University Press, London. Available from The Internet Archive at https://archive.org/details/in.ernet.dli.2015.28890/page/n3 [Accessed January 23, 2021].

February 9, 1949
Further Reading Related to Diary Entry:
- *Beethoven: Anguish and Triumph* by Jan Swafford

- *The Soul of Ann Rutledge Abraham Lincoln's Romance* by Bernie Babcock

- *Cosmology: A Very Short Introduction* by Peter Coles

- *The Physics of God: Unifying Quantum Physics, Consciousness, M-Theory, Heaven, Neuroscience and Transcendence* by Joseph Selbie

April 20, 1949
Further Reading Related to Diary Entry:
- *Look Homeward, Angel* by Thomas Wolfe

- *Of Time and the River: A Legend of Man's Hunger in His Youth* by Thomas Wolfe

- *The Depths of the Soul: Psycho-Analytic Studies* by Wilhelm Stekel

- *City of the Sacred Well* by T.A. Willard. Available from Internet Archive at https://archive.org/details/cityofsacredwell00will/page/n7 [Accessed January 23, 2021].

August 2, 1949
Further Reading Related to Diary Entry:
- *Castaways: The Penikese Island Experiment* by George Cadwalader
- *The Ocean of Life: The Fate of Man and the Sea* by Callum Roberts
- *The World Is Blue: How Our Fate and the Ocean's Are One* by Sylvia A. Earle
- *The Sea Around Us* by Rachel Carson

October 22, 1949
Further Reading Related to Diary Entry:
- *1934 Official Short Wave Radio Manual* by Hugo and H. Winfield Secor Gernsback; published by Short Wave Craft, New York, 1934.
- *The Empty Nest Chronicles: How to Have Fun (and Stop Annoying Your Spouse) After the Kids Move Out* by Jerry Zezima

December 28, 1949
Further Reading Related to Diary Entry:
- *The Flying Saucers are Real* by Donald Keyhoe
- *The Report On Unidentified Flying Objects* by Edward J. Ruppelt
- *Buck Rogers In The 25th Century: The Complete Newspaper Dailies, Vol. 5, 1935-1936* by John F. Dille
- *The War of the Worlds* by H.G. Wells
- *From the Earth to the Moon and Around the Moon* by Jules Verne
- *It's a Wonderful Christmas: The Best of the Holidays 1940-1965* by Susan Waggoner

A List of All the Suggested Popular Books by Year

1936

Popular Books Published in 1936:

Most Popular Books Published In 1936. Available from Goodreads.com at https://www.goodreads.com/book/popular_by_date/1936 [Accessed January 22, 2021].

- *Ramona* by Helen Hunt Jackson
- *The Diary of a Country Priest* by Georges Bernanos
- *Gone with the Wind* by Margaret Mitchell
- *Journey Without Maps* by Graham Greene
- *Drums Along the Mohawk* by Walter D. Edmonds
- *Keep the Aspidistra Flying* by George Orwell
- *In Dubious Battle* by John Steinbeck
- *Eyeless in Gaza* by Aldous Huxley
- *Fighting Angel* by Pearl S. Buck
- *Madame Curie: A Biography* by Evé Curie
- *How to Win Friends and Influence People* by Dale Carnegie
- *You Can't Take it With You* by Moss Hart
- *Language, Truth and Logic* by Alfred J. Ayer
- *The Snows of Kilimanjaro* by Ernest Hemingway
- *The Autobiography of G.K. Chesterton* by G.K. Chesterton
- *The Trouble I've Seen* by Martha Gellhorn
- *A Further Range* by Robert Frost
- *Fighting Angel* by Pearl S. Buck
- *Man Makes Himself* by V. Gordon Childe
- *Hamilton Fish: The Inner History of the Grant Administration* by Allan Nevins

1937

Popular Books Published in 1937:

Most Popular Books Published In 1937. Available from Goodreads.com at https://www.goodreads.com/book/popular_by_date/1937 [Accessed January 22, 2021].

- *The Cost of Discipleship* by Dietrich Bonhoeffer
- *Beat to Quarters* by C. S. Forester

- *Men of Mathematics* by Eric Temple Bell
- *The Importance Of Living* by Lin Yutang
- *The Bachelor of Arts* by R.K. Narayan
- *Northwest Passage* by Kenneth Roberts
- *The Complete Works of O. Henry* by O. Henry
- *The Devil and Daniel Webster* by Stephen Vincent Benét
- *The Flivver King: A Story of Ford-America* by Upton Sinclair
- *Pecos Bill: The Greatest Cowboy of All Time* by James Cloyd Bowman
- *A Hermit in the Himalayas: The Journal of a Lonely Exile* by Paul Brunton Inc.
- *Everybody's Enquire Within* (Volume 1) edited by Charles Ray
- *Last Flight* by Amelia Earhart
- *The Mystery of the Grail: Initiation and Magic in the Quest for the Spirit* by Julius Evola
- *Towers in the Mist* by Elizabeth Goudge
- *Think and Grow Rich* by Napoleon Hill
- *The Hobbit, Part One* by J.R.R. Tolkien
- *The Citadel* by A.J. Cronin

1938

Popular Books Published in 1938:

Most Popular Books Published In 1938. Available at Goodreads.com at https://www.goodreads.com/book/popular_by_date/1938 [Accessed January 22, 2021].

- *The Coming Victory of Democracy* by Thomas Mann
- *The Anatomy of Revolution* by Crane Brinton
- *The Evolution of Physics* by Albert Einstein and Leopold Infeld
- *Cause for Alarm* by Eric Ambler
- *Epitaph for a Spy* by Eric Ambler
- *Scoop* by Evelyn Waugh
- *The Unvanquished* by William Faulkner
- *Facing Mount Kenya* by Jomo Kenyatta

1939

Popular Books Published in 1939:

Most Popular Books Published In 1939. Available from Goodreads.com at https://www.goodreads.com/book/popular_by_date/1939 [Accessed January 22, 2021].

- *The Big Sleep* by Raymond Chandler
- *Alcoholics Anonymous, The Big Book* by Bill Wilson, Dr. Bob Smith
- *The Secret Life of Walter Mitty* by James Thurber
- *The Confidential Agent* by Graham Greene
- *Western Union* by Zane Grey
- *Johnny Got His Gun* by Dalton Trumbo
- *Gadsby* by Ernest Vincent Wright
- *Ask the Dust* by John Fante
- *Wind, Sand and Stars* by Antoine de Saint-Exupéry
- *Finnegans Wake* by James Joyce
- *After Many a Summer* by Aldous Huxley
- *Selected Poems* by W.B. Yeats, John Kelly (Editor)
- *Diets and Their Effects* by Weston A. Price
- *Systematic Theology* by Louis Berkhof
- *The Man Who Came to Dinner* by Moss Hart, George S. Kaufman
- *Lost on a Mountain in Maine* by Donn Fendler, Joseph B. Egan
- *Selected Writings* by Thomas Aquinas, Ralph McInerny

1940

Popular Books Published in 1940:

Most Popular Books Published In 1940. Available from Goodreads.com at https://www.goodreads.com/book/popular_by_date/1940 [Accessed January 22, 2021].

- *For Whom the Bells Toll* by Ernest Hemingway
- *How to Read a Book* by Mortimer J. Adler
- *A Mathematician's Apology* by G. H. Hardy
- *Country Squire in the White House* by John T. Flynn
- *The Transposed Heads* by Thomas Mann
- *Oliver Wiswell* by Kenneth Roberts
- *The Long Week-End* by Alan Hodge and Robert Graves
- *History of the Iranian Constitutional Revolution* by Ahmad Kasravi
- *Farewell My Lovely* by Raymond Chandler
- *To the Finland Station* by Edmund Wilson
- *The Trees* by Conrad Richter
- *The Ox-Bow Incident* by Walter Van Tilburg Clark
- *A Technique for Producing Ideas* by James Webb Young
- *Clock Without Hands* by Carson McCullers
- *Zen and Japanese Culture* by D.T. Suzuki

- *Miss Hargreaves* by Frank Baker
- *Darkness at Noon* by Arthur Koestler
- *New World Order* by H.G. Wells
- *Memory Hold-The-Door*. The Autobiography of John Buchanan by John Buchanan
- *Drums and Shadows* by Mary Granger
- *The Birth and Death of the Sun* by George Gamow
- *An Agricultural Testament* by Sir Albert Howard
- *The Artist's Handbook of Materials and Techniques* by Ralph Mayer
- *The Utrecht Atlas* by Marcel Minnaert, Gerard Mulders, Jakob Houtgast
- *Inside the Gestapo: Hitler's Shadow OverThe World* by Hansjrgen Koehler
- *The Encyclopedia of World History* compiled and edited by William L. Langer

1941

Popular Books Published in 1941:

Most Popular Books Published In 1941. Available from Goodreads.com at https://www.goodreads.com/book/popular_by_date/1941 [Accessed January 22, 2021].

- *Escape from Freedom* by Erich Fromm
- *The Mind of the Maker* by Dorothy L. Sayers
- *Under the Sea Wind: A Naturalist's Picture of Ocean Life* by Rachel Carson.
- *All in a Lifetime* by Frank Buck, with Ferrin Fraser
- *Mildred Pierce* by James M. Cain
- *The Keys of the Kingdom* by A. J. Cronin
- *The Physics of Blown Sand and Desert Dunes* by Ralph Alger Bagnold
- *Grey Eminence* by Aldous Huxley
- *The Snow Goose* by Paul Gallico
- *Strategy* by B.H. Liddell Hart
- *Blithe Spirit* by Noël Coward
- *Consider the Oyster* by M.F.K. Fisher
- *A Testament of Devotion* by Thomas R Kelly
- *Thomas the Obscure* by Maurice Blanchot
- *Space, Time and Architecture: The Growth of a New Tradition* by Siegfried Giedion
- *The Hammer of God* by Bo Giertz
- *The Impersonal Life* by Joseph Benner
- *Between Two Worlds* by Upton Sinclair
- *Clarence Darrow for the Defense* by Irving Stone
- *The Captain from Connecticut* by C.S. Forester

1942

Popular Books Published in 1942:

Most Popular Books Published In 1942. Available from Goodreads.com at https://www.goodreads.com/book/popular_by_date/1942 [Accessed January 22, 2021].

- *The Robe* by Lloyd C. Douglas
- *Calamity Town* by Ellery Queen (Frederic Dannay and Manfred B. Lee)
- *Chess Story* by Stefan Zweig, Joel Rotenberg (Translator)
- *Go Down, Moses* by William Faulkner
- *Capitalism, Socialism and Democracy* by Joseph Schumpeter
- *The Case for Christianity* by C.S. Lewis
- *The Art of Dramatic Writing: Its Basis in the Creative Interpretation of Human Motives* by Lajos Egri
- *The Secret Life of Salvador Dalí* by Salvador Dalí
- *The Skin of Our Teeth* by Thornton Wilder
- *Laura* by Vera Caspary
- *How to Cook a Wolf* by M.F.K. Fisher
- *Pied Piper* by Nevil Shute
- *We Took to the Woods* by Louise Dickinson Rich
- *Crazy Horse: The Strange Man of the Oglalas* by Mari Sandoz
- *Now and on Earth* by Jim Thompson
- *The Works of Henry David Thoreau* by Henry David Thoreau
- *30 Days to a More Powerful Vocabulary* by Wilfred Funk
- *The Life Divine* by Sri Aurobindo
- *The Fall of Paris* by Ilya Ehrenburg
- *Physics and Philosophy* by James Hopwood Jeans
- *The Screwtape Letters* by C.S. Lewis
- *The Theory of Capitalist Development* by Paul M. Sweezy
- *The Wisdom of China and India* by Lin Yutang (Editor)
- *Can Capitalism Survive? Creative Destruction and the Future of the Global Economy* by Joseph Schumpeter
- *The Puritan Family: Religion and Domestic Relations in Seventeenth-Century New England* by Edmund S. Morgan
- *I Saw The Fall Of The Philippines* by Carlos P. Romulo
- *Admiral of the Ocean Sea: A Life of Christopher Columbus* by Samuel Eliot Morison
- *Put Out More Flags* by Evelyn Waugh

1943

Popular Books Published in 1943:

Most Popular Books Published In 1943. Available from Goodreads.com at https://www.goodreads.com/book/popular_by_date/1943 [Accessed January 22, 2021].

- *Being and Nothingness* by Jean-Paul Sartre
- *Johnny Tremain* by Esther Forbes
- *The Greatest Gift* by Philip Van Doren Stern
- *The Human Comedy* by William Saroyan
- *Hungry Hill* by Daphne du Maurier
- *Journey in the Dark* by Martin Flavin
- *The Doctrine of Awakening* by Julius Evola
- *The Ship* by C. S. Forester
- *Colonel Effingham's Raid* by Berry Fleming
- *They Also Ran* by Irving Stone
- *Street Corner Society* by William Foote Whyte
- *The Fountainhead* by Ayn Rand
- *The God of the Machine* by Isabel Paterson
- *The Ministry of Fear* by Graham Greene
- *The Abolition of Man* by C. S. Lewis

1944

Popular Books Published in 1944:

Most Popular Books Published In 1944. Available at Goodreads.com at https://www.goodreads.com/book/popular_by_date/1944 [Accessed January 22, 2021].

- *A Bell for Adano* by John Hersey
- *The Razor's Edge* by William Somerset Maugham
- *The Lost Weekend* by Charles Jackson
- *Stick and Rudder: An Explanation of the Art of Flying* by Wolfgang Langewiesche
- *How to Stop Worrying and Start Living* by Dale Carnegie
- *Fascism: What It Is and How to Fight It* by Leon Trotsky
- *The Ashley Book of Knots* by Clifford W. Ashley
- *Can Do! The Story Of The Seabees* by William Bradford Huie
- *The Life and Selected Writings of Thomas Jefferson* by Thomas Jefferson
- *The Adventures of Sam Spade and Other Stories* by Dashiell Hammett

- *An Essay on Man: An Introduction to a Philosophy of Human Culture* by Ernst Cassirer
- *Story of a Secret State: My Report to the World* by Jan Karski
- *Brave Men* by Ernie Pyle
- *One Man's Meat* by E.B. White
- *Harvey* by Mary Chase
- *No Exit* by Jean-Paul Sartre

1945

Popular Books Published in 1945:

Most Popular Books Published In 1945. Available from Goodreads.com at https://www.goodreads.com/book/popular_by_date/1945 [Accessed January 22, 2021].

- *The Egg and I* by Betty MacDonald
- *Animal Farm* by George Orwell
- *Cannery Row* by John Steinbeck
- *The Black Rose* by Thomas B. Costain
- *The Portable Walt Whitman* by Walt Whitman
- *Pilates' Return to Life Through Contrology* by Joseph H. Pilates
- *The Adventures of Solar Pons* by August Derleth
- *The Pearl* by John Steinbeck
- *Brideshead Revisited: The Sacred and Profane Memories of Captain Charles Ryder* by Evelyn Waugh
- *Stuart Little* by E.B. White
- *Ross Poldark* by Winston Graham
- *The Age of Reason* by Jean-Paul Sartre
- *Arch of Triumph: A Novel of a Man Without a Country* by Erich Maria Remarque
- *Christ Stopped at Eboli: The Story of a Year* by Carlo Levi

1946

Popular Books Published in 1946:

Most Popular Books Published In 1946. Available from Goodreads.com at https://www.goodreads.com/book/popular_by_date/1946 [Accessed January 22, 2021].

- *Autobiography of a Yogi* by Paramahansa Yogananda
- *Man's Search for Meaning* by Viktor Frankl

- *All the King's Men* by Robert Penn Warren
- *Five Chimneys: A Woman Survivor's True Story of Auschwitz* by Olga Lengyel
- *Why I Write* by George Orwell
- *The Fields* by Conrad Richter
- *King Jesus* by Robert Graves
- *Gentleman's Agreement* by Laura Z. Hobson
- *Mr. Blandings Builds His Dream House* by Eric Hodgins
- *Three Came Home* by Agnes Newton Keith
- *The Tale of Beatrix Potter: A Biography* by Margaret Lane
- *If You Ask Me* by Eleanor Roosevelt
- *Mister Roberts* by Thomas Heggen
- *The Pianist: The Extraordinary Story of One Man's Survival in Warsaw, 1939-45* by Władysław Szpilman

1947

Popular Books Published in 1947:

Most Popular Books Published In 1947. Available from Goodreads.com at https://www.goodreads.com/book/popular_by_date/1947 [Accessed January 22, 2021].

- *The Diary of a Young Girl* by Anne Frank
- *Miracles* by C.S. Lewis
- *Survival in Auschwitz* by Primo Levi
- *Tales of the South Pacific* by James A. Michener
- *Exercises in Style* by Raymond Queneau
- *Company Commander: The Classic Infantry Memoir of World War II* by Charles B. MacDonald
- *War as I Knew It* by George S. Patton Jr.
- *Little Pilgrim's Progress: From John Bunyan's Classic* by Helen L. Taylor
- *Nuremberg Diary* by Gustave Mark Gilbert
- *The Chequer Board* by Nevil Shute
- *Battle for Leyte Gulf* by C. Vann Woodward
- *How I Raised Myself From Failure to Success in Selling* by Frank Bettger
- *The Wayward Bus* by John Steinbeck
- *Selections from the Prison Notebooks* by Antonio Gramsci,
- *The Psychology of Intelligence* by Jean Piaget
- *One, Two, Three...Infinity: Facts and Speculations of Science* by George Gamow
- *Rocket Ship Galileo* Robert A. Heinlein
- *With Folded Hands* by Jack Williamson

1948

Popular Books Published in 1948:

Most Popular Books Published In 1948. Available from Goodreads.com at https://www.goodreads.com/book/popular_by_date/1948 [Accessed January 22, 2021].

- *The Seven Storey Mountain* by Thomas Merton
- *Raintree County* by Ross Lockridge Jr.
- *Cheaper by the Dozen* by Ernestine Gilbreth Carey
- *The White Goddess* by Robert Graves
- *The Heart of the Matter* by Graham Greene
- *The Plague and I* by Betty MacDonald
- *Cry, the Beloved Country* by Alan Paton
- *No Highway* by Nevil Shute
- *The Celestial Plot* by Adolfo Bioy Casares
- *Catalina* by W. Somerset Maugham
- *City Boy: The Adventures of Herbie Bookbinder* by Herman Wouk
- *Last of the Conquerors* by William Gardner Smith

1949

Popular Books Published in 1949:

Most Popular Books Published In 1949. Available from Goodreads.com at https://www.goodreads.com/book/popular_by_date/1949 [Accessed January 22, 2021].

- *1984* by George Orwell
- *Jesus and the Disinherited* by Howard Thurman
- *The Sheltering Sky* by Paul Bowles
- *The Crow Comes Last* by Italo Calvino
- *The Hero with a Thousand Face* by Joseph Campbell
- *Death of a Salesman* by Arthur Miller
- *Death Be Not Proud* by John Gunther
- *A Sand County Almanac: And Sketches Here and There* by Aldo Leopold
- *The Art of Readable Writing* by Rudolf Flesch
- *The Historian's Craft* by Marc Bloch
- *To Hell and Back* by Audie Murphy

A List of All the Suggested Popular Movies by Year

1936

Popular Movies Released in 1936:

- *After the Thin Man* (Myrna Loy, William Powell)
- *Showboat* (Irene Dunne, Allan Jones)
- *Anything Goes* (Bing Crosby, Ethel Merman, Ida Lupino)
- *Ramona* (Loretta Young, Don Ameche, Kent Taylor)
- *My Man Godfrey* (Carole Lombard, William Powell)
- *Mr. Deeds Goes to Town* (Jean Arthur, Gary Cooper)
- *Earthworm Tractors* (Joe E. Brown, June Travis, Guy Kibbee)
- *Dodsworth* (Ruth Chatterton, Water Huston)
- *Little Lord Fauntleroy* (Freddie Bartholomew, Dolores Costello Barrymore)
- *Follow the Fleet* (Fred Astaire, Ginger Rogers, Lucille Ball)
- *Theodora Goes Wild* (Melvyn Douglas, Irene Dunne)
- *The Charge of the Light Brigade* (Errol Flynn, Olivia de Havilland)
- *Hopalong Cassidy Returns* (William Boyd, Gabby Hayes, Gail Sheridan)
- *Rose Marie* (Nelson Eddy, Jeanette MacDonald)
- *The Story of Louis Pasteur* (Paul Muni, Josephine Hutchinson, Anita Louise, Donald Woods)
- *The Amazing Adventure* (Cary Grant, Mary Brian)
- *Intermezzo* (Ingrid Bergman, Gösta Ekman)
- *Lloyd's of London* (Tyrone Power, Madeleine Carroll)
- *Meet Nero Wolfe* (Edward Arnold, Lionel Stander, Dennie Moore)
- *Secret Agent* (John Gielgud, Madeleine Carroll)
- *Flash Gordon* (Buster Crabbe, Jean Rogers)
- *San Francisco* (Clark Gable, Jeanette MacDonald, Spencer Tracy, Jack Holt, Jessie Ralph, Ted Healy)
- *The General Died at Dawn* (Gary Cooper, Madeleine Carroll)
- *Rembrandt* (Charles Laughton, Gertrude Lawrence)
- *Thank You, Jeeves!* (Arthur Treacher, Virginia Field, David Niven)
- *The Trail of the Lonesome Pine* (Sylvia Sidney, Fred MacMurray, Henry Fonda)
- *The Plainsman* (Jean Arthur, Gary Cooper)
- *Yellowstone* (Judith Barrett, Alan Hale)

1937

Popular Movies Released in 1937:

- *A Day at the Races* (The Marx Brothers)
- *Captains Courageous* (Spencer Tracy, Freddie Bartholomew, Lionel Barrymore)
- *The Emperor's Candlesticks* (William Powell, Luise Rainer, Robert Young, Maureen O'Sullivan, Frank Morgan)
- *Shall We Dance* Fed Astaire, Ginger Rogers)
- *Topper* (Cary Grant, Constance Bennett, Roland Young)
- *Green Light* (Errol Flynn, Anita Louise)
- *Black Legion* (Humphrey Bogart, Ann Sheridan)
- *You Only Live Once* (Sylvia Sidney, Henry Fonda)
- *Jim Hanvey, Detective* (Guy Kibbee, Tom Brown, Catherine Doucet)
- *The Prince and the Pauper* (Errol Flynn, Claude Rains, Henry Stephenson)
- *The Prisoner of Zenda* (Ronald Colman, Madeleine Carroll, C. Aubrey Smith)
- *The Life of Émile Zola* (Paul Muni, Joseph Schildkraut, Gale Sondergaard)
- *The Good Earth* (Paul Muni, Luise Rainer)
- *Make Way for Tomorrow* (Victor Moore, Beulah Bondi)
- *The Shadow* (Rita Hayworth, Charles Quigley)
- *Maytime* (Jeanette MacDonald, Nelson Eddy, John Barrymore)
- *Lost Horizon* (Ronald Colman, Jane Wyatt, Edward Everett Horton)
- *Super-Sleuth* (Jack Oakie, Ann Sothern, Paul Guilfoyle)
- *A Damsel in Distress* (Fred Astaire, George Burns, Gracie Allen)
- *Shall We Dance* (Fred Astaire, Ginger Rogers)
- *You're Only Young Once* (Mickey Rooney, Lewis Stone, Cecilia Parker)
- *Easy Living* (Jean Arthur, Edward Arnold, Ray Milland)
- *Think Fast Mr. Moto* (Peter Lorre, Virginia Field, Thomas Beck)
- *West Bound Limited* (Lyle Talbot, Polly Rowles)
- *True Confessions* (Carole Lombard, Fred MacMurray, John Barrymore)
- *Fire Over England* (Laurence Olivier, Flora Robson, Vivien Leigh)
- *Join the Marines* (Paul Kelly, June Travis, Reginald Denny)
- *Souls at Sea* (Gary Cooper, George Raft, Frances Dee)
- *A Family Affair* (Lionel Barrymore, Cecilia Parker, Eric Linden)
- *God's Country and the Woman* (George Brent, Beverly Roberts, Barton MacLane)

1938

Popular Movies Released in 1938:

- *The Adventures of Robin Hood* (Errol Flynn, Olivia de Havilland, Basil Rathbone, Claud Rains)

- *Boys Town* (Spencer Tracy, Mickey Rooney)
- *Love Finds Andy Hardy* (Mickey Rooney, Judy Garland, Lewis Stone)
- *White Banners* (Claude Rains, Fay Bainter, Jackie Cooper)
- *A Christmas Carol* (Reginald Owen, Gene Lockhart)
- *Algiers* (Charles Boyer, Hedy Lamarr)
- *Suez* (Tyrone Power, Loretta Young)
- *A Yank at oxford* (Robert Taylor, Vivien Leigh, Lionel Barrymore)
- *The Dawn Patrol* (Errol Flynn, Basil Rathbone, David Niven)
- *Young Doctor Kildare* (Lionel Barrymore, Lew Ayres, Lynne Carver)
- *The Saint in New York* (Louis Hayward, Kay Sutton, Sig Ruman)
- *Of Human Hearts* (Walter Huston, James Stewart, Beulah Bondi)
- *Room Service* (The Marx Brothers)
- *Cipher Bureau* (Leon Ames, Charlotte Wynters, Joan Woodbury)
- *Angels with Dirty Faces* (James Cagney, Pat O'Brien, Humphrey Bogart)
- *Alexander's Ragtime Band* (Alice Faye, Tyrone Power)
- *The Lady Vanishes* (Margaret Lockwood, Michael Redgrave, Paul Lukas)

1939

Popular Movies Released in 1939:

- *Mr. Smith Goes to Washington* (James Stewart, Jean Arthur, Claude Rains)
- *The Wizard of Oz* (Judy Garland, Frank Morgan, Ray Bolger)
- *Gone with the Wind* (Clark Gable, Vivien Leigh, Leslie Howard, Olivia de Havilland, Hatie McDaniel, Butterfly McQueen)
- *Only Angels Have Wings* (Jean Arthur, Cary Grant)
- *Young Mr. Lincoln* (Henry Fonda, Alice Brady)
- *It's a Wonderful World* (Jimmy Stewart, Claudette Colbert)
- *The Hunchback of Notre Dame* (Charles Laughton, Maureen O'Hara, Cedric Hardwicke)
- *Gunga Din* (Cary Grant, Joan Fontaine, Victor McLaglen)
- *Goodbye, Mr. Chips* (Robert Donat, Greer Garson, Terry Kilburn)
- *Another Thin Man* (Myrna Loy, William Powell)
- *The Four Feathers* (John Clements, Ralph Richardson, C. Aubrey Smith)
- *Dark Victory* (Bette Davis, Humphrey Bogart, George Brent)
- *The Adventures of Sherlock Holmes* (Basil Rathbone, Nigel Bruce, Ida Lupino)
- *Union Pacific* (Barbara Stanwyck, Joel McCrea, Akim Tamiroff)
- *Babes in Arms* (Mickey Rooney, Judy Garland)
- *Stanley and Livingstone* (Spencer Tracy, Nancy Kelly, Richard Greene)
- *Confessions of a Nazi Spy* (Edward G. Robinson, George Sanders, Francis Lederer)
- *Jesse James* (Tyrone Power, Henry Fonda, Nancy Kelly, Randolph Scott)

- *Andy Hardy Gets Spring Fever* (Lewis Stone, Mickey Rooney, Cecilia Parker, Fay Holden)
- *The Hound of the Baskervilles* (Basil Rathbone, Nigel Bruce)
- *The Three Musketeers* (Don Ameche, Gloria Stuart, The Ritz Brothers, Binnie Barnes)
- *Buck Rogers* (Buster Crabbe, Constance Moore, Jackie Moran)
- *Destry Rides Again* (James Stewart, Marlene Dietrich)
- *It's a Wonderful World* (James Stewart, Claudette Colbert)
- *On Borrowed Time* (Lionel Barrymore, Sir Cedric Hardwicke, Beulah Bondi)
- *Idiot's Delight* (Clark Gable, Norma Shearer, Edward Arnold, Charles Coburn)

1940

Popular Movies Released in 1940:

- *The Grapes of Wrath* (Henry Fonda, Jane Darwell, John Carradine)
- *The Long Voyage Home* (John Wayne, Thomas Mitchell, Ian Hunter)
- *Night Train to Munich* (Margaret Lockwood, Rex Harrison, Paul Henreid)
- *The House of Seven Gables* (George Sanders, Margaret Lindsay, Vincent Price)
- *Pride and Prejudice* (Greer Garson, Laurence Olivier, Mary Boland)
- *Broadway Melody of 1940* (Fred Astaire, Eleanor Powell, George Murphy, Frank Morgan)
- *Stranger on the Third Floor* (Peter Lorre, John McGuire, Margaret Tallichet)
- *Boom Town* (Clark Gable, Spencer Tracy, Claudette Colbert)
- *The Shop Around the Corner* (Jimmy Stewart, Margaret Sullivan)
- *The Santa Fe Trail* (Errol Flynn, Olivia de Havilland, Raymond Massey)
- *Our Town* (William Holden, Martha Scott, Fay Bainter)
- *The Westerner* (Gary Cooper, Walter Brennan, Doris Davenport)
- *Road to Singapore* (Bing Crosby, Bob Hope, Dorothy Lamour)
- *Waterloo Bridge* (Vivien Leigh, Robert Taylor, Lucile Watson)
- *The Bank Dick* (W.C. Fields, Cora Witherspoon, Una Merkel)
- *The Sea Hawk* (Errol Flynn, Brenda Marshall, Claude Rains)
- *The Mark of Zorro* (Tyrone Power, Linda Darnell, Basil Rathbone)
- *The Ghost Breakers* (Bob Hope, Paulette Goddard)
- *Behind the News* (Lloyd Nolan, Doris Davenport, Frank Albertson)
- *Edison, the Man* (Spencer Tracy, Rita Johnson, Charles Coburn)
- *The Great McGinty* (Brian Donlevy, Muriel Angelus, Akim Tamiroff)
- *Foreign Correspondent* (Joel McCrea, Laraine Day, Herbert Marshall)
- *Rebecca* (Laurence Olivier, Joan Fontaine)
- *Escape* (Robert Taylor, Norma Shearer, Conrad Veidt)
- *The Philadelphia Story* (Cary Grant, Katharine Hepburn, James Stewart)
- *The Mortal Storm* (James Stewart, Margaret Sullavan, Robert Young)

- *The Howards of Virginia* (Cary Grant, Martha Scott)
- *The Great Dictator* (Charlie Chaplin)
- *Brother Orchid* (Edward G. Robinson, Ann Sothern, Humphrey Bogart)
- *Northwest Passage* (Spencer Tracy, Robert Young)
- *Charlie Chan at the Wax Museum* (Sidney Toler, Victor Sen Yung, C. Henry Gordon, Marc Lawrence)
- *Christmas in July* (Dick Powell, Ellen Drew)
- *Strange Cargo* (Clark Gable, Joan Crawford, Peter Lorre, Paul Lukas)
- *A Dispatch from Reuters* (Edward G. Robinson, Edna Best)
- *East Side Kids* (Leon Ames, Dennis Moore, Joyce Bryant, East Side Kids)
- *My Favorite Wife* (Cary Grant, Irene Dunn)
- *His Girl Friday* (Cary Grant, Rosalind Russell)
- *The Marines Fly High* (Richard Dix, Chester Morris, Lucille Ball)
- *Rhythm on the River* (Bing Crosby and Mary Martin)
- *Pastor Hall* (Wilfrid Lawson, Nova Pilbeam, Seymour Hicks)
- *Remember the Night* (Barbara Stanwyck, Fred MacMurray)
- *Turnabout* (Adolphe Menjou, Carole Landis, John Hubbard)

1941

Popular Movies Released in 1941:

- *The Maltese Falcon* (Humphrey Bogart, Mary Astor, Sydney Greenstreet, Peter Lorre, Elisha Cook Jr., Ward Bond)
- *Adventure in Washington* (Herbert Marshall, Virginia Bruce)
- *Arkansas Judge* (Roy Rogers, Veda Ann Borg)
- *All Through the Night* (Humphrey Bogart, Kaaren Verne, Conrad Veidt, Jane Darwell)
- *The Big Store* (Marx Brothers, Tony Martin)
- *Citizen Kane* (Orson Welles, Joseph Cotten, Everett Sloane, Paul Stewart, Dorothy Comingore, Agnes Moorehead)
- *Confessions of Boston Blackie* (Chester Morris, Harriet Hilliard)
- *Dangerously They Live* (John Garfield, Nancy Coleman)
- *Dive Bomber* (Errol Flynn, Fred MacMurray)
- *Footsteps in the Dark* (Errol Flynn, Brenda Marshall, Ralph Bellamy)
- *High Sierra* (Ida Lupino, Humphrey Bogart, Joan Leslie, Arthur Kennedy, Cornel Wilde, Henry Travers)
- *The Lady Eve* (Barbara Stanwyck, Henry Fonda)
- *Mr. And Mrs. Smith* (Carole Lombard, Robert Montgomery)
- *No Hands on the Clock* (Jean Parker, Chester Morris)
- *One Foot in Heaven* (Fredric March, Martha Scott, Beulah Bondi, Gene Lockhart)

- *Penny Serenade* (Irene Dunne, Cary Grant, Beulah Bondi, Edgar Buchanan)
- *Red River Valley* (Roy Rogers, Gabby Hayes)
- *The Sea Wolf* (Edward G. Robinson, Ida Lupino, John Garfield)
- *Sergeant York* (Gary Cooper, Walter Brennan, Joan Leslie)
- *The Shepherd of the Hills* (John Wayne, Betty Field)
- *Sullivan's Travels* (Joel McCrea, Veronica Lake)
- *Suspicion* (Cary Grant, Joan Fontaine, Nigel Bruce, Cedric Hardwicke, Dame May Whitty, Leo G. Carroll)
- *Western Union* (Randolph Scott, Robert Young)
- *Sun Valley Serenade* (Sonja Henie, John Payne, Glenn Miller)
- *You're in the Army Now* (Jimmy Durante, Jane Wyman, Phil Silvers)
- *Topper Returns* (Joan Blondell, Roland Young, Carole Landis, Dennis O'Keefe)
- *Here Comes Mr. Jordan* (Robert Montgomery, Evelyn Keyes, Claude Rains)
- *Harvard, Here I Come* (Maxie Rosenbloom, Arline Judge)
- *Dr. Jekyll and Mr. Hyde* (Spencer Tracy, Ingrid Bergman, Lana Turner)
- *The Devil and Miss Jones* (Jean Arthur, Charles Coburn)

1942

Popular Movies Released in 1942:

- *Casablanca* (Humphrey Bogart, Ingrid Bergman, Claude Rains, Paul Henreid, Dooley Wilson, Peter Lorre)
- *Across the Pacific* (Humphrey Bogart, Mary Astor, Sydney Greenstreet, Charles Halton)
- *Bells of Capistrano* (Gene Autry, Virginia Grey)
- *Blondie Goes to College* (Penny Singleton, Arthur Lake, Janet Blair)
- *Captains of the Clouds* (James Cagney, Dennis Morgan, Brenda Marshall)
- *A Date with the Falcon* (George Sanders, Wendy Barrie, Allen Jenkins)
- *Eyes in the Night* (Edward Arnold, Ann Harding, Donna Reed)
- *Flying Tigers* (John Wayne, John Carroll, Anna Lee)
- *The Forest Rangers* (Fred MacMurray, Susan Hayward, Paulette Goddard)
- *George Washington Slept Here* (Jack Benny, Ann Sheridan, Charles Coburn)
- *Holiday Inn* (Bing Crosby, Fred Astaire, Marjorie Reynolds, Virginia Dale)
- *King's Row* (Ann Sheridan, Ronald Reagan, Robert Cummings)
- *The Magnificent Ambersons* (Joseph Cotten, Anne Baxter, Dolores Costello, Agnes Moorehead, Tim Holt)
- *The Man Who Came to Dinner* (Monty Woolley, Bette Davis, Ann Sheridan, Billie Burke)
- *Mrs. Miniver* (Greer Garson, Walter Pidgeon, Teresa Wright)
- *My Favorite Blonde* (Bob Hope, Madeleine Carroll, Gale Sondergaard, George Zucco)

- *A Night to Remember* (Loretta Young, Brian Aherne)
- *The Old Chisholm Trail* (Johnny Mack Brown, Tex Ritter, Jennifer Holt)
- *Paris Calling* (Basil Rathbone, Randolph Scott, Elisabeth Bergner)
- *The Pride of the Yankees* (Gary Cooper, Teresa Wright, Walter Brennan, Babe Ruth)
- *Reap the Wild Wind* (John Wayne, Paulette Goddard, Ray Milland)
- *Reunion in France* (Joan Crawford, John Wayne, Philip Dorn)
- *Sherlock Holmes and the Secret Weapon* (Basil Rathbone, Nigel Bruce, Lionel Atwill)
- *The Talk of the Town* (Cary Grant, Jean Arthur, Ronald Colman)
- *To the Shores of Tripoli* (Maureen O'Hara, John Payne, Randolph Scott)
- *Woman of the Year* (Spencer Tracy, Katharine Hepburn, Reginald Owen)
- *Wake Island* (Brian Donlevy, Robert Preston)
- *Thunderbirds* (Gene Tierney, Preston Foster, John Sutton)
- *Saboteur* (Robert Cummings, Priscilla Lane, Norman Lloyd)
- *Once Upon a Honeymoon* (Cary Grant, Ginger Rogers, Walter Slezak)
- *Maisie Gets Her Man* (Ann Sothern, Red Skelton, Allen Jenkins)
- *The Major and the Minor* (Ginger Rogers, Ray Milland, Rita Johnson)
- *Life Begins at Eight-Thirty* (Ida Lupino, Monty Woolley, Cornel Wilde)
- *Joe Smith, American* (Robert Young, Marsha Hunt)
- *Eagle Squadron* (Robert Stack, Diana Barrymore)
- *Dr. Kildare's Victory* (Lew Ayres, Ann Ayars, Lionel Barrymore)
- *The Dawn Express* (Michael Whalen, Anne Nagel, Constance Worth)
- *The Courtship of Andy Hardy* (Lewis Stone, Mickey Rooney, Cecilia Parker, Donna Reed)
- *Cairo* (Jeanette MacDonald, Robert Young, Lionel Atwill)
- *The Bugle Sounds* (Wallace Beery, Marjorie Main, Donna Reed)
- *The Big Street* (Henry Fonda, Lucille Ball, Barton MacLane)
- *Cadet Girl* (Carole Landis, George Montgomery)
- *Crossroads* (William Powell, Hedy Lamarr, Claire Trevor)
- *The Falcon's Brother* (George Sanders, Tom Conway, Jane Randolph)

1943

Popular Movies Released in 1943:
- *Action in the North Atlantic* (Humphrey Bogart, Raymond Massey, Alan Hale Sr.)
- *Edge of Darkness* (Errol Flynn, Ann Sheridan, Walter Huston)
- *The Gang's All Here* (Alice Faye, Carmen Miranda)
- *Above Suspicion* (Joan Crawford, Fred MacMurray, Conrad Veidt)
- *Five Graves to Cairo* (Franchot Tone, Anne Baxter)
- *Girl Crazy* (Judy Garland and Mickey Rooney)

- *This is the Army* (George Murphy, Joan Leslie, Ronald Reagan)
- *Destination Tokyo* (Cary Grant, John Garfield)
- *Watch on the Rhine* (Bette Davis, Paul Lukas, Geraldine Fitzgerald)
- *The Song of Bernadette* (Jennifer Jones, William Eythe)
- *Whistling in Brooklyn* (Red Skelton, Ann Rutherford, Jean Rogers)
- *Immortal Sergeant* (Henry Fonda, Maureen O'Hara)
- *Air Force* (John Garfield, John Ridgely, Gig Young)
- *Bombardier* (Pat O'Brien, Randolph Scott, Anne Shirley, Eddie Albert)
- *China* (Loretta Young, Alan Ladd, William Bendix)
- *Coney Island* (Betty Grable, George Montgomery, Cesar Romero, Phil Silvers)
- *Cosmo Jones, Crime Smasher* (Richard Cromwell, Gale Storm)
- *The Desperadoes* (Randolph Scott, Claire Trevor, Glenn Ford)
- *The Fallen Sparrow* (Maureen O'Hara, John Garfield, Walter Slezak, Patricia Morison)
- *For Whom the Bell Tolls* (Gary Cooper, Ingrid Bergman, Arturo de Córdova)
- *Heaven Can Wait* (Don Ameche, Gene Tierney)

1944

Popular Movies Released in 1944:

- *Double Indeminity* (Fred MacMurray, Edward G. Robinson, Barbara Stanwyck)
- *Going My Way* (Bing Crosby and Barry Fitzgerald)
- *Passage to Marseille* (Humphrey Bogart, Claude Rains, Michèle Morgan)
- *The Fighting Seabees* (John Wayne, Susan Hayward, Dennis O'Keefe)
- *The Fighting Sullivans* (Anne Baxter, Thomas Mitchell, Selena Royle)
- *National Velvet* (Mickey Rooney, Elizabeth Taylor, Donald Crisp)
- *Andy Hardy's Blonde Trouble* (Lewis Stone, Mickey Rooney, Fay Holden)
- *Buffalo Bill* (Joel McCrea, Maureen O'Hara, Linda Darnell, Anthony Quinn, Thomas Mitchell)
- *The Canterville Ghost* (Charles Laughton, Margaret O'Brien)
- *The Conspirators* (Hedy Lamarr, Paul Henreid)
- *Gaslight* (Charles Boyer, Ingrid Bergman, Angela Lansbury)
- *Hail the Conquering Hero* (Eddie Bracken, Ella Raines, William Demarest)
- *The Hour Before the Dawn* (Veronica Lake, Franchot Tone, Binnie Barnes)
- *The Keys of the Kingdom* (Gregory Peck, Thomas Mitchell, Roddy McDowall)
- *Lifeboat* (Tallulah Bankhead, William Bendix)
- *Meet Me in St. Louis* (Judy Garland, Margaret O'Brien, Mary Astor)
- *Thirty Seconds over Tokyo* (Spencer Tracy, Van Johnson)
- *Rationing* (Wallace Beery, Marjorie Main)
- *Murder, My Sweet* (Dick Powell, Claire Trevor)
- *Mr. Winkle Goes to War* (Edward G. Robinson, Ruth Warrick)

- *The Miracle of Morgan's Creek* (Eddie Bracken, Betty Hutton, William Demarest)
- *Ministry of Fear* (Ray Milland, Marjorie Reynolds, Carl Esmond)
- *Lights of Old Santa Fe* (Roy Rogers, Dale Evans)
- *Laura* (Gene Tierney, Dana Andrews, Clifton Webb, Vincent Price, Judith Anderson)
- *Ladies Courageous* (Loretta Young, Diana Barrymore, Anne Gwynne, Geraldine Fitzgerald)
- *The Heavenly Body* (William Powell, Hedy Lamarr)
- *The Adventures of Mark Twain* (Fredric March, Alexis Smith)

1945

Popular Movies Released in 1945:

- *Mildred Pierce* (Joan Crawford, Jack Carson, Zachary Scott, Eve Arden
- *And Then There Were None* (Barry Fitzgerald, Walter Huston, Louis Hayward, Roland Young)
- *State Fair* (Jeanne Crain, Dana Andrews, Dick Haymes, Vivian Blaine)
- *And Now Tomorrow* (Alan Ladd, Loretta Young)
- *They Were Expendable* (Robert Montgomery, John Wayne, Donna Reed, Jack Holt)
- *Anchors Aweigh* (Frank Sinatra, Kathryn Grayson, Gene Kelly, José Iturbi)
- *The Clock* (Judy Garland, Robert Walker, James Gleason)
- *A Song to Remember* (Paul Muni, Merle Oberon, Cornel Wilde)
- *Story of G.I. Joe* (Burgess Meredith, Robert Mitchum, Freddie Steele, Wally Cassell)
- *Confidential Agent* (Charles Boyer, Lauren Bacall, Victor Francen, Wanda Hendrix)
- *The House on 92nd Street* (William Eythe, Lloyd Nolan, Signe Hasso, Gene Lockhart)
- *Pursuit to Algiers* (Basil Rathbone, Nigel Bruce, Marjorie Riordan, Rosalind Ivan)
- *Lady on a Train* (Deanna Durbin, Ralph Bellamy, Edward Everett Horton, Allen Jenkins)
- *Duffy's Tavern* (Ed Gardner, Bing Crosby, Betty Hutton, Paulette Goddard)
- *Spellbound* (Ingrid Bergman, Gregory Peck, Michael Chekhov, Leo G. Carroll)
- *The Picture of Dorian Gray* (George Sanders, Hurd Hatfield, Donna Reed)
- *I Know Where I'm Going!* (Wendy Hiller, Roger Livesey, George Carney, Walter Hudd)
- *Back to Bataan* (John Wayne, Anthony Quinn, Beulah Bondi)
- *Eyes In The Night* (Edward Arnold, Ann Harding, Dona Reed [released in 1942)
- *Her Highness and the Bellboy* (Hedy Lamarr, Robert Walker, and June Allyson)
- *The Corn is Green* (Bette Davis, John Dall, Nigel Bruce)

- *The Bells of St. Mary's* (Bing Crosby, Ingrid Bergman, Henry Travers, William Gargan)
- *Christmas in Connecticut* (Barbara Stanwyck, Dennis Morgan, Sydney Greenstreet, Reginald Gardiner)
- *An Angel Comes to Brooklyn* (Barbara Perry, Charles Kemper)

1946

Popular Movies Released in 1946:

- *The Big Sleep* (Humphrey Bogart, Lauren Bacall)
- *The Yearling* (Gregory Peck, Jane Wyman, Claude Jarman Jr.)
- *The Razor's Edge* (Tyrone Power, Gene Tierney, John Payne)
- *Till the Clouds Roll By* (June Allyson, Lucille Bremer, Judy Garland, Kathryn Grayson, Van Heflin, Lena Horne, Van Johnson, Angela Lansbury)
- *Blue Skies* (Fred Astaire, Bing Crosby, Joan Caulfield)
- *Notorious* (Cary Grant, Ingrid Bergman, Claude Rains, Louis Calhern
- *The Stranger* (Orson Welles, Edward G. Robinson, Loretta Young, Philip Merivale)
- *The Best Years of Our Lives* (Myrna Loy, Dana Andrews, Fredric March, Teresa Wright)
- *Terror by Night* (Basil Rathbone, Nigel Bruce, Alan Mowbray, Dennis Hoey)
- *Cloak and Dagger* (Gary Cooper, Robert Alda, Lilli Palmer, Vladimir Sokoloff)
- *Till the End of Time* (Dorothy McGuire, Robert Mitchum, Guy Madison, Bill Williams)
- *Night and Day* (Cary Grant, Alexis Smith, Monty Woolley, Ginny Simms)
- *Humoresque* (Joan Crawford, John Garfield, Oscar Levant, J. Carrol Naish)
- *The Show-Off* (Red Skelton, Marilyn Maxwell, Marjorie Main, Virginia O'Brien)
- *A Stolen Life* (Bette Davis, Glenn Ford, Dane Clark, Walter Brennan)
- *The Harvey Girls* (Judy Garland, Ray Bolger, John Hodiak, Angela Lansbury)
- *The Dark Corner* (Lucille Ball, Clifton Webb, William Bendix, Mark Stevens)
- *The Strange Love of Martha Ivers* (Barbara Stanwyck, Van Heflin, Lizabeth Scott, Kirk Douglas)
- *Somewhere in the Night* (John Hodiak, Nancy Guild, Lloyd Nolan, Richard Conte)
- *A Matter of Life and Death* (David Niven, Kim Hunter, Robert Coote, Kathleen Byron)
- *It's a Wonderful Life* (James Stewart, Donna Reed, Lionel Barrymore)
- *Duel in the Sun* (Jennifer Jones, Joseph Cotten, Gregory Peck, Lionel Barrymore)
- *Lady in the Lake* (Robert Montgomery, Audrey Totter, Lloyd Nolan, Tom Tully)
- *My Darling Clementine* (Henry Fonda, Linda Darnell, Victor Mature)

1947

Popular Movies Released in 1947:

- *Gentleman's Agreement* (Gregory Peck, John Garfield, Dorothy McGuire, Celeste Holm, Jane Wyatt)
- *Song of the Thin Man* (Myna Loy, William Powell)
- *The Secret Life of Walter Mitty* (Danny Kaye, Virginia Mayo, Boris Karloff)
- *Road to Rio* (Bob Hope, Bing Crosby, Dorothy Lamour)
- *Bommerang* (Dana Andrews, Jane Wyatt, Lee J. Cobb)
- *Dead Reckoning* (Humphrey Bogart, Lizabeth Scott, Morris Carnovsky)
- *My Favorite Brunette* (Bon Hope, Dorothy Lamour, Peter Lorre, Lon Chaney Jr.)
- *The Farmer's Daughter* (Loretta Young, Joseph Cotten, Ethel Barrymore)
- *Angel and the Badman* (John Wayne, Gail Russell, Harry Carey)
- *The Bachelor and the Bobby-Soxer* (Cary Grant, Myrna Loy, Shirley Temple)
- *Apache Rose* (Roy Rogers, Dale Evans)
- *Her Husband's Affairs* (Lucille Ball, Franchot Tone, Edward Everett Horton)
- *The Hucksters* (Clark Gable, Deborah Kerr, Sydney Greenstreet, Adolphe Menjou, Keenan Wynn, Edward Arnold and Ava Gardner)
- *Magic Town* (James Stewart, Jane Wyman)
- *The Perils of Pauline* (Betty Hutton, John Lund)
- *The Return of Rin Tin Tin* (Donald Woods, Claudia Drake, Rin Tin Tin)
- *Merton of the Movies* (Red Skelton, Virginia O'Brien, Gloria Grahame)
- *Living in a Big Way* (Gene Kelly, Marie McDonald, Charles Winninger)
- *It Happened in Brooklyn* (Frank Sinatra, Kathryn Grayson, Peter Lawford, Jimmy Durante)
- *Hollywood Barn Dance* (Ernest Tubb, Helen Boyce)
- *The Ghost and Mrs. Muir* (Gene Tierney, Rex Harrison)
- *The Yearling* (Gregory Peck, Jane Wyman, Claude Jarman Jr.)
- *Life with Father* (William Powell, Irene Dunne, Elizabeth Taylor)
- *Winter Wonderland* (Lynne Roberts, Charles Drake, Eric Blore)
- *Blondie in the Dough* (Penny Singleton, Arthur Lake)
- *Captain from Castile* (Tyrone Power, Jean Peters, Cesar Romero)
- *Buffalo Bill Rides Again* (Richard Arlen, Jennifer Holt)
- *The Egg and I* (Claudette Colbert, Fred MacMurray, Marjorie Main, Percy Kilbride)
- *It Happened on Fifth Avenue* (Don DeFore, Ann Harding, Charles Ruggles)
- *The Guilt of Janet Ames* (Rosalind Russell, Melvyn Douglas)
- *The Fabulous Dorseys* (Tommy Dorsey, Jimmy Dorsey, Janet Blair)
- *Stallion Road* (Ronald Reagan, Alexis Smith, Zachary Scott)
- *Miracle on 34th Street* (Edmund Gwenn, Maureen O'Hara, John Payne, Natalie Wood)

- *The Bishop's Wife* (Cary Grant, Loretta Young, David Niven)
- *Christmas Eve* (George Raft, Randolph Scott, George Brent, Joan Blondell)

1948

Popular Movies Released in 1948:

- *Bicycle Thieves* (Lamberto Maggiorani, Enzo Staiola, Lianella Carell)
- *Oliver Twist* (Robert Newton, Alec Guinness, Kay Walsh)
- *Albuquerque* (Randolph Scott, Barbara Britton, George "Gabby" Hayes)
- *Red River* (John Wayne, Montgomery Clift, Joanne Dru)
- *Easter Parade* (Judy Garland, Fred Astaire, Peter Lawford)
- *Blondie's Secret* (Penny Singleton, Arthur Lake)
- *The Treasure of the Sierra Madre* (Humphrey Bogart, Walter Huston, Tim Holt)
- *Fort Apache* (John Wayne, Henry Fonda, Shirley Temple)
- *The Bride Goes Wild* (June Allyson, Van Johnson)
- *A Foreign Affair* (Jean Arthur, Marlene Dietrich, John Lund)
- *State of the Union* (Spencer Tracy, Katharine Hepburn, Van Johnson)
- *The Fuller Brush Man* (Red Skelton, Janet Blair, Hillary Brooke, Adele Jergens)
- *Good Sam* (Gary Cooper, Ann Sheridan, Edmund Lowe)
- *Homecoming* (Clark Gable, Lana Turner, Anne Baxter)
- *The Iron Curtain* (Dana Andrews, Gene Tierney, June Havoc)
- *Joan of Arc* (Ingrid Bergman, José Ferrer)
- *June Bride* (Bette Davis, Robert Montgomery)
- *The Miracle of the Bells* (Alida Valli, Fred MacMurray, Frank Sinatra)
- *Apartment for Peggy* (Jeanne Crain, William Holden, Edmund Gwenn)

1949

Popular Movies Released in 1949:

- *The Secret Garden* (Margaret O'Brien, Herbert Marshall, Dean Stockwell)
- *Come to the Stable* (Loretta Young, Celeste Holm, Hugh Marlowe)
- *A Connecticut Yankee in King Arthur's Court* (Bing Crosby, Rhonda Fleming, Cedric Hardwicke)
- *Sands of Iwo Jima* (John Wayne, John Agar, Adele Mara)
- *On the Town* (Gene Kelly, Frank Sinatra, Betty Garrett)
- *I Was a Male War Bride* (Cary Grant, Ann Sheridan, Marion Marshall)
- *Twelve O'Clock High* (Gregory Peck, Hugh Marlowe, Gary Merrill)
- *She Wore a Yellow Ribbon* (John Wayne, Joanne Dru, John Agar)
- *Ma and Pa Kettle* (Marjorie Main, Percy Kilbride)
- *The Life of Riley* (William Bendix, Rosemary DeCamp)
- *The Third Man* (Orson Welles, Joseph Cotten, Alida Valli)

- *Riders of the Whistling Pines* (Gene Autry, Patricia Barry)
- *My Friend Irma* (Dean Martin, Jerry Lewis)
- *Blondie Hits the Jackpot* (Penny Singleton, Arthur Lake)
- *Outpost in Morocco* (George Raft, Marie Windsor)

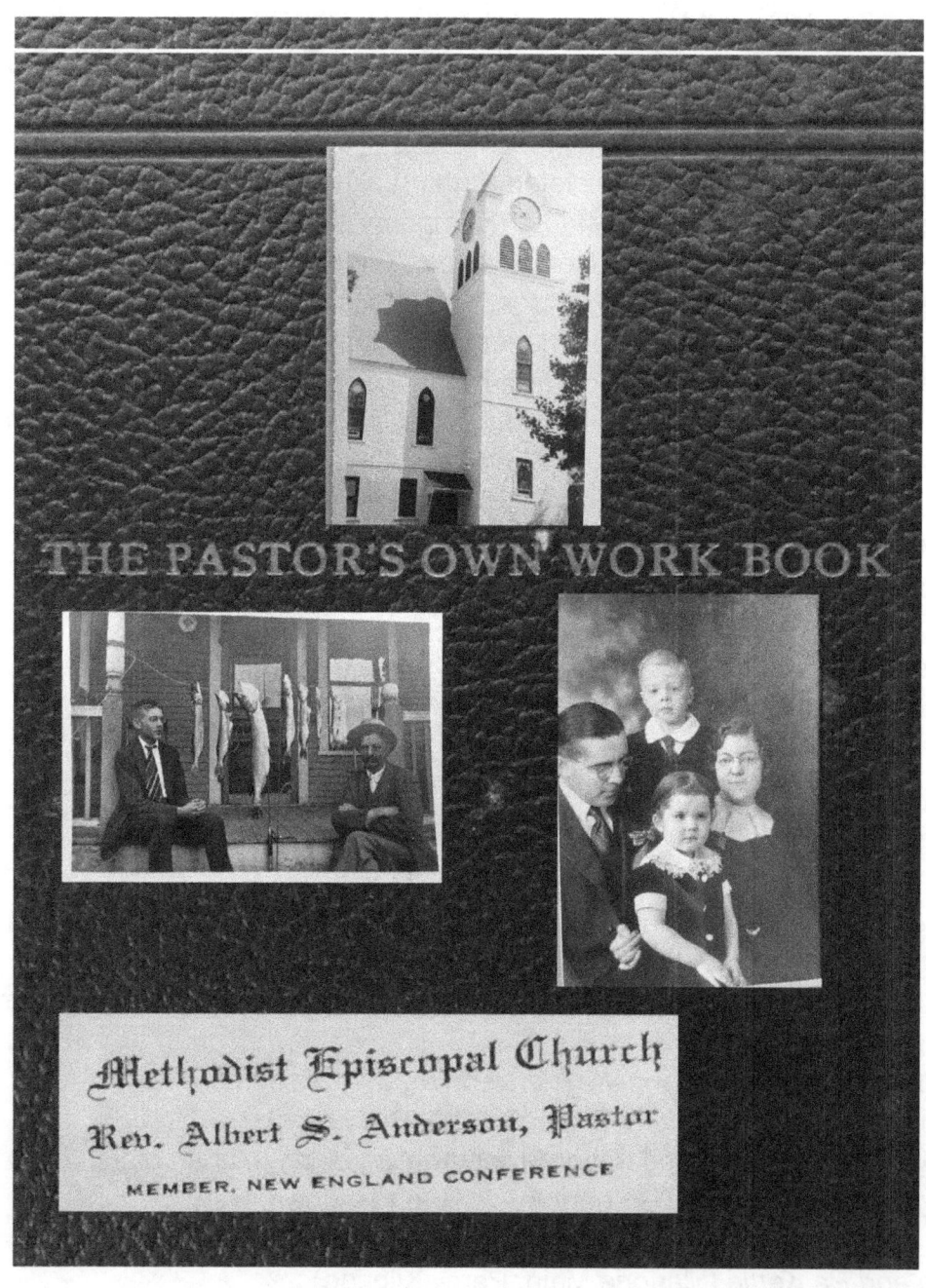

www.ingramcontent.com/pod-product-compliance
Lightning Source LLC
Chambersburg PA
CBHW080833230426
43665CB00021B/2823